DARK HORSE BOOKS presents

BLACKSAD ™

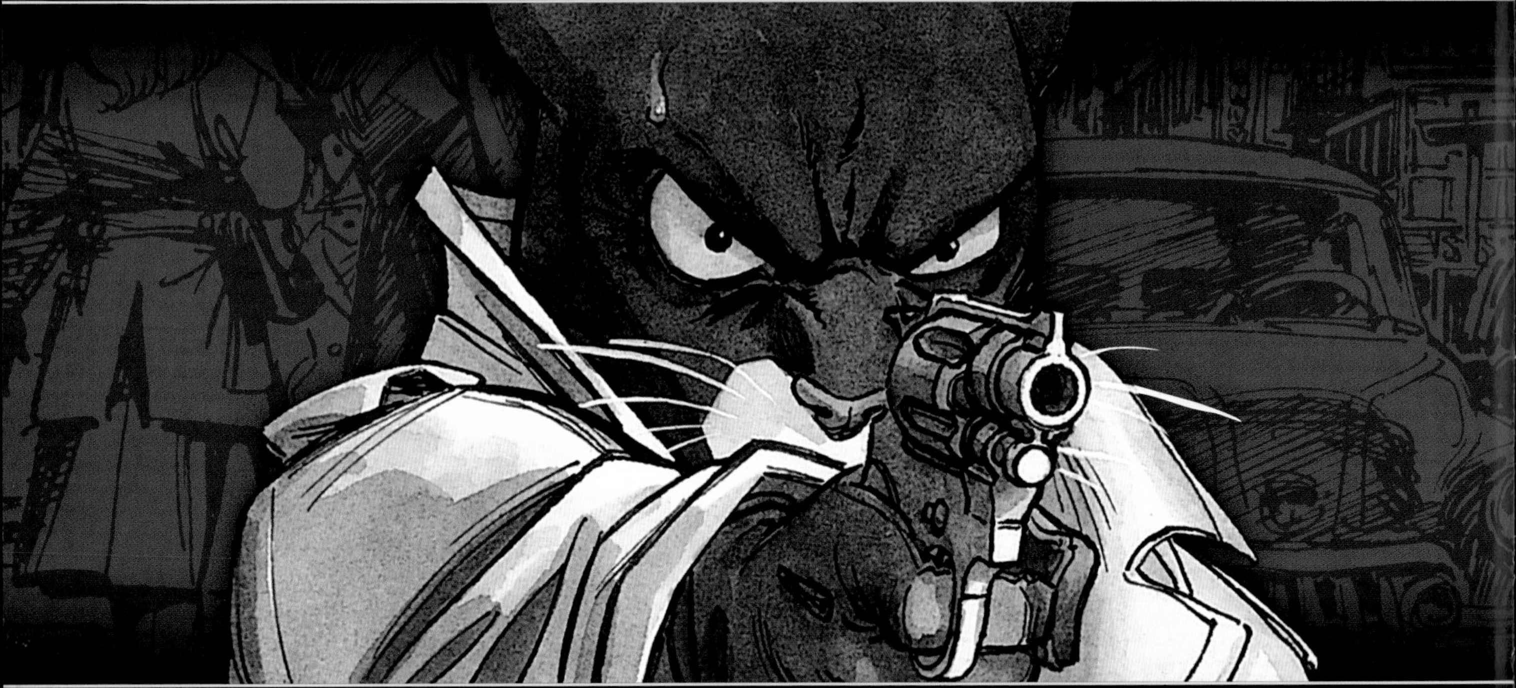

DARK HORSE BOOKS *presents*

BLACKSAD™

Written by
JUAN DÍAZ CANALES

Illustrated by
JUANJO GUARNIDO

Lettering by
STUDIO CUTIE

Dark Horse Books®

To Byron Preiss, who believed in Blacksad

Publisher - Mike Richardson
Collection Editor – Katie Moody
Assistant Editor – Patrick Thorpe
English Translations – Anthya Flores and Patricia Rivera
Collection Designer – Scott Cook
Digital Retouch – Susan Tardif and Matt Dryer

Special thanks to Stuart Ng, Jemiah Jefferson, and Dargaud's Sophie Castille

Published by
Dark Horse Books
A division of Dark Horse Comics, Inc.
10956 SE Main Street
Milwaukie, OR 97222

darkhorse.com

To find a comics shop in your area, call the Comic Shop Locator Service: (888) 266-4226

First edition: June 2010
ISBN 978-1-59582-393-9

10 9 8 7 6 5 4 3 2
Printed at Midas Printing International, Ltd., Huizhou, China

BLACKSAD
Blacksad 1 - Quelque part entre les ombres
© DARGAUD 2000, by Díaz Canales, Guarnido;
Blacksad 2 - Arctic-Nation
© DARGAUD 2002, by Díaz Canales, Guarnido;
Blacksad 3 - Âme rouge
© DARGAUD 2005, by Díaz Canales, Guarnido.
www.dargaud.com
All rights reserved

This volume collects the first three *Blacksad* albums: *Quelque part entre les ombres*, *Arctic-Nation*,
and *Âme rouge*, originally published in France in 2000, 2003, and 2005 by Dargaud.

3 9547 00347 8091

TABLE OF CONTENTS

If it's true that cats have nine lives, then John Blacksad must have a few dozen.

While there's a long aesthetic tradition of animals in the comics, Guarnido and Díaz Canales are obviously in the process of establishing their own. Initially defined by the term "funny animals"—which suggests a range between cute and cuddly—the genre was never quite devoid of sledgehammer violence, mysterious doings, and sometimes even a little sex. And that was prior to the liberation of the form in the 1960s, after which four-footed creatures behaved more like real people than most comic-book characters, thanks to Crumb and company.

Blacksad takes the trend to another level. Rather than animals who act like people, the creators' approach is predicated on people who resemble animals. There's a major difference and it's not as remote as it seems. Who hasn't likened a shrill librarian to a bird or a construction worker to a bear or an old aunt to a cow? By animalizing their characters, Guarnido and Díaz Canales invite readers to enter an arena where the animals are somewhat less than funny—one that's relatively easy to accept because the premise is so charming and skillfully conceived, not unlike James Gurney's Dinotopia or Bob Zemeckis's Who Framed Roger Rabbit.

In Blacksad's world, the characters are generally unconcerned about their zoological differences; they are cast for their natures and personalities. To the perceptive reader, it's almost impossible not to see a trace of slinky Lauren Bacall in Natalia Wilford or burly Ernie Borgnine in Jake Ostiombe or slippery James Woods in the lizard. It's no accident that, down to the last bit player, they've all been visually crafted to reflect their intrinsic qualities—which might just qualify as overt symbolism. Or simple typecasting.

While his draftsmanship is as superb as it is appealing, Guarnido's sharpest and most persuasive ability is apparent in the emotional nuances and facial expressions of his characters, easily the equal of any Disney effort on record. There is a compelling maturity about his art that seems to invest his anthropomorphic cast with experience, vitality, and even dignity. He gets more out of his animal faces than most artists do from people faces. The trick, of course, is making it look easy, like a trapeze artist who throws a triple so flawlessly that the audience believes they could do it, too.

That is no easy task. Here's the universal equation: the easier it looks, the more study, the more practice, the more dedication it takes.

The real pros, however, never allow their relentless quest for discipline and sacrifice to show. But it's there, if you know how to look for it. And while you're looking, don't miss the interesting narrative approach that Guarnido lavishes on his pages, an amalgam of traditional European comics storytelling and American cinematic style. The latter is a critical aspect in the artist's vision and one he leans on heavily in both concept and execution.

Blacksad's adventures are, in many ways, like films on paper. Díaz Canales taps into the dark heart of stateside noir thrillers (not to suggest that Europe, especially France, doesn't have its fair share) for his structural elements: first-person narration, revealing flashbacks, and a nightmarish chiaroscuro of predatory characters in stark silhouette, cluttered offices, grids of venetian blinds, shadowy stairwells, and architectural canyons of iron and concrete illuminated by a maze of flashing neon.

Classic noir themes developed in the pulps by Hammett, Chandler, Goodis, Whitfield, Nebel, Woolrich, and Cain, among others, are manifest in Blacksad's search for justice. His bitter manhunt thrusts him through a gauntlet of corruption, betrayal, obsessive sexuality, alienation, and revenge that mirrors the most memorable genre efforts of RKO Pictures and Warner Bros. during the era of black-and-white B movies.

Particularly notable are Guarnido's muted color passages, giving the impression of the '40s and '50s crime thrillers that have come to define the noir experience. His use of light and shadow is no less memorable, and he often utilizes illumination—sometimes the lack of it—to underscore the drama twisting Blacksad through an urban landscape riddled with mystery, violence, and passion.

Curiosity may have killed some cats, but not this one.

He's too tough.

STERANKO

World-renowned Renaissance man Jim Steranko is a painter and illustrator who, among his many achievements, revolutionized American comic-book storytelling in the late 1960s and designed the look of adventurer Indiana Jones.

SOMEWHERE *within the* SHADOWS

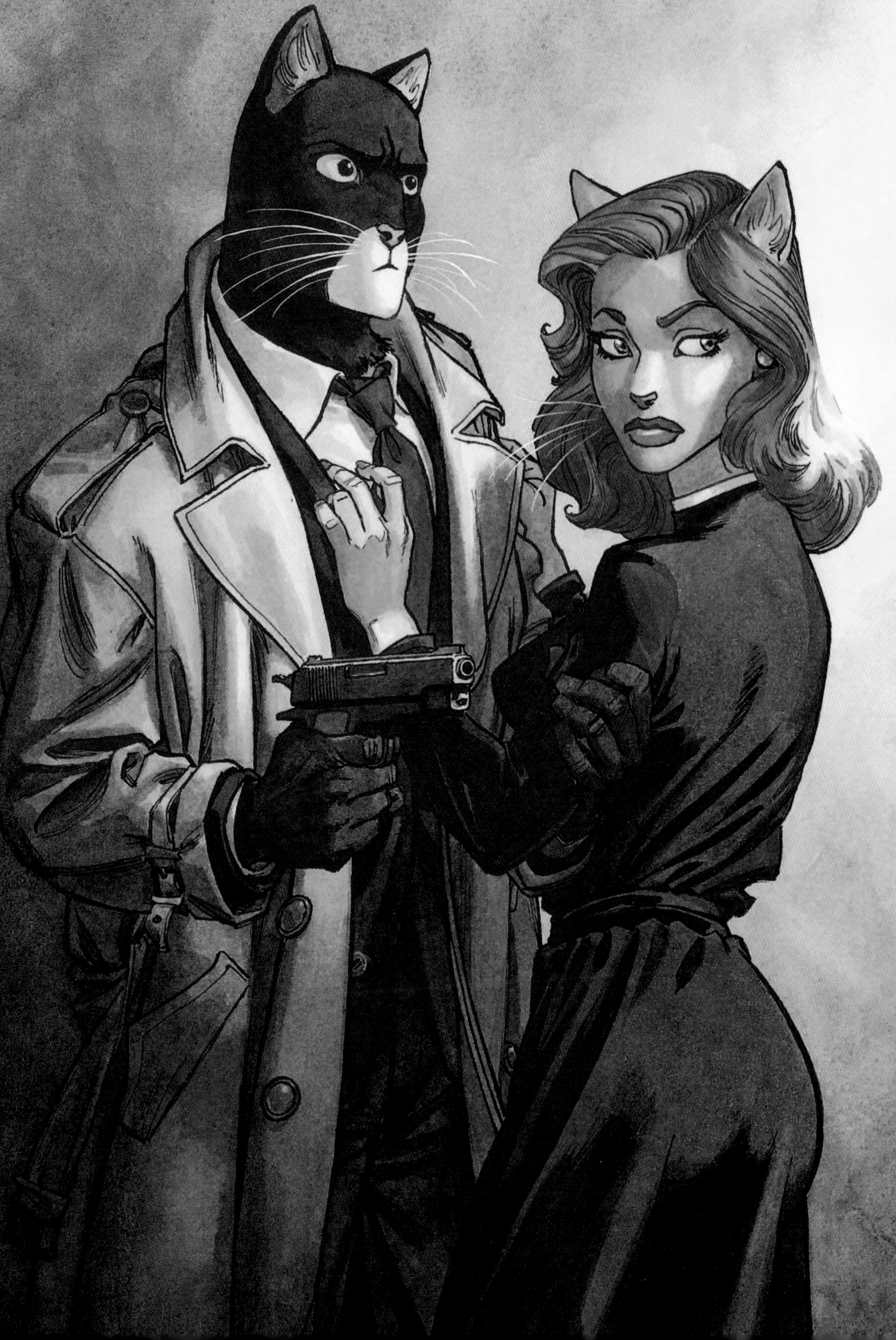

Preceding:
The American cover to this album as
published by iBooks, December 2003

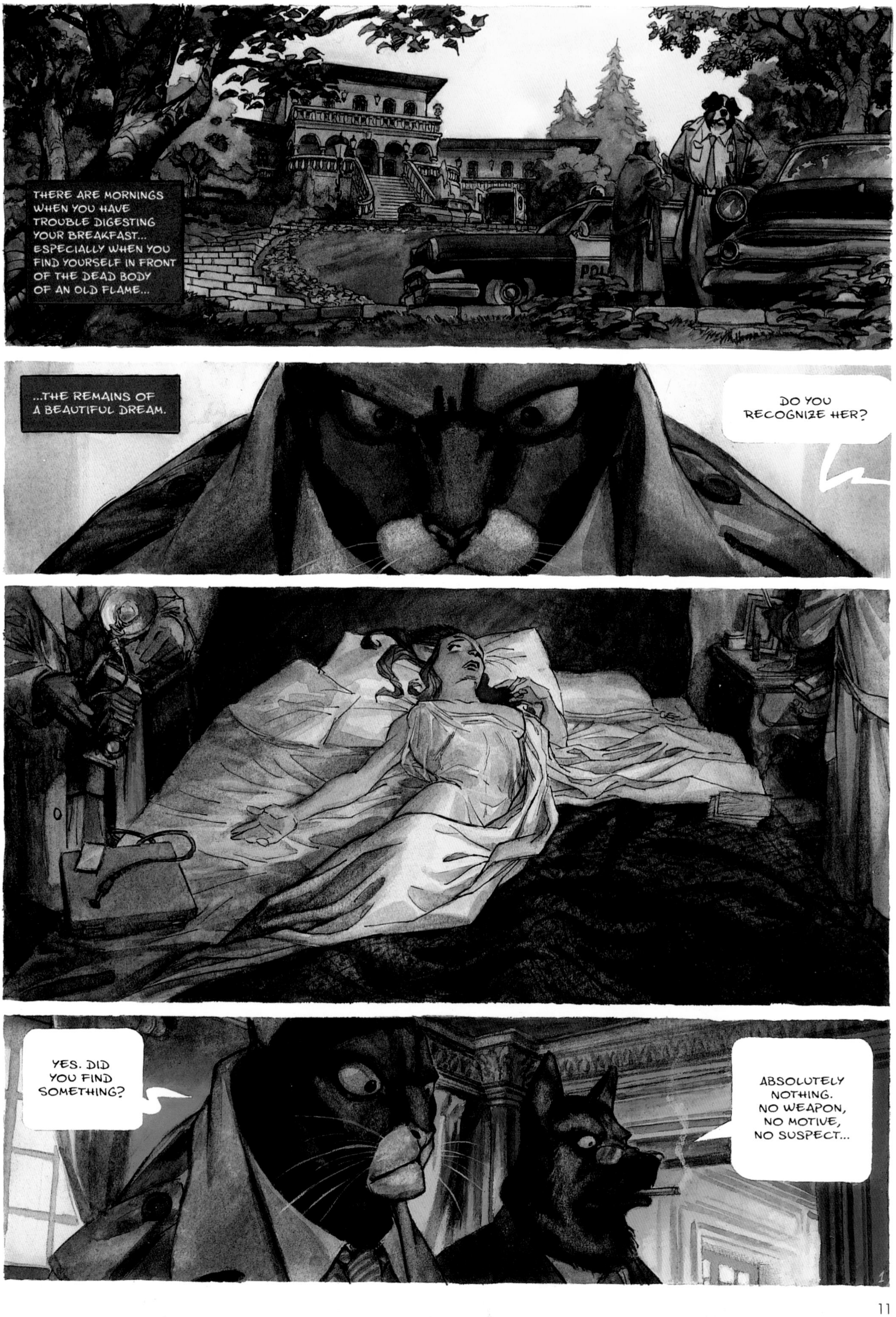
THERE ARE MORNINGS WHEN YOU HAVE TROUBLE DIGESTING YOUR BREAKFAST... ESPECIALLY WHEN YOU FIND YOURSELF IN FRONT OF THE DEAD BODY OF AN OLD FLAME...
...THE REMAINS OF A BEAUTIFUL DREAM.
DO YOU RECOGNIZE HER?
YES. DID YOU FIND SOMETHING?
ABSOLUTELY NOTHING. NO WEAPON, NO MOTIVE, NO SUSPECT...

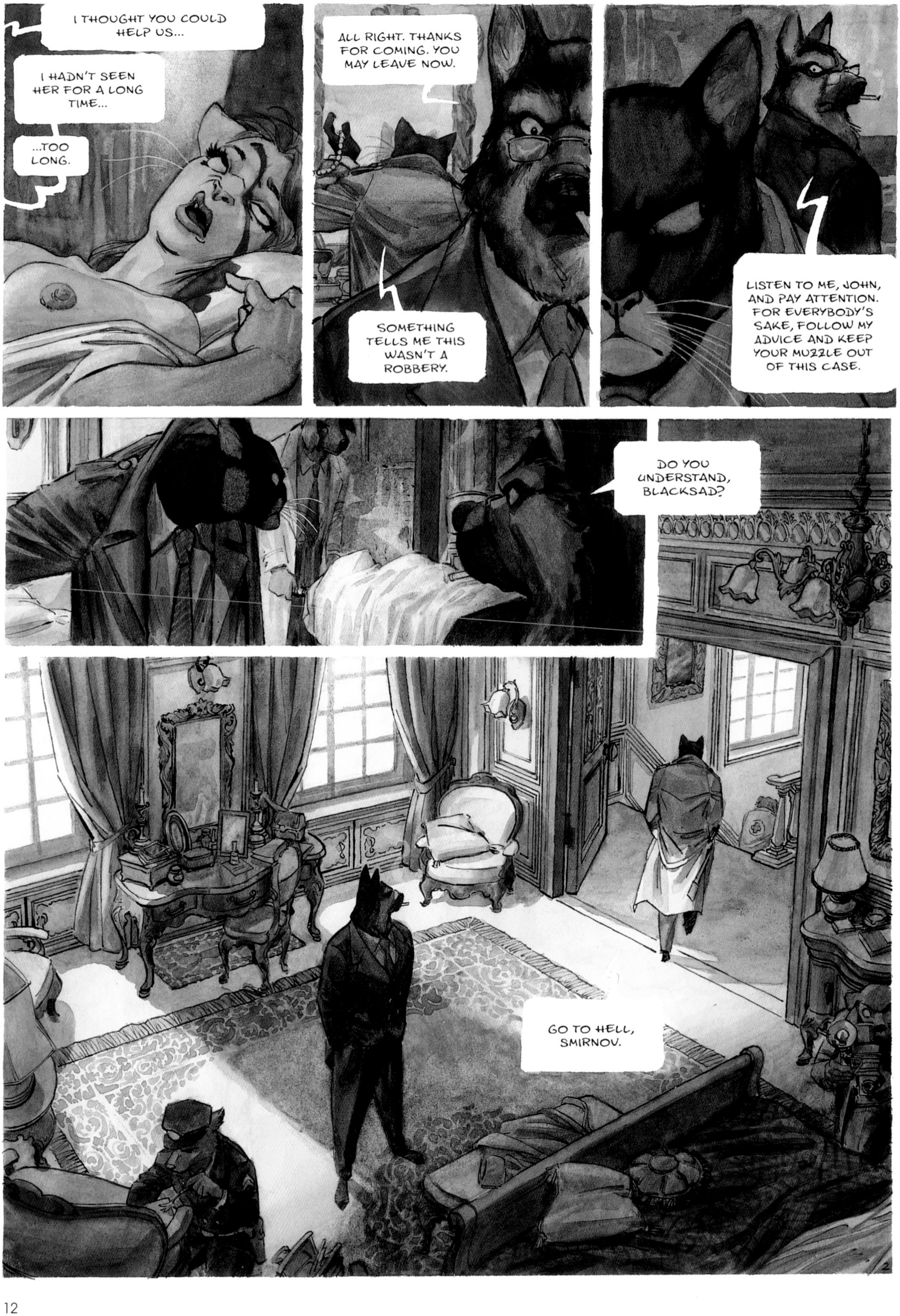
I THOUGHT YOU COULD HELP US...
I HADN'T SEEN HER FOR A LONG TIME...
...TOO LONG.
ALL RIGHT. THANKS FOR COMING. YOU MAY LEAVE NOW.
SOMETHING TELLS ME THIS WASN'T A ROBBERY.
LISTEN TO ME, JOHN, AND PAY ATTENTION. FOR EVERYBODY'S SAKE, FOLLOW MY ADVICE AND KEEP YOUR MUZZLE OUT OF THIS CASE.
DO YOU UNDERSTAND, BLACKSAD?
GO TO HELL, SMIRNOV.

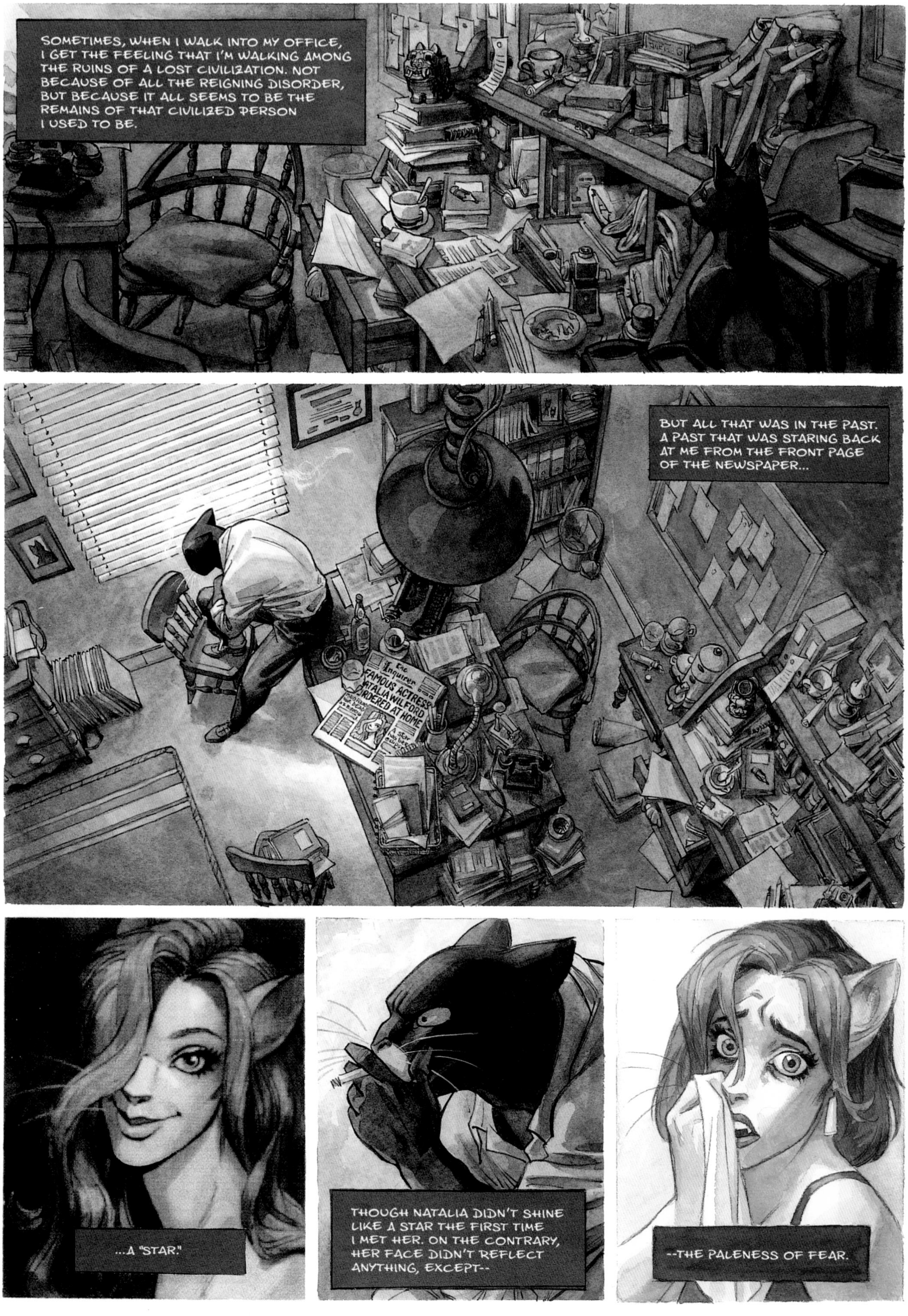
SOMETIMES, WHEN I WALK INTO MY OFFICE, I GET THE FEELING THAT I'M WALKING AMONG THE RUINS OF A LOST CIVILIZATION. NOT BECAUSE OF ALL THE REIGNING DISORDER, BUT BECAUSE IT ALL SEEMS TO BE THE REMAINS OF THAT CIVILIZED PERSON I USED TO BE.
BUT ALL THAT WAS IN THE PAST. A PAST THAT WAS STARING BACK AT ME FROM THE FRONT PAGE OF THE NEWSPAPER...
The Inquirer
FAMOUS ACTRESS
...A "STAR."
THOUGH NATALIA DIDN'T SHINE LIKE A STAR THE FIRST TIME I MET HER. ON THE CONTRARY, HER FACE DIDN'T REFLECT ANYTHING, EXCEPT--
--THE PALENESS OF FEAR.

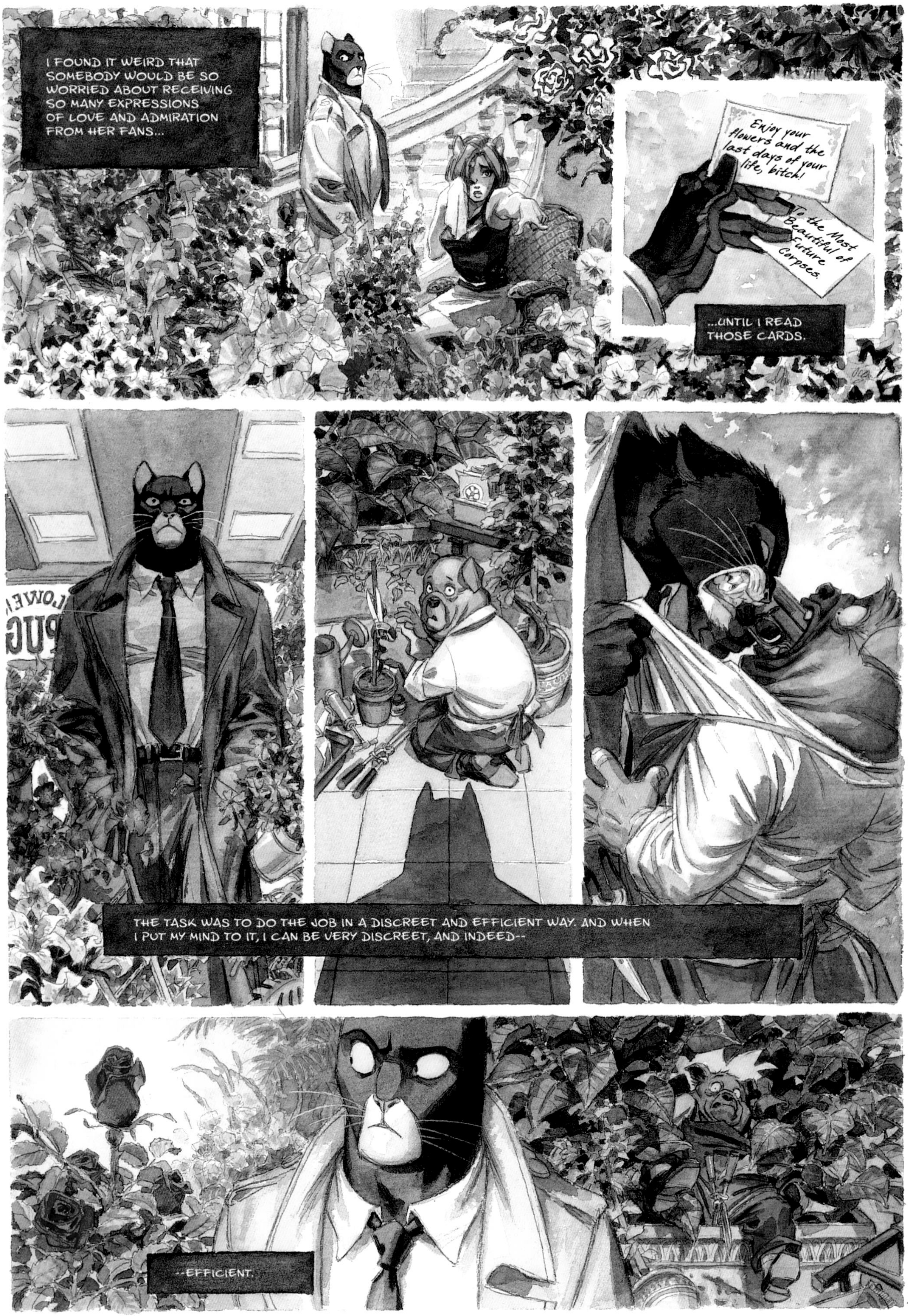
I FOUND IT WEIRD THAT SOMEBODY WOULD BE SO WORRIED ABOUT RECEIVING SO MANY EXPRESSIONS OF LOVE AND ADMIRATION FROM HER FANS...
Enjoy your flowers and the last days of your life, bitch!
To the Most Beautiful of Future Corpses.
...UNTIL I READ THOSE CARDS.
THE TASK WAS TO DO THE JOB IN A DISCREET AND EFFICIENT WAY. AND WHEN I PUT MY MIND TO IT, I CAN BE VERY DISCREET, AND INDEED--
--EFFICIENT.

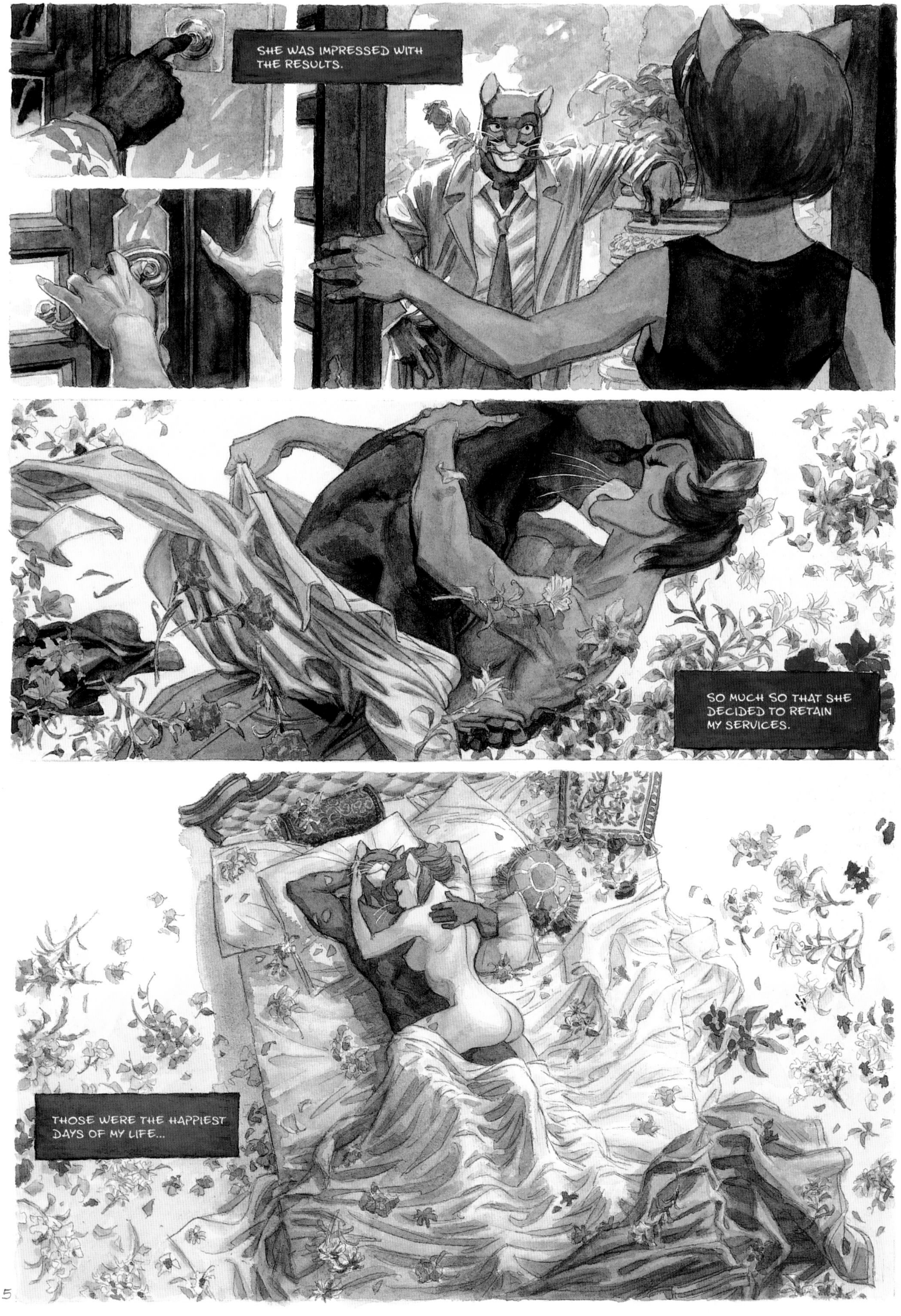
SHE WAS IMPRESSED WITH THE RESULTS.
SO MUCH SO THAT SHE DECIDED TO RETAIN MY SERVICES.
THOSE WERE THE HAPPIEST DAYS OF MY LIFE...

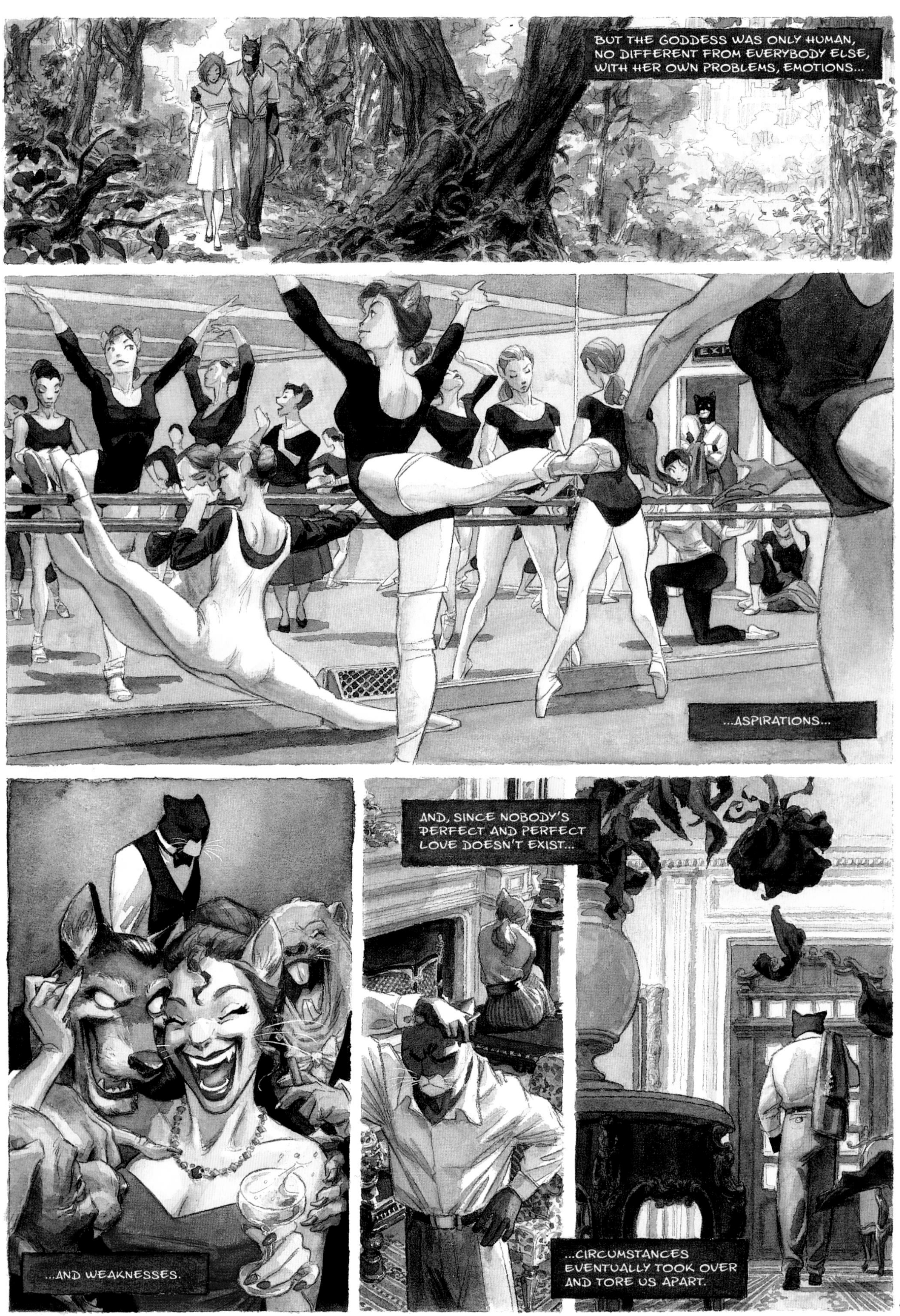
BUT THE GODDESS WAS ONLY HUMAN, NO DIFFERENT FROM EVERYBODY ELSE, WITH HER OWN PROBLEMS, EMOTIONS...
EXIT
...ASPIRATIONS...
...AND WEAKNESSES.
AND, SINCE NOBODY'S PERFECT AND PERFECT LOVE DOESN'T EXIST...
...CIRCUMSTANCES EVENTUALLY TOOK OVER AND TORE US APART.
6

SINCE THEN, I HADN'T SEEN HER...

A star has been eclipsed

...UNTIL THAT DAY.

A STAR HAD BEEN ECLIPSED, LEAVING MY PAST IN THE DARKNESS, LOST SOMEWHERE WITHIN THE SHADOWS. AND NOBODY CAN LIVE WITHOUT A PAST.

OUT THERE, HIDING SOMEWHERE, WAS THE GUILTY PARTY. GUILTY OF AT LEAST TWO MURDERS-- HE'D BOTH KILLED A PERSON AND DESTROYED MY MEMORIES.

AND THAT BASTARD WAS GOING TO PAY!

17

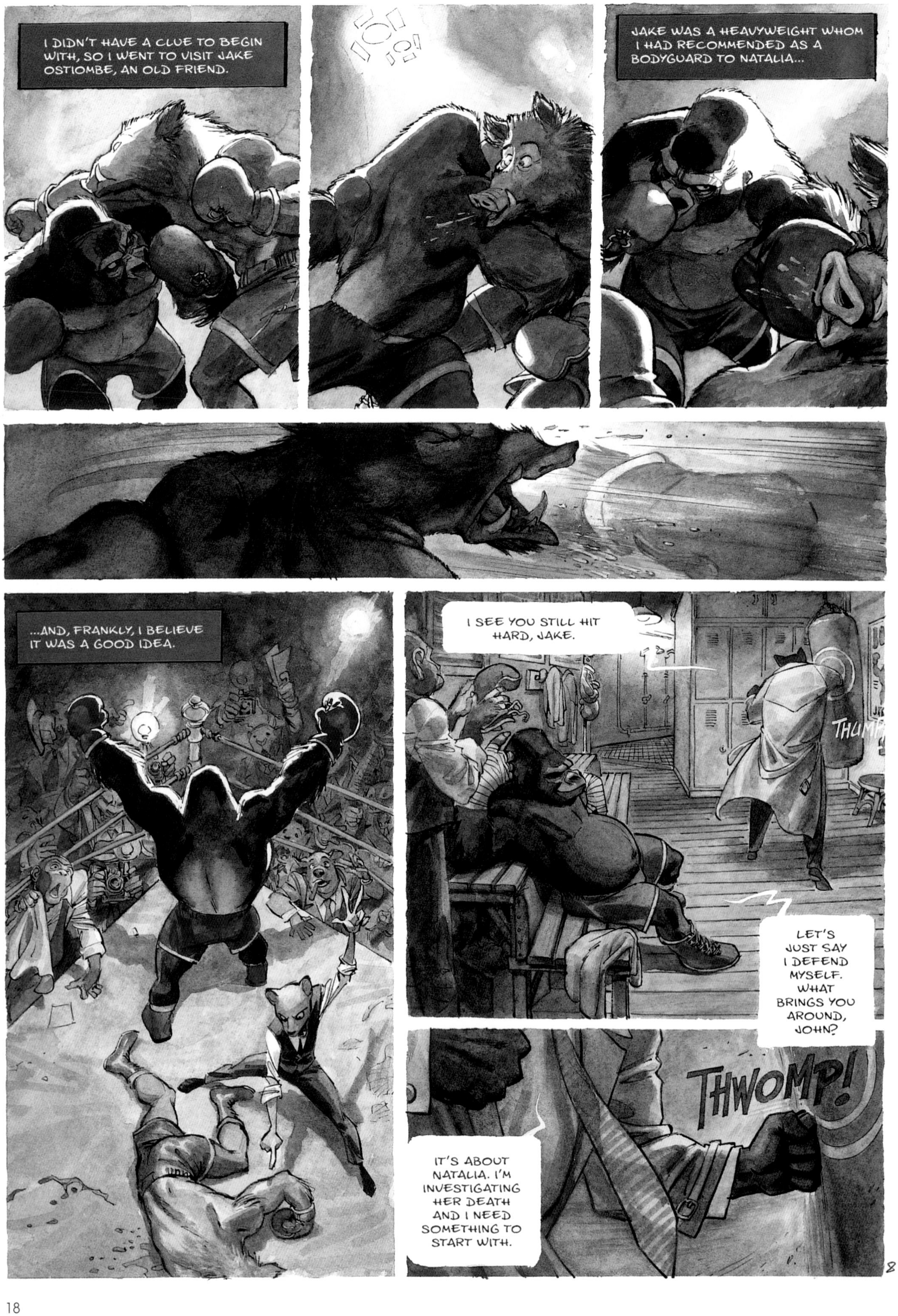
I DIDN'T HAVE A CLUE TO BEGIN WITH, SO I WENT TO VISIT JAKE OSTIOMBE, AN OLD FRIEND.
JAKE WAS A HEAVYWEIGHT WHOM I HAD RECOMMENDED AS A BODYGUARD TO NATALIA...
...AND, FRANKLY, I BELIEVE IT WAS A GOOD IDEA.
I SEE YOU STILL HIT HARD, JAKE.
THUMP
LET'S JUST SAY I DEFEND MYSELF. WHAT BRINGS YOU AROUND, JOHN?
THWOMP!
IT'S ABOUT NATALIA. I'M INVESTIGATING HER DEATH AND I NEED SOMETHING TO START WITH.
8

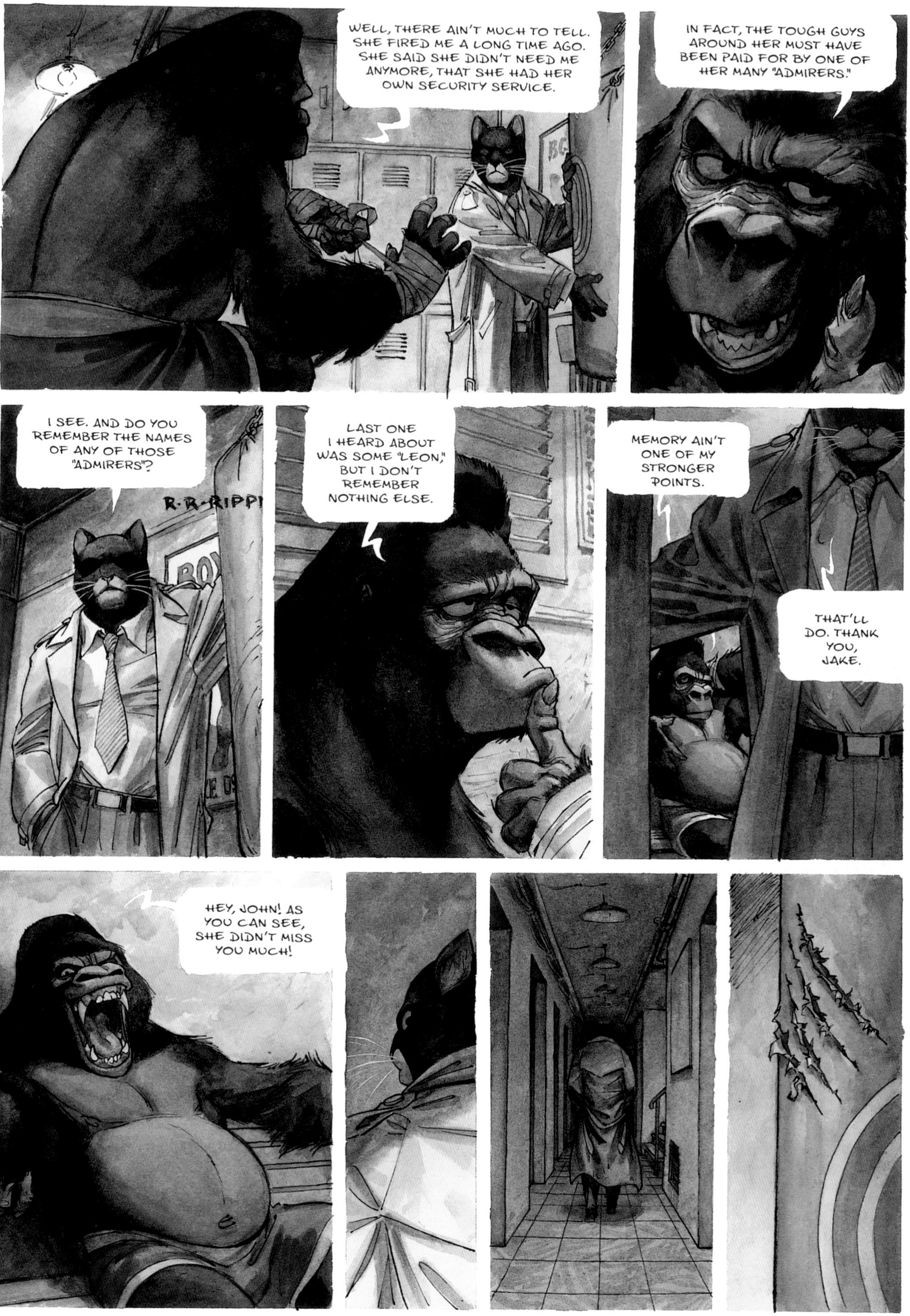
WELL, THERE AIN'T MUCH TO TELL. SHE FIRED ME A LONG TIME AGO. SHE SAID SHE DIDN'T NEED ME ANYMORE, THAT SHE HAD HER OWN SECURITY SERVICE.
IN FACT, THE TOUGH GUYS AROUND HER MUST HAVE BEEN PAID FOR BY ONE OF HER MANY "ADMIRERS."
I SEE. AND DO YOU REMEMBER THE NAMES OF ANY OF THOSE "ADMIRERS"?
LAST ONE I HEARD ABOUT WAS SOME "LEON," BUT I DON'T REMEMBER NOTHING ELSE.
MEMORY AIN'T ONE OF MY STRONGER POINTS.
THAT'LL DO. THANK YOU, JAKE.
HEY, JOHN! AS YOU CAN SEE, SHE DIDN'T MISS YOU MUCH!

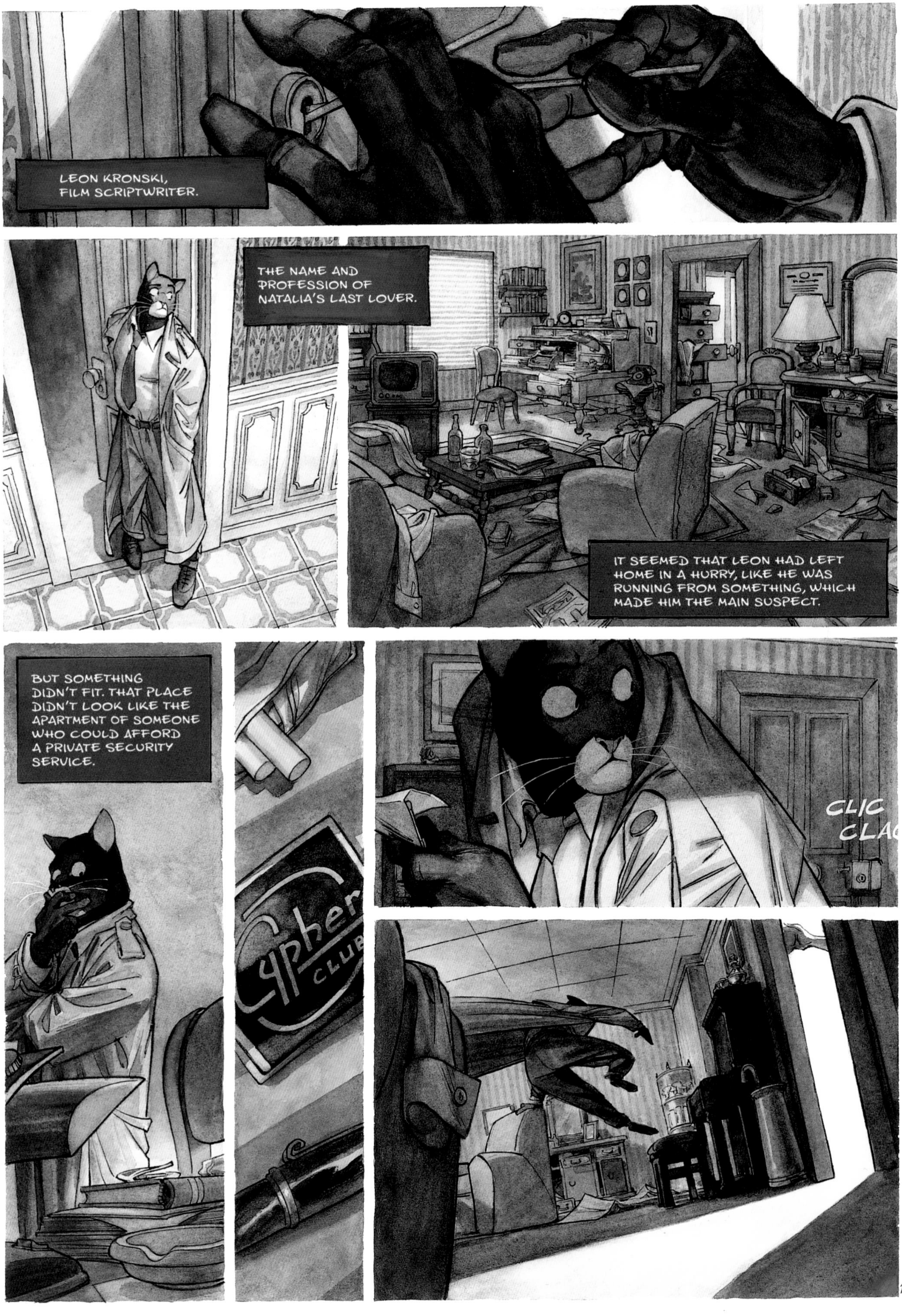
LEON KRONSKI,
FILM SCRIPTWRITER.
THE NAME AND
PROFESSION OF
NATALIA'S LAST LOVER.
IT SEEMED THAT LEON HAD LEFT
HOME IN A HURRY, LIKE HE WAS
RUNNING FROM SOMETHING, WHICH
MADE HIM THE MAIN SUSPECT.
BUT SOMETHING
DIDN'T FIT. THAT PLACE
DIDN'T LOOK LIKE THE
APARTMENT OF SOMEONE
WHO COULD AFFORD
A PRIVATE SECURITY
SERVICE.
CLIC
CLAC

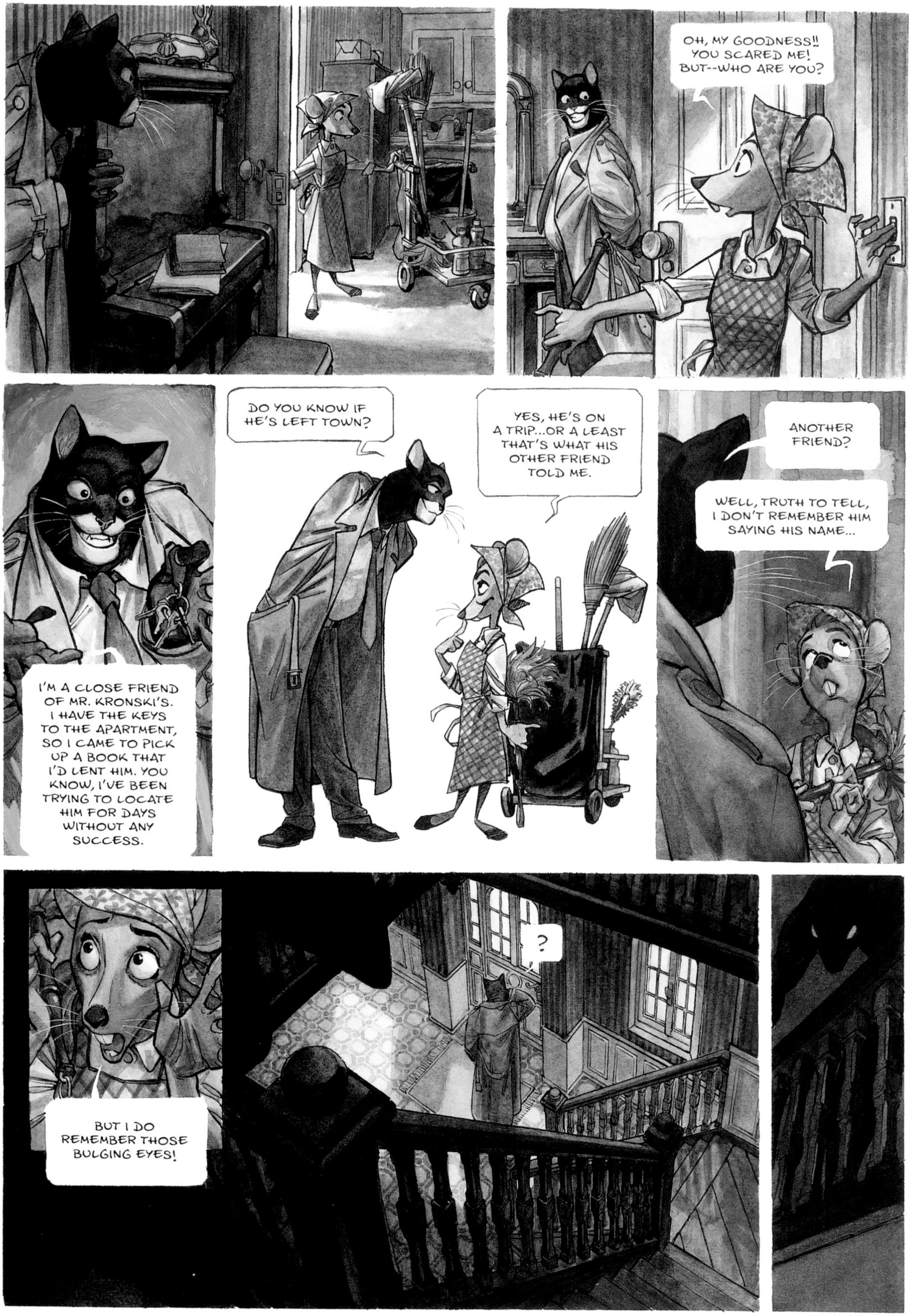
OH, MY GOODNESS!! YOU SCARED ME! BUT--WHO ARE YOU?
I'M A CLOSE FRIEND OF MR. KRONSKI'S. I HAVE THE KEYS TO THE APARTMENT, SO I CAME TO PICK UP A BOOK THAT I'D LENT HIM. YOU KNOW, I'VE BEEN TRYING TO LOCATE HIM FOR DAYS WITHOUT ANY SUCCESS.
DO YOU KNOW IF HE'S LEFT TOWN?
YES, HE'S ON A TRIP...OR A LEAST THAT'S WHAT HIS OTHER FRIEND TOLD ME.
ANOTHER FRIEND?
WELL, TRUTH TO TELL, I DON'T REMEMBER HIM SAYING HIS NAME...
BUT I DO REMEMBER THOSE BULGING EYES!
?
11

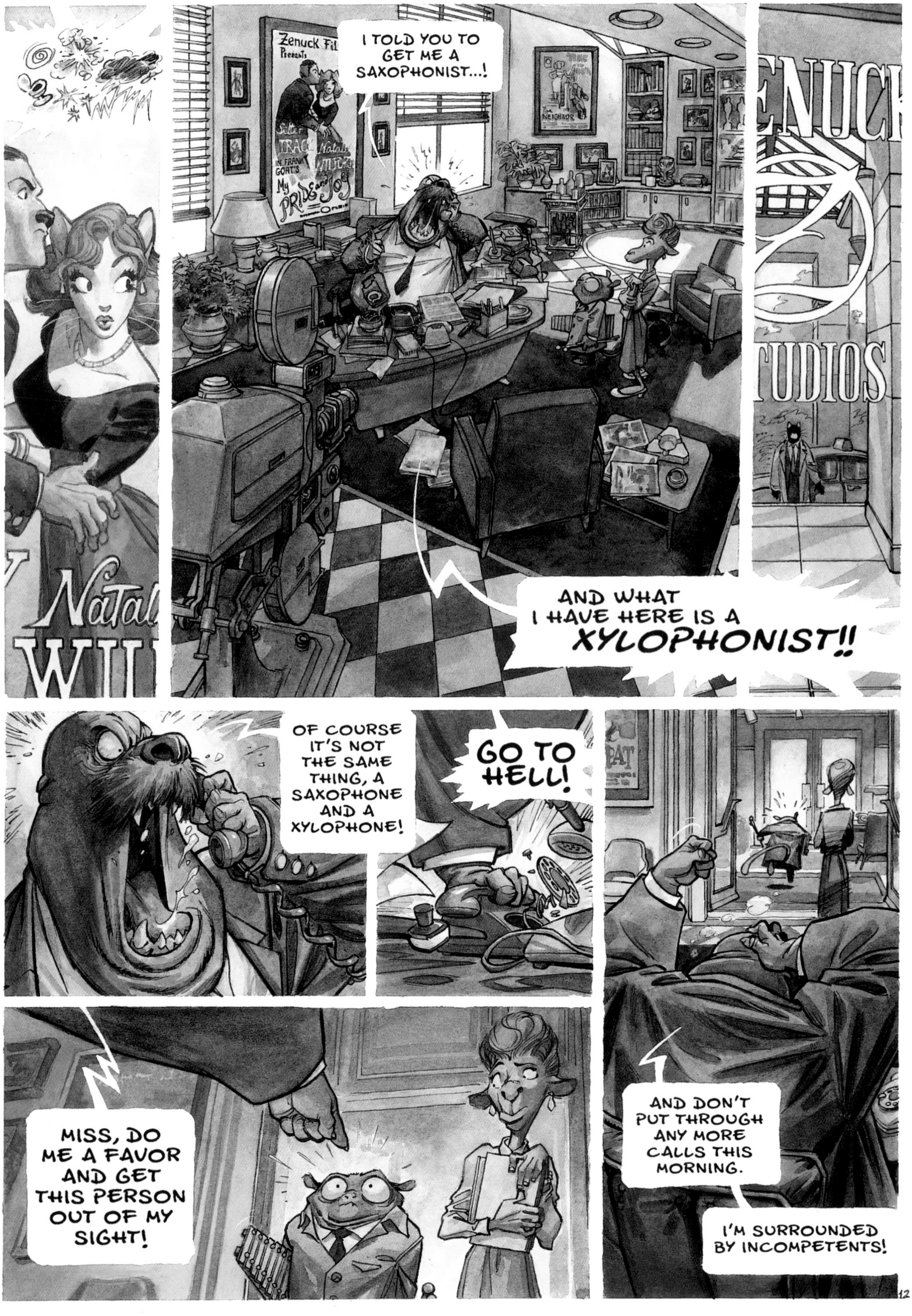
I TOLD YOU TO GET ME A SAXOPHONIST...!
AND WHAT I HAVE HERE IS A XYLOPHONIST!!
OF COURSE IT'S NOT THE SAME THING, A SAXOPHONE AND A XYLOPHONE!
GO TO HELL!
MISS, DO ME A FAVOR AND GET THIS PERSON OUT OF MY SIGHT!
AND DON'T PUT THROUGH ANY MORE CALLS THIS MORNING.
I'M SURROUNDED BY INCOMPETENTS!
ZENUCK STUDIOS
12

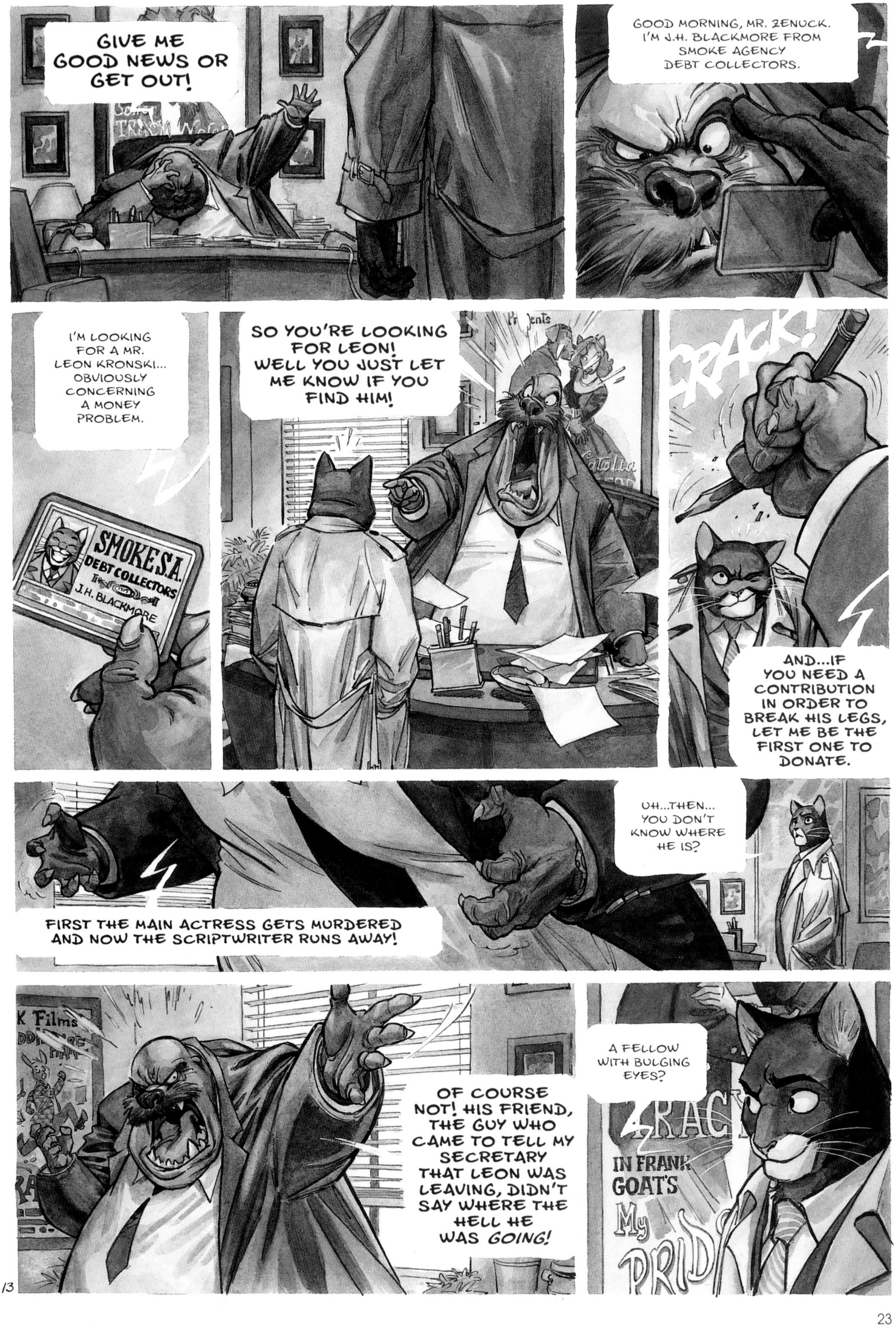
GIVE ME GOOD NEWS OR GET OUT!
GOOD MORNING, MR. ZENUCK. I'M J.H. BLACKMORE FROM SMOKE AGENCY DEBT COLLECTORS.
I'M LOOKING FOR A MR. LEON KRONSKI... OBVIOUSLY CONCERNING A MONEY PROBLEM.
SMOKE S.A.
DEBT COLLECTORS
J.H. BLACKMORE
SO YOU'RE LOOKING FOR LEON! WELL YOU JUST LET ME KNOW IF YOU FIND HIM!
CRACK!
AND...IF YOU NEED A CONTRIBUTION IN ORDER TO BREAK HIS LEGS, LET ME BE THE FIRST ONE TO DONATE.
FIRST THE MAIN ACTRESS GETS MURDERED AND NOW THE SCRIPTWRITER RUNS AWAY!
UH...THEN... YOU DON'T KNOW WHERE HE IS?
OF COURSE NOT! HIS FRIEND, THE GUY WHO CAME TO TELL MY SECRETARY THAT LEON WAS LEAVING, DIDN'T SAY WHERE THE HELL HE WAS *GOING*!
A FELLOW WITH BULGING EYES?
IN FRANK GOAT'S
My
13

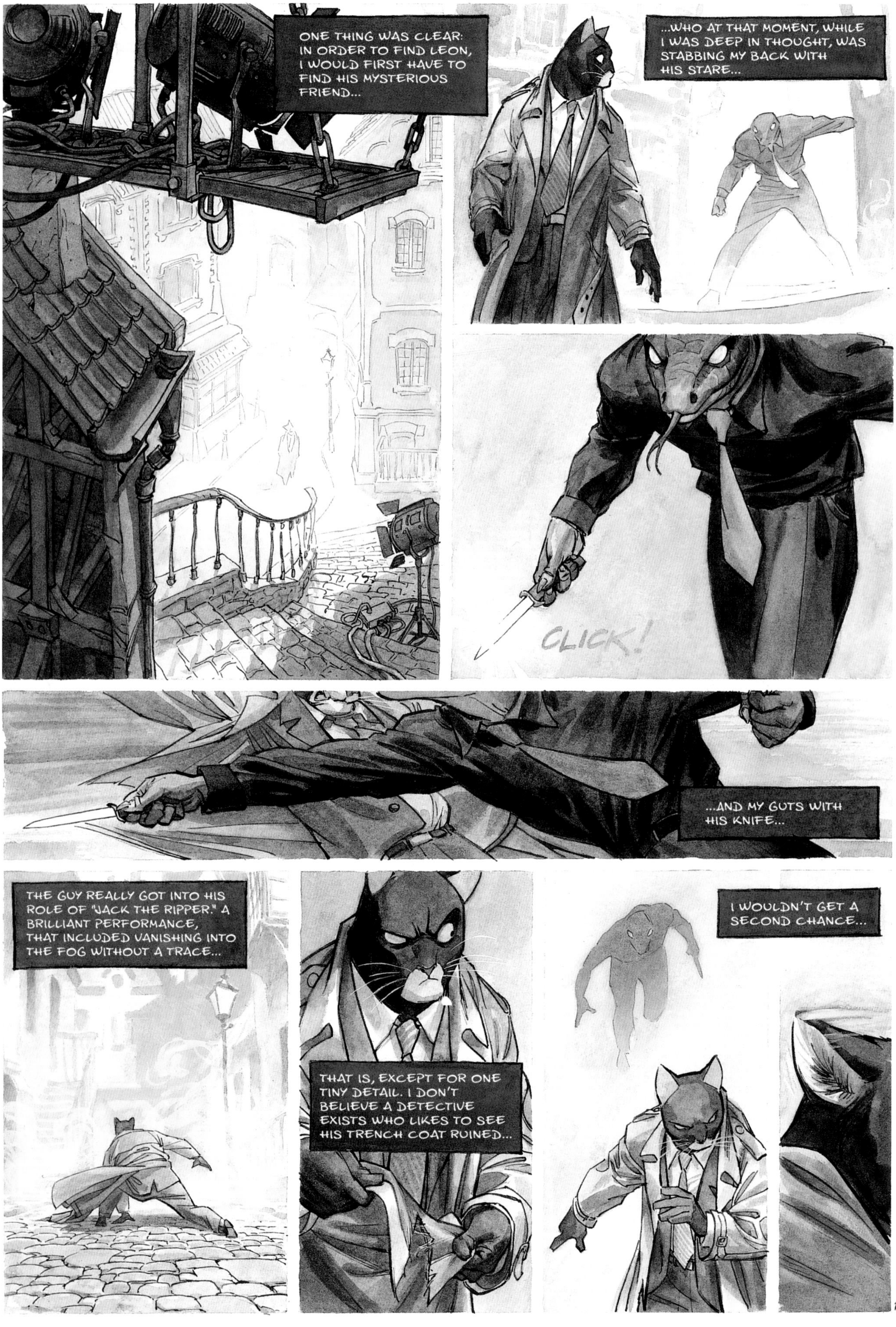

ONE THING WAS CLEAR: IN ORDER TO FIND LEON, I WOULD FIRST HAVE TO FIND HIS MYSTERIOUS FRIEND...
...WHO AT THAT MOMENT, WHILE I WAS DEEP IN THOUGHT, WAS STABBING MY BACK WITH HIS STARE...
CLICK!
...AND MY GUTS WITH HIS KNIFE...
THE GUY REALLY GOT INTO HIS ROLE OF "JACK THE RIPPER." A BRILLIANT PERFORMANCE, THAT INCLUDED VANISHING INTO THE FOG WITHOUT A TRACE...
THAT IS, EXCEPT FOR ONE TINY DETAIL. I DON'T BELIEVE A DETECTIVE EXISTS WHO LIKES TO SEE HIS TRENCH COAT RUINED...
I WOULDN'T GET A SECOND CHANCE...
14

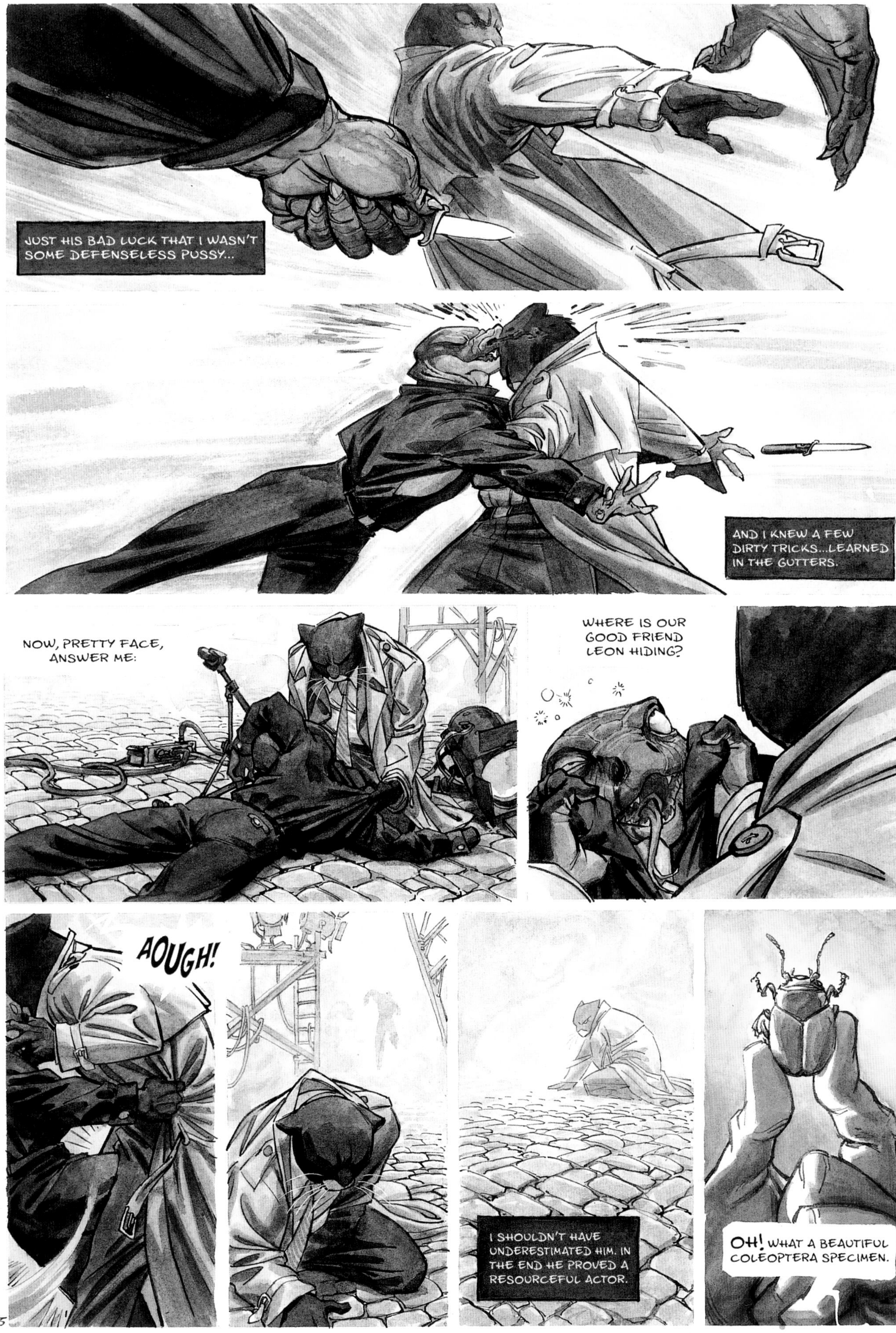
JUST HIS BAD LUCK THAT I WASN'T SOME DEFENSELESS PUSSY...
AND I KNEW A FEW DIRTY TRICKS...LEARNED IN THE GUTTERS.
NOW, PRETTY FACE, ANSWER ME:
WHERE IS OUR GOOD FRIEND LEON HIDING?
AOUGH!
I SHOULDN'T HAVE UNDERESTIMATED HIM. IN THE END HE PROVED A RESOURCEFUL ACTOR.
OH! WHAT A BEAUTIFUL COLEOPTERA SPECIMEN.
15

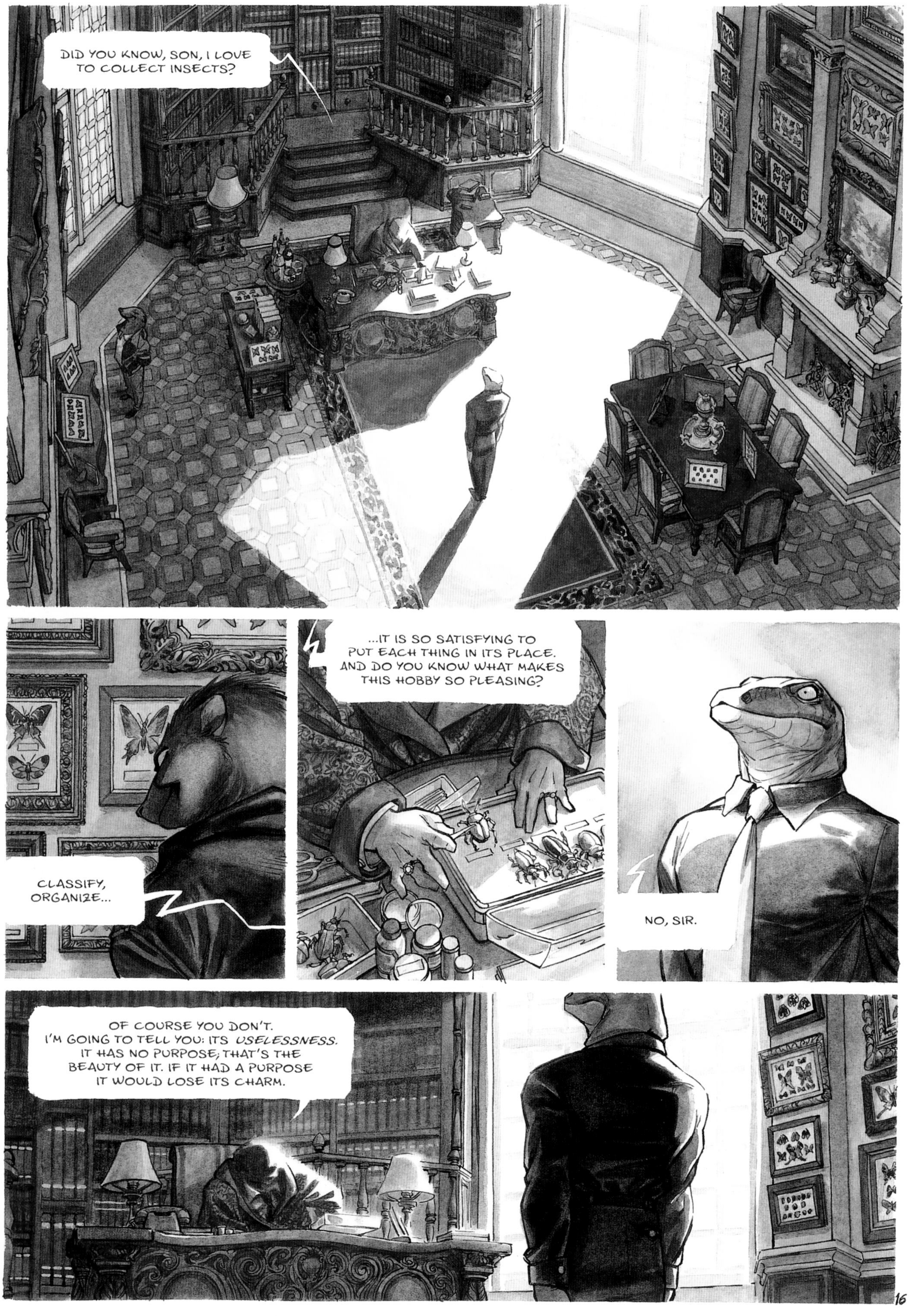
DID YOU KNOW, SON, I LOVE TO COLLECT INSECTS?
CLASSIFY, ORGANIZE...
...IT IS SO SATISFYING TO PUT EACH THING IN ITS PLACE. AND DO YOU KNOW WHAT MAKES THIS HOBBY SO PLEASING?
NO, SIR.
OF COURSE YOU DON'T. I'M GOING TO TELL YOU: ITS *USELESSNESS.* IT HAS NO PURPOSE; THAT'S THE BEAUTY OF IT. IF IT HAD A PURPOSE IT WOULD LOSE ITS CHARM.
16

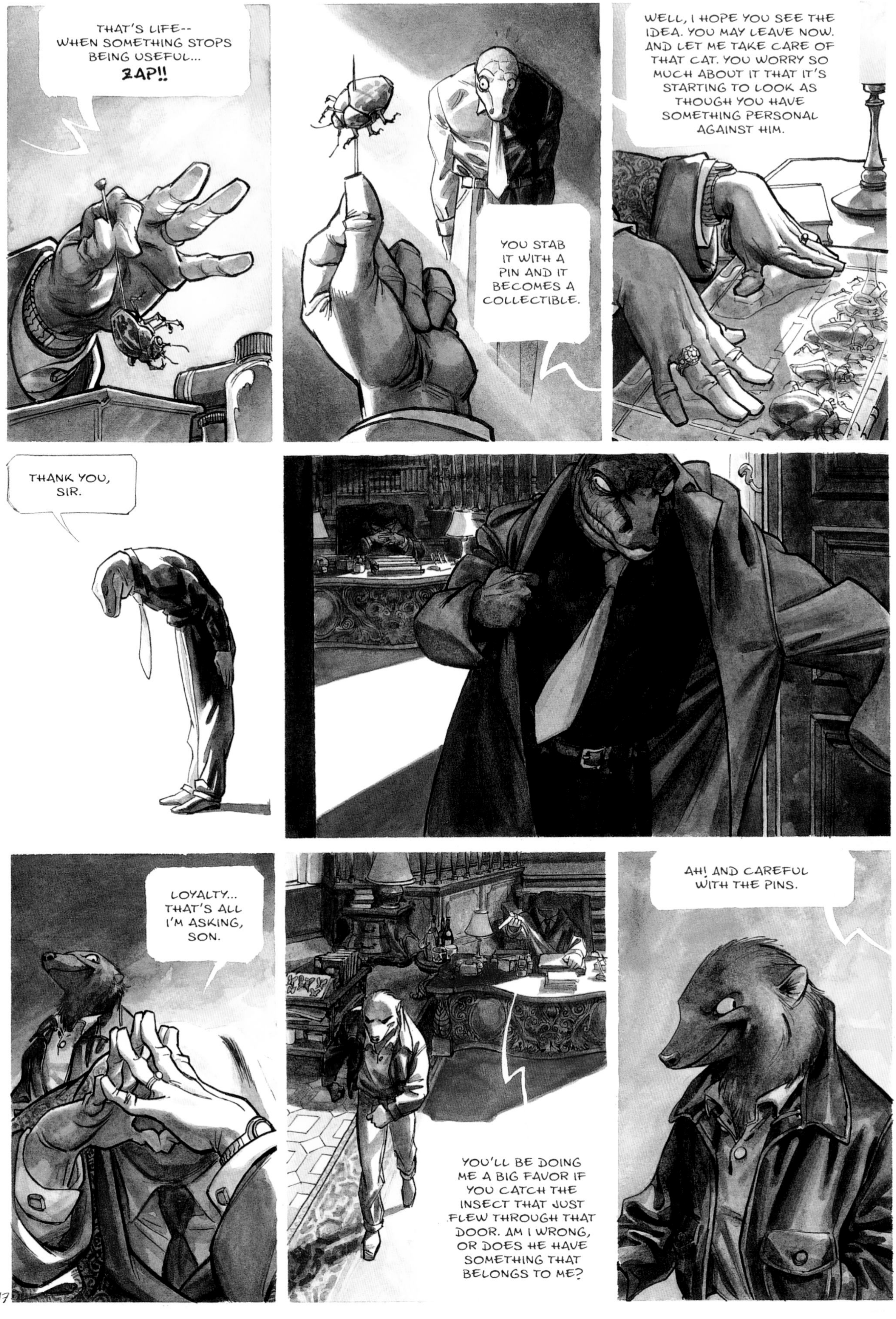
THAT'S LIFE-- WHEN SOMETHING STOPS BEING USEFUL... ZAP!!
YOU STAB IT WITH A PIN AND IT BECOMES A COLLECTIBLE.
WELL, I HOPE YOU SEE THE IDEA. YOU MAY LEAVE NOW. AND LET ME TAKE CARE OF THAT CAT. YOU WORRY SO MUCH ABOUT IT THAT IT'S STARTING TO LOOK AS THOUGH YOU HAVE SOMETHING PERSONAL AGAINST HIM.
THANK YOU, SIR.
LOYALTY... THAT'S ALL I'M ASKING, SON.
YOU'LL BE DOING ME A BIG FAVOR IF YOU CATCH THE INSECT THAT JUST FLEW THROUGH THAT DOOR. AM I WRONG, OR DOES HE HAVE SOMETHING THAT BELONGS TO ME?
AH! AND CAREFUL WITH THE PINS.
17

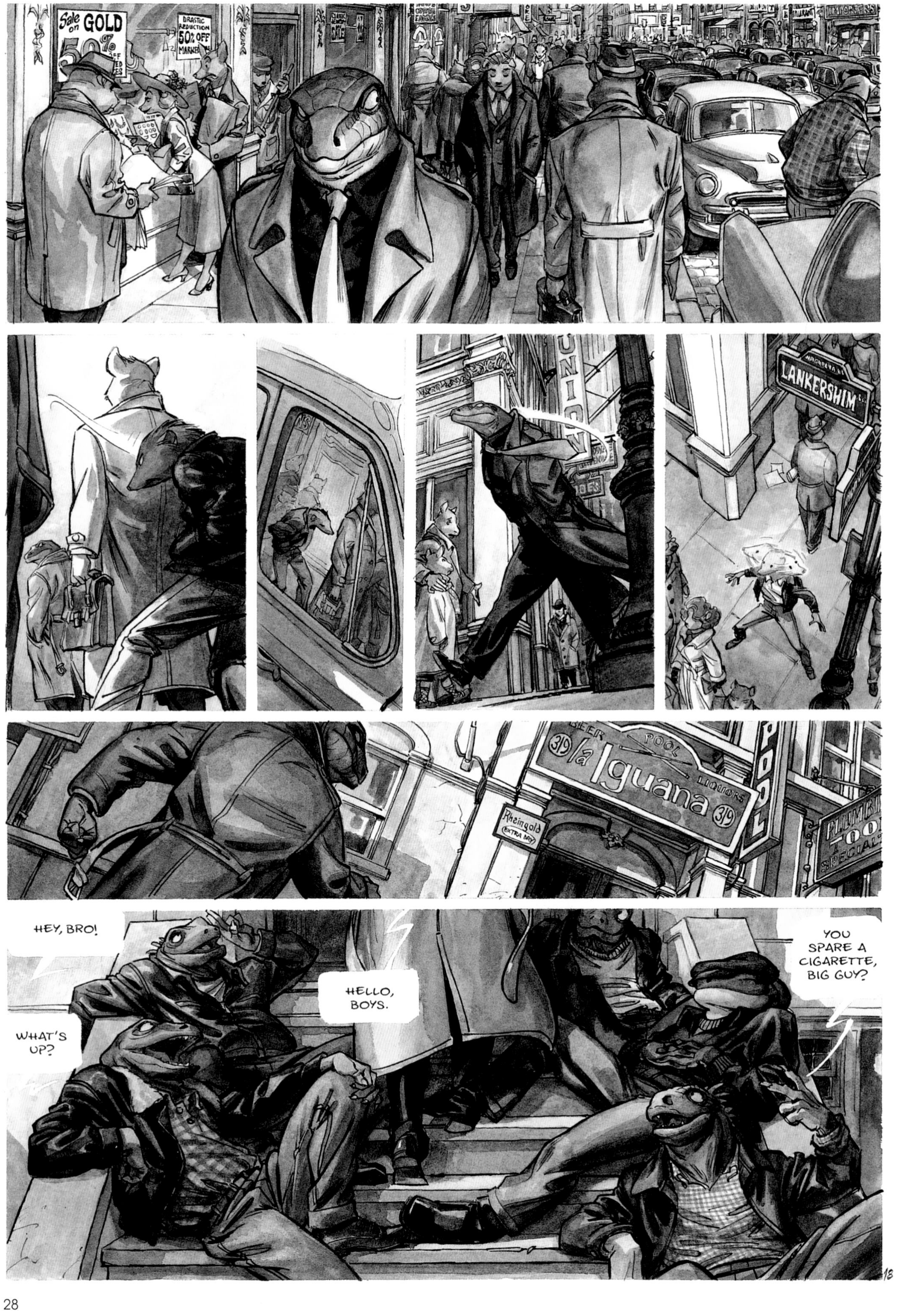
Sale on GOLD
DRASTIC REDUCTION 50% OFF
LANKERSHIM
UNION
BEER
POOL
319 La Iguana 319
LIQUORS
Rheingold
EXTRA DRY
POOL
HEY, BRO!
WHAT'S UP?
HELLO, BOYS.
YOU SPARE A CIGARETTE, BIG GUY?
18

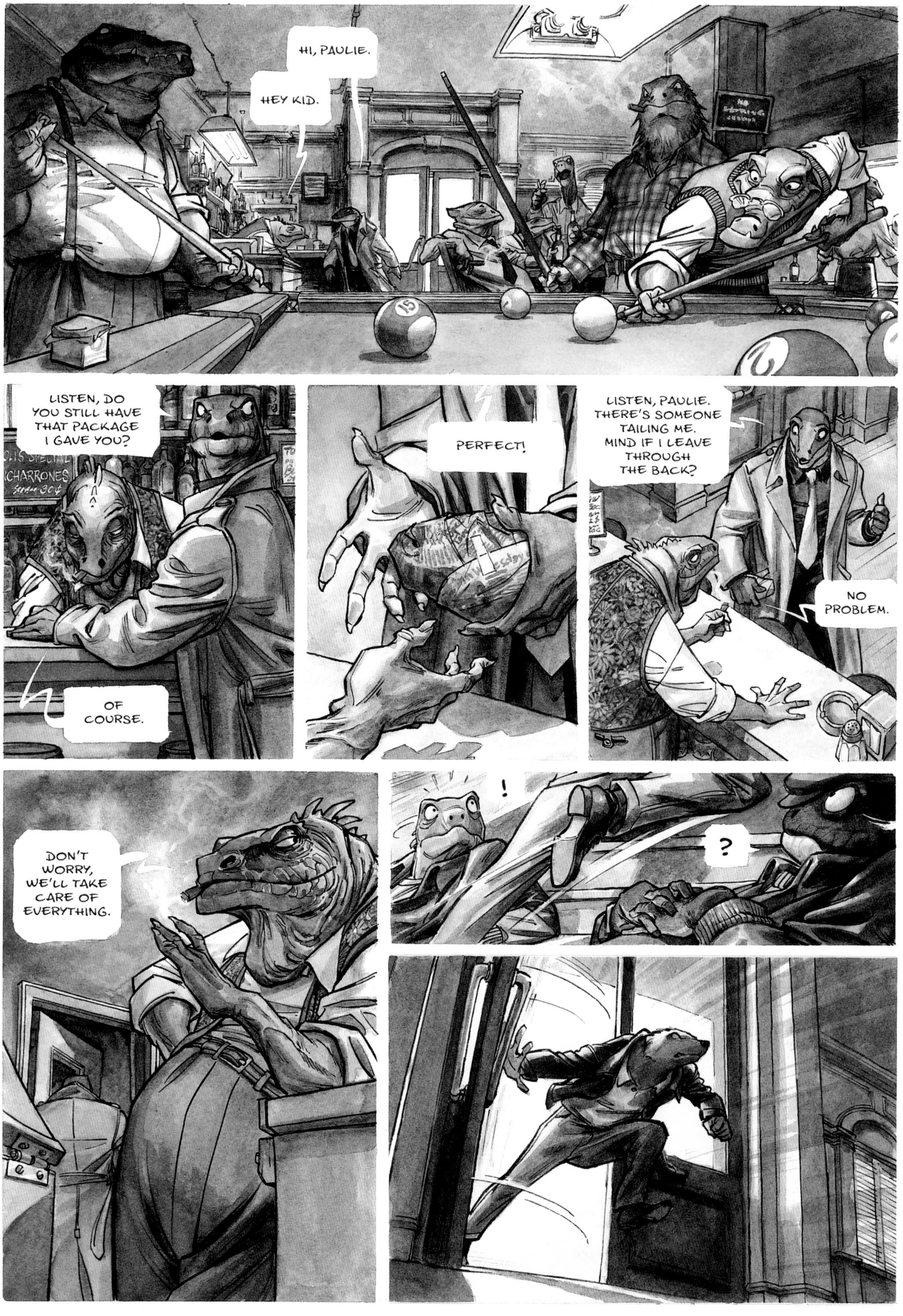
HI, PAULIE.
HEY KID.
LISTEN, DO YOU STILL HAVE THAT PACKAGE I GAVE YOU?
OF COURSE.
PERFECT!
LISTEN, PAULIE. THERE'S SOMEONE TAILING ME. MIND IF I LEAVE THROUGH THE BACK?
NO PROBLEM.
DON'T WORRY, WE'LL TAKE CARE OF EVERYTHING.
!
?

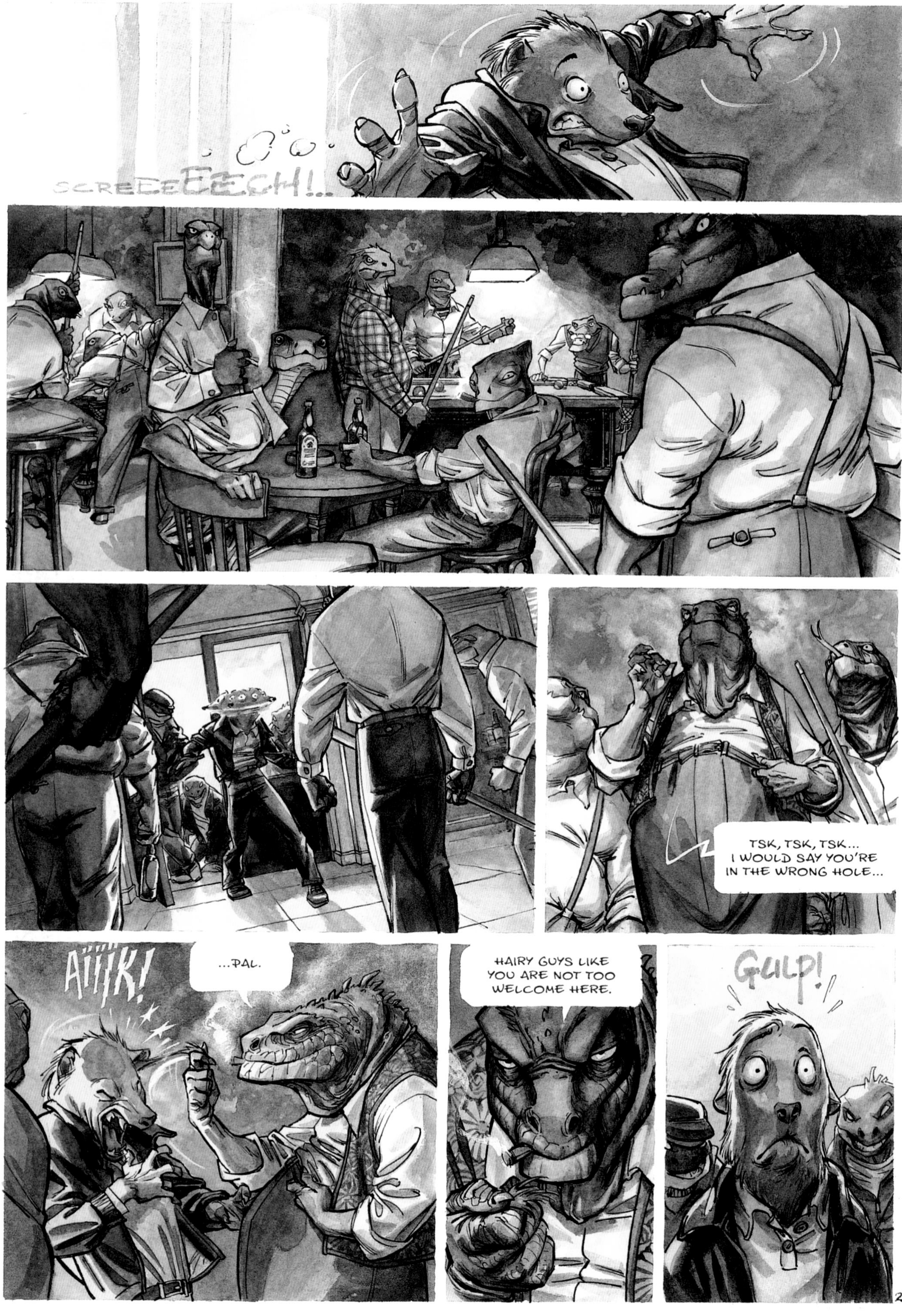
SCREEEEEECH!..
TSK, TSK, TSK... I WOULD SAY YOU'RE IN THE WRONG HOLE...
AIIIK!
...PAL.
HAIRY GUYS LIKE YOU ARE NOT TOO WELCOME HERE.
GULP!
20

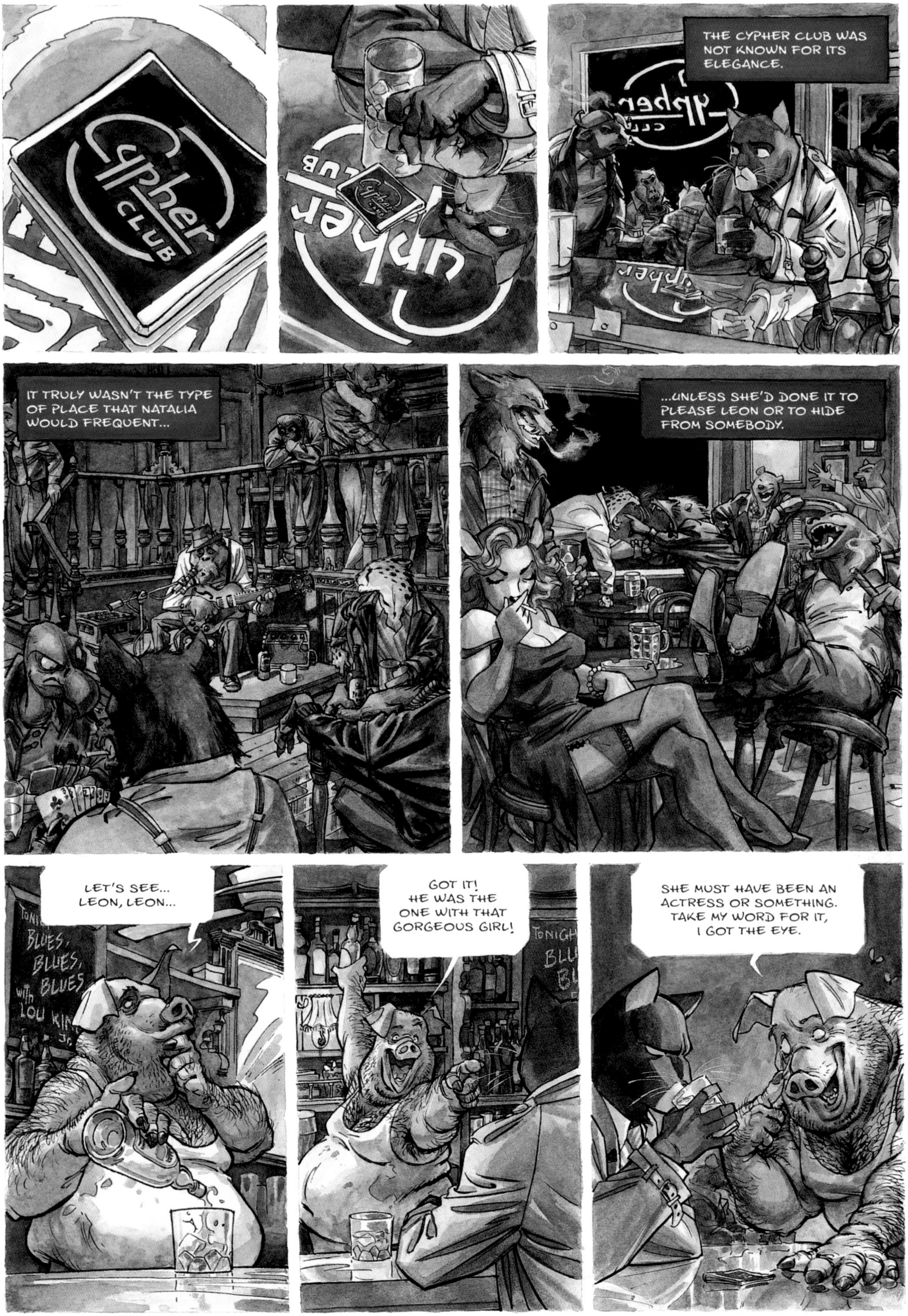

Cypher CLUB
Cypher CLUB
THE CYPHER CLUB WAS NOT KNOWN FOR ITS ELEGANCE.
IT TRULY WASN'T THE TYPE OF PLACE THAT NATALIA WOULD FREQUENT...
...UNLESS SHE'D DONE IT TO PLEASE LEON OR TO HIDE FROM SOMEBODY.
LET'S SEE... LEON, LEON...
TONIGHT BLUES, BLUES, with BLUES LOU KIN
GOT IT! HE WAS THE ONE WITH THAT GORGEOUS GIRL!
SHE MUST HAVE BEEN AN ACTRESS OR SOMETHING. TAKE MY WORD FOR IT, I GOT THE EYE.

21

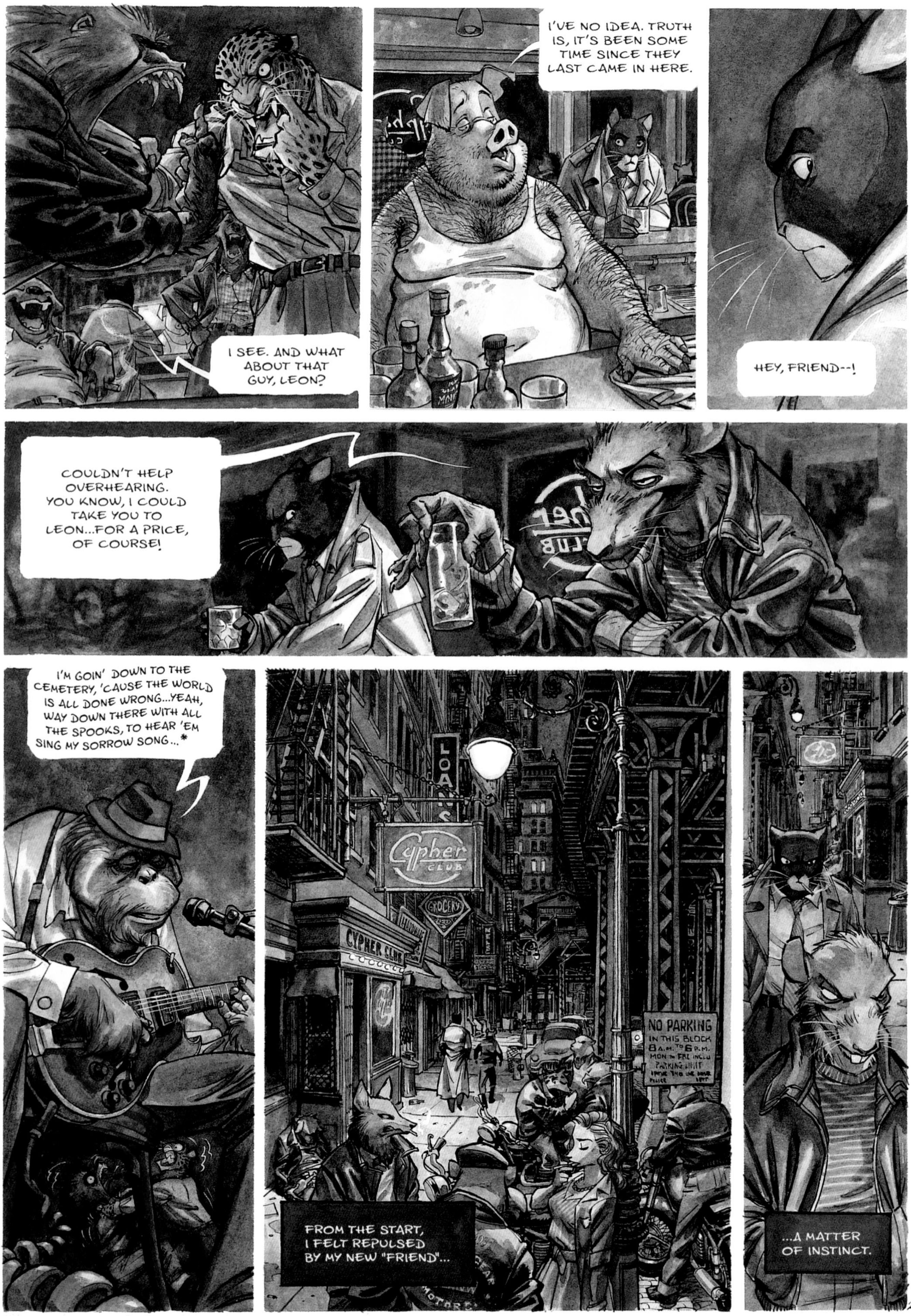
I SEE. AND WHAT ABOUT THAT GUY, LEON?
I'VE NO IDEA. TRUTH IS, IT'S BEEN SOME TIME SINCE THEY LAST CAME IN HERE.
HEY, FRIEND--!
COULDN'T HELP OVERHEARING. YOU KNOW, I COULD TAKE YOU TO LEON...FOR A PRICE, OF COURSE!
I'M GOIN' DOWN TO THE CEMETERY, 'CAUSE THE WORLD IS ALL DONE WRONG...YEAH, WAY DOWN THERE WITH ALL THE SPOOKS, TO HEAR 'EM SING MY SORROW SONG...*
Cypher CLUB
GROCERY
CYPHER CLUB
NO PARKING IN THIS BLOCK 8 A.M. TO 6 P.M.
FROM THE START, I FELT REPULSED BY MY NEW "FRIEND"...
...A MATTER OF INSTINCT.
22

* "CEMETERY BLUES," WRITTEN BY SID LANEY IN 1923.

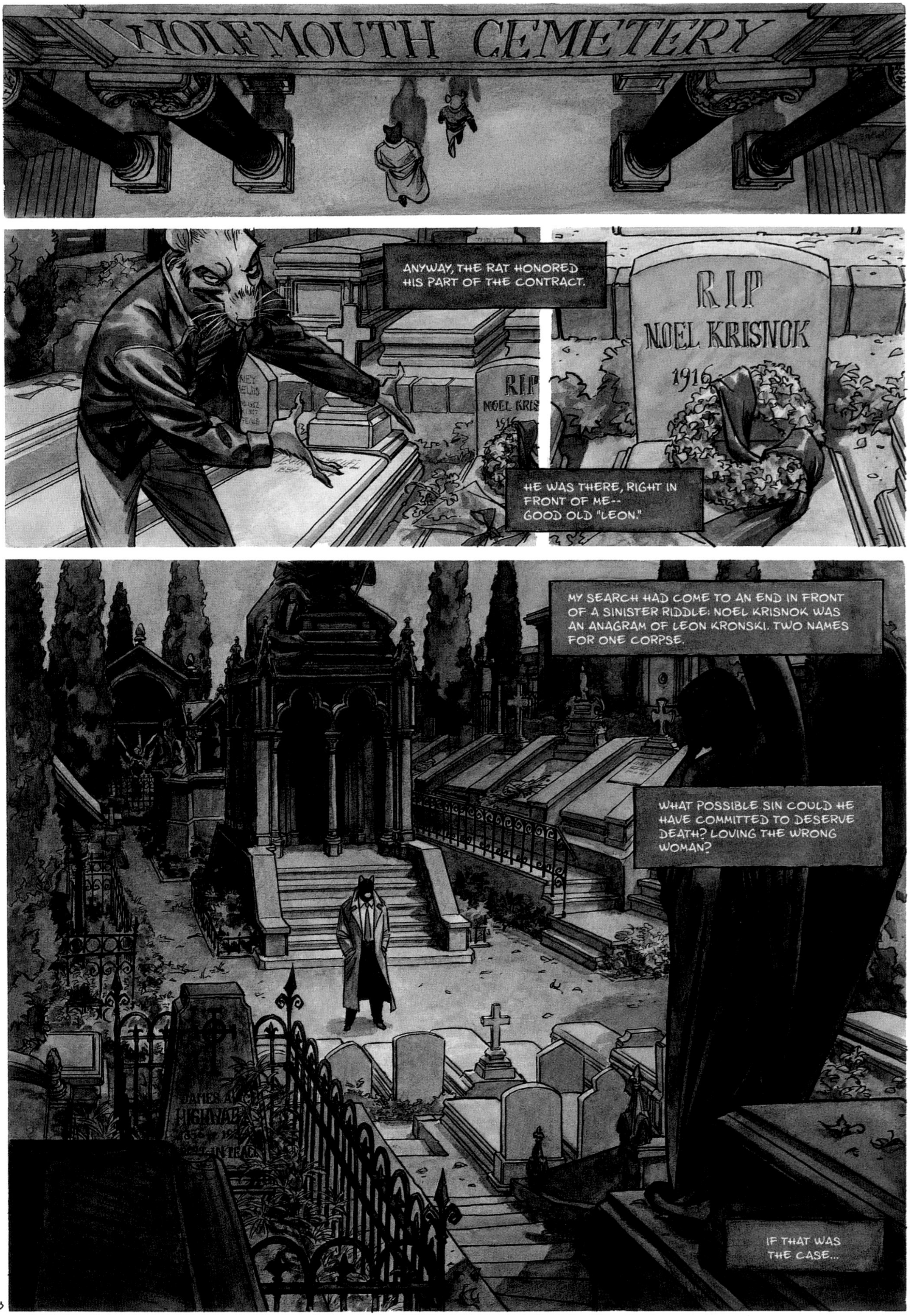
WOLFMOUTH CEMETERY
ANYWAY, THE RAT HONORED HIS PART OF THE CONTRACT.
RIP
NOEL KRISNOK
1916
HE WAS THERE, RIGHT IN FRONT OF ME-- GOOD OLD "LEON."
MY SEARCH HAD COME TO AN END IN FRONT OF A SINISTER RIDDLE: NOEL KRISNOK WAS AN ANAGRAM OF LEON KRONSKI. TWO NAMES FOR ONE CORPSE.
WHAT POSSIBLE SIN COULD HE HAVE COMMITTED TO DESERVE DEATH? LOVING THE WRONG WOMAN?
IF THAT WAS THE CASE...

23

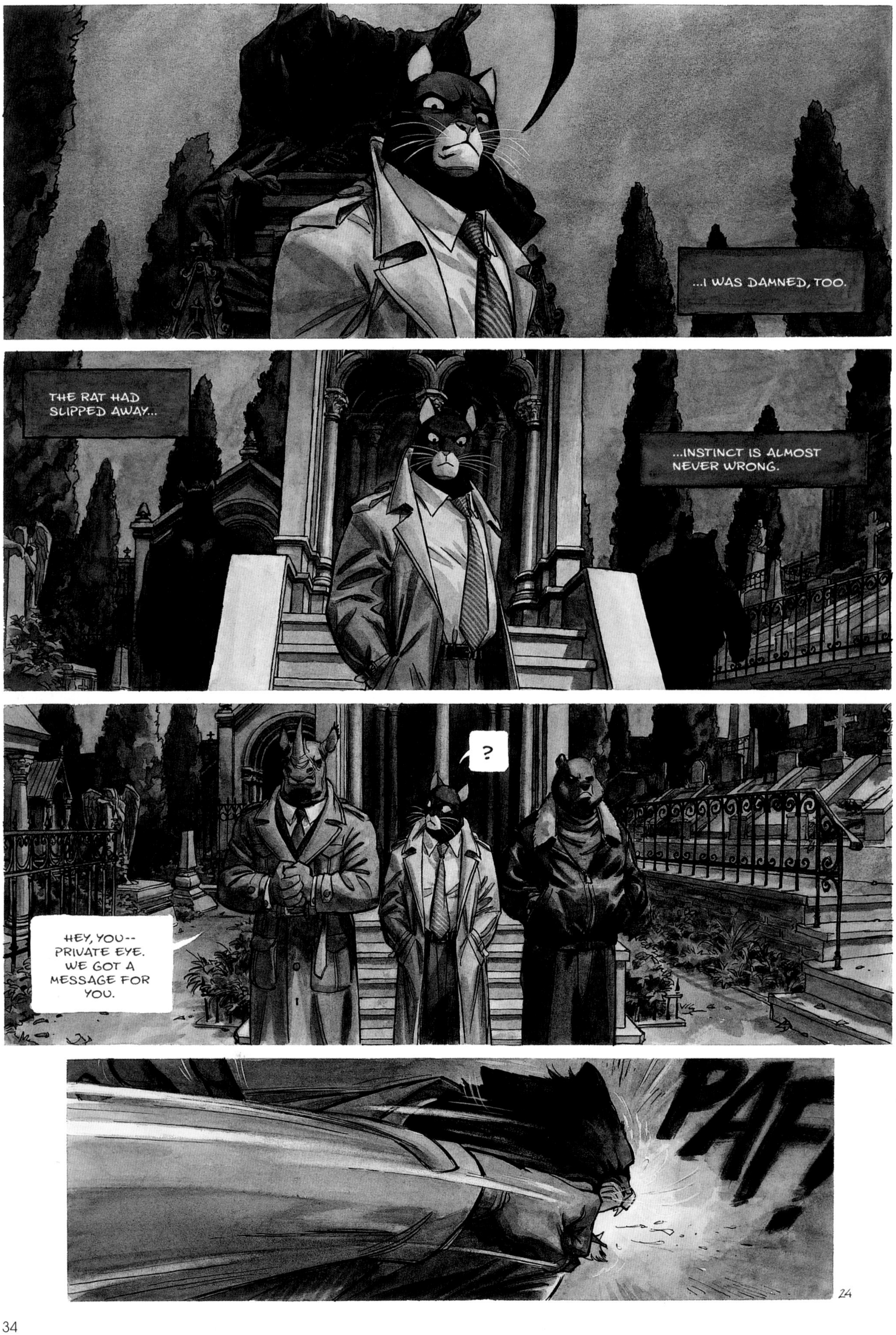
...I WAS DAMNED, TOO.
THE RAT HAD SLIPPED AWAY...
...INSTINCT IS ALMOST NEVER WRONG.
?
HEY, YOU-- PRIVATE EYE. WE GOT A MESSAGE FOR YOU.
PAF!
24

HOW TO DESCRIBE THOSE GUYS?

IT WAS AS IF THE TOMBS' MARBLE GARGOYLES HAD SUDDENLY COME TO LIFE.

AND THIS WAS LESS FROM THEIR SCARY LOOKS THAN THEIR HARDNESS.

PUNCHING BACK WAS LIKE HITTING A STONE WALL.

ALL THE SAME, THERE'S A WORD THAT WOULD DESCRIBE THEM PERFECTLY:

PROFESSIONAL.

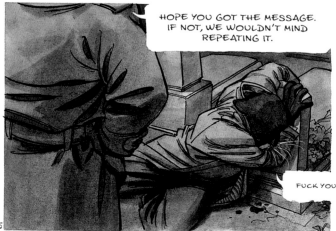

HOPE YOU GOT THE MESSAGE. IF NOT, WE WOULDN'T MIND REPEATING IT.

FUCK YOU...

IDIOT!

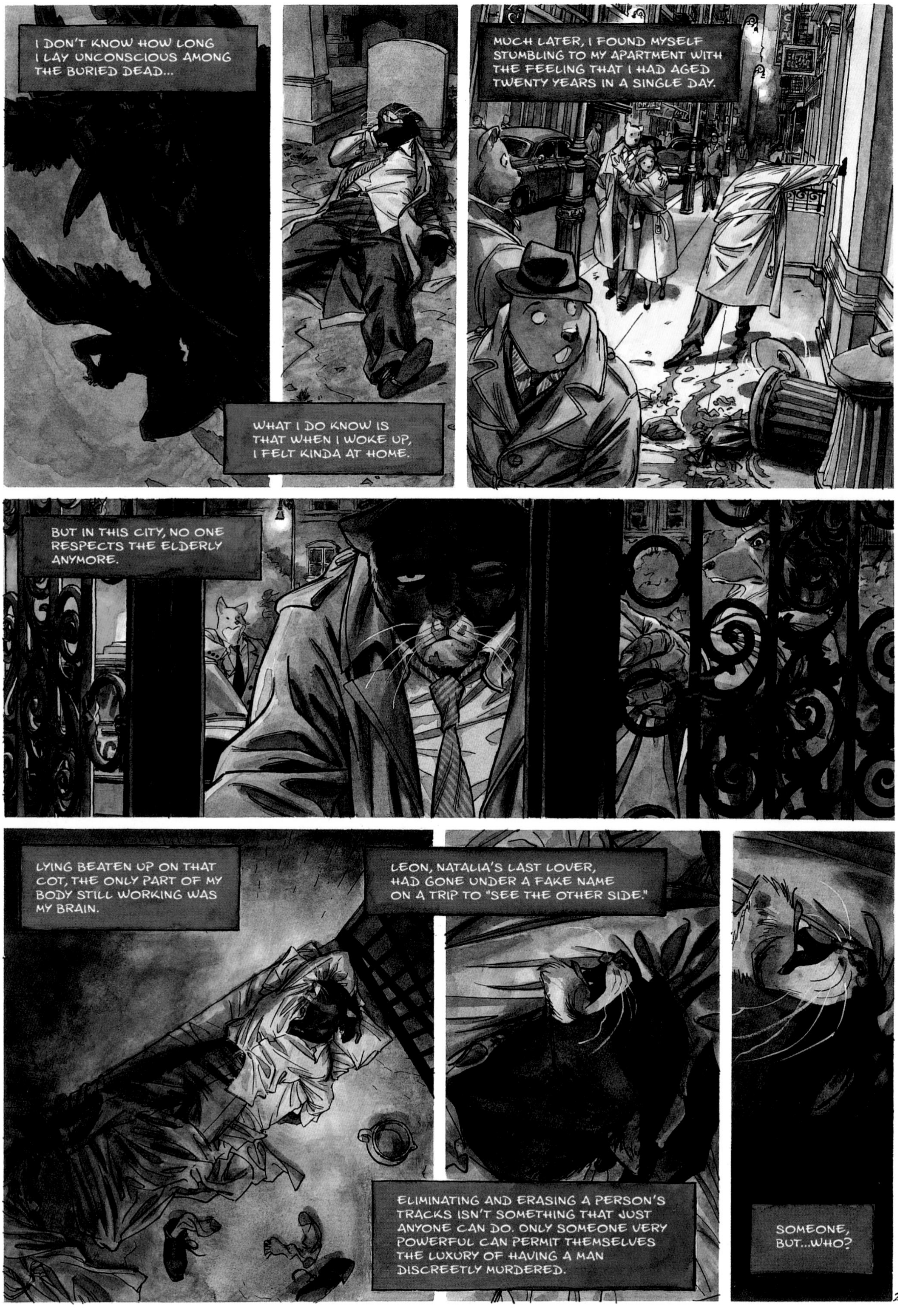
I DON'T KNOW HOW LONG I LAY UNCONSCIOUS AMONG THE BURIED DEAD...
WHAT I DO KNOW IS THAT WHEN I WOKE UP, I FELT KINDA AT HOME.
MUCH LATER, I FOUND MYSELF STUMBLING TO MY APARTMENT WITH THE FEELING THAT I HAD AGED TWENTY YEARS IN A SINGLE DAY.
BUT IN THIS CITY, NO ONE RESPECTS THE ELDERLY ANYMORE.
LYING BEATEN UP ON THAT COT, THE ONLY PART OF MY BODY STILL WORKING WAS MY BRAIN.
LEON, NATALIA'S LAST LOVER, HAD GONE UNDER A FAKE NAME ON A TRIP TO "SEE THE OTHER SIDE."
ELIMINATING AND ERASING A PERSON'S TRACKS ISN'T SOMETHING THAT JUST ANYONE CAN DO. ONLY SOMEONE VERY POWERFUL CAN PERMIT THEMSELVES THE LUXURY OF HAVING A MAN DISCREETLY MURDERED.
SOMEONE, BUT...WHO?
26

THE HUMIDITY SEEPED INTO MY BONES AND IT WOULDN'T BE TOO LONG BEFORE SMIRNOV STARTED GNAWING ON WHAT WAS LEFT OF THEM. WITH THIS COMFORTING IMAGE IN MY HEAD, I FELL ASLEEP.

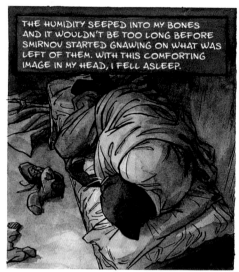

I DREAMT OF HER.

IN THE MORNING, I WOKE UP DEPRESSED.

GOOD MORNING, BLACKSAD.

COME IN AND GET COMFORTABLE, CHIEF. MAKE YOURSELF AT HOME.

I IMAGINE...

...YOU'RE CURIOUS TO KNOW WHY YOU'RE IN JAIL.

WELL YOU KNOW, SMIRNOV, I'M STARTING TO BELIEVE THAT OLD SAYING, "CURIOSITY KILLED THE CAT."

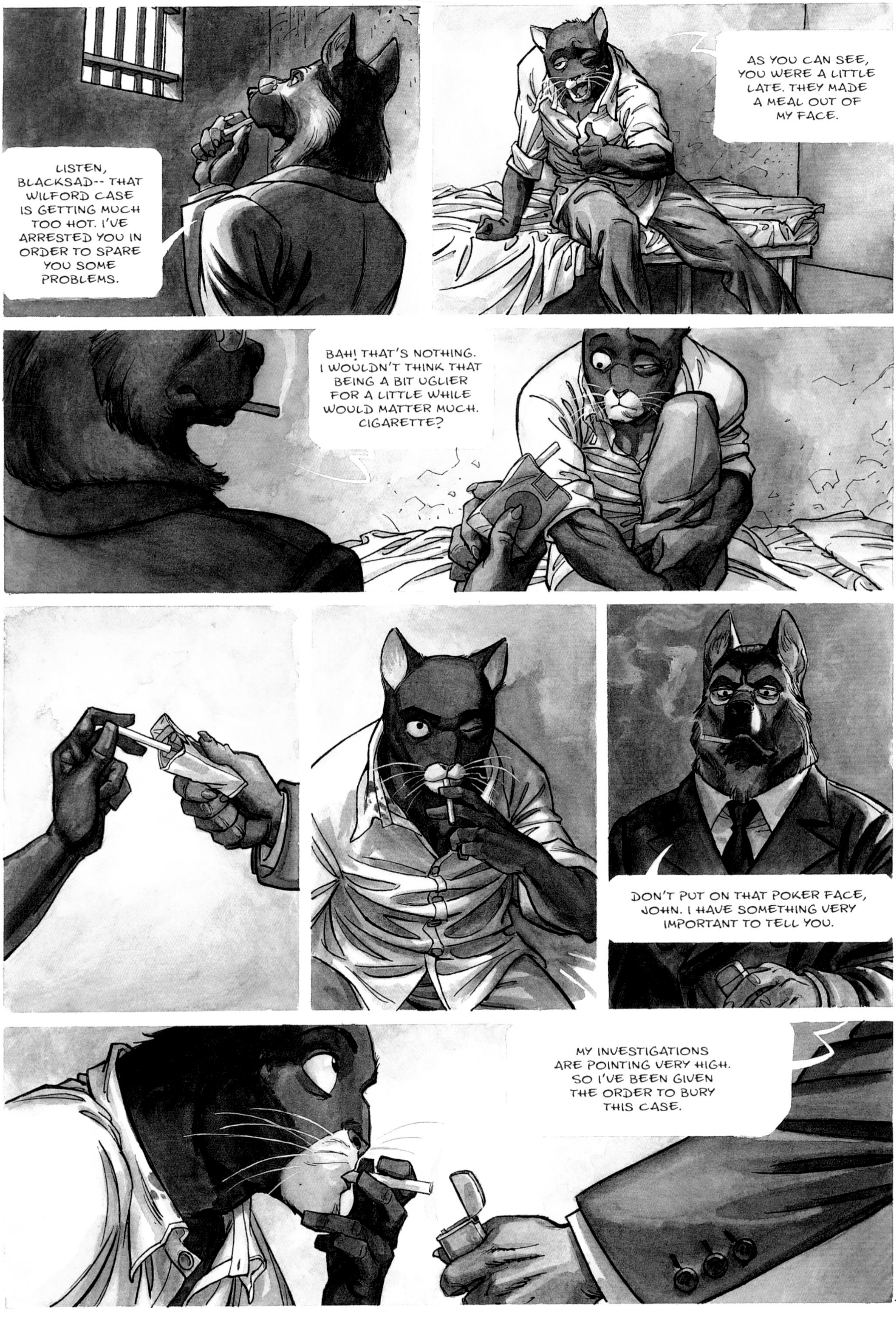
LISTEN, BLACKSAD-- THAT WILFORD CASE IS GETTING MUCH TOO HOT. I'VE ARRESTED YOU IN ORDER TO SPARE YOU SOME PROBLEMS.
AS YOU CAN SEE, YOU WERE A LITTLE LATE. THEY MADE A MEAL OUT OF MY FACE.
BAH! THAT'S NOTHING. I WOULDN'T THINK THAT BEING A BIT UGLIER FOR A LITTLE WHILE WOULD MATTER MUCH. CIGARETTE?
DON'T PUT ON THAT POKER FACE, JOHN. I HAVE SOMETHING VERY IMPORTANT TO TELL YOU.
MY INVESTIGATIONS ARE POINTING VERY HIGH. SO I'VE BEEN GIVEN THE ORDER TO BURY THIS CASE.
28

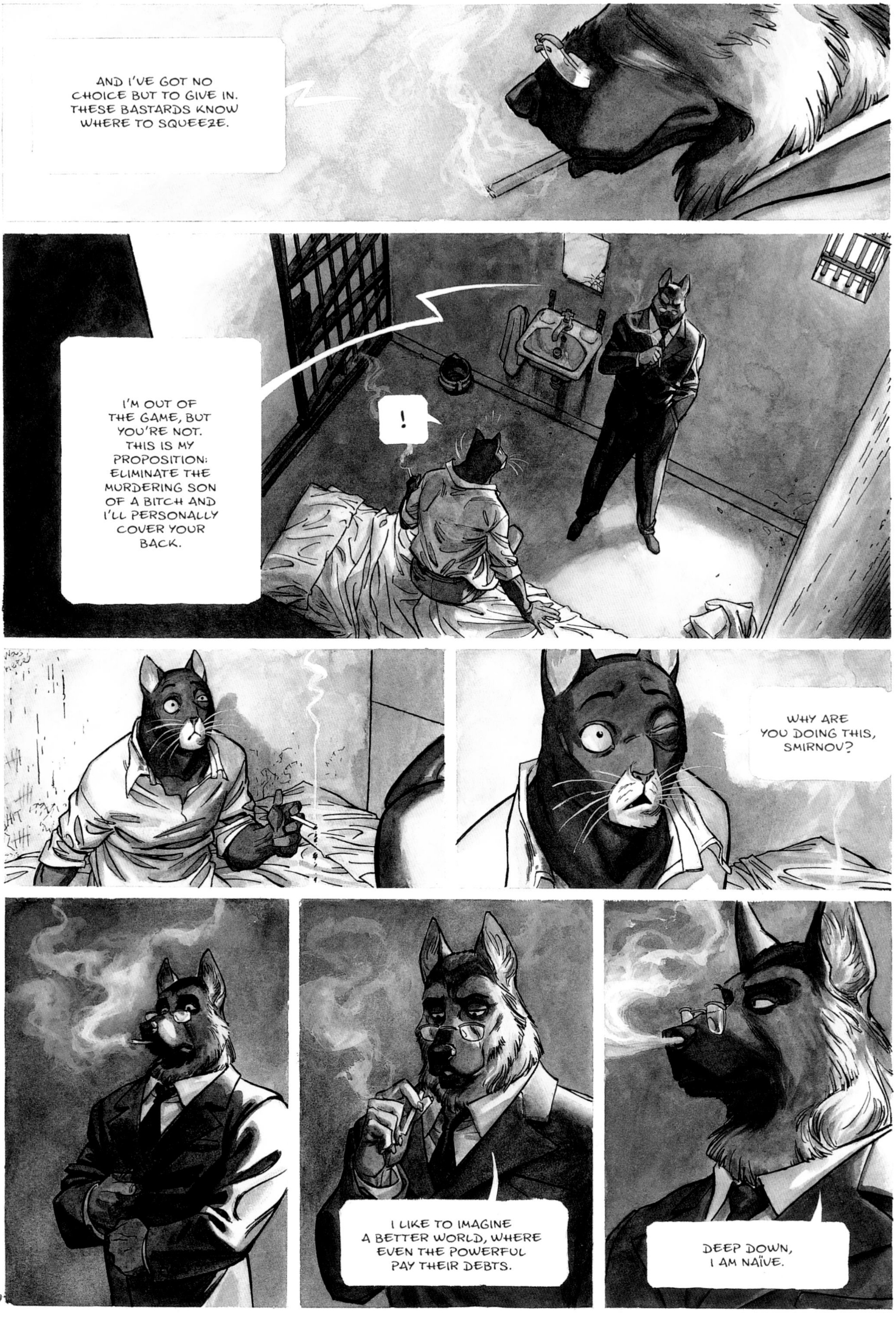
AND I'VE GOT NO CHOICE BUT TO GIVE IN. THESE BASTARDS KNOW WHERE TO SQUEEZE.
I'M OUT OF THE GAME, BUT YOU'RE NOT. THIS IS MY PROPOSITION: ELIMINATE THE MURDERING SON OF A BITCH AND I'LL PERSONALLY COVER YOUR BACK.
!
WHY ARE YOU DOING THIS, SMIRNOV?
I LIKE TO IMAGINE A BETTER WORLD, WHERE EVEN THE POWERFUL PAY THEIR DEBTS.
DEEP DOWN, I AM NAÏVE.

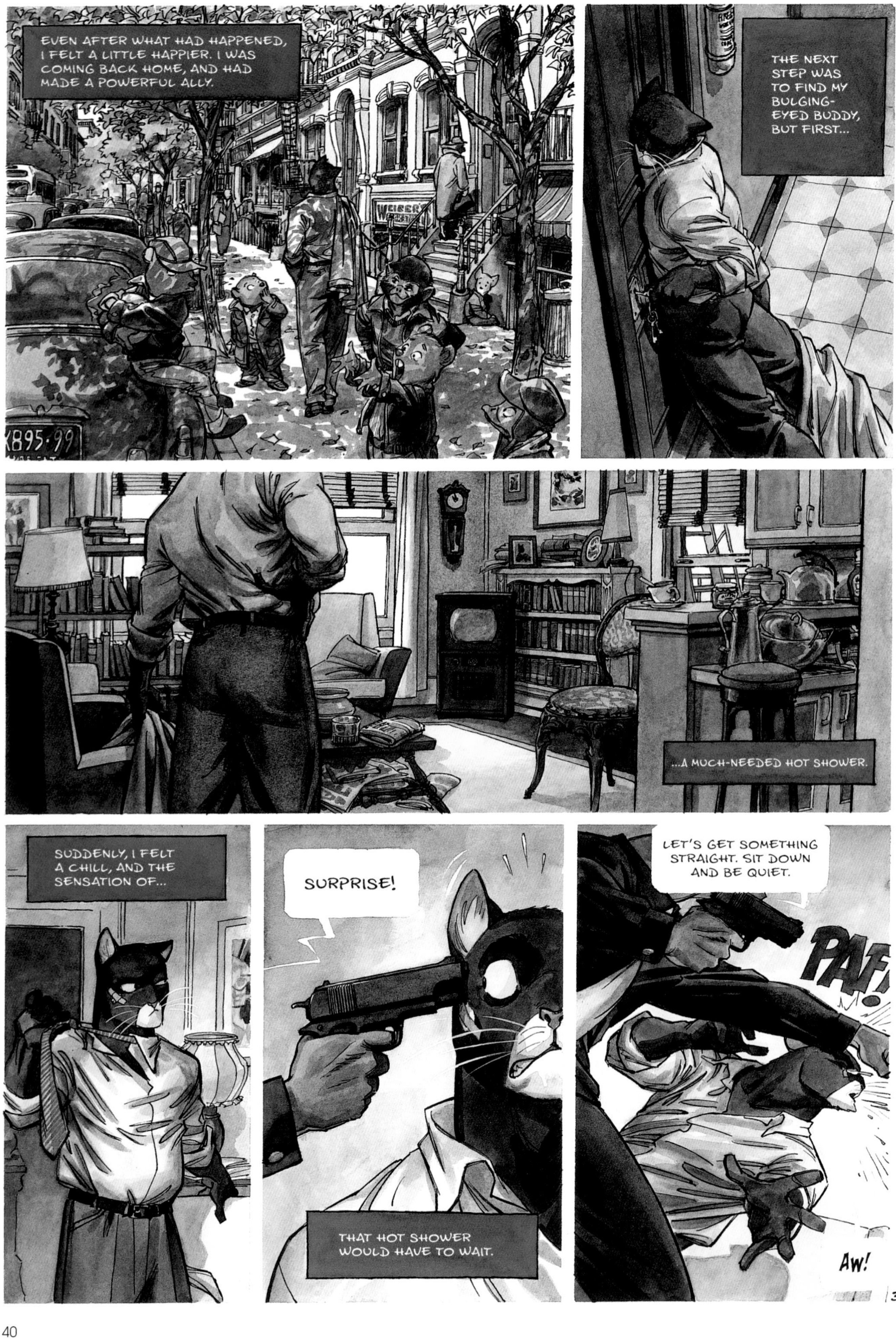
EVEN AFTER WHAT HAD HAPPENED, I FELT A LITTLE HAPPIER. I WAS COMING BACK HOME, AND HAD MADE A POWERFUL ALLY.
WEIBERT'S
XB95-99
THE NEXT STEP WAS TO FIND MY BULGING-EYED BUDDY, BUT FIRST...
...A MUCH-NEEDED HOT SHOWER.
SUDDENLY, I FELT A CHILL, AND THE SENSATION OF...
SURPRISE!
THAT HOT SHOWER WOULD HAVE TO WAIT.
LET'S GET SOMETHING STRAIGHT. SIT DOWN AND BE QUIET.
PAF!
AW!

YOU AND I HAVE A COMPATABILITY PROBLEM.

AND FRANKLY, I DON'T INTEND TO GIVE UP A SINGLE DOLLAR.

I'VE BEEN THAT BASTARD'S RIGHT HAND FOR TOO MANY YEARS. FAR TOO MANY TO ALLOW A JACKASS LIKE YOU TO COME IN AND TRY TO STEAL MY GAME NOW.

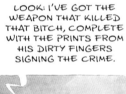

LOOK: I'VE GOT THE WEAPON THAT KILLED THAT BITCH, COMPLETE WITH THE PRINTS FROM HIS DIRTY FINGERS SIGNING THE CRIME.

THE LIZARD WAS A BLACKMAILER. AND, KNOWING I WAS WORKING ALONE, HE FIGURED THAT I ALSO WANTED TO MAKE MONEY OFF THE AFFAIR.

AND YOU. WHAT DO YOU HAVE? THE GUN HE USED TO KILL LEON, MAYBE?

ANSWER ME!!

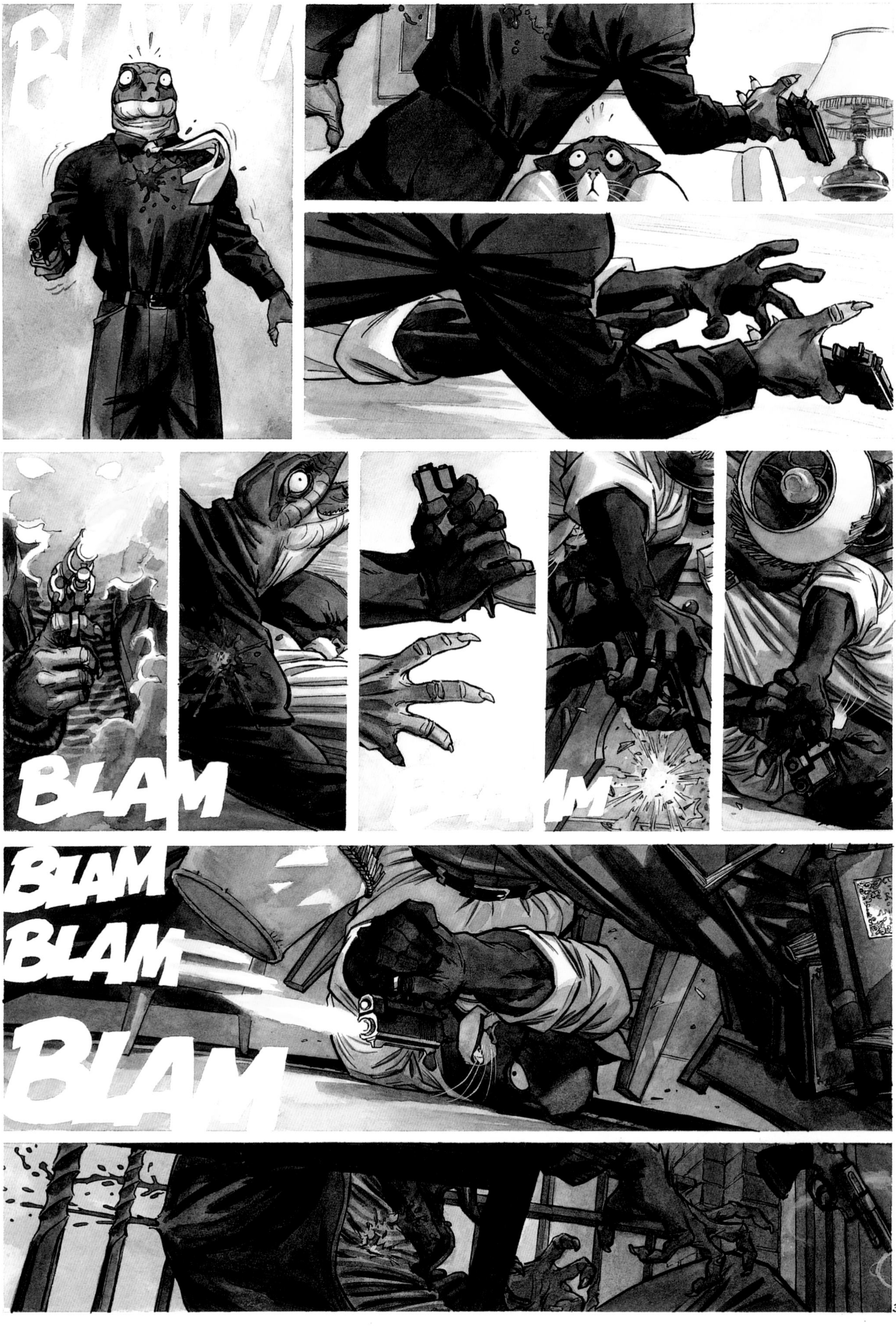
BLAM
BLAM
BLAM
BLAM

32

THERE ARE A LOT OF CLICHÉS ABOUT US CATS. ONE SAYS THAT WE HAVE NINE LIVES.

I'VE HONESTLY NEVER REALLY WANTED TO FIND OUT IF THAT'S TRUE OR NOT.

IT'S ALSO SAID THAT WE'VE GOT SOMETHING PERSONAL AGAINST RATS. THAT ONE'S TRUE. EVEN MORE SO IF THEY MAKE THE MISTAKE OF SLIPPING INTO YOUR DEN WITH A GUN.

WE ARE NOTHING... RIGHT, CAT?

SPENT SO MUCH TIME WAITING FOR MY CHANCE AND WHEN IT FINALLY HAPPENS, IT ALL FALLS TO PIECES...

I'VE ENDURED ALL KINDS OF HUMILIATION, BUT I ALWAYS THOUGHT ABOUT THE DAY WHEN I WOULD GET EVEN...

HUH... NO THANKS, DON'T SMOKE.

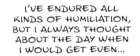

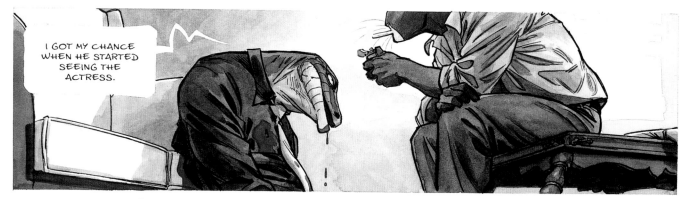

I GOT MY CHANCE WHEN HE STARTED SEEING THE ACTRESS.

"EVERYTHING WAS GOING SMOOTHLY, KEPT PERFECTLY QUIET, THE WAY *HE* HAD ORDERED IT. I WAS IN CHARGE OF DISCREETLY DELIVERING HER TO AND RETURNING HER FROM THEIR DATES, AVOIDING ALL PUBLICITY.

"STILL, BEING THE JEALOUS TYPE BY NATURE, HE HIRED THE RAT TO SPY ON HER. IT SEEMS SHE WASN'T A ONE-MAN WOMAN-- UNFORTUNATELY FOR HER AND LEON.

"IT'S NOT VERY PLEASANT TO WATCH SOMEONE DIE, AND EVEN LESS SO THE WAY HE WENT. I CAN STILL HEAR HIS SCREAMS. *HE* TOOK HIS TIME WITH GIVING LEON THE COUP DE GRÂCE.

34

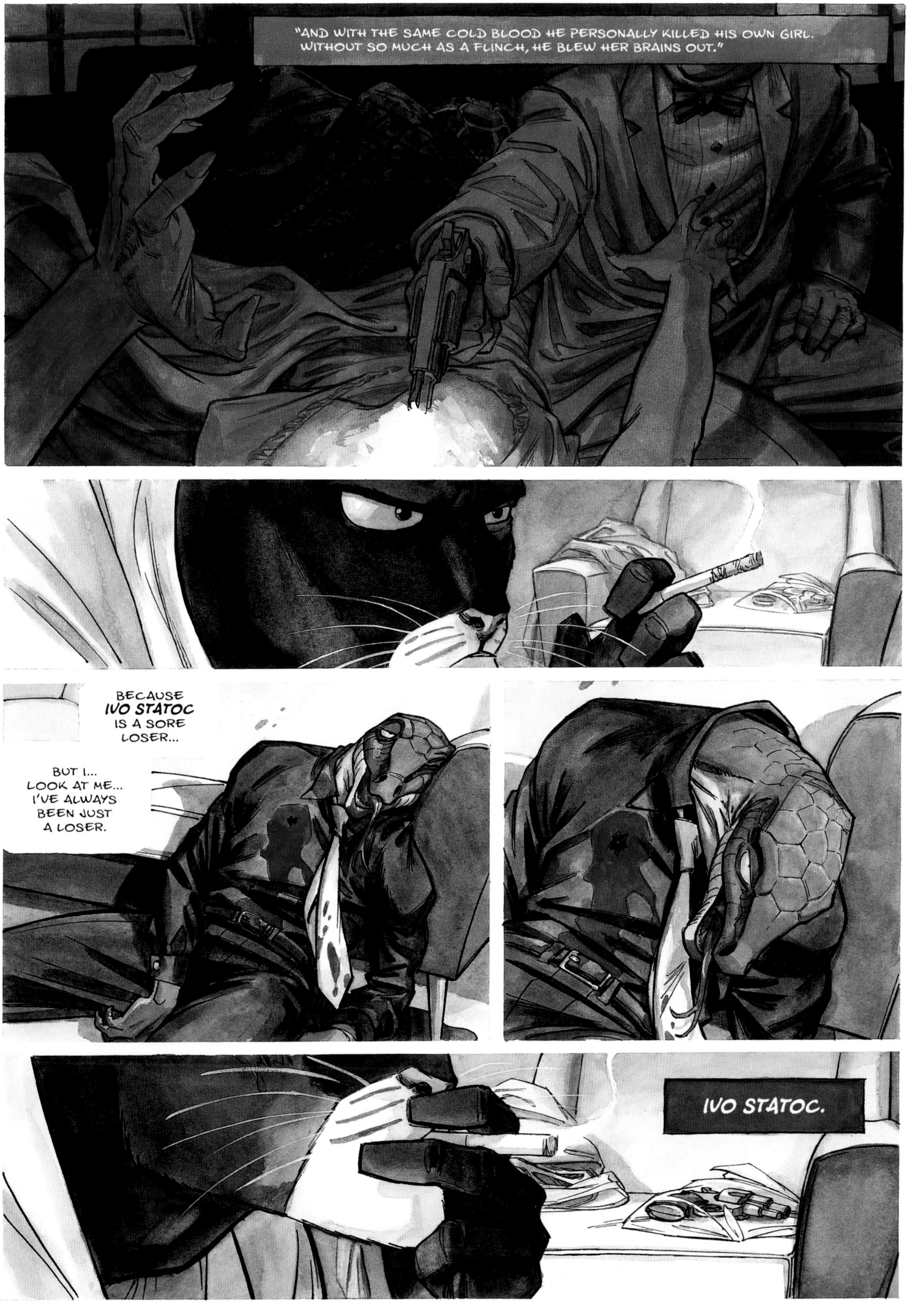
"AND WITH THE SAME COLD BLOOD HE PERSONALLY KILLED HIS OWN GIRL. WITHOUT SO MUCH AS A FLINCH, HE BLEW HER BRAINS OUT."
BECAUSE IVO STATOC IS A SORE LOSER...
BUT I... LOOK AT ME... I'VE ALWAYS BEEN JUST A LOSER.
IVO STATOC.
35

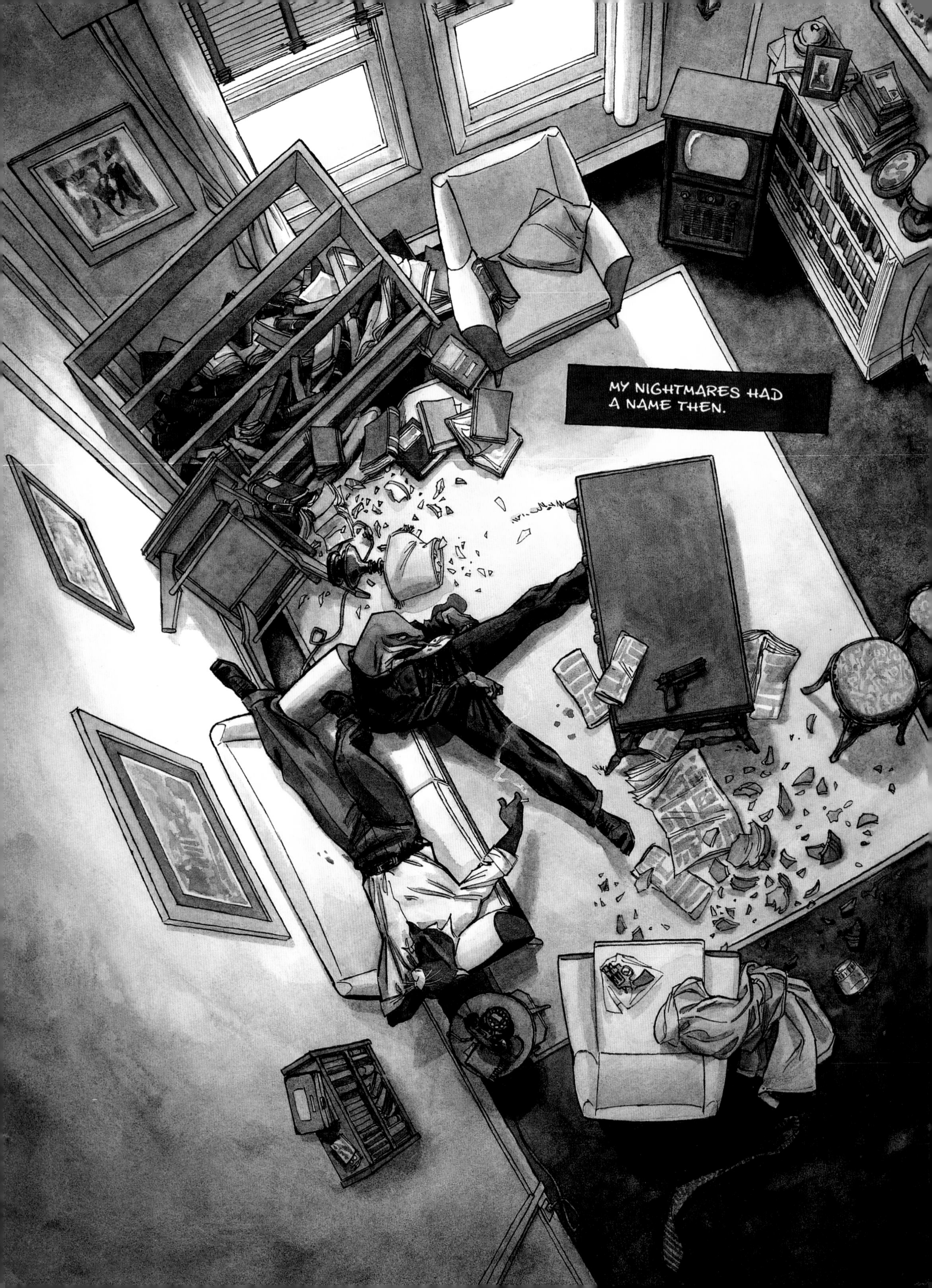
MY NIGHTMARES HAD A NAME THEN.

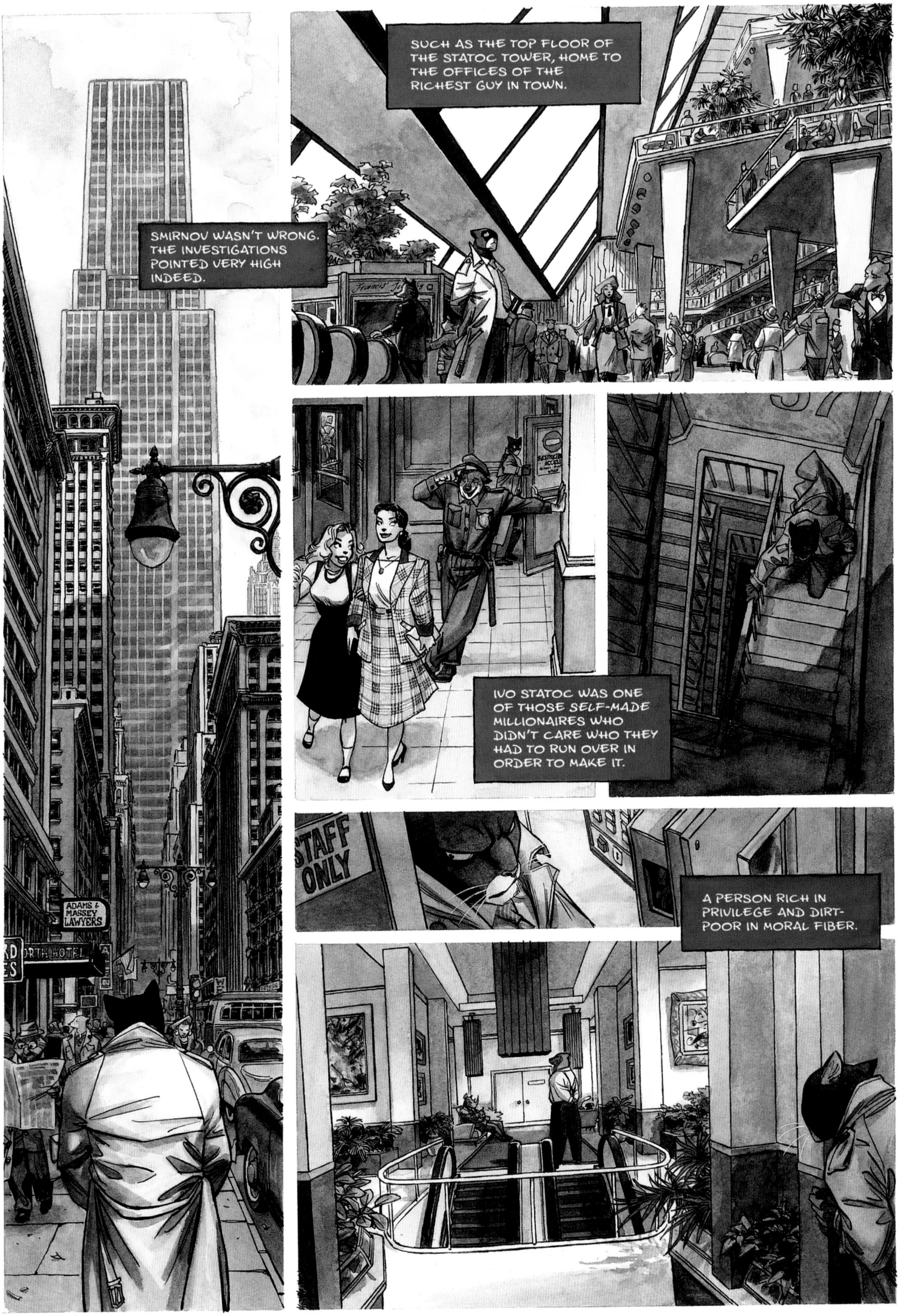
SMIRNOV WASN'T WRONG. THE INVESTIGATIONS POINTED VERY HIGH INDEED.
ADAMS & MASSEY LAWYERS
SUCH AS THE TOP FLOOR OF THE STATOC TOWER, HOME TO THE OFFICES OF THE RICHEST GUY IN TOWN.
IVO STATOC WAS ONE OF THOSE *SELF-MADE* MILLIONAIRES WHO DIDN'T CARE WHO THEY HAD TO RUN OVER IN ORDER TO MAKE IT.
STAFF ONLY
A PERSON RICH IN PRIVILEGE AND DIRT-POOR IN MORAL FIBER.

37

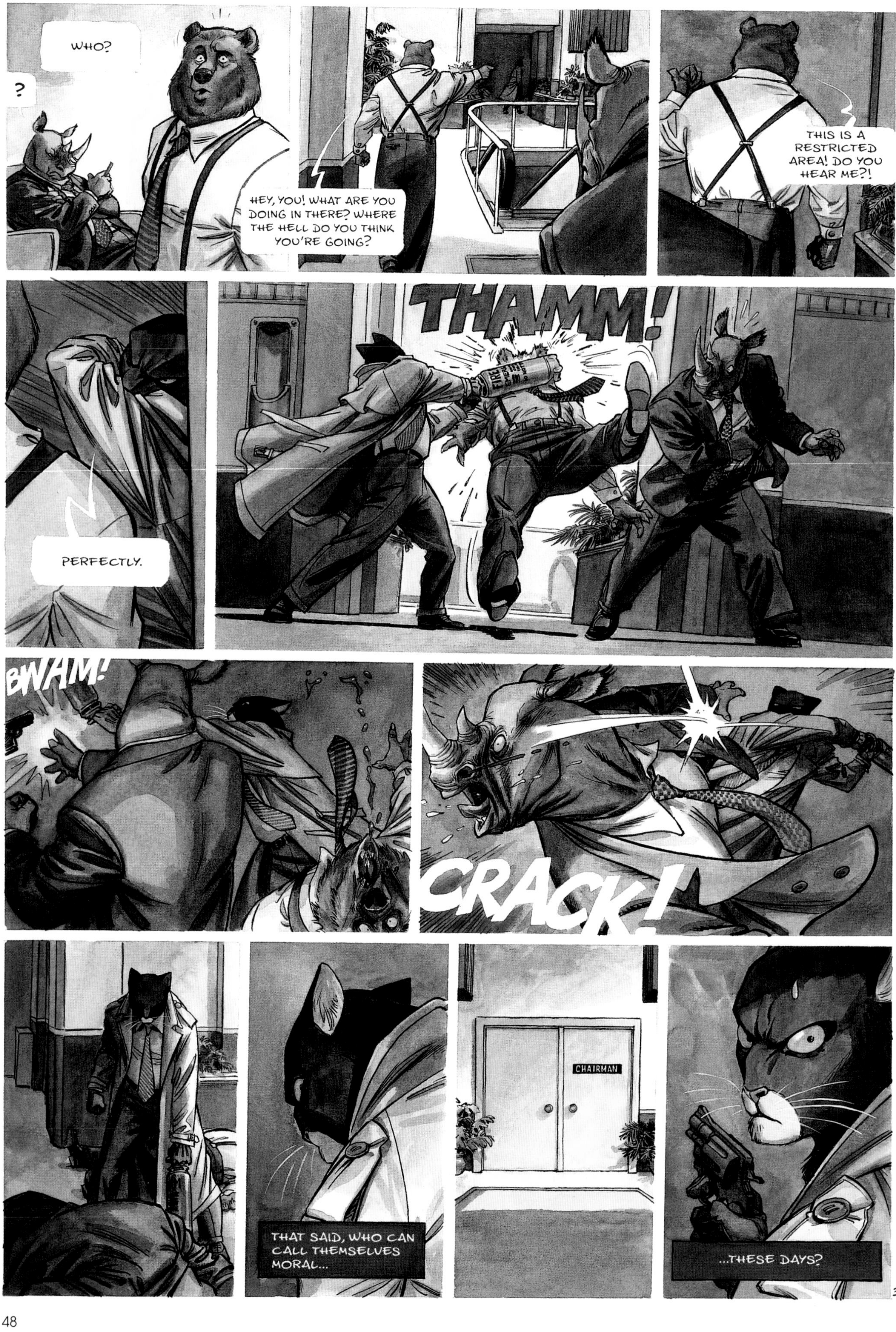
WHO?
?
HEY, YOU! WHAT ARE YOU DOING IN THERE? WHERE THE HELL DO YOU THINK YOU'RE GOING?
THIS IS A RESTRICTED AREA! DO YOU HEAR ME?!
PERFECTLY.
THAMM!
FIRE
BWAM!
CRACK!
CHAIRMAN
THAT SAID, WHO CAN CALL THEMSELVES MORAL...
...THESE DAYS?
38

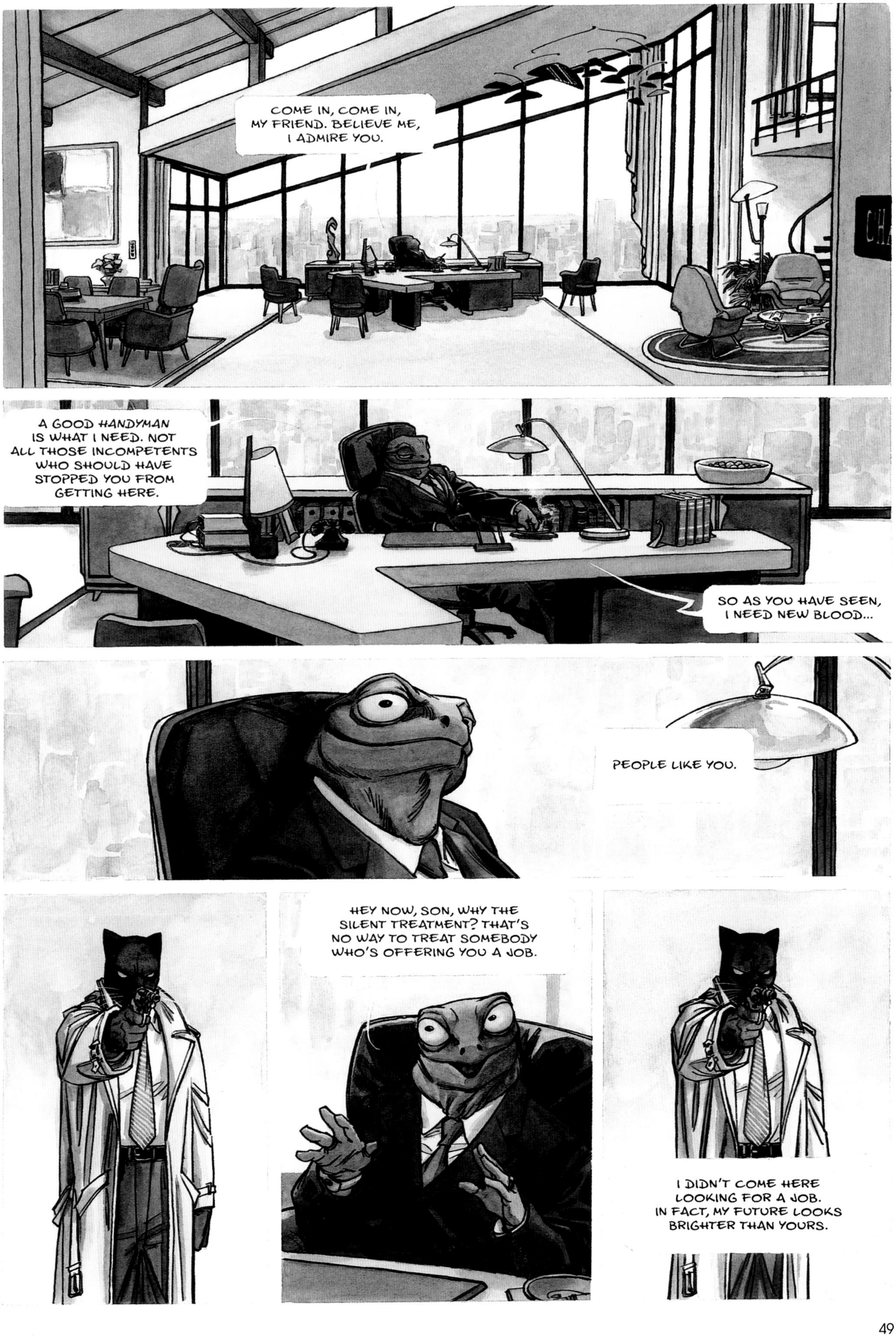
COME IN, COME IN, MY FRIEND. BELIEVE ME, I ADMIRE YOU.
A GOOD HANDYMAN IS WHAT I NEED. NOT ALL THOSE INCOMPETENTS WHO SHOULD HAVE STOPPED YOU FROM GETTING HERE.
SO AS YOU HAVE SEEN, I NEED NEW BLOOD...
PEOPLE LIKE YOU.
HEY NOW, SON, WHY THE SILENT TREATMENT? THAT'S NO WAY TO TREAT SOMEBODY WHO'S OFFERING YOU A JOB.
I DIDN'T COME HERE LOOKING FOR A JOB. IN FACT, MY FUTURE LOOKS BRIGHTER THAN YOURS.
39

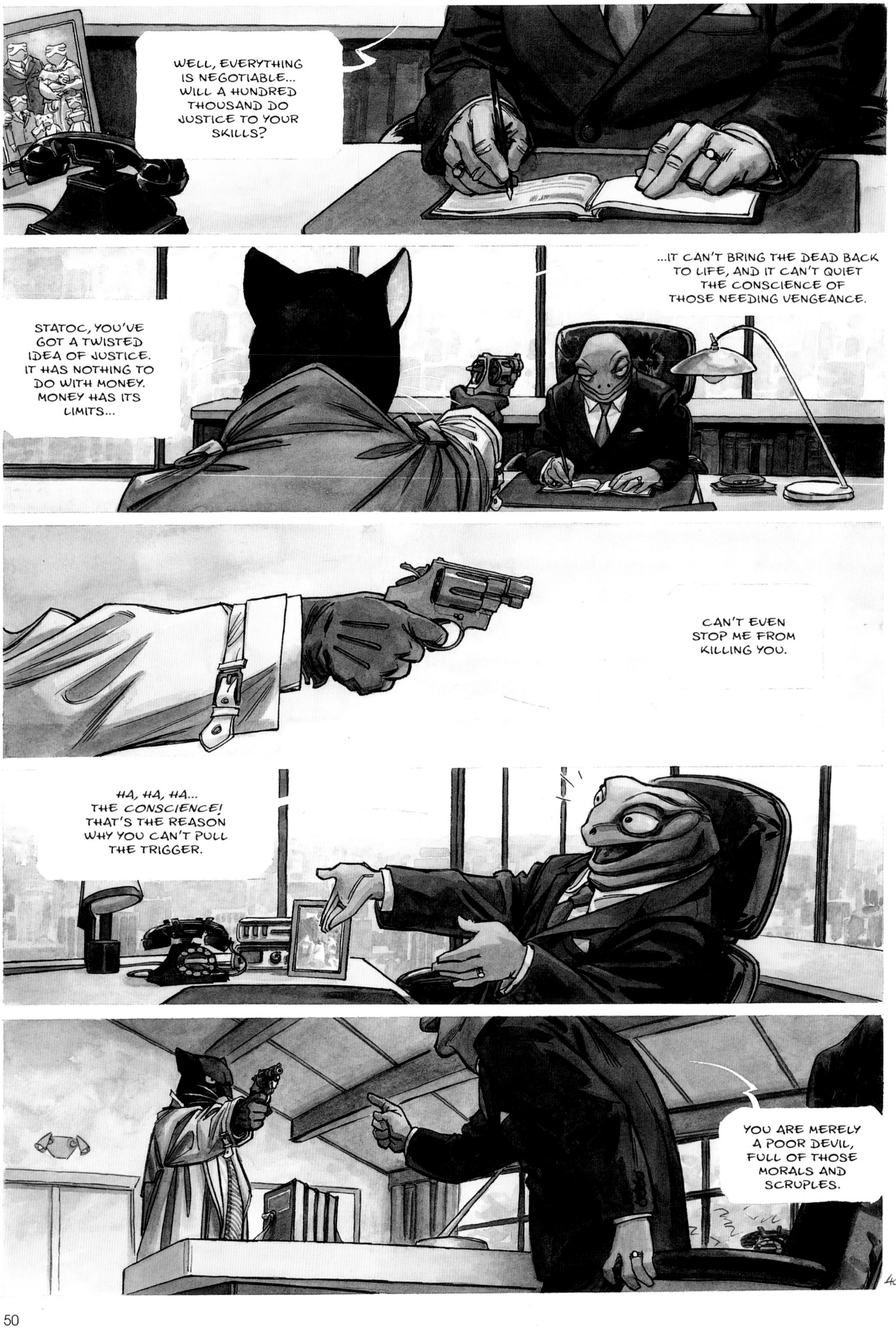
WELL, EVERYTHING IS NEGOTIABLE... WILL A HUNDRED THOUSAND DO JUSTICE TO YOUR SKILLS?
STATOC, YOU'VE GOT A TWISTED IDEA OF JUSTICE. IT HAS NOTHING TO DO WITH MONEY. MONEY HAS ITS LIMITS...
...IT CAN'T BRING THE DEAD BACK TO LIFE, AND IT CAN'T QUIET THE CONSCIENCE OF THOSE NEEDING VENGEANCE.
CAN'T EVEN STOP ME FROM KILLING YOU.
HA, HA, HA... THE *CONSCIENCE!* THAT'S THE REASON WHY YOU CAN'T PULL THE TRIGGER.
YOU ARE MERELY A POOR DEVIL, FULL OF THOSE MORALS AND SCRUPLES.

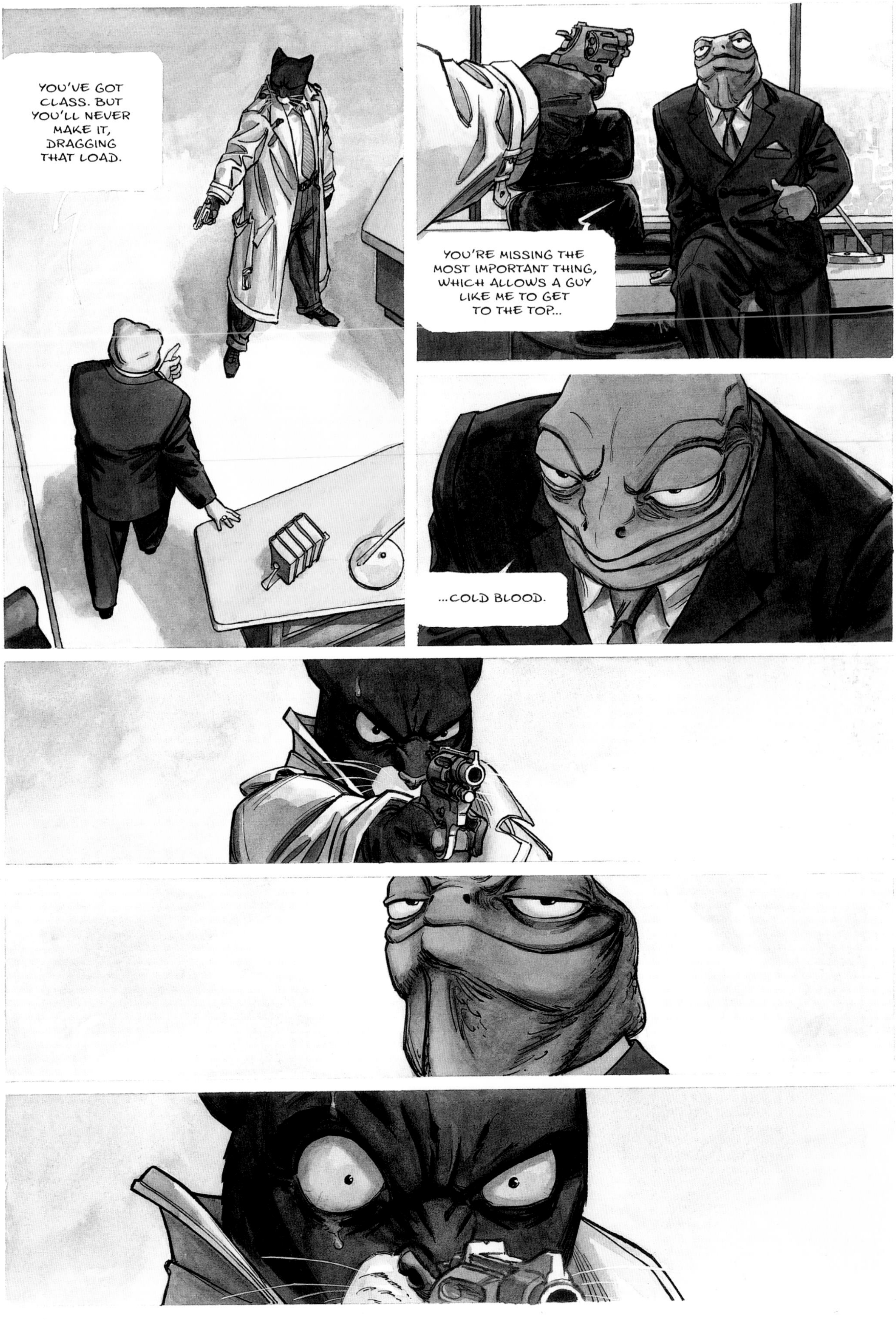
YOU'VE GOT CLASS. BUT YOU'LL NEVER MAKE IT, DRAGGING THAT LOAD.
YOU'RE MISSING THE MOST IMPORTANT THING, WHICH ALLOWS A GUY LIKE ME TO GET TO THE TOP...
...COLD BLOOD.
41

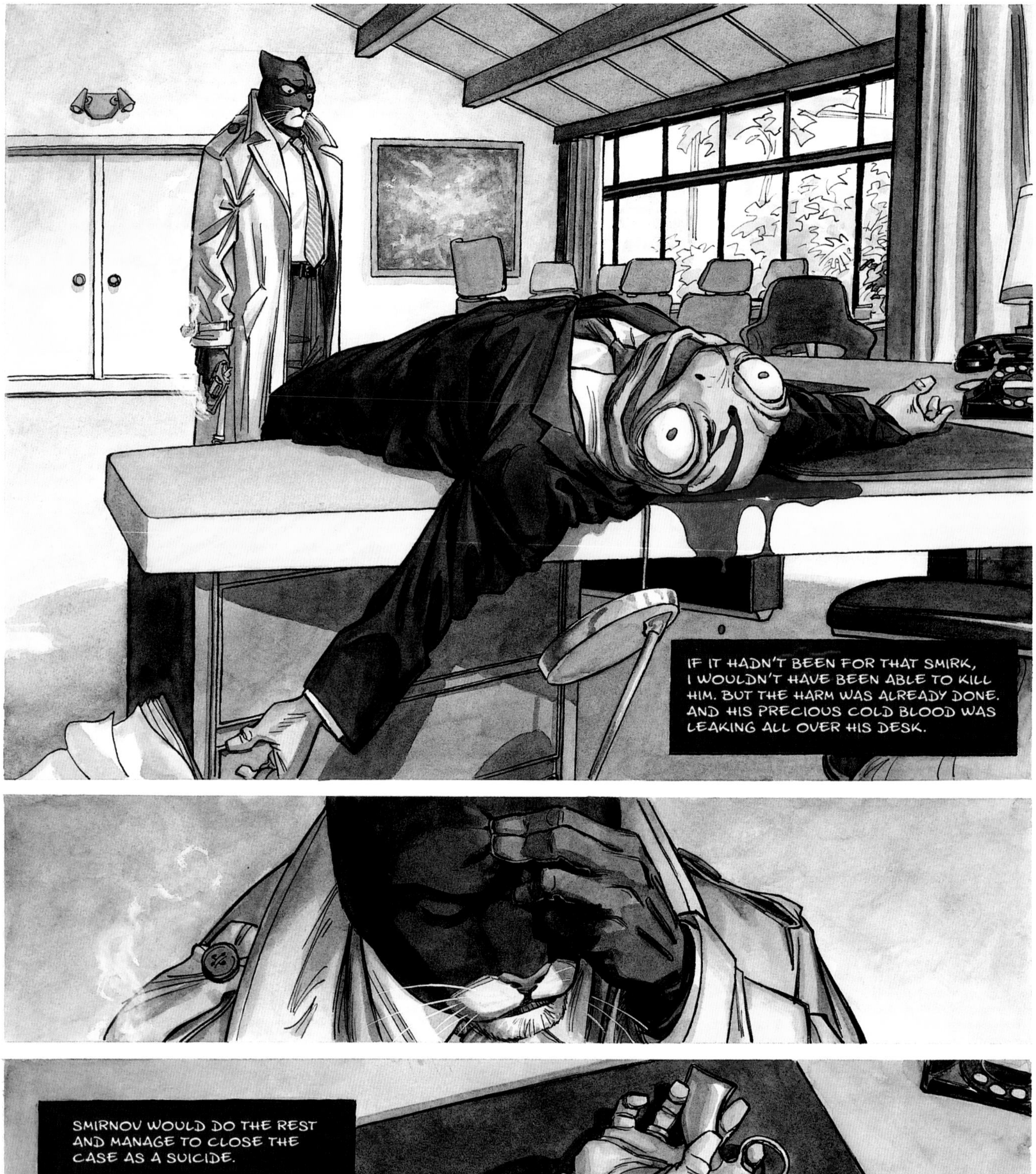
IF IT HADN'T BEEN FOR THAT SMIRK, I WOULDN'T HAVE BEEN ABLE TO KILL HIM. BUT THE HARM WAS ALREADY DONE. AND HIS PRECIOUS COLD BLOOD WAS LEAKING ALL OVER HIS DESK.
SMIRNOV WOULD DO THE REST AND MANAGE TO CLOSE THE CASE AS A SUICIDE.

42

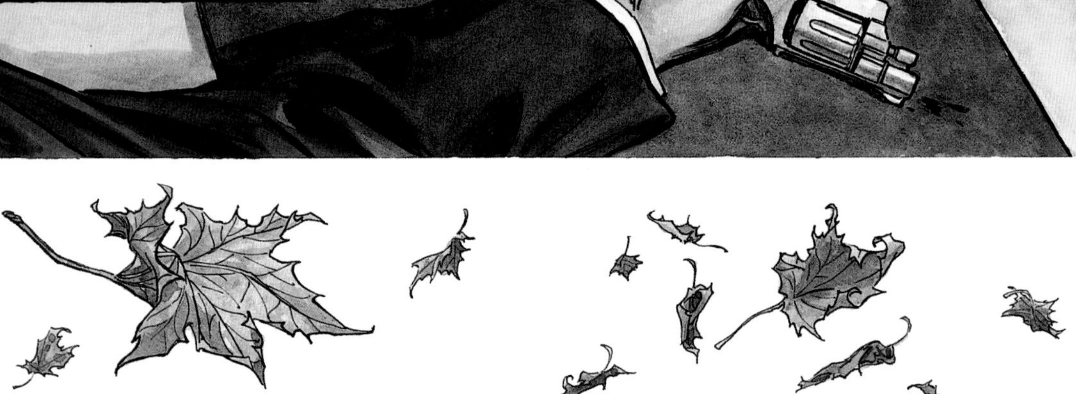

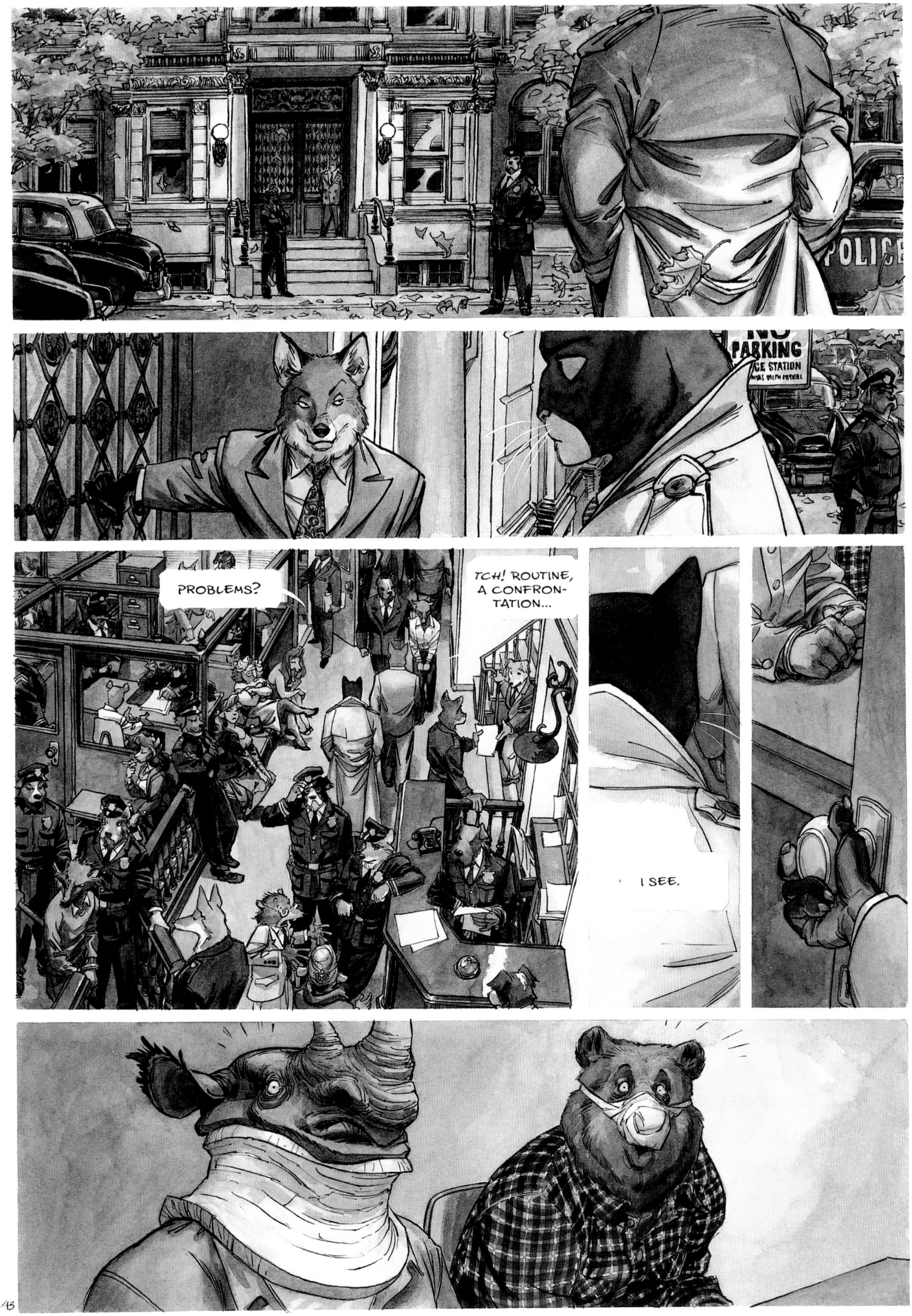
POLICE
PARKING
PROBLEMS?
TCH! ROUTINE, A CONFRONTATION...
I SEE.

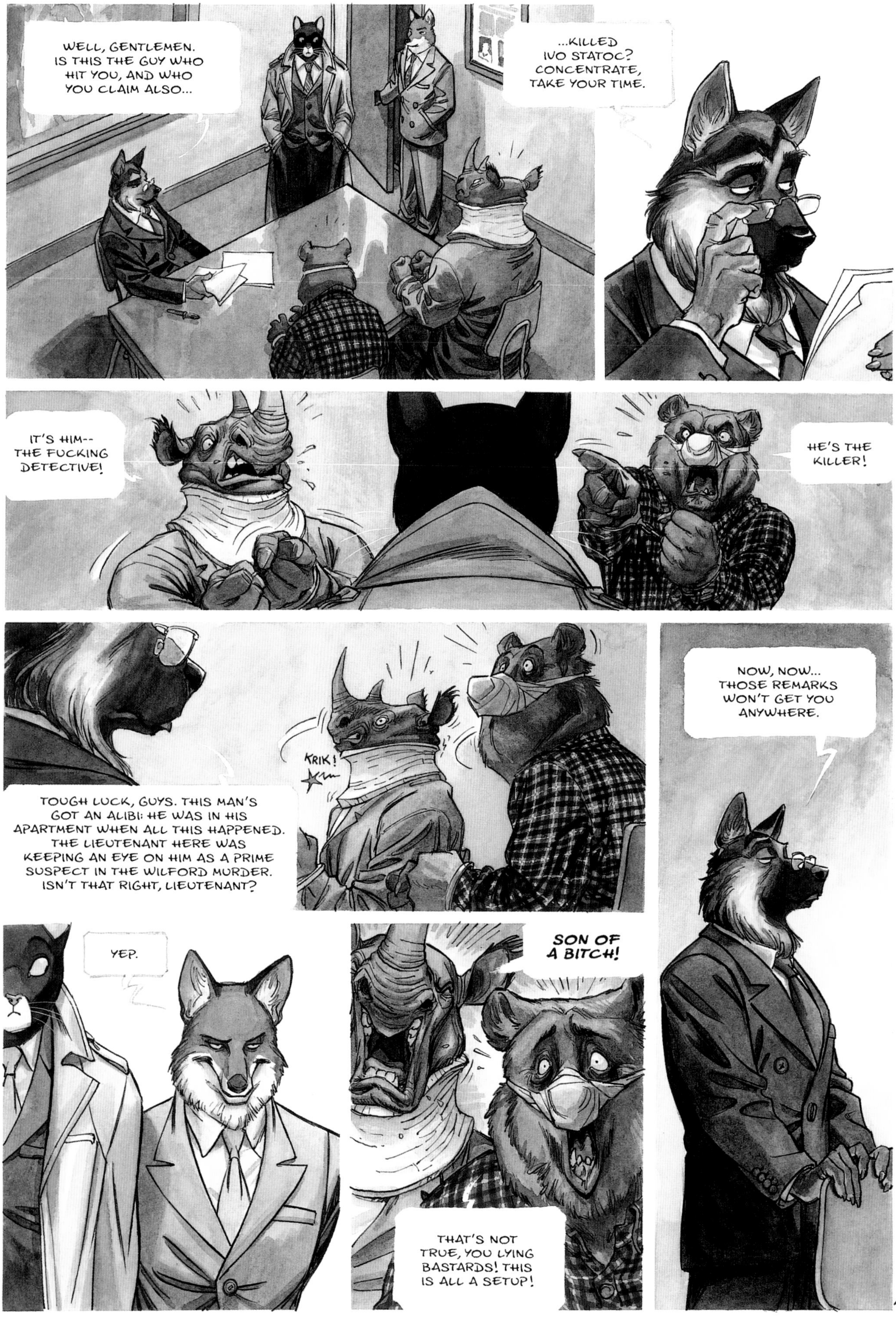
WELL, GENTLEMEN. IS THIS THE GUY WHO HIT YOU, AND WHO YOU CLAIM ALSO...
...KILLED IVO STATOC? CONCENTRATE, TAKE YOUR TIME.
IT'S HIM-- THE FUCKING DETECTIVE!
HE'S THE KILLER!
KRIK!
TOUGH LUCK, GUYS. THIS MAN'S GOT AN ALIBI: HE WAS IN HIS APARTMENT WHEN ALL THIS HAPPENED. THE LIEUTENANT HERE WAS KEEPING AN EYE ON HIM AS A PRIME SUSPECT IN THE WILFORD MURDER. ISN'T THAT RIGHT, LIEUTENANT?
NOW, NOW... THOSE REMARKS WON'T GET YOU ANYWHERE.
YEP.
SON OF A BITCH!
THAT'S NOT TRUE, YOU LYING BASTARDS! THIS IS ALL A SETUP!
44

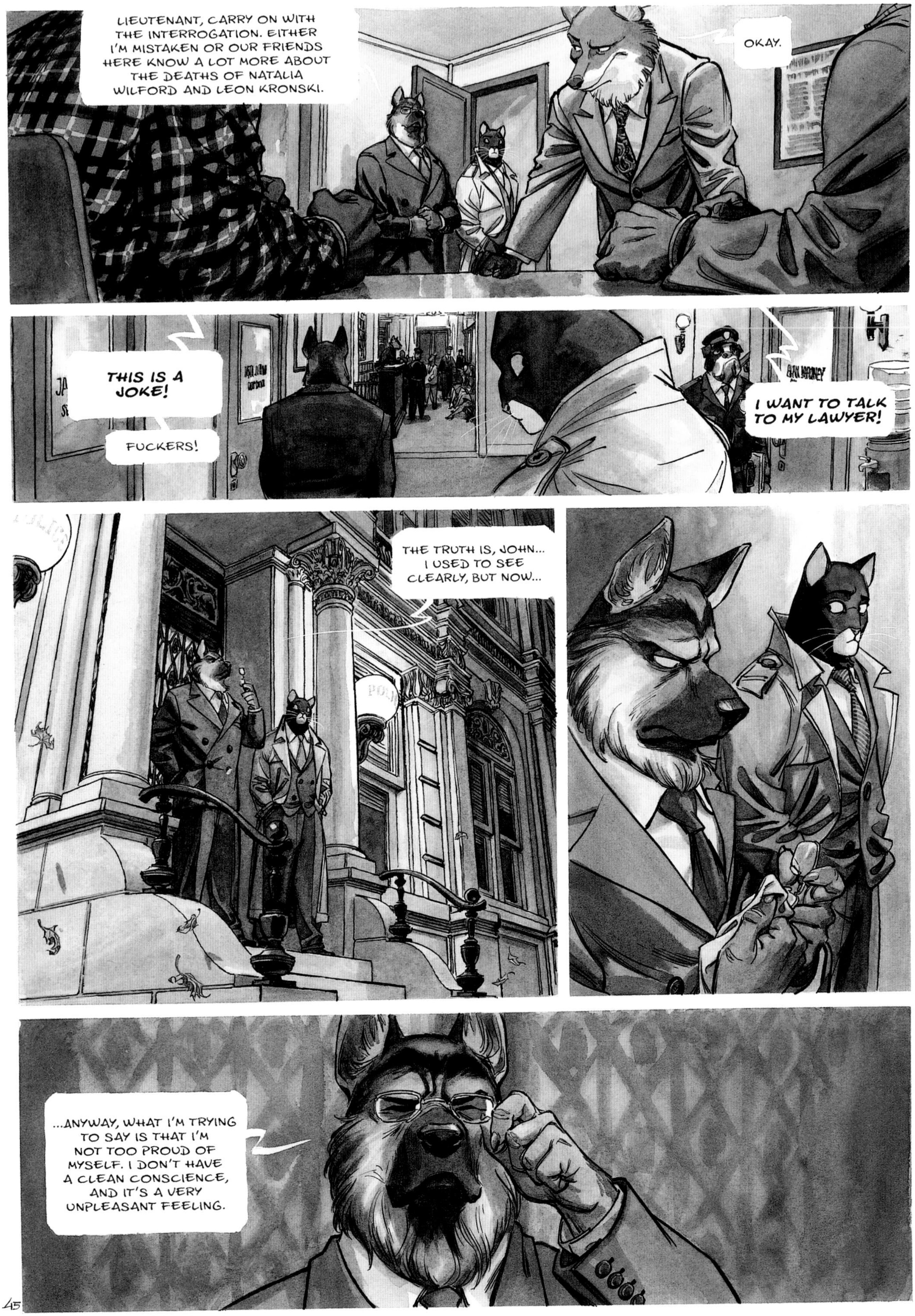

LIEUTENANT, CARRY ON WITH THE INTERROGATION. EITHER I'M MISTAKEN OR OUR FRIENDS HERE KNOW A LOT MORE ABOUT THE DEATHS OF NATALIA WILFORD AND LEON KRONSKI.
OKAY.
THIS IS A JOKE!
FUCKERS!
I WANT TO TALK TO MY LAWYER!
THE TRUTH IS, JOHN... I USED TO SEE CLEARLY, BUT NOW...
...ANYWAY, WHAT I'M TRYING TO SAY IS THAT I'M NOT TOO PROUD OF MYSELF. I DON'T HAVE A CLEAN CONSCIENCE, AND IT'S A VERY UNPLEASANT FEELING.
45

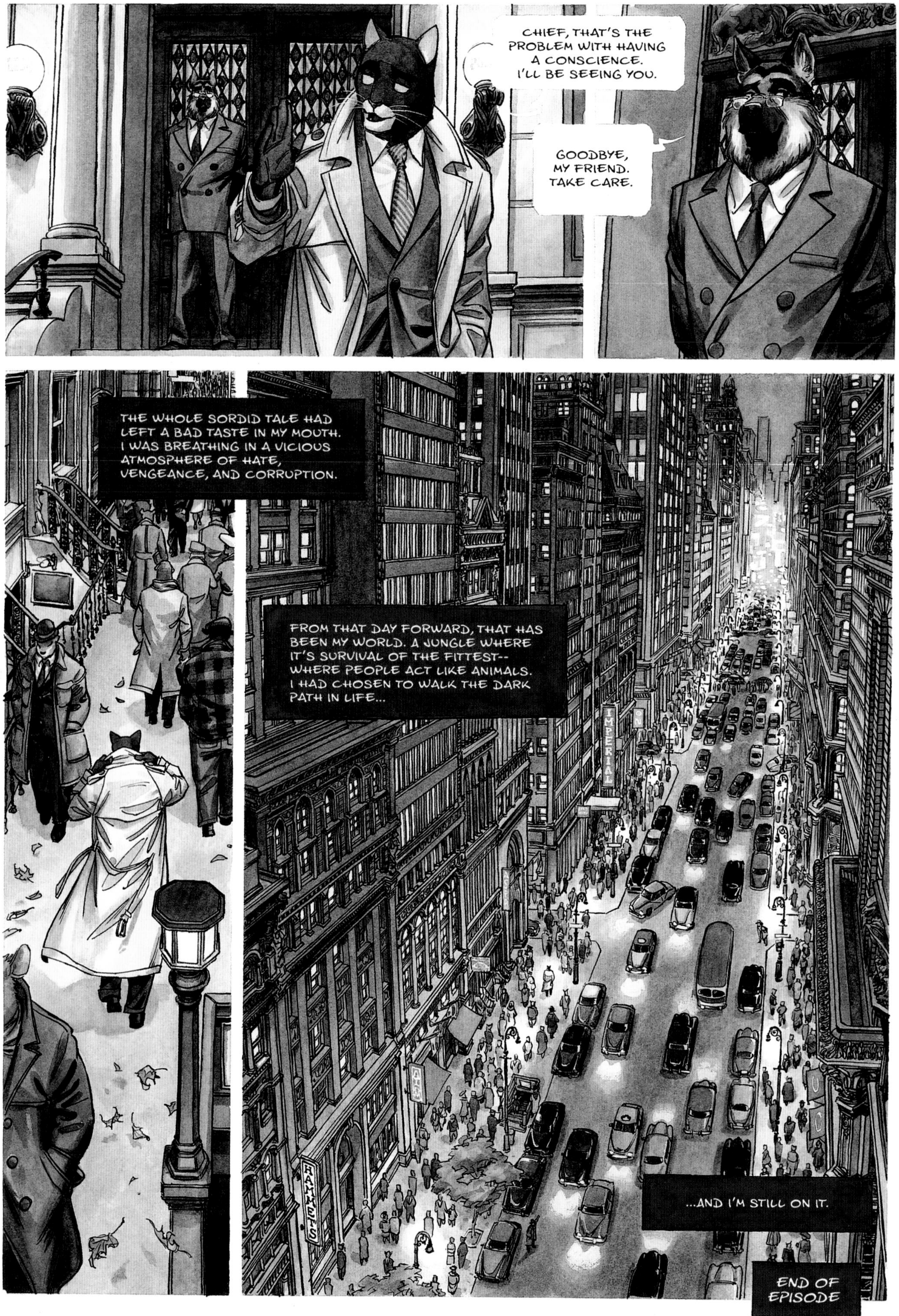
CHIEF, THAT'S THE PROBLEM WITH HAVING A CONSCIENCE. I'LL BE SEEING YOU.
GOODBYE, MY FRIEND. TAKE CARE.
THE WHOLE SORDID TALE HAD LEFT A BAD TASTE IN MY MOUTH. I WAS BREATHING IN A VICIOUS ATMOSPHERE OF HATE, VENGEANCE, AND CORRUPTION.
FROM THAT DAY FORWARD, THAT HAS BEEN MY WORLD. A JUNGLE WHERE IT'S SURVIVAL OF THE FITTEST-- WHERE PEOPLE ACT LIKE ANIMALS. I HAD CHOSEN TO WALK THE DARK PATH IN LIFE...
IMPERIAL
...AND I'M STILL ON IT.
END OF EPISODE

Juanjo Guarnido & Juan Diaz Canales - 2000

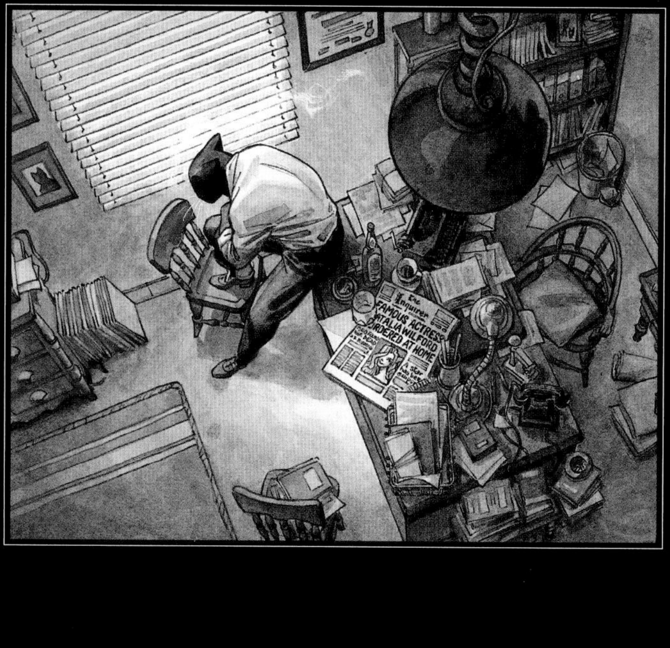
The Inquirer
FAMOUS ACTRESS
AT HOME

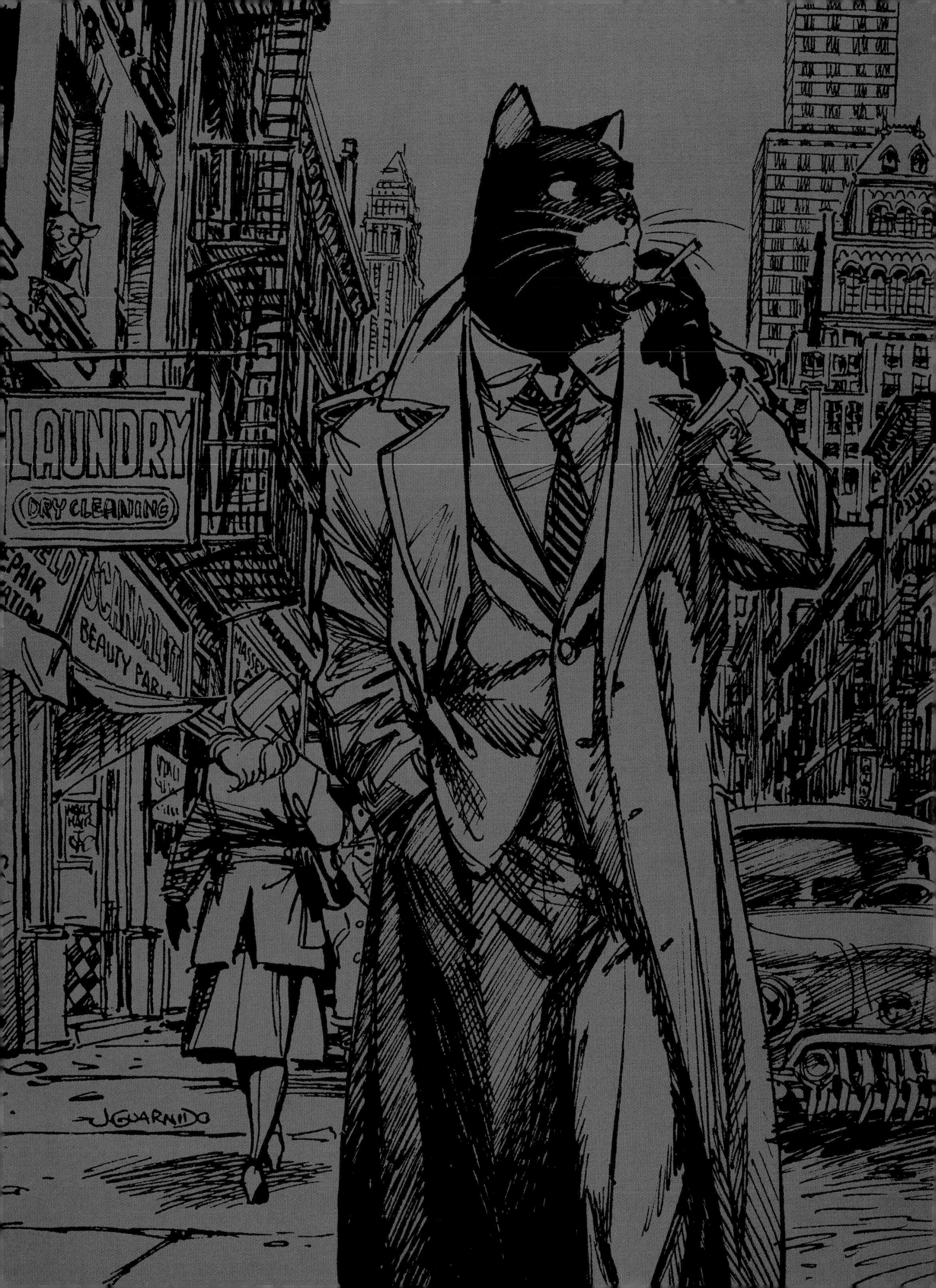

LAUNDRY
DRY CLEANING
BEAUTY PAR
J.GUARNIDO

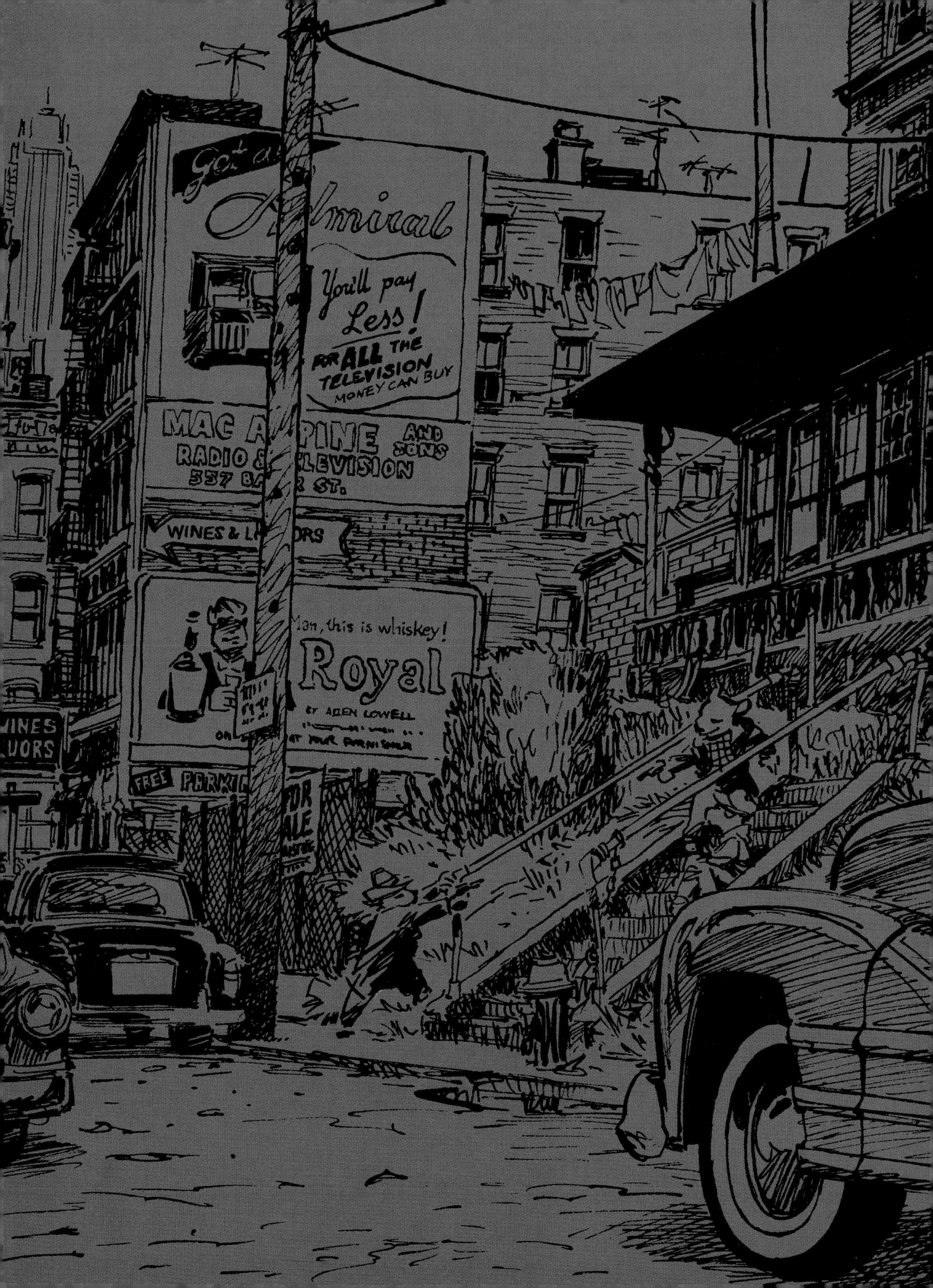
You'll pay Less!
FOR ALL THE TELEVISION MONEY CAN BUY
AND SONS
Man, this is whiskey!
Royal
BY ALLEN LOWELL
FREE

ARCTIC NATION

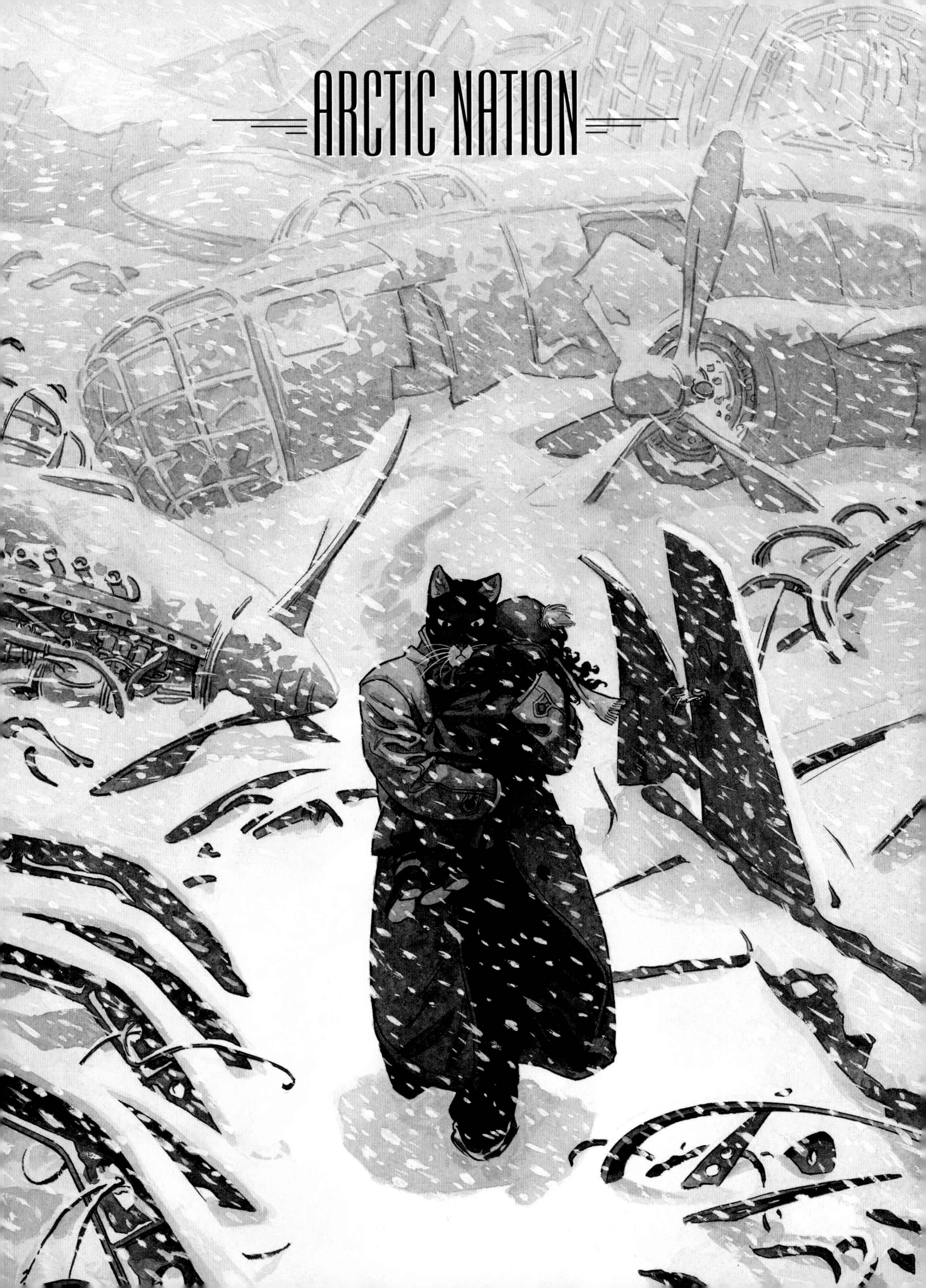

Preceding:
The original cover to this album as
published by Dargaud, March 2003

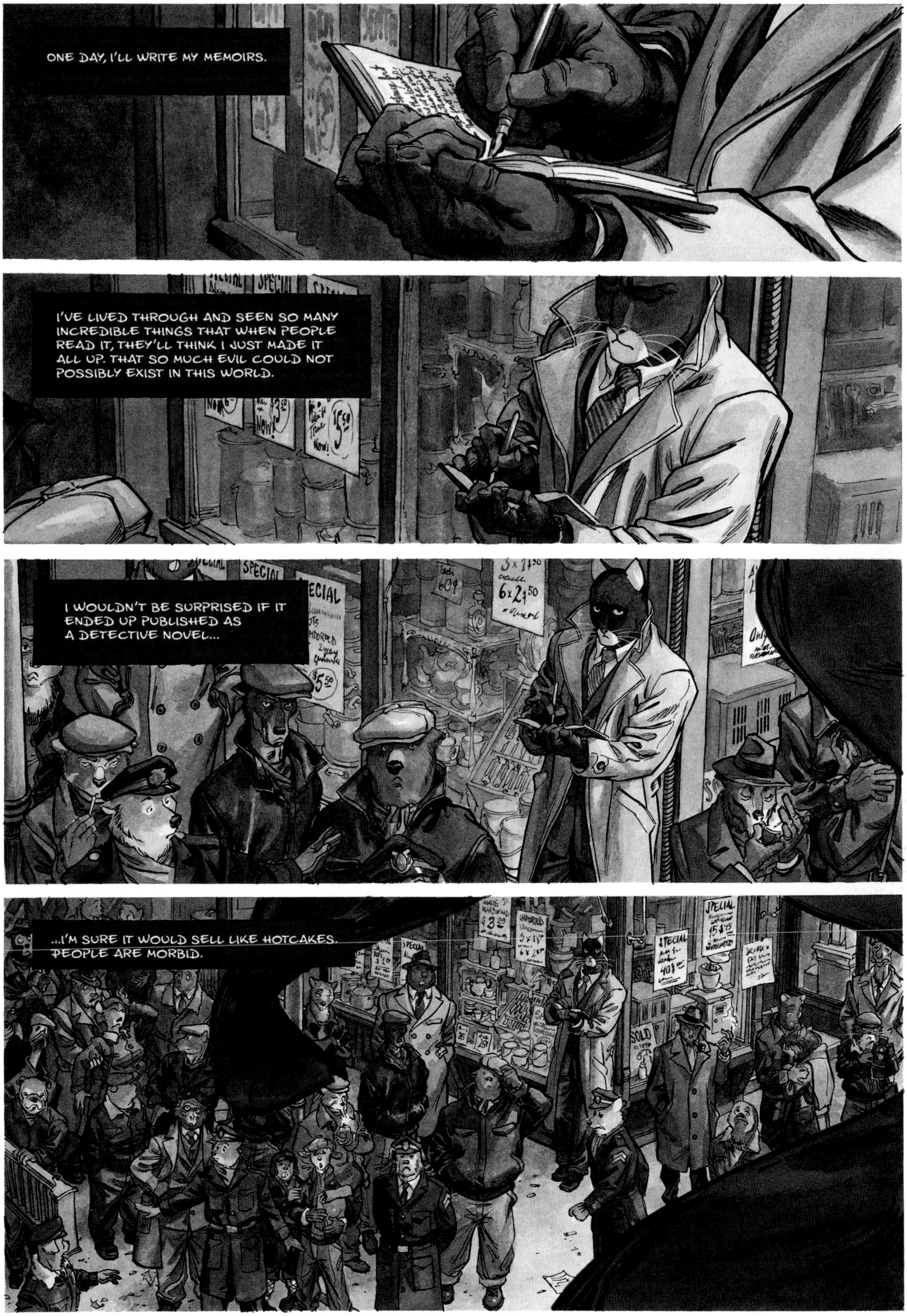
ONE DAY, I'LL WRITE MY MEMOIRS.
I'VE LIVED THROUGH AND SEEN SO MANY INCREDIBLE THINGS THAT WHEN PEOPLE READ IT, THEY'LL THINK I JUST MADE IT ALL UP. THAT SO MUCH EVIL COULD NOT POSSIBLY EXIST IN THIS WORLD.
I WOULDN'T BE SURPRISED IF IT ENDED UP PUBLISHED AS A DETECTIVE NOVEL...
...I'M SURE IT WOULD SELL LIKE HOTCAKES. PEOPLE ARE MORBID.

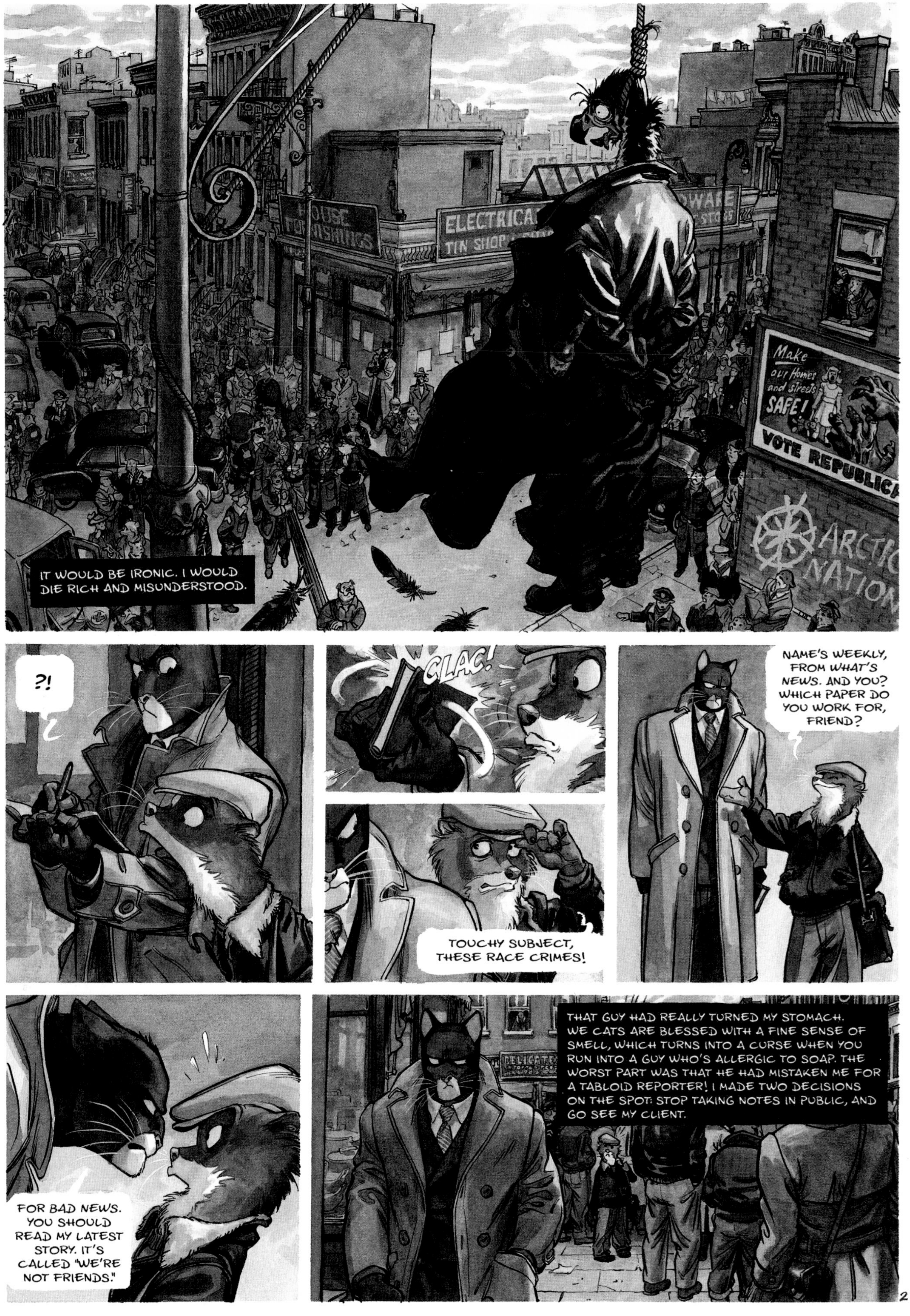

ELECTRICAL
TIN SHOP
HOUSE FURNISHINGS
Make our Homes and Streets SAFE!
VOTE REPUBLICA
ARCTIC NATION
IT WOULD BE IRONIC. I WOULD DIE RICH AND MISUNDERSTOOD.
?!
CLAC!
NAME'S WEEKLY, FROM WHAT'S NEWS. AND YOU? WHICH PAPER DO YOU WORK FOR, FRIEND?
TOUCHY SUBJECT, THESE RACE CRIMES!
!
FOR BAD NEWS. YOU SHOULD READ MY LATEST STORY. IT'S CALLED "WE'RE NOT FRIENDS."
THAT GUY HAD REALLY TURNED MY STOMACH. WE CATS ARE BLESSED WITH A FINE SENSE OF SMELL, WHICH TURNS INTO A CURSE WHEN YOU RUN INTO A GUY WHO'S ALLERGIC TO SOAP. THE WORST PART WAS THAT HE HAD MISTAKEN ME FOR A TABLOID REPORTER! I MADE TWO DECISIONS ON THE SPOT: STOP TAKING NOTES IN PUBLIC, AND GO SEE MY CLIENT.
2

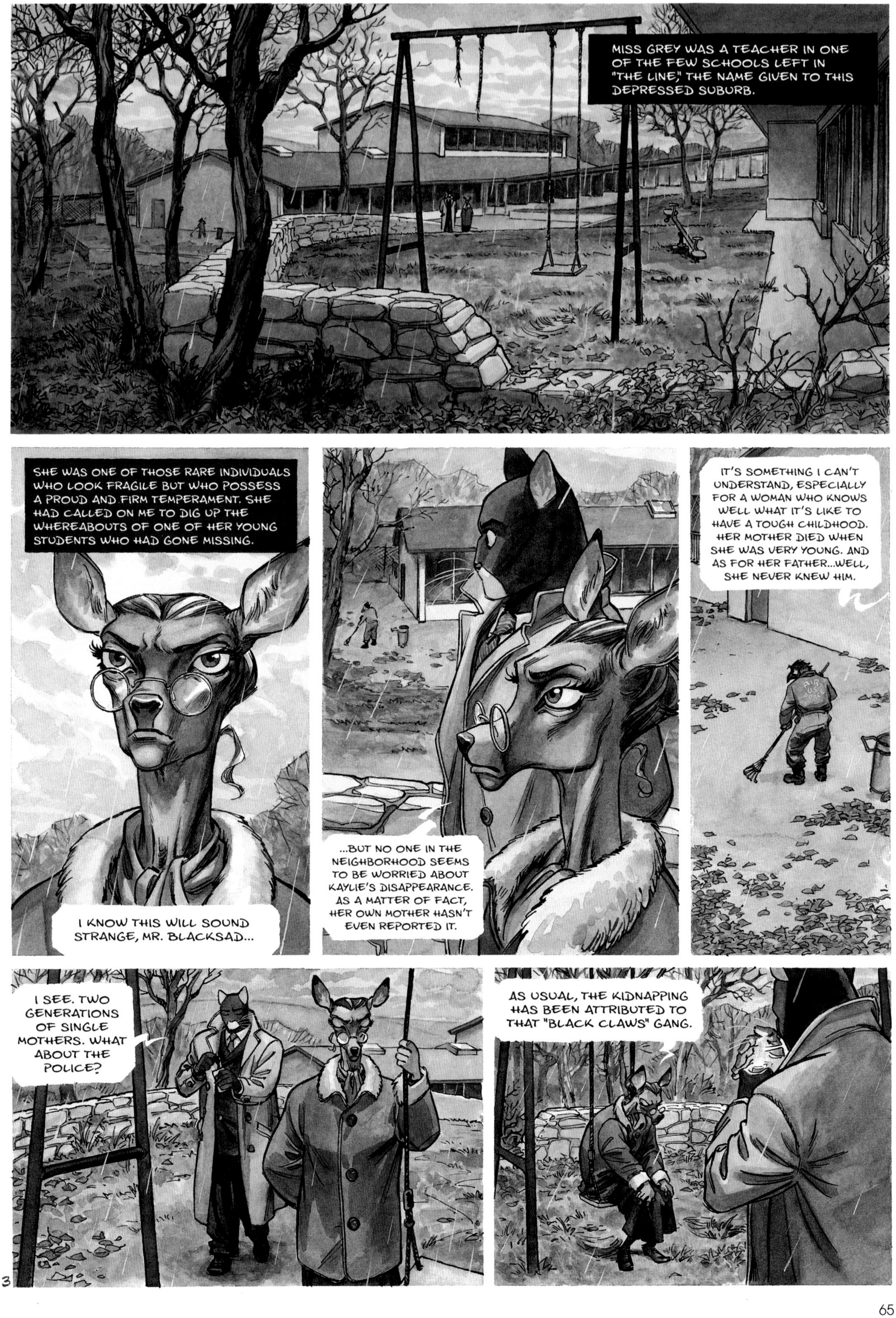
MISS GREY WAS A TEACHER IN ONE OF THE FEW SCHOOLS LEFT IN "THE LINE," THE NAME GIVEN TO THIS DEPRESSED SUBURB.
SHE WAS ONE OF THOSE RARE INDIVIDUALS WHO LOOK FRAGILE BUT WHO POSSESS A PROUD AND FIRM TEMPERAMENT. SHE HAD CALLED ON ME TO DIG UP THE WHEREABOUTS OF ONE OF HER YOUNG STUDENTS WHO HAD GONE MISSING.
I KNOW THIS WILL SOUND STRANGE, MR. BLACKSAD...
...BUT NO ONE IN THE NEIGHBORHOOD SEEMS TO BE WORRIED ABOUT KAYLIE'S DISAPPEARANCE. AS A MATTER OF FACT, HER OWN MOTHER HASN'T EVEN REPORTED IT.
IT'S SOMETHING I CAN'T UNDERSTAND, ESPECIALLY FOR A WOMAN WHO KNOWS WELL WHAT IT'S LIKE TO HAVE A TOUGH CHILDHOOD. HER MOTHER DIED WHEN SHE WAS VERY YOUNG. AND AS FOR HER FATHER...WELL, SHE NEVER KNEW HIM.
I SEE. TWO GENERATIONS OF SINGLE MOTHERS. WHAT ABOUT THE POLICE?
AS USUAL, THE KIDNAPPING HAS BEEN ATTRIBUTED TO THAT "BLACK CLAWS" GANG.
3

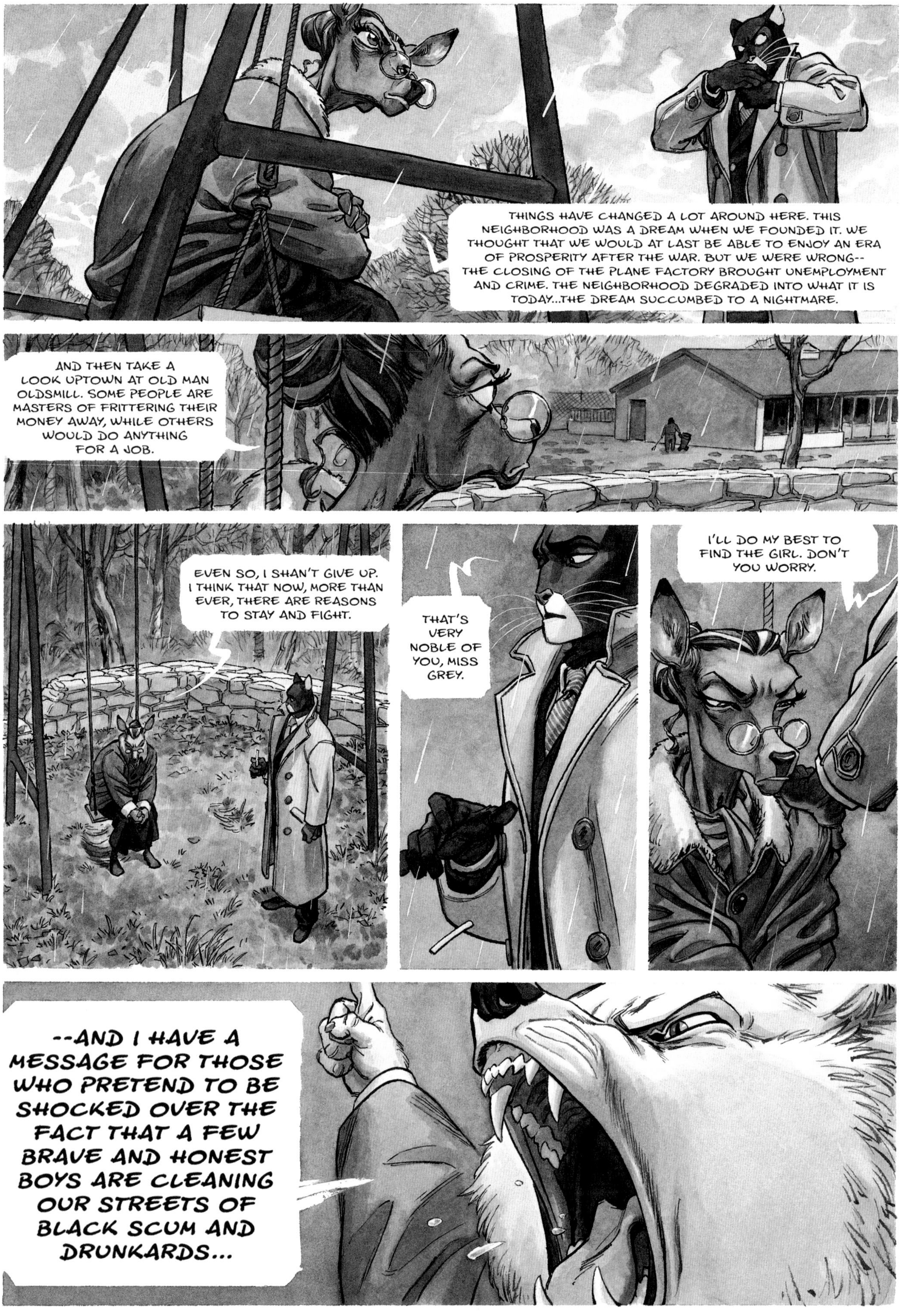
THINGS HAVE CHANGED A LOT AROUND HERE. THIS NEIGHBORHOOD WAS A DREAM WHEN WE FOUNDED IT. WE THOUGHT THAT WE WOULD AT LAST BE ABLE TO ENJOY AN ERA OF PROSPERITY AFTER THE WAR. BUT WE WERE WRONG-- THE CLOSING OF THE PLANE FACTORY BROUGHT UNEMPLOYMENT AND CRIME. THE NEIGHBORHOOD DEGRADED INTO WHAT IT IS TODAY...THE DREAM SUCCUMBED TO A NIGHTMARE.
AND THEN TAKE A LOOK UPTOWN AT OLD MAN OLDSMILL. SOME PEOPLE ARE MASTERS OF FRITTERING THEIR MONEY AWAY, WHILE OTHERS WOULD DO ANYTHING FOR A JOB.
EVEN SO, I SHAN'T GIVE UP. I THINK THAT NOW, MORE THAN EVER, THERE ARE REASONS TO STAY AND FIGHT.
THAT'S VERY NOBLE OF YOU, MISS GREY.
I'LL DO MY BEST TO FIND THE GIRL. DON'T YOU WORRY.
--AND I HAVE A MESSAGE FOR THOSE WHO PRETEND TO BE SHOCKED OVER THE FACT THAT A FEW BRAVE AND HONEST BOYS ARE CLEANING OUR STREETS OF BLACK SCUM AND DRUNKARDS...

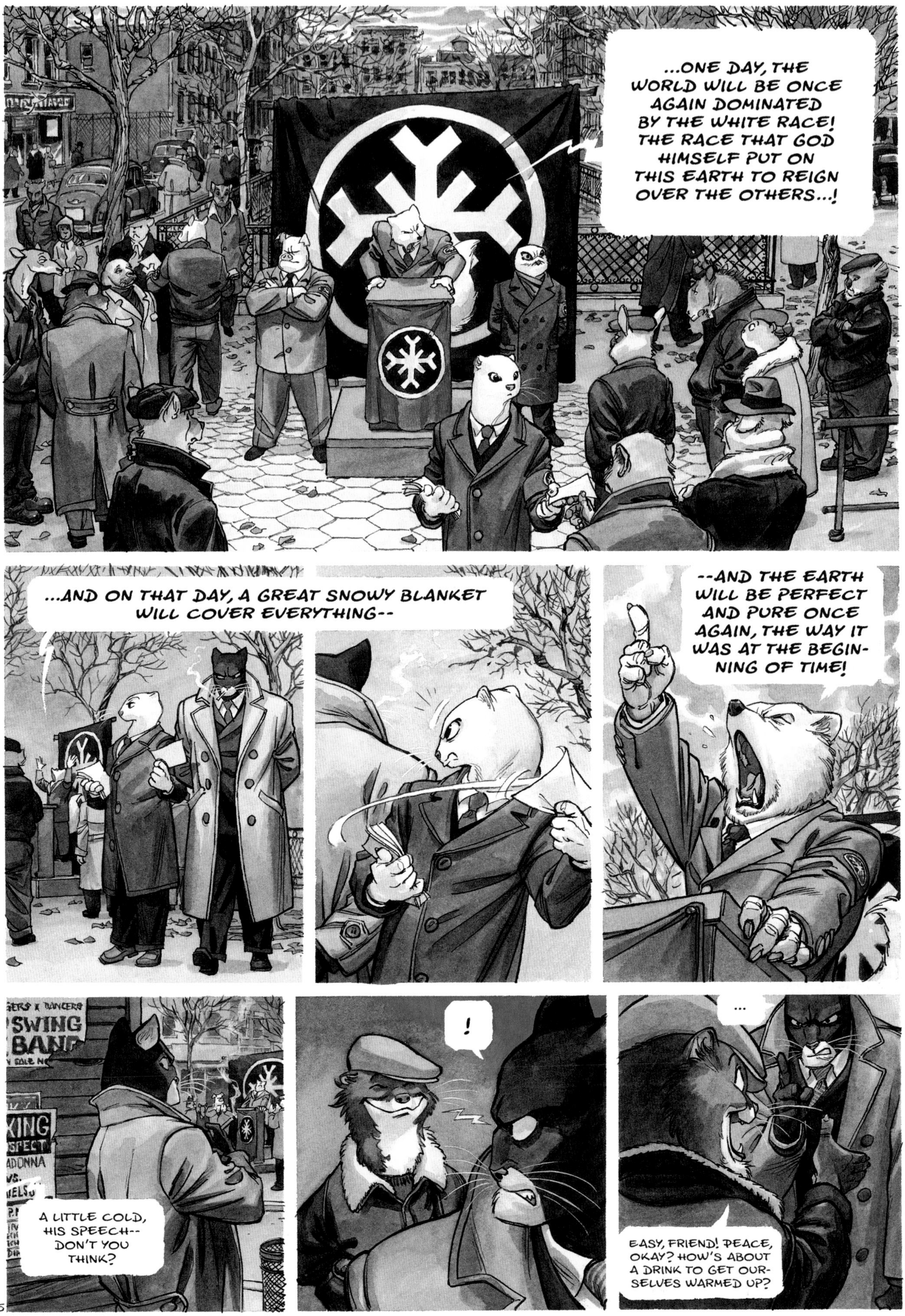
...ONE DAY, THE WORLD WILL BE ONCE AGAIN DOMINATED BY THE WHITE RACE! THE RACE THAT GOD HIMSELF PUT ON THIS EARTH TO REIGN OVER THE OTHERS...!
...AND ON THAT DAY, A GREAT SNOWY BLANKET WILL COVER EVERYTHING--
--AND THE EARTH WILL BE PERFECT AND PURE ONCE AGAIN, THE WAY IT WAS AT THE BEGINNING OF TIME!
SWING
A LITTLE COLD, HIS SPEECH-- DON'T YOU THINK?
!
...
EASY, FRIEND! PEACE, OKAY? HOW'S ABOUT A DRINK TO GET OURSELVES WARMED UP?

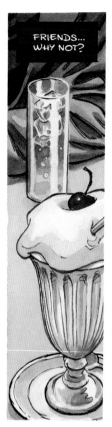

FRIENDS... WHY NOT?

AFTER ALL, WE WERE A PAIR OF OUTSIDERS IN AN INHOSPITABLE ENVIRONMENT.

THE LINE IS ON THE VERGE OF EXPLODING. ON THE ONE HAND, WE'VE GOT THESE HUELESS DIMWITS WHO THINK THAT THE WORLD BEGINS AND ENDS AT THE NORTH POLE...

...AND ON THE OTHER HAND WE'VE GOT THE CLAWS, EVERY SINGLE ONE OF 'EM AS BLACK AS COAL.

THEY'RE ALL CRAZY--! *SLURRRP!*

SNIF SNIFF

MMM! THIS BOURBON MILKSHAKE IS DELICIOUS! YOU WANNA TASTE IT?

NO THANKS. I DON'T LIKE MILK.

SAY--YOU'RE NOT REALLY A REPORTER, ARE YOU?

CLANG DING DONG

NOT REALLY. I'M ACTUALLY A TOPOGRAPHER.

6

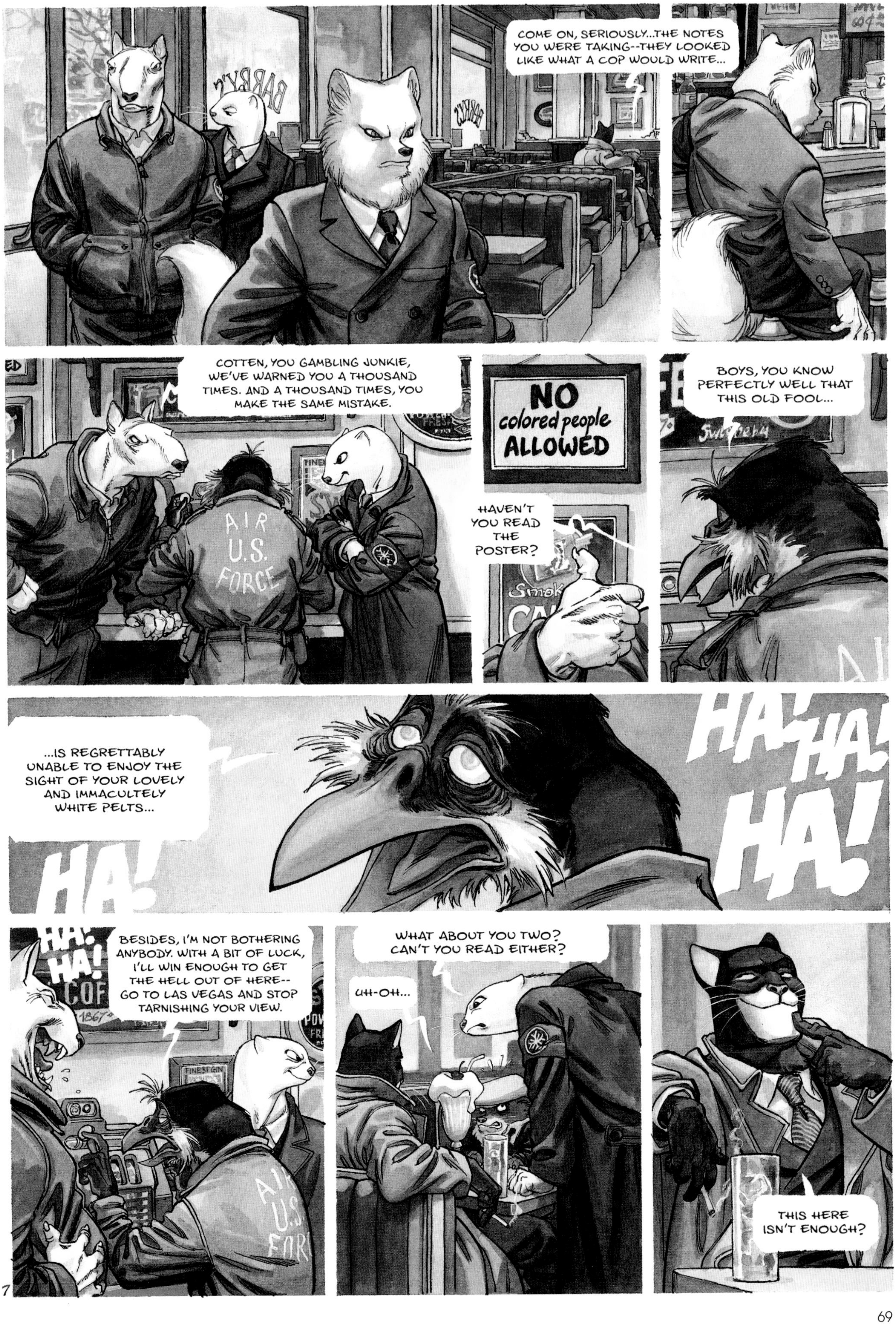
COME ON, SERIOUSLY...THE NOTES YOU WERE TAKING--THEY LOOKED LIKE WHAT A COP WOULD WRITE...
COTTEN, YOU GAMBLING JUNKIE, WE'VE WARNED YOU A THOUSAND TIMES. AND A THOUSAND TIMES, YOU MAKE THE SAME MISTAKE.
NO colored people ALLOWED
HAVEN'T YOU READ THE POSTER?
BOYS, YOU KNOW PERFECTLY WELL THAT THIS OLD FOOL...
AIR U.S. FORCE
...IS REGRETTABLY UNABLE TO ENJOY THE SIGHT OF YOUR LOVELY AND IMMACULTELY WHITE PELTS...
HA! HA! HA! HA!
HA! HA!
BESIDES, I'M NOT BOTHERING ANYBODY. WITH A BIT OF LUCK, I'LL WIN ENOUGH TO GET THE HELL OUT OF HERE--GO TO LAS VEGAS AND STOP TARNISHING YOUR VIEW.
WHAT ABOUT YOU TWO? CAN'T YOU READ EITHER?
UH-OH...
THIS HERE ISN'T ENOUGH?

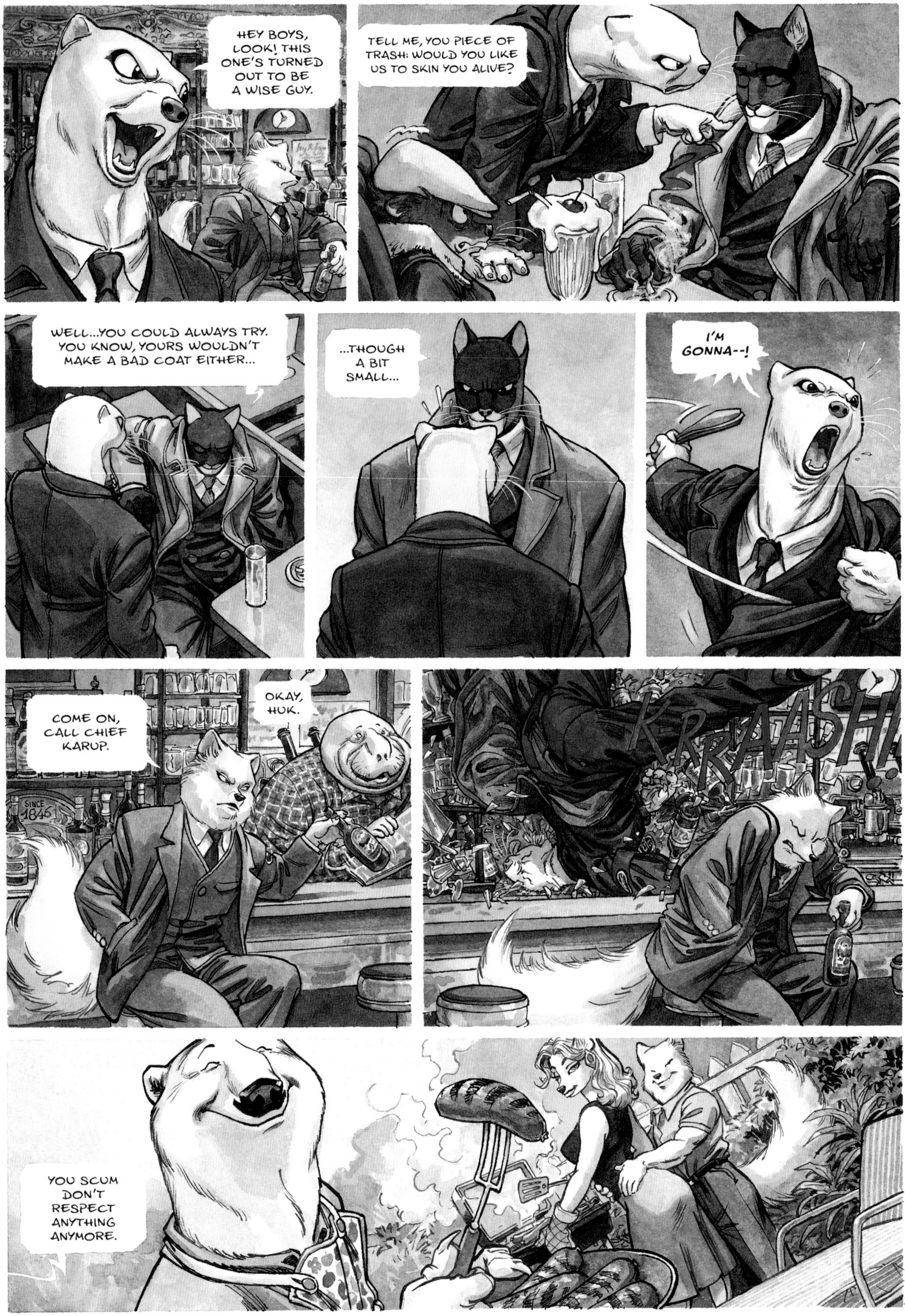
HEY BOYS, LOOK! THIS ONE'S TURNED OUT TO BE A WISE GUY.
TELL ME, YOU PIECE OF TRASH: WOULD YOU LIKE US TO SKIN YOU ALIVE?
WELL...YOU COULD ALWAYS TRY. YOU KNOW, YOURS WOULDN'T MAKE A BAD COAT EITHER...
...THOUGH A BIT SMALL...
I'M GONNA--!
COME ON, CALL CHIEF KARUP.
OKAY, HUK.
SINCE 1846
KRRAASH!
YOU SCUM DON'T RESPECT ANYTHING ANYMORE.
8

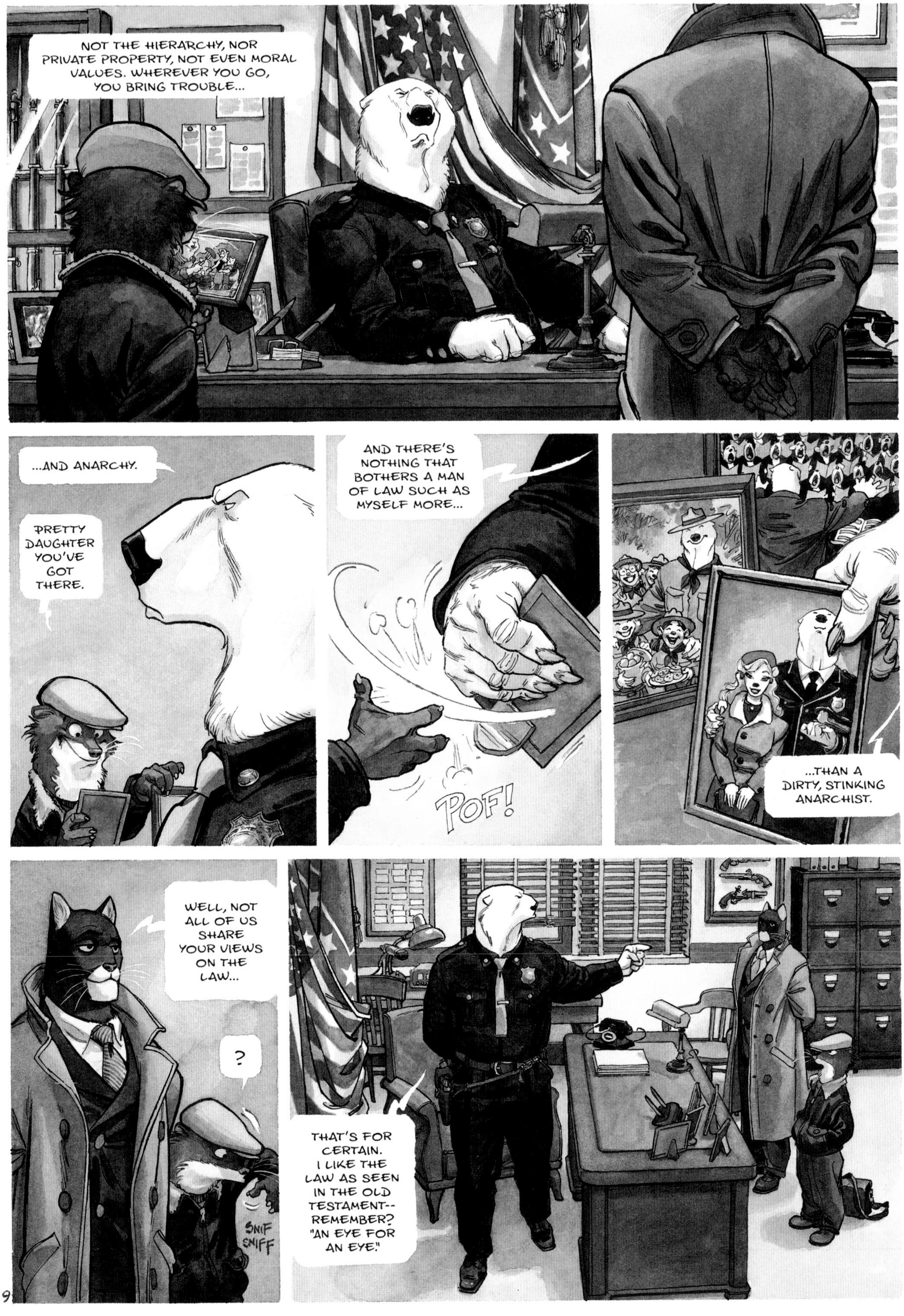
NOT THE HIERARCHY, NOR PRIVATE PROPERTY, NOT EVEN MORAL VALUES. WHEREVER YOU GO, YOU BRING TROUBLE...
...AND ANARCHY.
PRETTY DAUGHTER YOU'VE GOT THERE.
AND THERE'S NOTHING THAT BOTHERS A MAN OF LAW SUCH AS MYSELF MORE...
POF!
...THAN A DIRTY, STINKING ANARCHIST.
WELL, NOT ALL OF US SHARE YOUR VIEWS ON THE LAW...
?
SNIF SNIFF
THAT'S FOR CERTAIN. I LIKE THE LAW AS SEEN IN THE OLD TESTAMENT-- REMEMBER? "AN EYE FOR AN EYE."

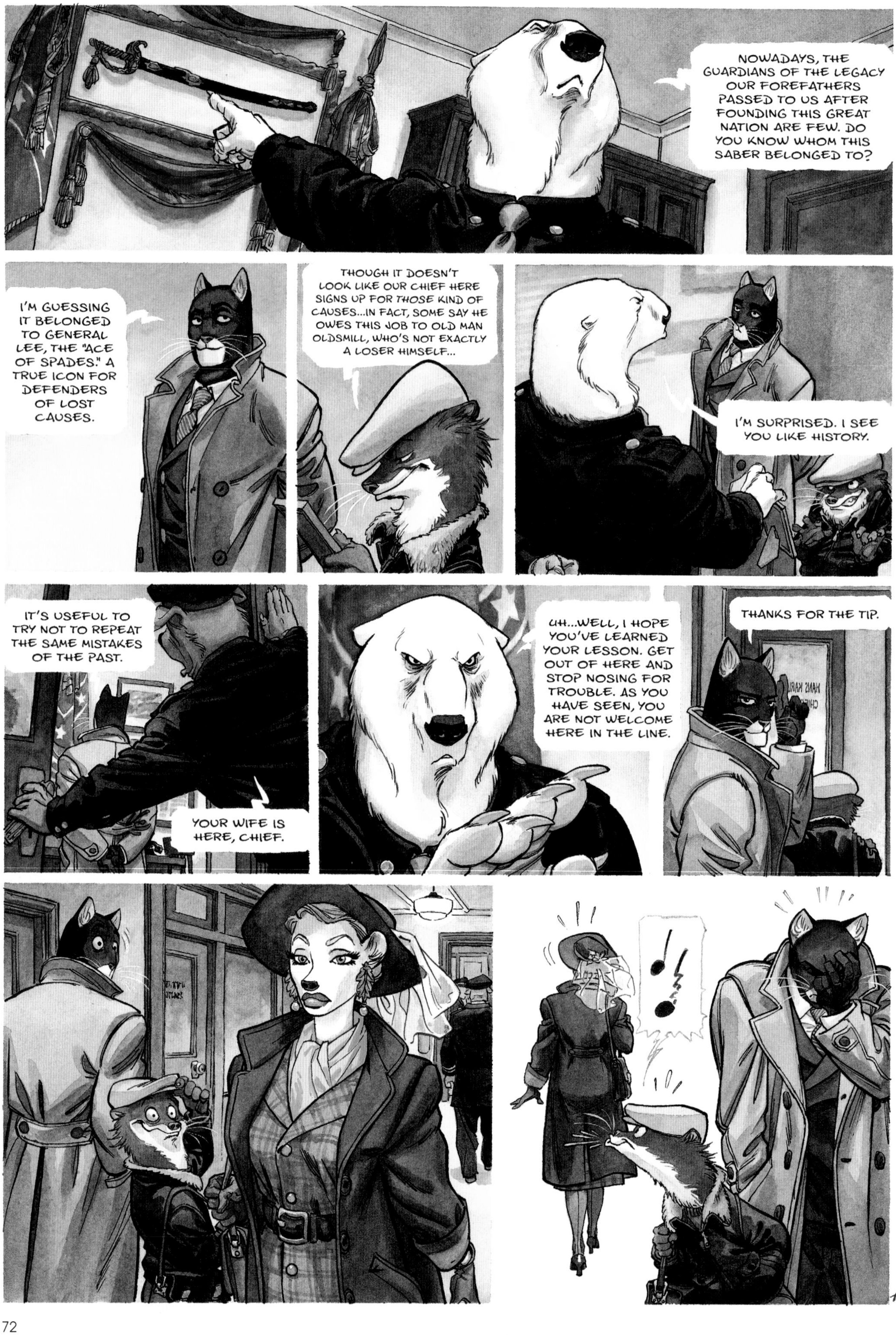

NOWADAYS, THE GUARDIANS OF THE LEGACY OUR FOREFATHERS PASSED TO US AFTER FOUNDING THIS GREAT NATION ARE FEW. DO YOU KNOW WHOM THIS SABER BELONGED TO?
I'M GUESSING IT BELONGED TO GENERAL LEE, THE "ACE OF SPADES." A TRUE ICON FOR DEFENDERS OF LOST CAUSES.
THOUGH IT DOESN'T LOOK LIKE OUR CHIEF HERE SIGNS UP FOR *THOSE* KIND OF CAUSES...IN FACT, SOME SAY HE OWES THIS JOB TO OLD MAN OLDSMILL, WHO'S NOT EXACTLY A LOSER HIMSELF...
I'M SURPRISED. I SEE YOU LIKE HISTORY.
IT'S USEFUL TO TRY NOT TO REPEAT THE SAME MISTAKES OF THE PAST.
YOUR WIFE IS HERE, CHIEF.
UH...WELL, I HOPE YOU'VE LEARNED YOUR LESSON. GET OUT OF HERE AND STOP NOSING FOR TROUBLE. AS YOU HAVE SEEN, YOU ARE NOT WELCOME HERE IN THE LINE.
THANKS FOR THE TIP.
10

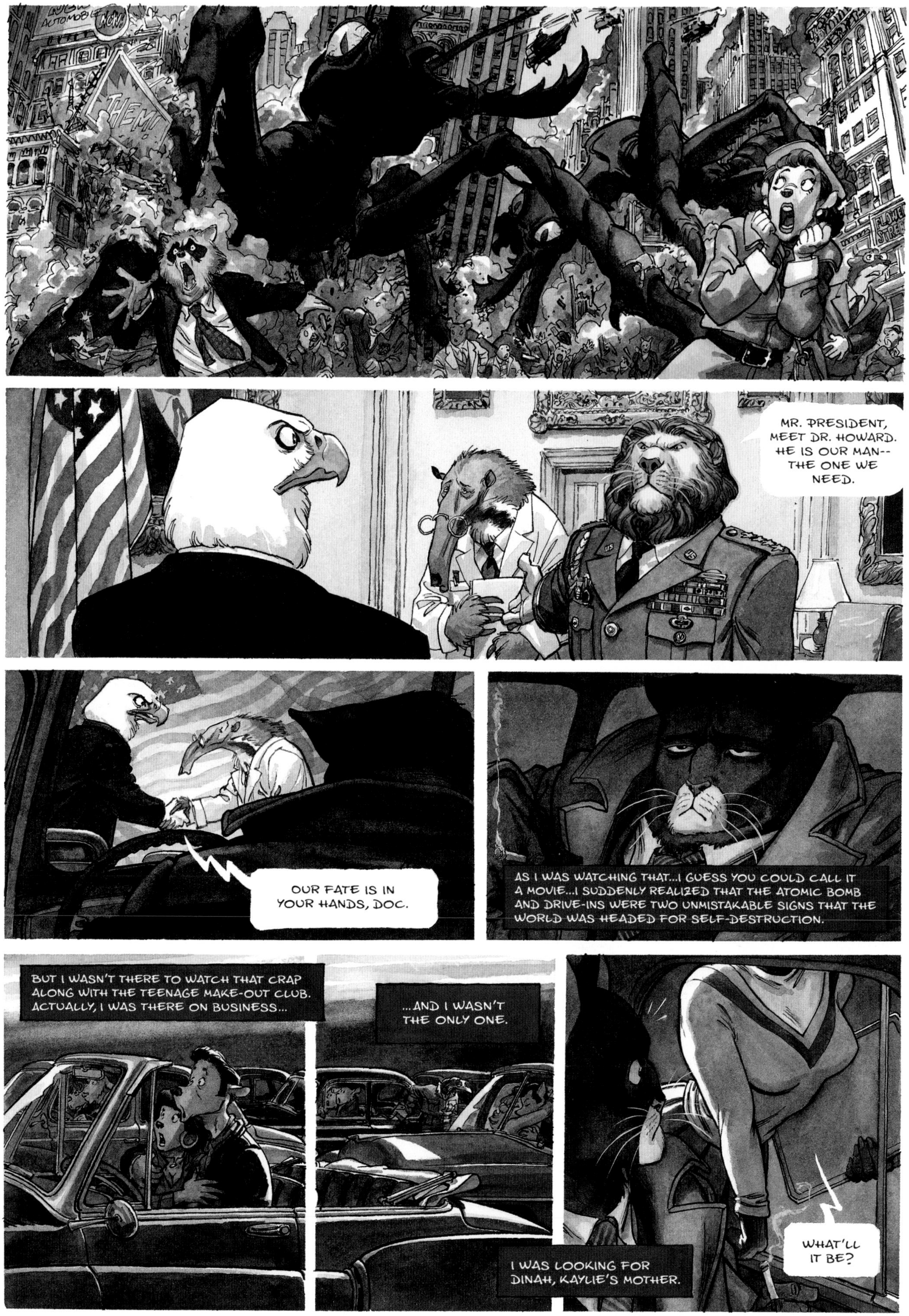
NEW AUTOMOBILE
THEM!
FLOWER STREET
MR. PRESIDENT, MEET DR. HOWARD. HE IS OUR MAN--THE ONE WE NEED.
OUR FATE IS IN YOUR HANDS, DOC.
AS I WAS WATCHING THAT...I GUESS YOU COULD CALL IT A MOVIE...I SUDDENLY REALIZED THAT THE ATOMIC BOMB AND DRIVE-INS WERE TWO UNMISTAKABLE SIGNS THAT THE WORLD WAS HEADED FOR SELF-DESTRUCTION.
BUT I WASN'T THERE TO WATCH THAT CRAP ALONG WITH THE TEENAGE MAKE-OUT CLUB. ACTUALLY, I WAS THERE ON BUSINESS...
...AND I WASN'T THE ONLY ONE.
I WAS LOOKING FOR DINAH, KAYLIE'S MOTHER.
WHAT'LL IT BE?
11

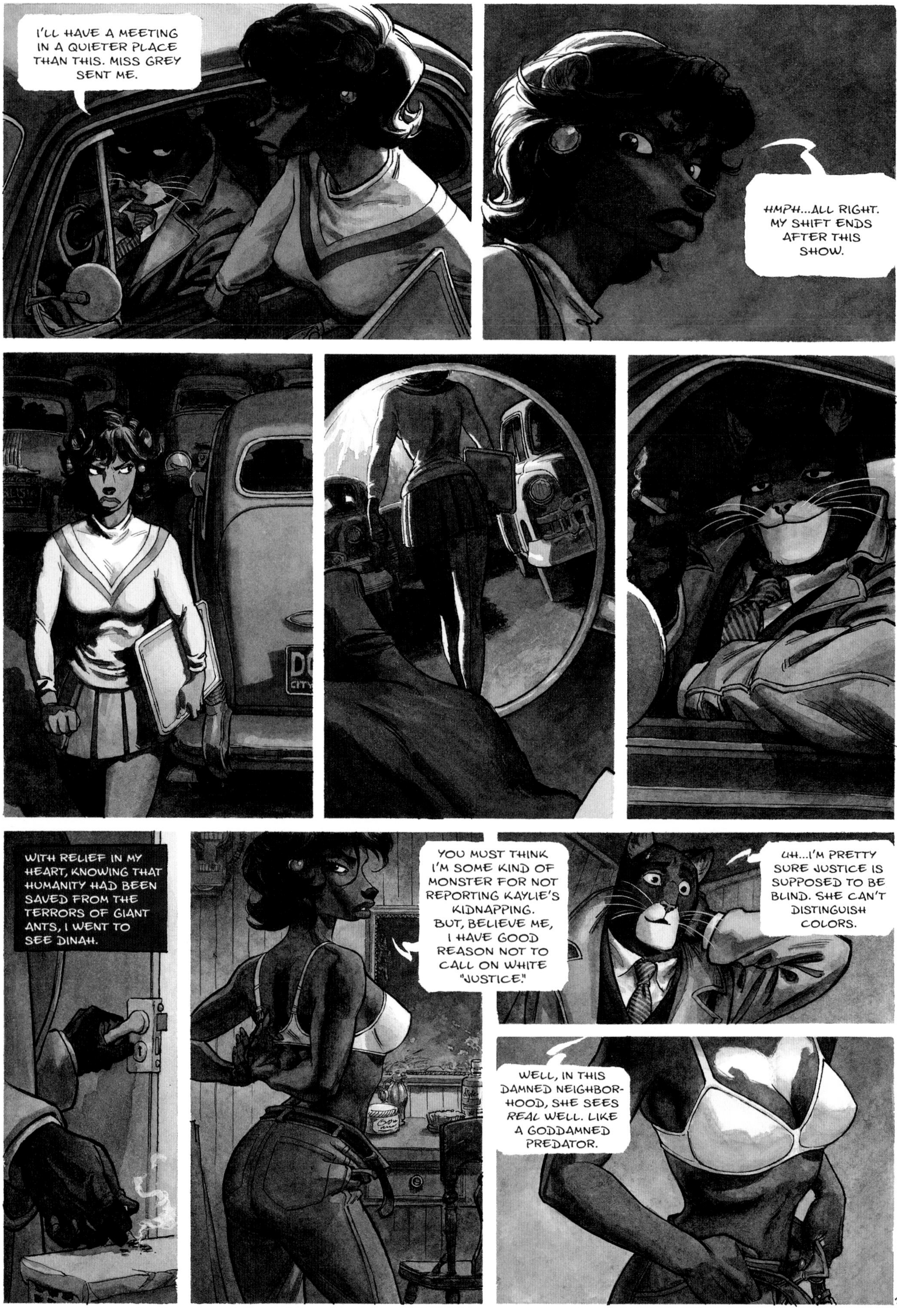
I'LL HAVE A MEETING IN A QUIETER PLACE THAN THIS. MISS GREY SENT ME.
HMPH...ALL RIGHT. MY SHIFT ENDS AFTER THIS SHOW.
WITH RELIEF IN MY HEART, KNOWING THAT HUMANITY HAD BEEN SAVED FROM THE TERRORS OF GIANT ANTS, I WENT TO SEE DINAH.
YOU MUST THINK I'M SOME KIND OF MONSTER FOR NOT REPORTING KAYLIE'S KIDNAPPING. BUT, BELIEVE ME, I HAVE GOOD REASON NOT TO CALL ON WHITE "JUSTICE."
UH...I'M PRETTY SURE JUSTICE IS SUPPOSED TO BE BLIND. SHE CAN'T DISTINGUISH COLORS.
WELL, IN THIS DAMNED NEIGHBOR-HOOD, SHE SEES *REAL* WELL. LIKE A GODDAMNED PREDATOR.
12

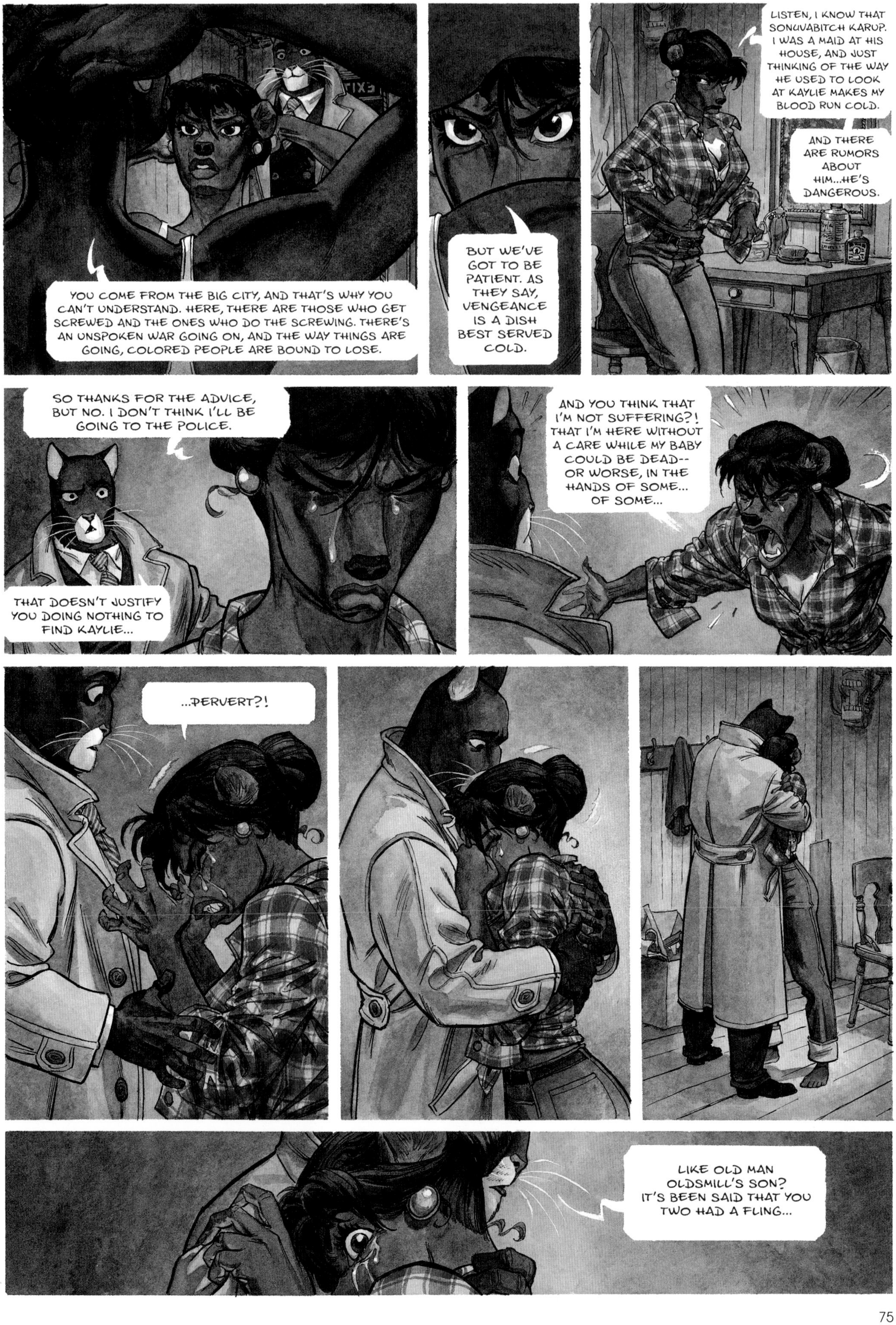

YOU COME FROM THE BIG CITY, AND THAT'S WHY YOU CAN'T UNDERSTAND. HERE, THERE ARE THOSE WHO GET SCREWED AND THE ONES WHO DO THE SCREWING. THERE'S AN UNSPOKEN WAR GOING ON, AND THE WAY THINGS ARE GOING, COLORED PEOPLE ARE BOUND TO LOSE.
BUT WE'VE GOT TO BE PATIENT. AS THEY SAY, VENGEANCE IS A DISH BEST SERVED COLD.
LISTEN, I KNOW THAT SONUVABITCH KARUP. I WAS A MAID AT HIS HOUSE, AND JUST THINKING OF THE WAY HE USED TO LOOK AT KAYLIE MAKES MY BLOOD RUN COLD.
AND THERE ARE RUMORS ABOUT HIM...HE'S DANGEROUS.
SO THANKS FOR THE ADVICE, BUT NO. I DON'T THINK I'LL BE GOING TO THE POLICE.
THAT DOESN'T JUSTIFY YOU DOING NOTHING TO FIND KAYLIE...
AND YOU THINK THAT I'M NOT SUFFERING?! THAT I'M HERE WITHOUT A CARE WHILE MY BABY COULD BE DEAD-- OR WORSE, IN THE HANDS OF SOME... OF SOME...
...PERVERT?!
LIKE OLD MAN OLDSMILL'S SON? IT'S BEEN SAID THAT YOU TWO HAD A FLING...

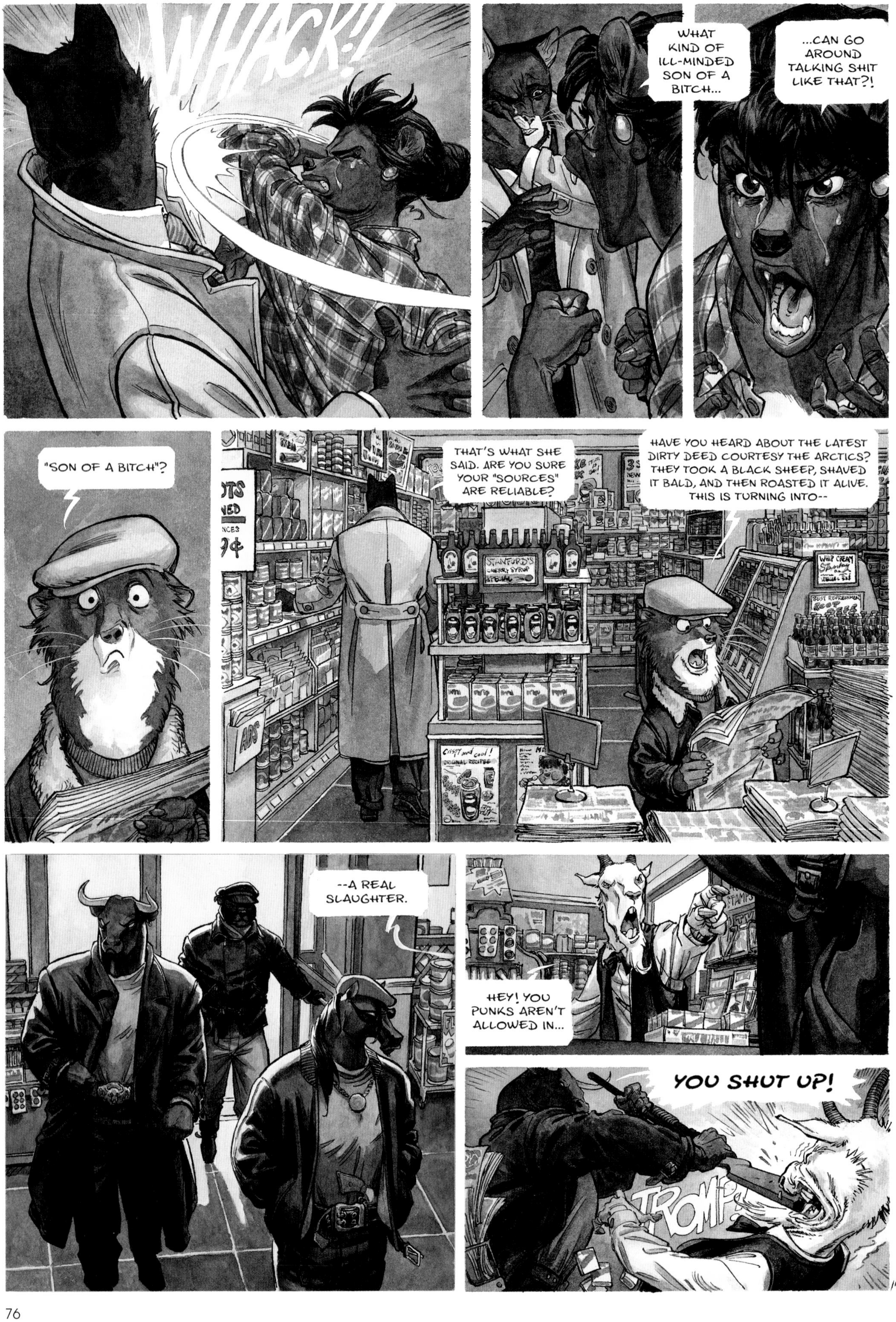
WHACK!!
WHAT KIND OF ILL-MINDED SON OF A BITCH...
...CAN GO AROUND TALKING SHIT LIKE THAT?!
"SON OF A BITCH"?
THAT'S WHAT SHE SAID. ARE YOU SURE YOUR "SOURCES" ARE RELIABLE?
HAVE YOU HEARD ABOUT THE LATEST DIRTY DEED COURTESY THE ARCTICS? THEY TOOK A BLACK SHEEP, SHAVED IT BALD, AND THEN ROASTED IT ALIVE. THIS IS TURNING INTO--
STANFORD'S CHERRY SYRUP
WHIP CREAM
CRISPY and cool! ORIGINAL RECIPE
--A REAL SLAUGHTER.
HEY! YOU PUNKS AREN'T ALLOWED IN...
YOU SHUT UP!
TROMP!
14

E-E-E-EEEH!

OH-OH-OH-OH!

AAAAA!!

SPECIAL!!

O-OWWW...

YOU'RE A REPORTER, RIGHT?

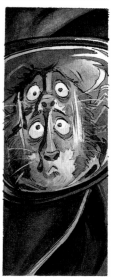

GOOD-- YOU'RE GOING TO DO US A FAVOR.

RUN THIS IN THE PAPER. WE WANT THOSE WHITE BASTARDS TO KNOW THAT WE DON'T GO AROUND KIDNAPPING KIDS. IF THEY WANT TO KNOW WHAT HAPPENED TO HER, LET THEM ASK THAT KARUP PRICK.

I'M SURE HE'S COVERING UP FOR OLDSMILL AND THAT RETARDED SON OF HIS AGAIN.

WHAT HAPPENED TO YOUR SNOUT, BROTHER?

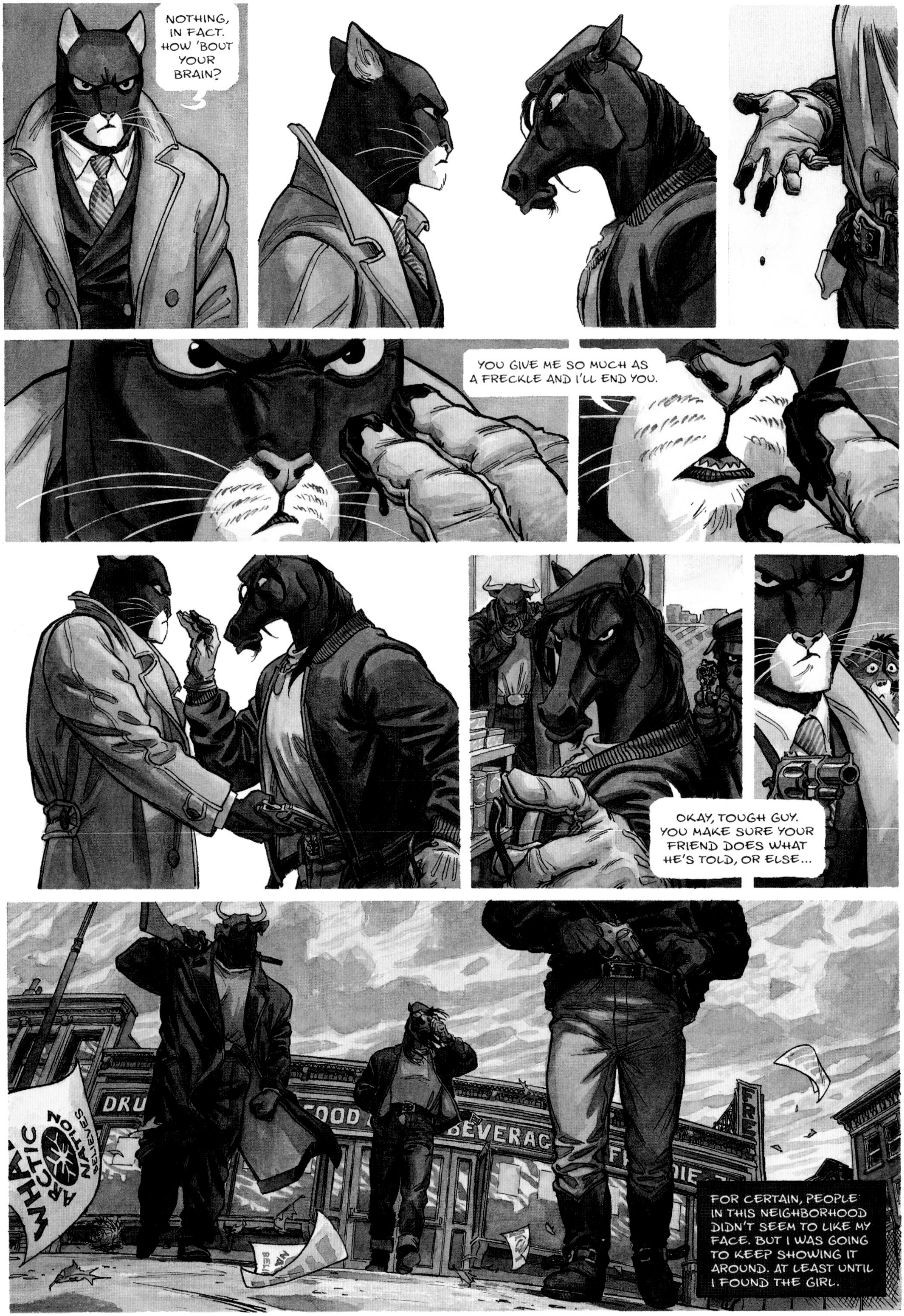

NOTHING, IN FACT. HOW 'BOUT YOUR BRAIN?
YOU GIVE ME SO MUCH AS A FRECKLE AND I'LL END YOU.
OKAY, TOUGH GUY. YOU MAKE SURE YOUR FRIEND DOES WHAT HE'S TOLD, OR ELSE...
FOR CERTAIN, PEOPLE IN THIS NEIGHBORHOOD DIDN'T SEEM TO LIKE MY FACE. BUT I WAS GOING TO KEEP SHOWING IT AROUND. AT LEAST UNTIL I FOUND THE GIRL.

16

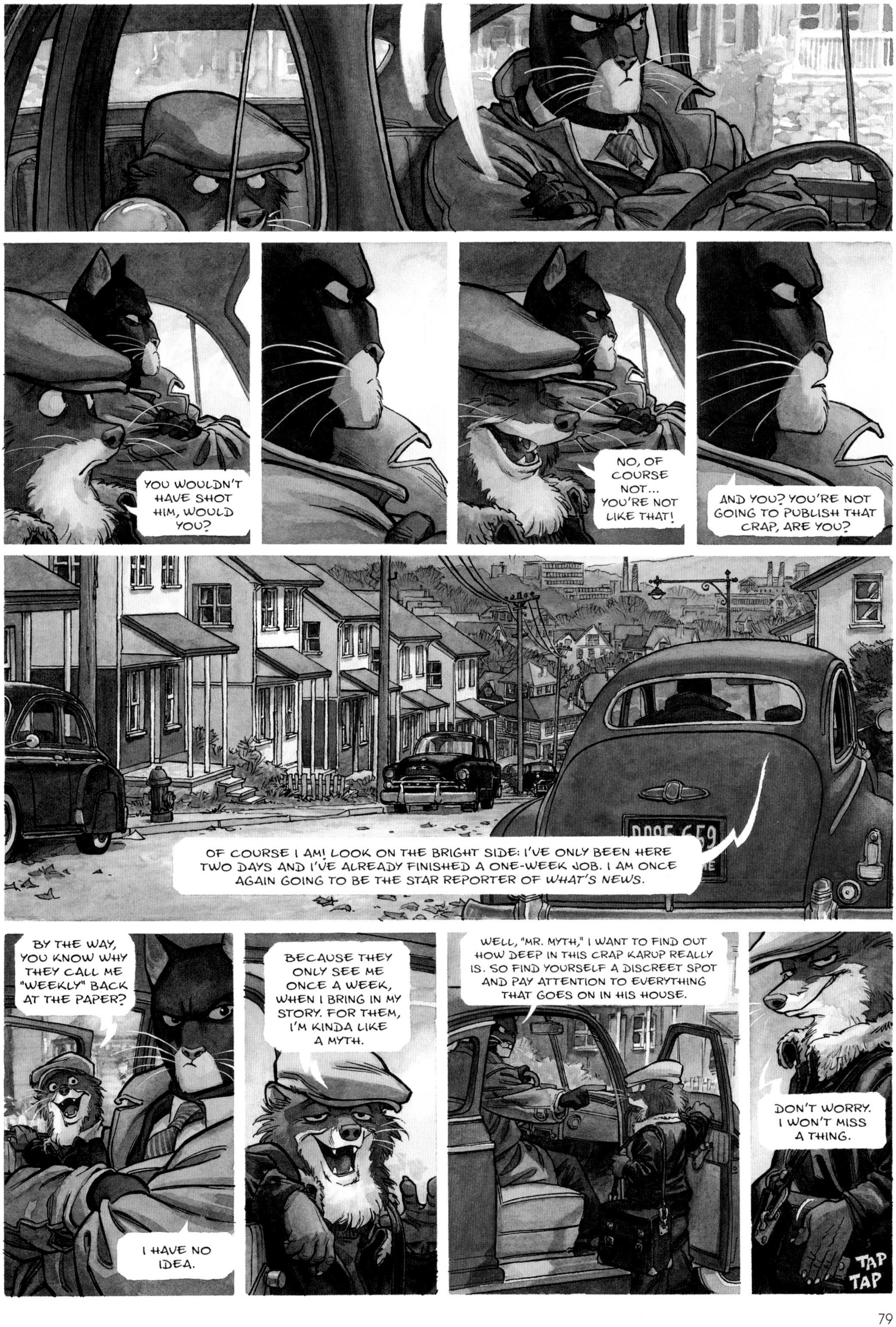

YOU WOULDN'T HAVE SHOT HIM, WOULD YOU?
NO, OF COURSE NOT... YOU'RE NOT LIKE THAT!
AND YOU? YOU'RE NOT GOING TO PUBLISH THAT CRAP, ARE YOU?
OF COURSE I AM! LOOK ON THE BRIGHT SIDE: I'VE ONLY BEEN HERE TWO DAYS AND I'VE ALREADY FINISHED A ONE-WEEK JOB. I AM ONCE AGAIN GOING TO BE THE STAR REPORTER OF WHAT'S NEWS.
BY THE WAY, YOU KNOW WHY THEY CALL ME "WEEKLY" BACK AT THE PAPER?
I HAVE NO IDEA.
BECAUSE THEY ONLY SEE ME ONCE A WEEK, WHEN I BRING IN MY STORY. FOR THEM, I'M KINDA LIKE A MYTH.
WELL, "MR. MYTH," I WANT TO FIND OUT HOW DEEP IN THIS CRAP KARUP REALLY IS. SO FIND YOURSELF A DISCREET SPOT AND PAY ATTENTION TO EVERYTHING THAT GOES ON IN HIS HOUSE.
DON'T WORRY. I WON'T MISS A THING.
TAP TAP
17

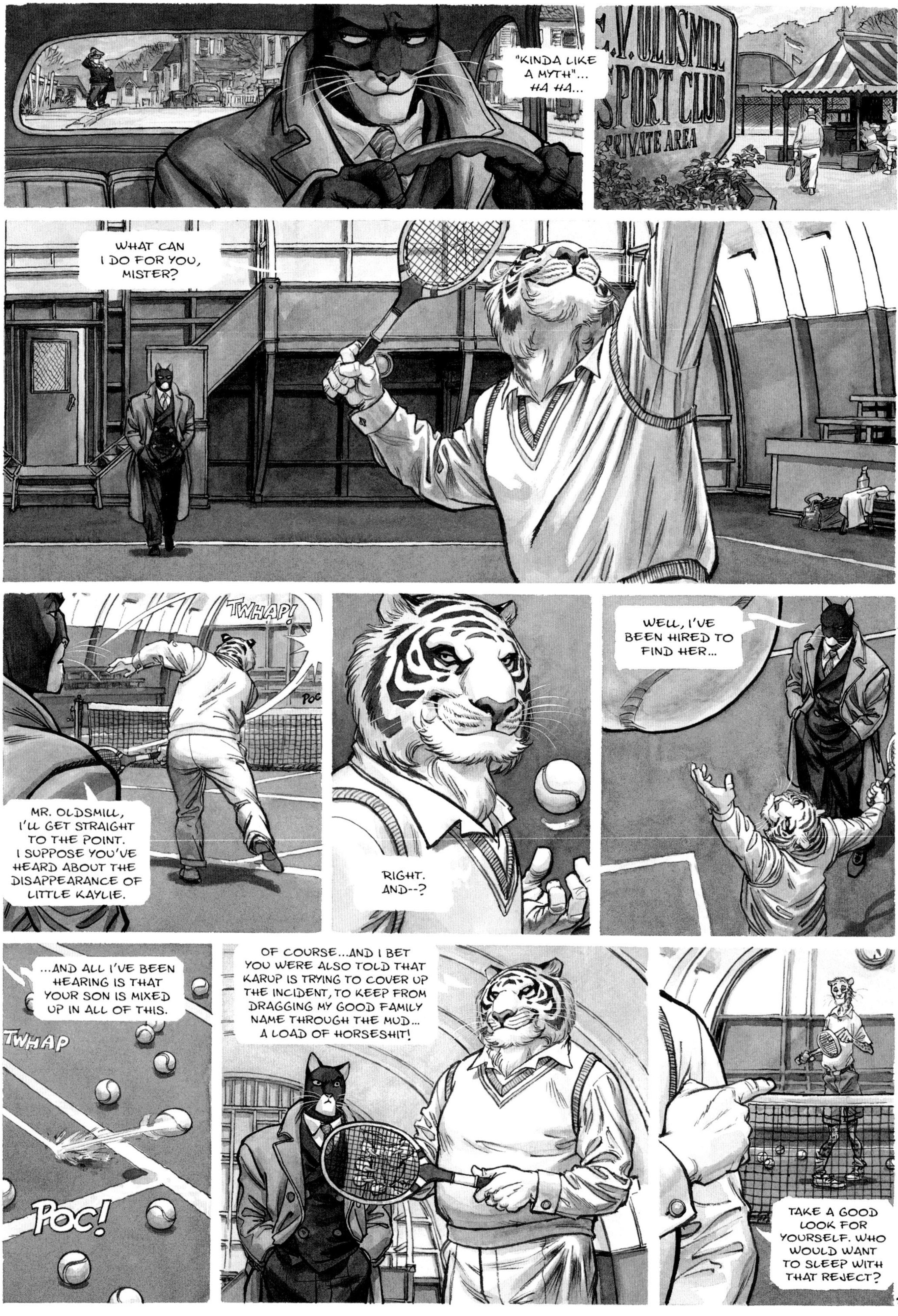
"KINDA LIKE A MYTH"... HA HA...
C.V. OLDSMILL SPORT CLUB
PRIVATE AREA
WHAT CAN I DO FOR YOU, MISTER?
TWHAP!
POC
MR. OLDSMILL, I'LL GET STRAIGHT TO THE POINT. I SUPPOSE YOU'VE HEARD ABOUT THE DISAPPEARANCE OF LITTLE KAYLIE.
RIGHT. AND--?
WELL, I'VE BEEN HIRED TO FIND HER...
...AND ALL I'VE BEEN HEARING IS THAT YOUR SON IS MIXED UP IN ALL OF THIS.
TWHAP
POC!
OF COURSE...AND I BET YOU WERE ALSO TOLD THAT KARUP IS TRYING TO COVER UP THE INCIDENT, TO KEEP FROM DRAGGING MY GOOD FAMILY NAME THROUGH THE MUD... A LOAD OF HORSESHIT!
TAKE A GOOD LOOK FOR YOURSELF. WHO WOULD WANT TO SLEEP WITH THAT REJECT?
18

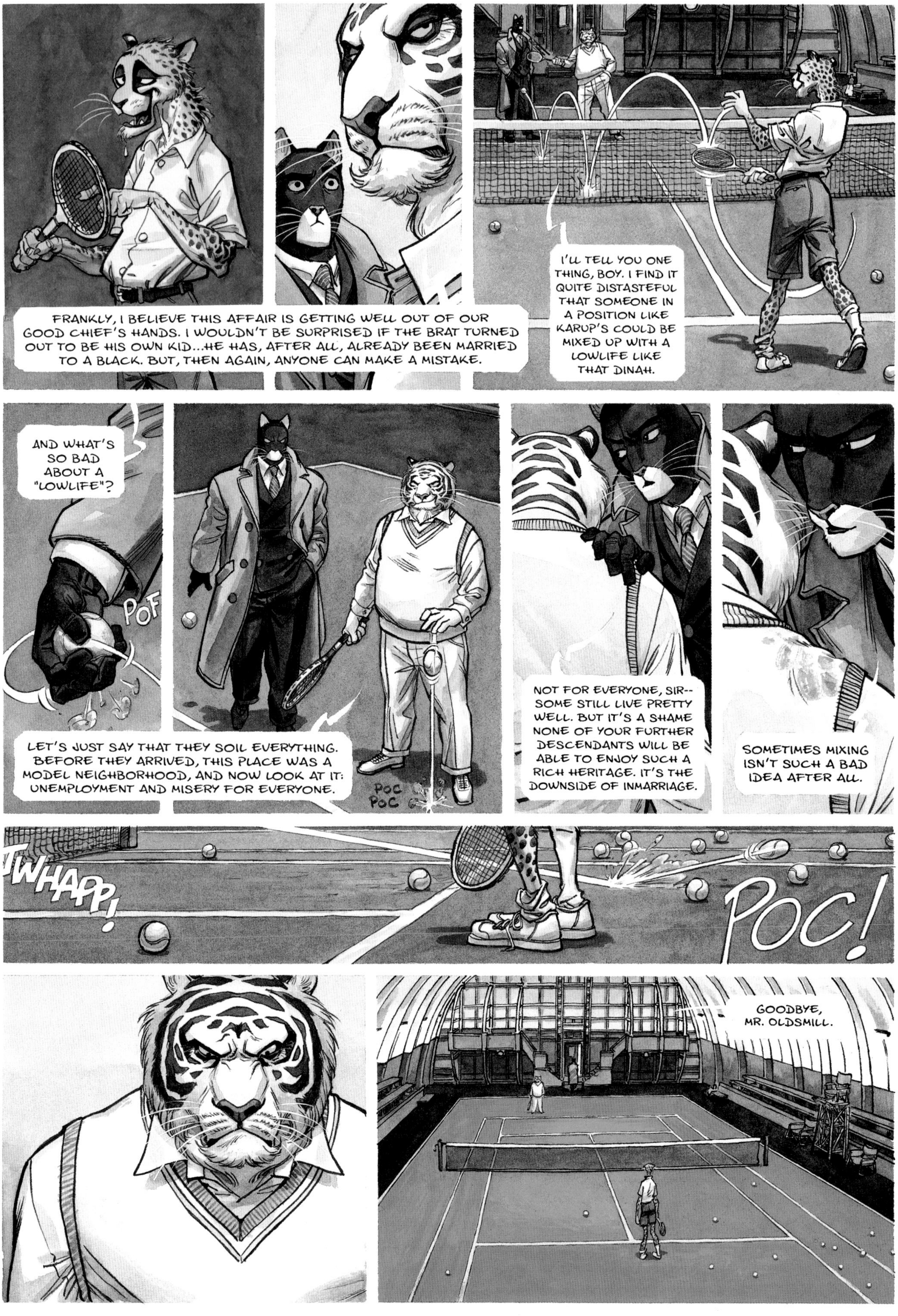

FRANKLY, I BELIEVE THIS AFFAIR IS GETTING WELL OUT OF OUR GOOD CHIEF'S HANDS. I WOULDN'T BE SURPRISED IF THE BRAT TURNED OUT TO BE HIS OWN KID...HE HAS, AFTER ALL, ALREADY BEEN MARRIED TO A BLACK. BUT, THEN AGAIN, ANYONE CAN MAKE A MISTAKE.
I'LL TELL YOU ONE THING, BOY. I FIND IT QUITE DISTASTEFUL THAT SOMEONE IN A POSITION LIKE KARUP'S COULD BE MIXED UP WITH A LOWLIFE LIKE THAT DINAH.
AND WHAT'S SO BAD ABOUT A "LOWLIFE"?
POF
LET'S JUST SAY THAT THEY SOIL EVERYTHING. BEFORE THEY ARRIVED, THIS PLACE WAS A MODEL NEIGHBORHOOD, AND NOW LOOK AT IT: UNEMPLOYMENT AND MISERY FOR EVERYONE.
POC POC
NOT FOR EVERYONE, SIR-- SOME STILL LIVE PRETTY WELL. BUT IT'S A SHAME NONE OF YOUR FURTHER DESCENDANTS WILL BE ABLE TO ENJOY SUCH A RICH HERITAGE. IT'S THE DOWNSIDE OF INMARRIAGE.
SOMETIMES MIXING ISN'T SUCH A BAD IDEA AFTER ALL.
TWHAPP!
POC!
GOODBYE, MR. OLDSMILL.
19

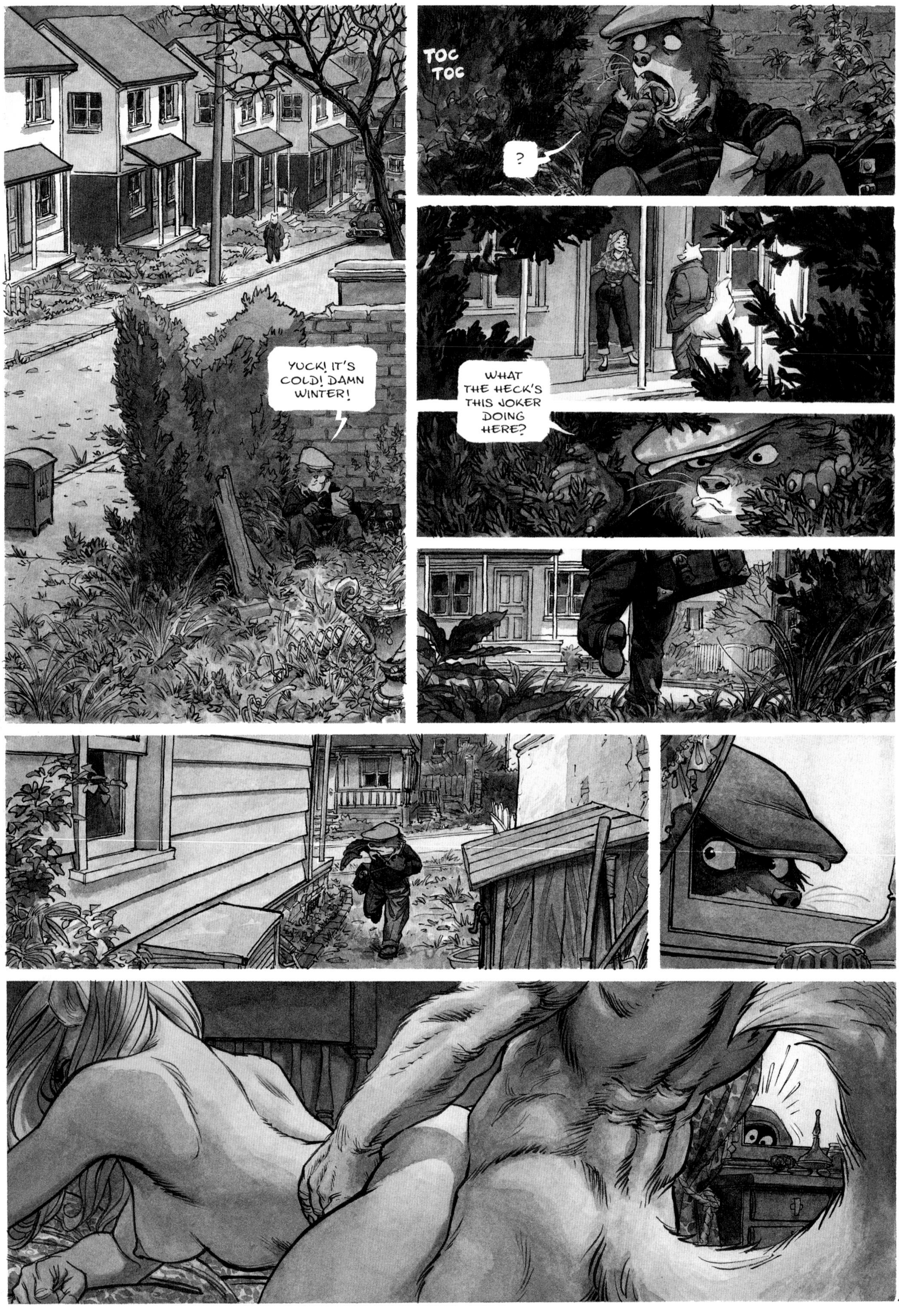
YUCK! IT'S COLD! DAMN WINTER!
TOC TOC
?
WHAT THE HECK'S THIS JOKER DOING HERE?

20

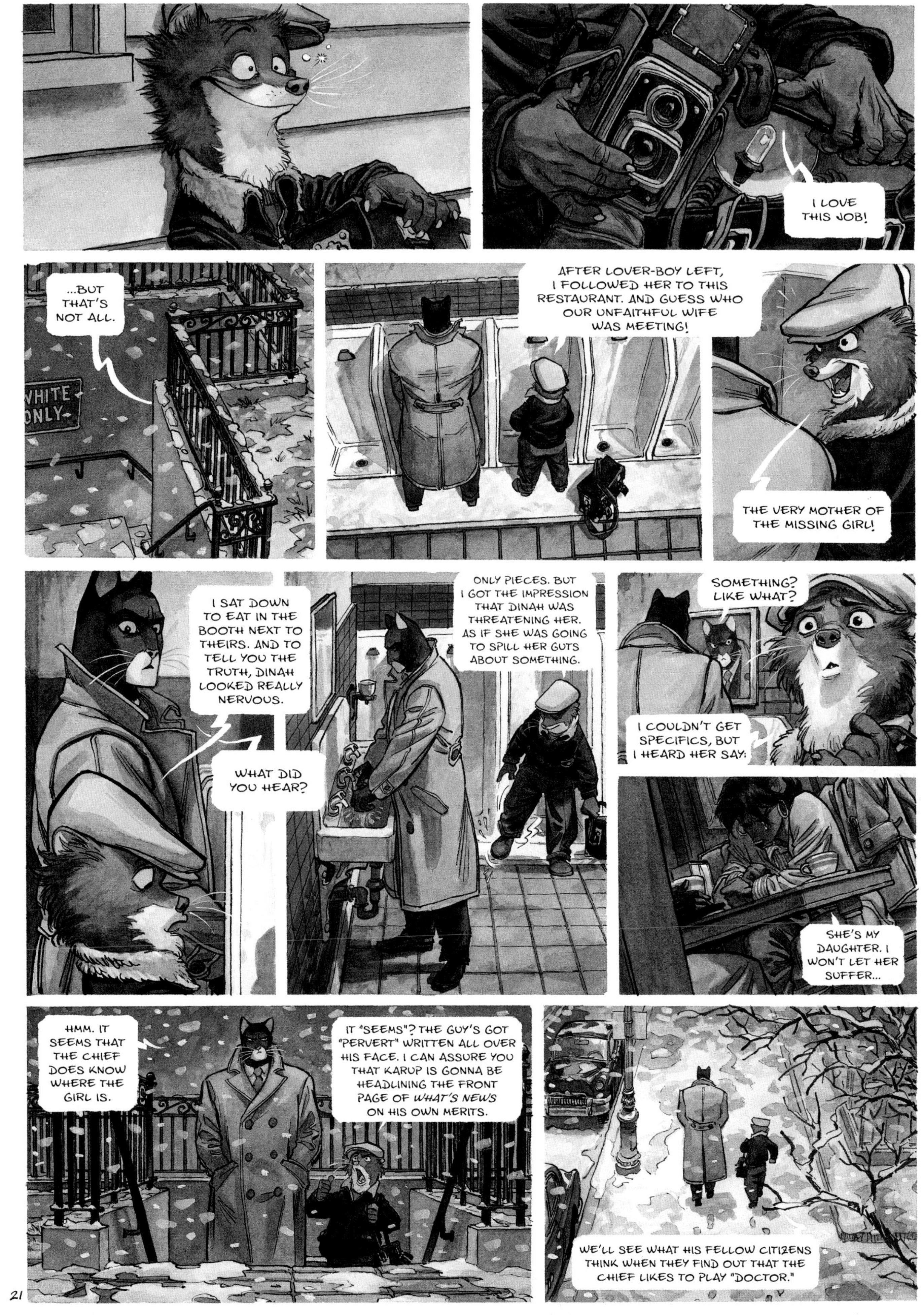
I LOVE THIS JOB!
...BUT THAT'S NOT ALL.
WHITE ONLY
AFTER LOVER-BOY LEFT, I FOLLOWED HER TO THIS RESTAURANT. AND GUESS WHO OUR UNFAITHFUL WIFE WAS MEETING!
THE VERY MOTHER OF THE MISSING GIRL!
I SAT DOWN TO EAT IN THE BOOTH NEXT TO THEIRS. AND TO TELL YOU THE TRUTH, DINAH LOOKED REALLY NERVOUS.
WHAT DID YOU HEAR?
ONLY PIECES. BUT I GOT THE IMPRESSION THAT DINAH WAS THREATENING HER. AS IF SHE WAS GOING TO SPILL HER GUTS ABOUT SOMETHING.
SOMETHING? LIKE WHAT?
I COULDN'T GET SPECIFICS, BUT I HEARD HER SAY:
SHE'S MY DAUGHTER. I WON'T LET HER SUFFER...
HMM. IT SEEMS THAT THE CHIEF DOES KNOW WHERE THE GIRL IS.
IT "SEEMS"? THE GUY'S GOT "PERVERT" WRITTEN ALL OVER HIS FACE. I CAN ASSURE YOU THAT KARUP IS GONNA BE HEADLINING THE FRONT PAGE OF *WHAT'S NEWS* ON HIS OWN MERITS.
WE'LL SEE WHAT HIS FELLOW CITIZENS THINK WHEN THEY FIND OUT THAT THE CHIEF LIKES TO PLAY "DOCTOR."
21

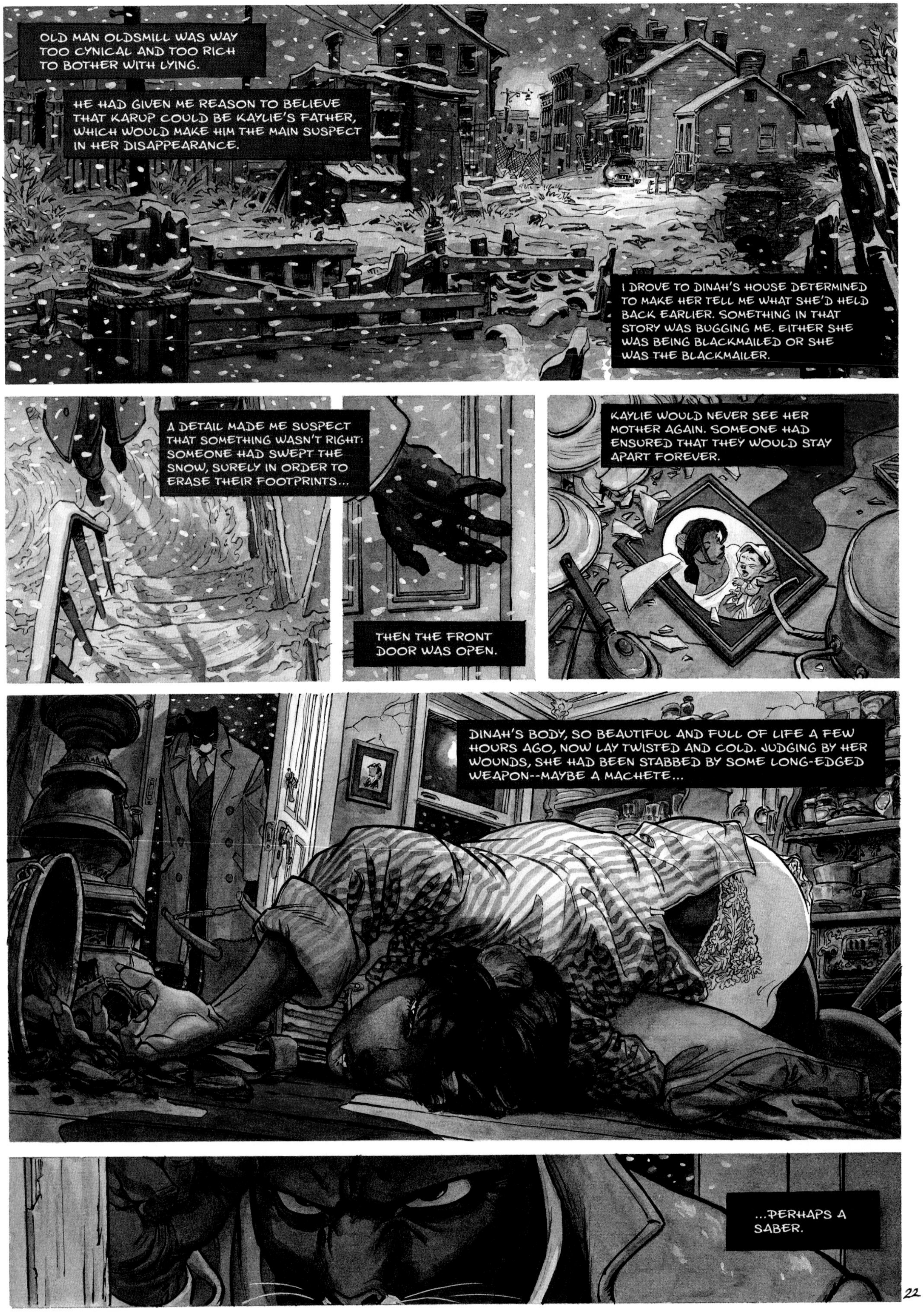
OLD MAN OLDSMILL WAS WAY TOO CYNICAL AND TOO RICH TO BOTHER WITH LYING.
HE HAD GIVEN ME REASON TO BELIEVE THAT KARUP COULD BE KAYLIE'S FATHER, WHICH WOULD MAKE HIM THE MAIN SUSPECT IN HER DISAPPEARANCE.
I DROVE TO DINAH'S HOUSE DETERMINED TO MAKE HER TELL ME WHAT SHE'D HELD BACK EARLIER. SOMETHING IN THAT STORY WAS BUGGING ME. EITHER SHE WAS BEING BLACKMAILED OR SHE WAS THE BLACKMAILER.
A DETAIL MADE ME SUSPECT THAT SOMETHING WASN'T RIGHT: SOMEONE HAD SWEPT THE SNOW, SURELY IN ORDER TO ERASE THEIR FOOTPRINTS...
THEN THE FRONT DOOR WAS OPEN.
KAYLIE WOULD NEVER SEE HER MOTHER AGAIN. SOMEONE HAD ENSURED THAT THEY WOULD STAY APART FOREVER.
DINAH'S BODY, SO BEAUTIFUL AND FULL OF LIFE A FEW HOURS AGO, NOW LAY TWISTED AND COLD. JUDGING BY HER WOUNDS, SHE HAD BEEN STABBED BY SOME LONG-EDGED WEAPON--MAYBE A MACHETE...
...PERHAPS A SABER.
22

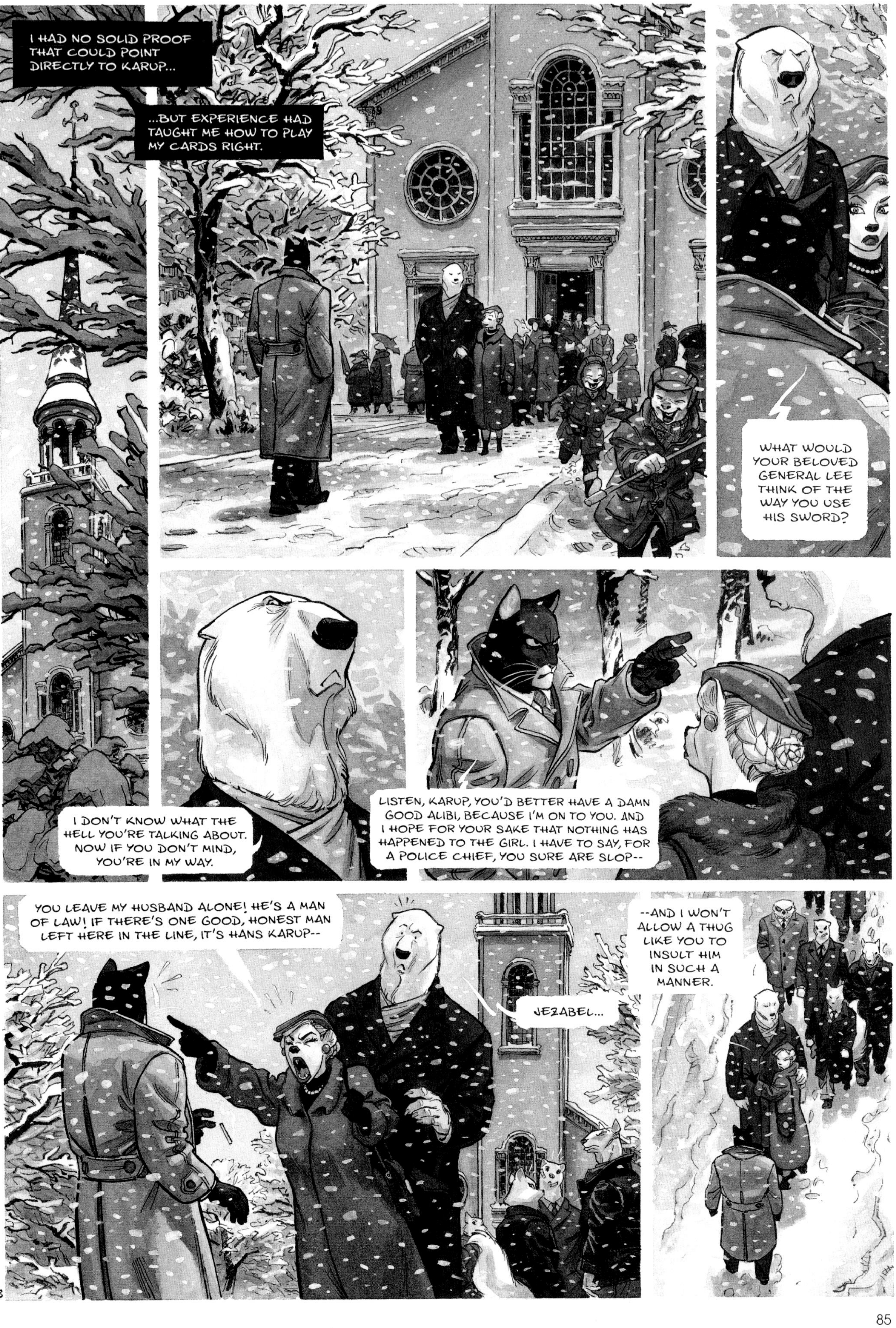
I HAD NO SOLID PROOF THAT COULD POINT DIRECTLY TO KARUP...
...BUT EXPERIENCE HAD TAUGHT ME HOW TO PLAY MY CARDS RIGHT.
WHAT WOULD YOUR BELOVED GENERAL LEE THINK OF THE WAY YOU USE HIS SWORD?
I DON'T KNOW WHAT THE HELL YOU'RE TALKING ABOUT. NOW IF YOU DON'T MIND, YOU'RE IN MY WAY.
LISTEN, KARUP, YOU'D BETTER HAVE A DAMN GOOD ALIBI, BECAUSE I'M ON TO YOU. AND I HOPE FOR YOUR SAKE THAT NOTHING HAS HAPPENED TO THE GIRL. I HAVE TO SAY, FOR A POLICE CHIEF, YOU SURE ARE SLOP--
YOU LEAVE MY HUSBAND ALONE! HE'S A MAN OF LAW! IF THERE'S ONE GOOD, HONEST MAN LEFT HERE IN THE LINE, IT'S HANS KARUP--
JEZABEL...
--AND I WON'T ALLOW A THUG LIKE YOU TO INSULT HIM IN SUCH A MANNER.
23

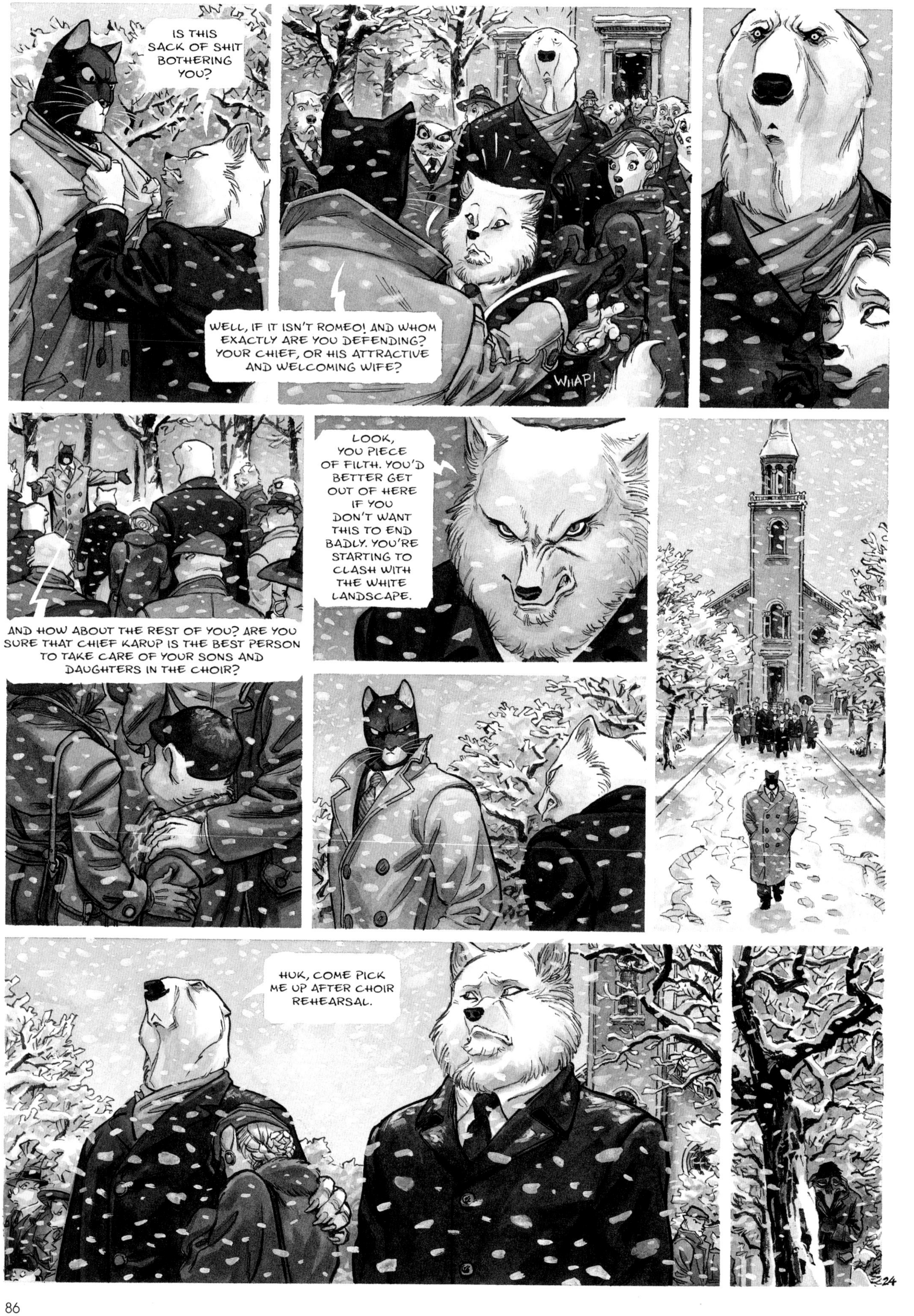
IS THIS SACK OF SHIT BOTHERING YOU?
WELL, IF IT ISN'T ROMEO! AND WHOM EXACTLY ARE YOU DEFENDING? YOUR CHIEF, OR HIS ATTRACTIVE AND WELCOMING WIFE?
WHAP!
LOOK, YOU PIECE OF FILTH. YOU'D BETTER GET OUT OF HERE IF YOU DON'T WANT THIS TO END BADLY. YOU'RE STARTING TO CLASH WITH THE WHITE LANDSCAPE.
AND HOW ABOUT THE REST OF YOU? ARE YOU SURE THAT CHIEF KARUP IS THE BEST PERSON TO TAKE CARE OF YOUR SONS AND DAUGHTERS IN THE CHOIR?
HUK, COME PICK ME UP AFTER CHOIR REHEARSAL.
24

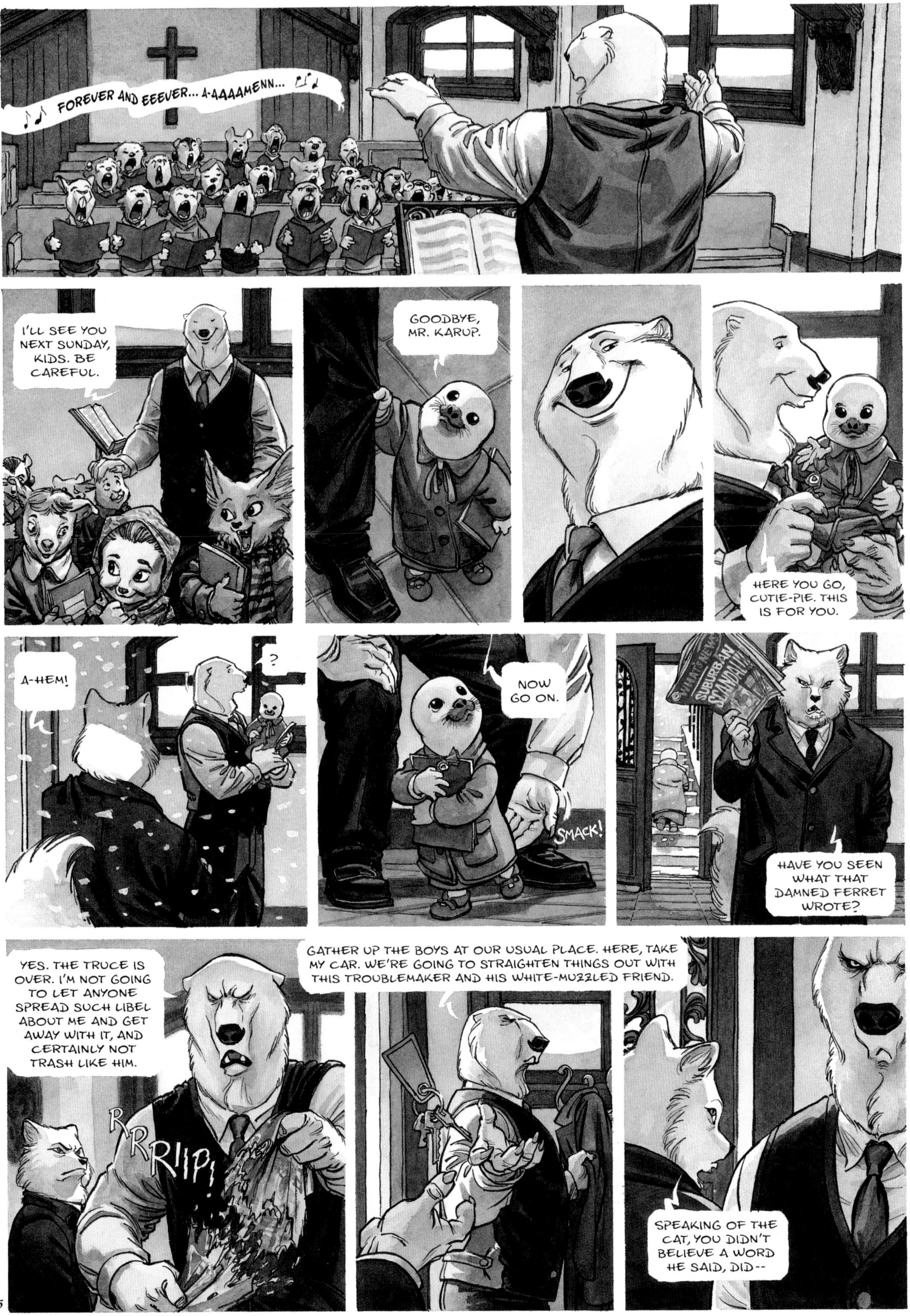

FOREVER AND EEEVER... A-AAAAMENN...
I'LL SEE YOU NEXT SUNDAY, KIDS. BE CAREFUL.
GOODBYE, MR. KARUP.
HERE YOU GO, CUTIE-PIE. THIS IS FOR YOU.
A-HEM!
?
NOW GO ON.
SMACK!
WHAT'S NEWS
SUBURBAN SCANDAL
HAVE YOU SEEN WHAT THAT DAMNED FERRET WROTE?
YES. THE TRUCE IS OVER. I'M NOT GOING TO LET ANYONE SPREAD SUCH LIBEL ABOUT ME AND GET AWAY WITH IT, AND CERTAINLY NOT TRASH LIKE HIM.
RRRIIIP!
GATHER UP THE BOYS AT OUR USUAL PLACE. HERE, TAKE MY CAR. WE'RE GOING TO STRAIGHTEN THINGS OUT WITH THIS TROUBLEMAKER AND HIS WHITE-MUZZLED FRIEND.
SPEAKING OF THE CAT, YOU DIDN'T BELIEVE A WORD HE SAID, DID--
25

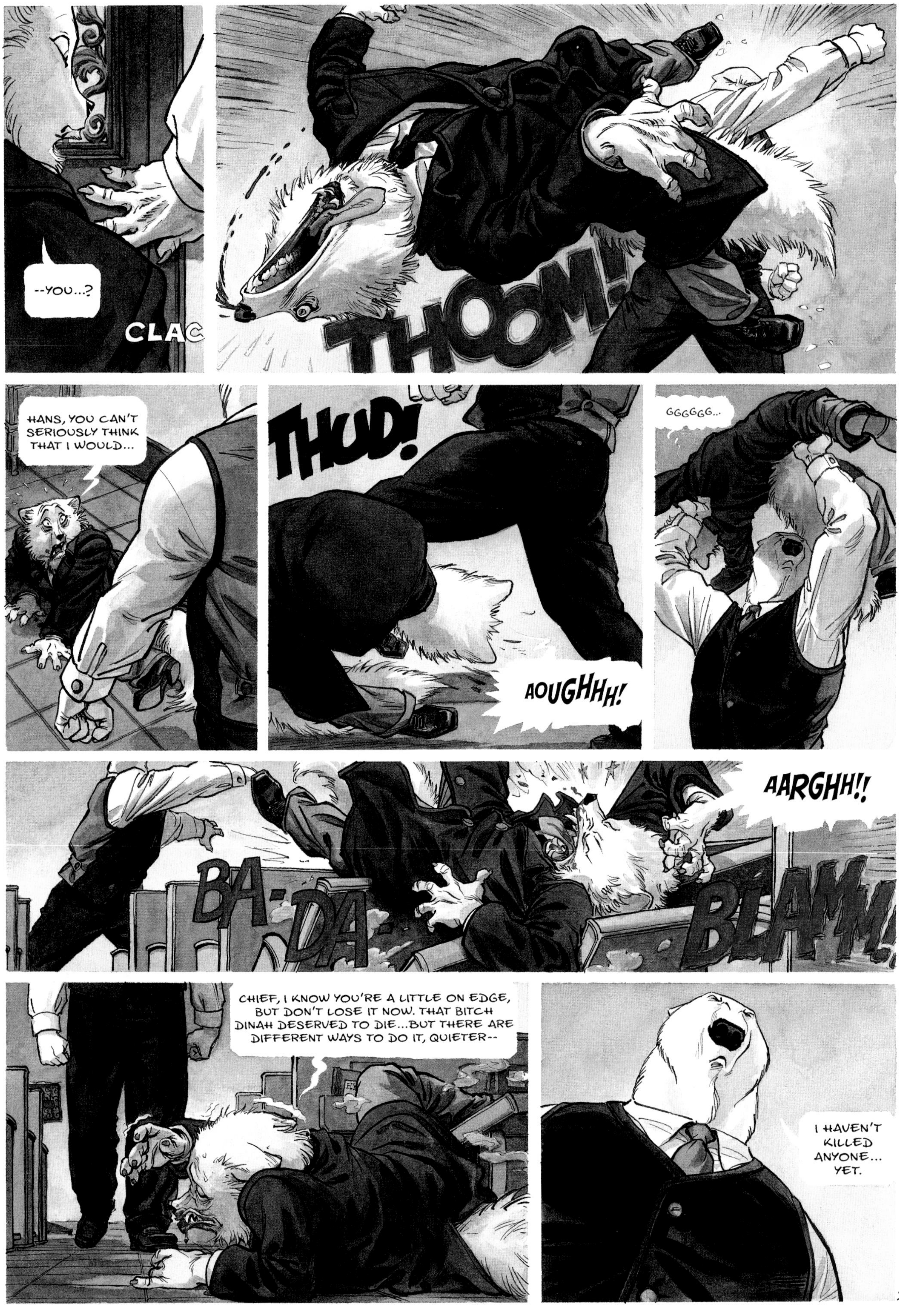
--YOU...?
CLAC
THOOM!
HANS, YOU CAN'T SERIOUSLY THINK THAT I WOULD...
THUD!
AOUGHHH!
GGGGGG...
AARGHH!!
BA-DA-BLAMM!
CHIEF, I KNOW YOU'RE A LITTLE ON EDGE, BUT DON'T LOSE IT NOW. THAT BITCH DINAH DESERVED TO DIE...BUT THERE ARE DIFFERENT WAYS TO DO IT, QUIETER--
I HAVEN'T KILLED ANYONE... YET.
26

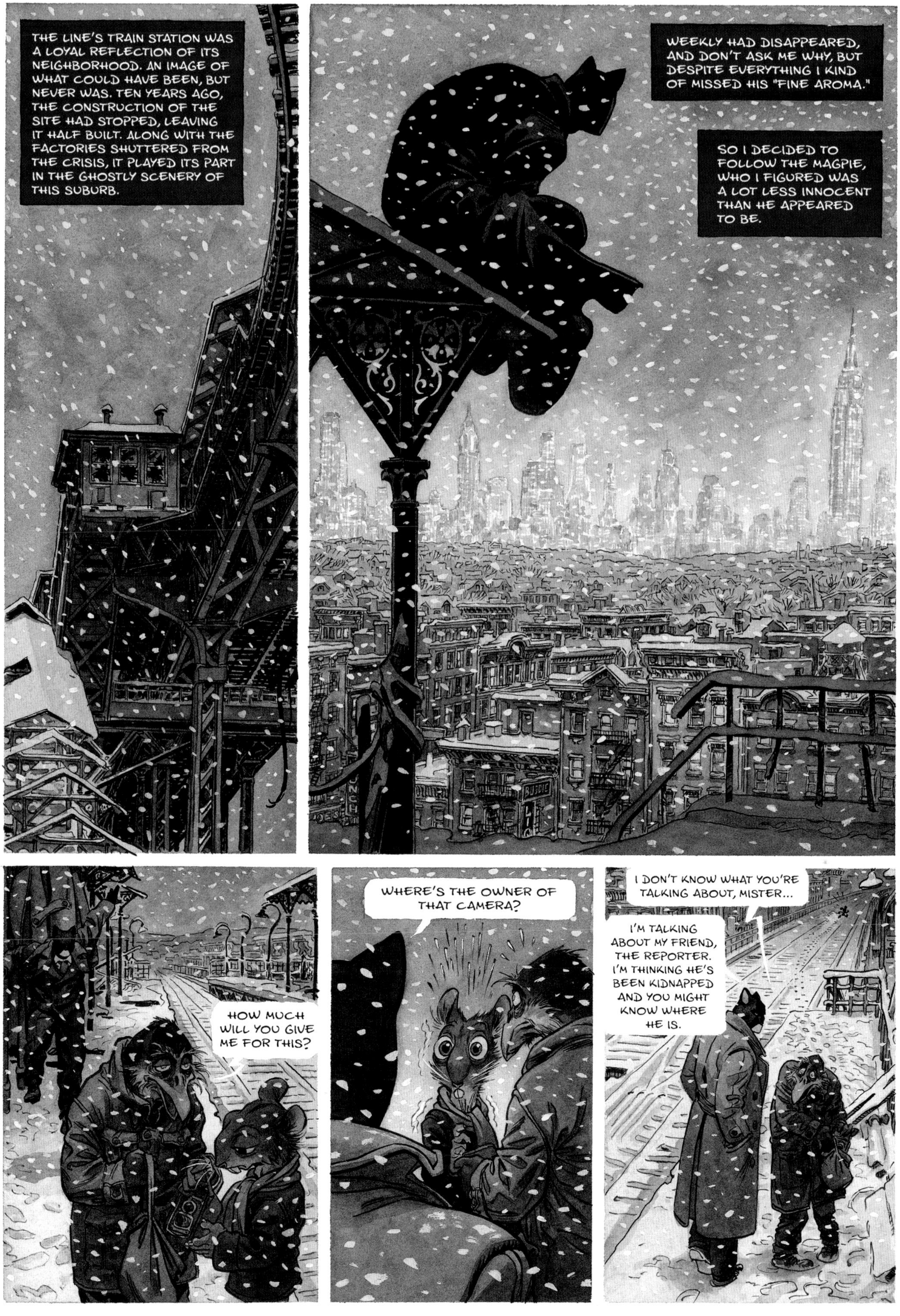
THE LINE'S TRAIN STATION WAS A LOYAL REFLECTION OF ITS NEIGHBORHOOD. AN IMAGE OF WHAT COULD HAVE BEEN, BUT NEVER WAS. TEN YEARS AGO, THE CONSTRUCTION OF THE SITE HAD STOPPED, LEAVING IT HALF BUILT. ALONG WITH THE FACTORIES SHUTTERED FROM THE CRISIS, IT PLAYED ITS PART IN THE GHOSTLY SCENERY OF THIS SUBURB.
WEEKLY HAD DISAPPEARED, AND DON'T ASK ME WHY, BUT DESPITE EVERYTHING I KIND OF MISSED HIS "FINE AROMA."
SO I DECIDED TO FOLLOW THE MAGPIE, WHO I FIGURED WAS A LOT LESS INNOCENT THAN HE APPEARED TO BE.
HOW MUCH WILL YOU GIVE ME FOR THIS?
WHERE'S THE OWNER OF THAT CAMERA?
I DON'T KNOW WHAT YOU'RE TALKING ABOUT, MISTER...
I'M TALKING ABOUT MY FRIEND, THE REPORTER. I'M THINKING HE'S BEEN KIDNAPPED AND YOU MIGHT KNOW WHERE HE IS.

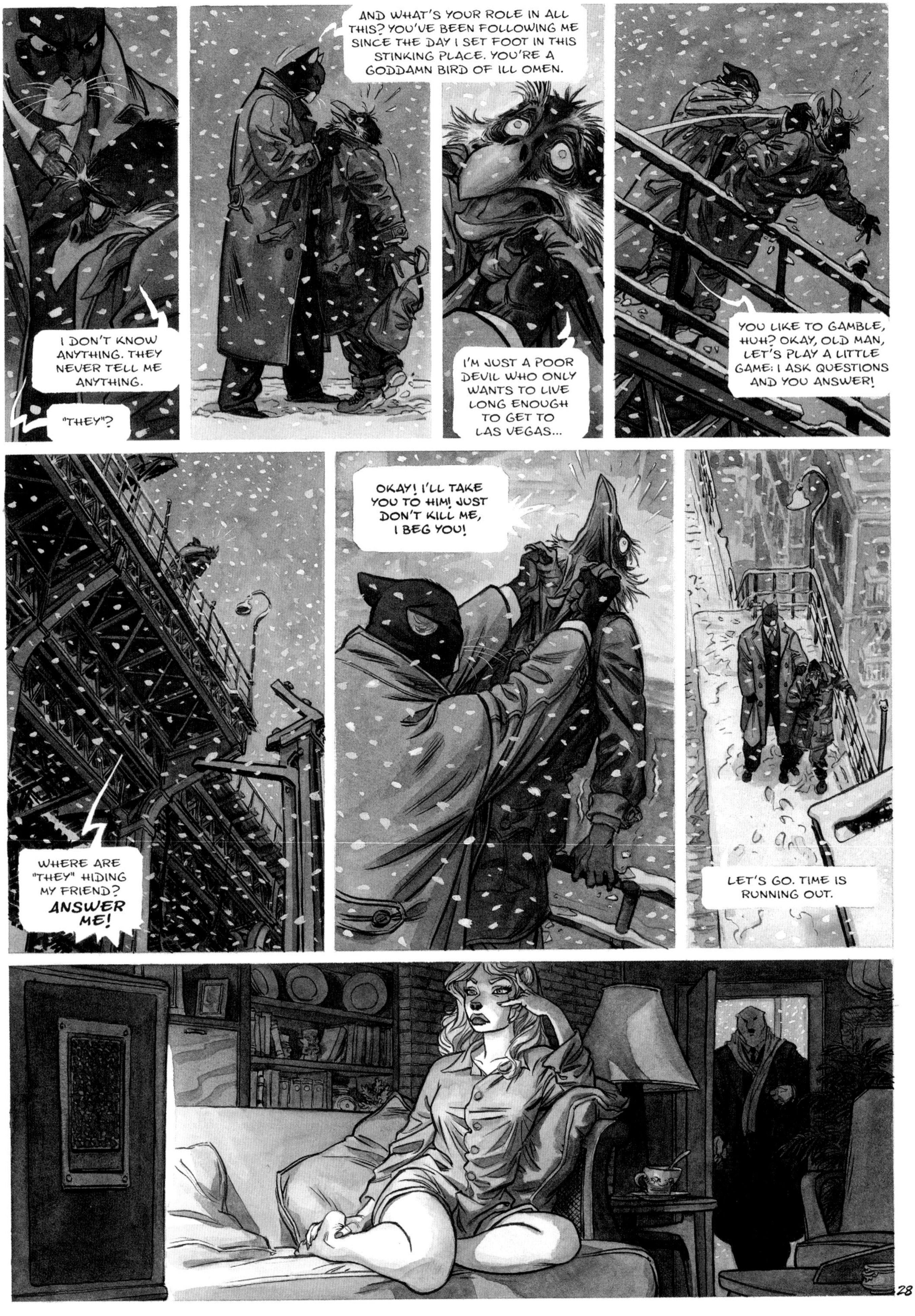
I DON'T KNOW ANYTHING. THEY NEVER TELL ME ANYTHING.
"THEY"?
AND WHAT'S YOUR ROLE IN ALL THIS? YOU'VE BEEN FOLLOWING ME SINCE THE DAY I SET FOOT IN THIS STINKING PLACE. YOU'RE A GODDAMN BIRD OF ILL OMEN.
I'M JUST A POOR DEVIL WHO ONLY WANTS TO LIVE LONG ENOUGH TO GET TO LAS VEGAS...
YOU LIKE TO GAMBLE, HUH? OKAY, OLD MAN, LET'S PLAY A LITTLE GAME: I ASK QUESTIONS AND YOU ANSWER!
WHERE ARE "THEY" HIDING MY FRIEND? ANSWER ME!
OKAY! I'LL TAKE YOU TO HIM! JUST DON'T KILL ME, I BEG YOU!
LET'S GO. TIME IS RUNNING OUT.
28

TELL ME THAT THERE'S NOTHING BETWEEN YOU AND HUK.

I'M SURPRISED YOU EVEN PAID ATTENTION TO THAT OAF. YOU KNOW BETTER THAN ANYONE THAT I'D NEVER LET ANY MAN TOUCH ME. IT DISGUSTS ME FAR TOO MUCH!

GOD, JEZ! IT'S UNBEARABLE TO THINK THAT SOMEONE ELSE IS ENJOYING WHAT I'VE BEEN DENIED FOR SO LONG...

OH, CALM DOWN, HANS! YOU KNEW EXACTLY WHAT WAS IN STORE FOR YOU WHEN WE ARRANGED THIS MARRIAGE. ANYWAY, IT LOOKS LIKE YOU'VE FOUND SOMETHING TO CONSOLE YOU, HAVEN'T YOU?

I MEAN, THOSE CHOIR KIDS TO WHOM YOU ARE SO DEVOTED--

--OH!

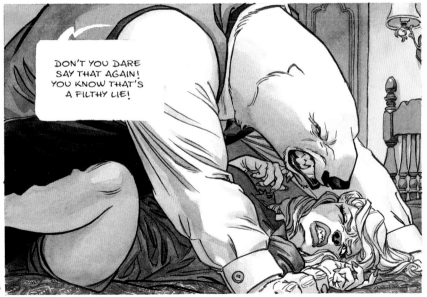

DON'T YOU DARE SAY THAT AGAIN! YOU KNOW THAT'S A FILTHY LIE!

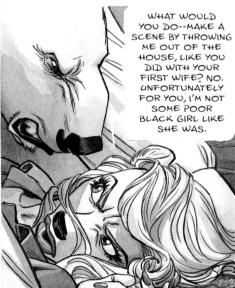

WHAT WOULD YOU DO--MAKE A SCENE BY THROWING ME OUT OF THE HOUSE, LIKE YOU DID WITH YOUR FIRST WIFE? NO. UNFORTUNATELY FOR YOU, I'M NOT SOME POOR BLACK GIRL LIKE SHE WAS.

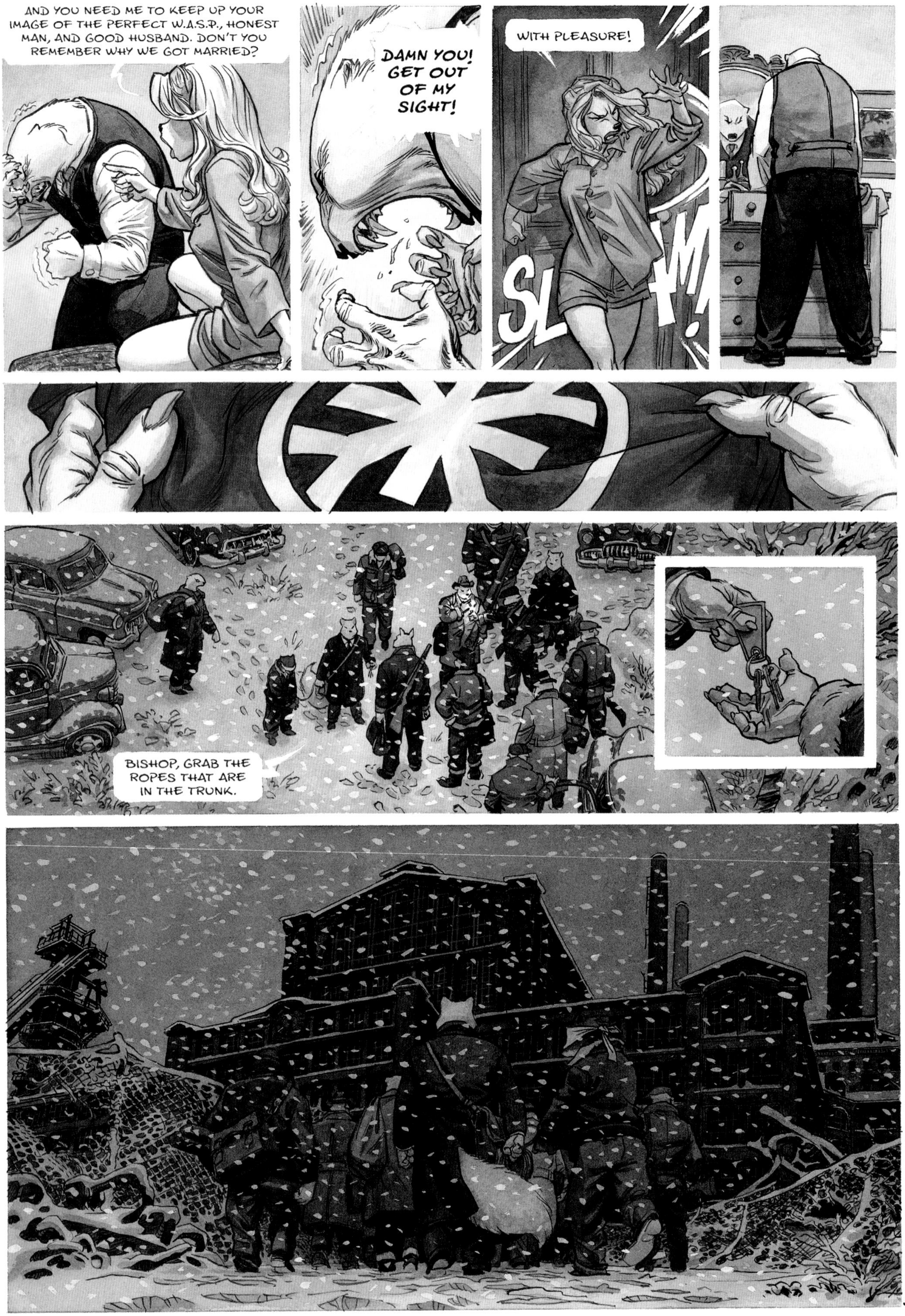
AND YOU NEED ME TO KEEP UP YOUR IMAGE OF THE PERFECT W.A.S.P., HONEST MAN, AND GOOD HUSBAND. DON'T YOU REMEMBER WHY WE GOT MARRIED?
DAMN YOU! GET OUT OF MY SIGHT!
WITH PLEASURE!
SLAM!
BISHOP, GRAB THE ROPES THAT ARE IN THE TRUNK.
30

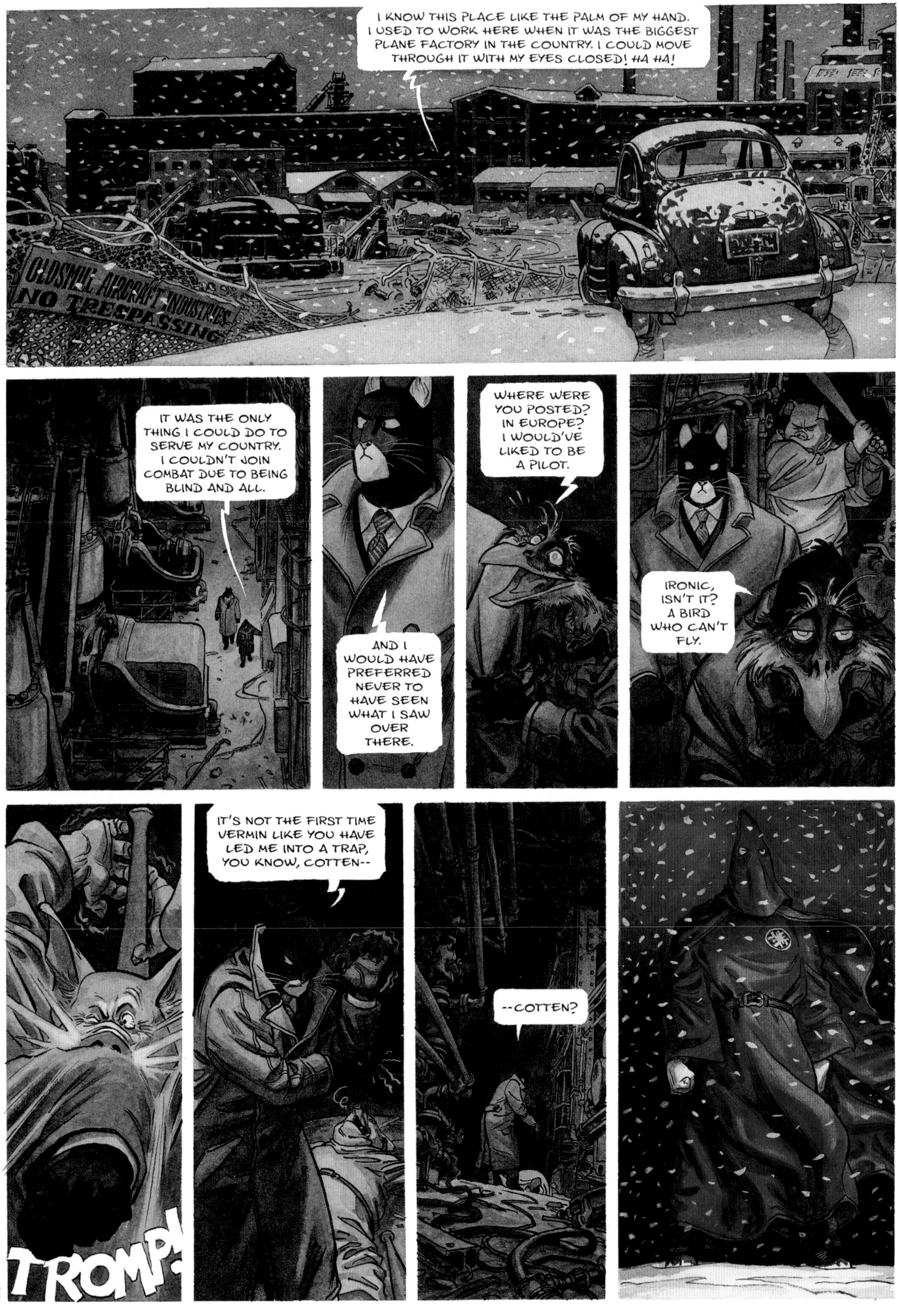
I KNOW THIS PLACE LIKE THE PALM OF MY HAND. I USED TO WORK HERE WHEN IT WAS THE BIGGEST PLANE FACTORY IN THE COUNTRY. I COULD MOVE THROUGH IT WITH MY EYES CLOSED! HA HA!
OLDSMILL AIRCRAFT INDUSTRIES
NO TRESPASSING
IT WAS THE ONLY THING I COULD DO TO SERVE MY COUNTRY. I COULDN'T JOIN COMBAT DUE TO BEING BLIND AND ALL.
AND I WOULD HAVE PREFERRED NEVER TO HAVE SEEN WHAT I SAW OVER THERE.
WHERE WERE YOU POSTED? IN EUROPE? I WOULD'VE LIKED TO BE A PILOT.
IRONIC, ISN'T IT? A BIRD WHO CAN'T FLY.
TROMP!
IT'S NOT THE FIRST TIME VERMIN LIKE YOU HAVE LED ME INTO A TRAP, YOU KNOW, COTTEN--
--COTTEN?
31

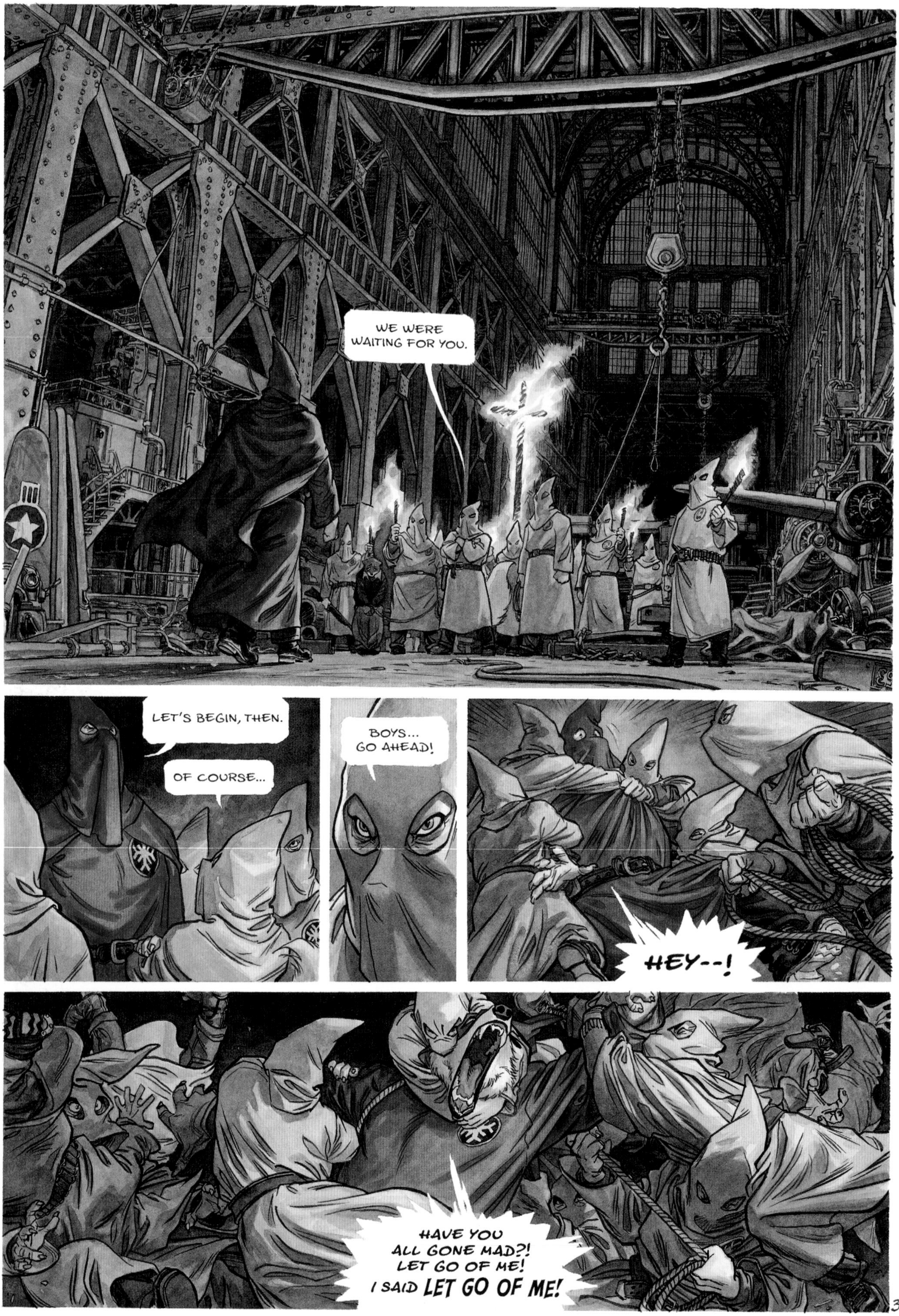
WE WERE WAITING FOR YOU.
LET'S BEGIN, THEN.
OF COURSE...
BOYS... GO AHEAD!
HEY--!
HAVE YOU ALL GONE MAD?! LET GO OF ME! I SAID LET GO OF ME!
32

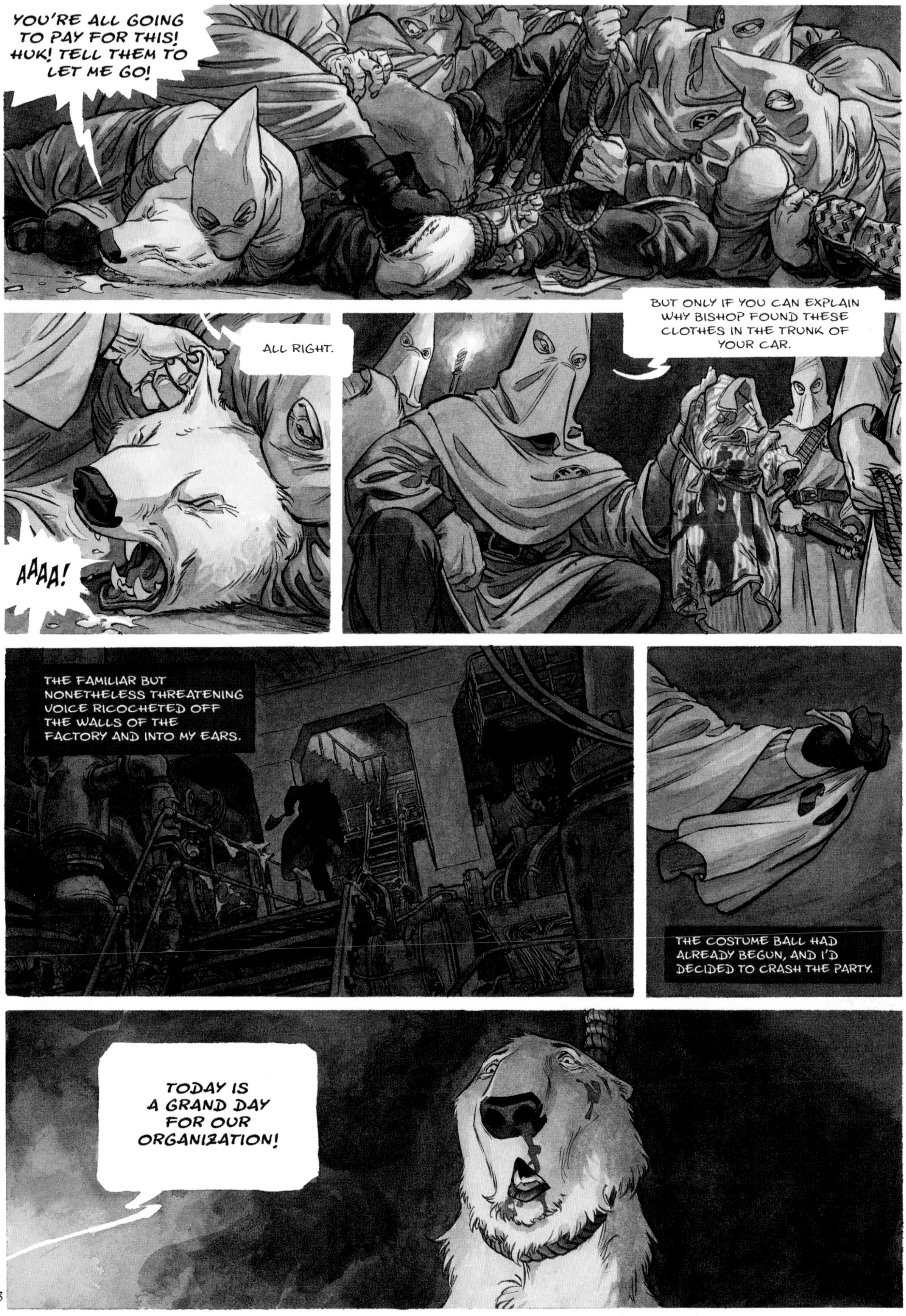
YOU'RE ALL GOING TO PAY FOR THIS! HUK! TELL THEM TO LET ME GO!
ALL RIGHT.
AAAA!
BUT ONLY IF YOU CAN EXPLAIN WHY BISHOP FOUND THESE CLOTHES IN THE TRUNK OF YOUR CAR.
THE FAMILIAR BUT NONETHELESS THREATENING VOICE RICOCHETED OFF THE WALLS OF THE FACTORY AND INTO MY EARS.
THE COSTUME BALL HAD ALREADY BEGUN, AND I'D DECIDED TO CRASH THE PARTY.
TODAY IS A GRAND DAY FOR OUR ORGANIZATION!
33

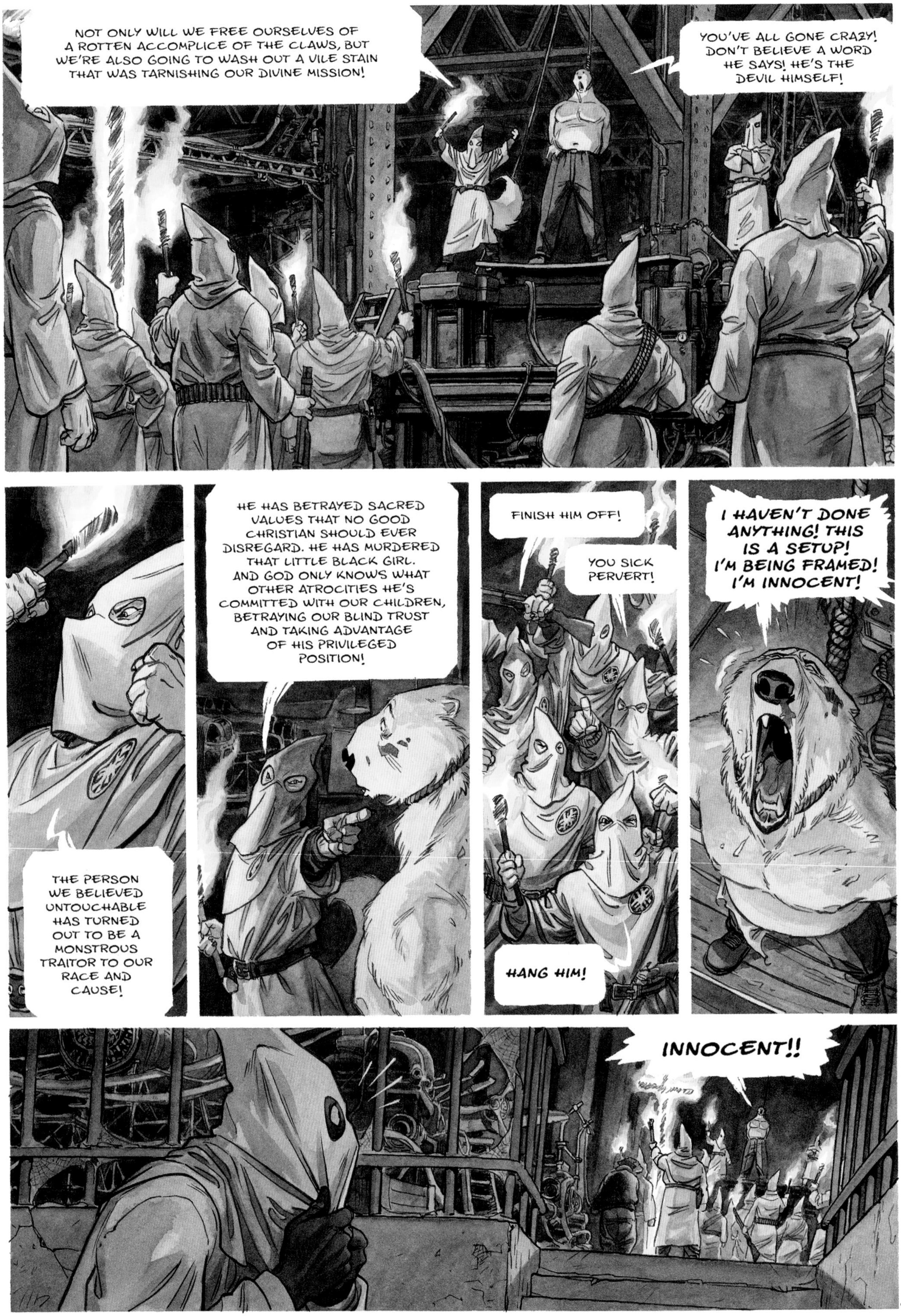

NOT ONLY WILL WE FREE OURSELVES OF A ROTTEN ACCOMPLICE OF THE CLAWS, BUT WE'RE ALSO GOING TO WASH OUT A VILE STAIN THAT WAS TARNISHING OUR DIVINE MISSION!
YOU'VE ALL GONE CRAZY! DON'T BELIEVE A WORD HE SAYS! HE'S THE DEVIL HIMSELF!
THE PERSON WE BELIEVED UNTOUCHABLE HAS TURNED OUT TO BE A MONSTROUS TRAITOR TO OUR RACE AND CAUSE!
HE HAS BETRAYED SACRED VALUES THAT NO GOOD CHRISTIAN SHOULD EVER DISREGARD. HE HAS MURDERED THAT LITTLE BLACK GIRL. AND GOD ONLY KNOWS WHAT OTHER ATROCITIES HE'S COMMITTED WITH OUR CHILDREN, BETRAYING OUR BLIND TRUST AND TAKING ADVANTAGE OF HIS PRIVILEGED POSITION!
FINISH HIM OFF!
YOU SICK PERVERT!
HANG HIM!
I HAVEN'T DONE ANYTHING! THIS IS A SETUP! I'M BEING FRAMED! I'M INNOCENT!
INNOCENT!!

34

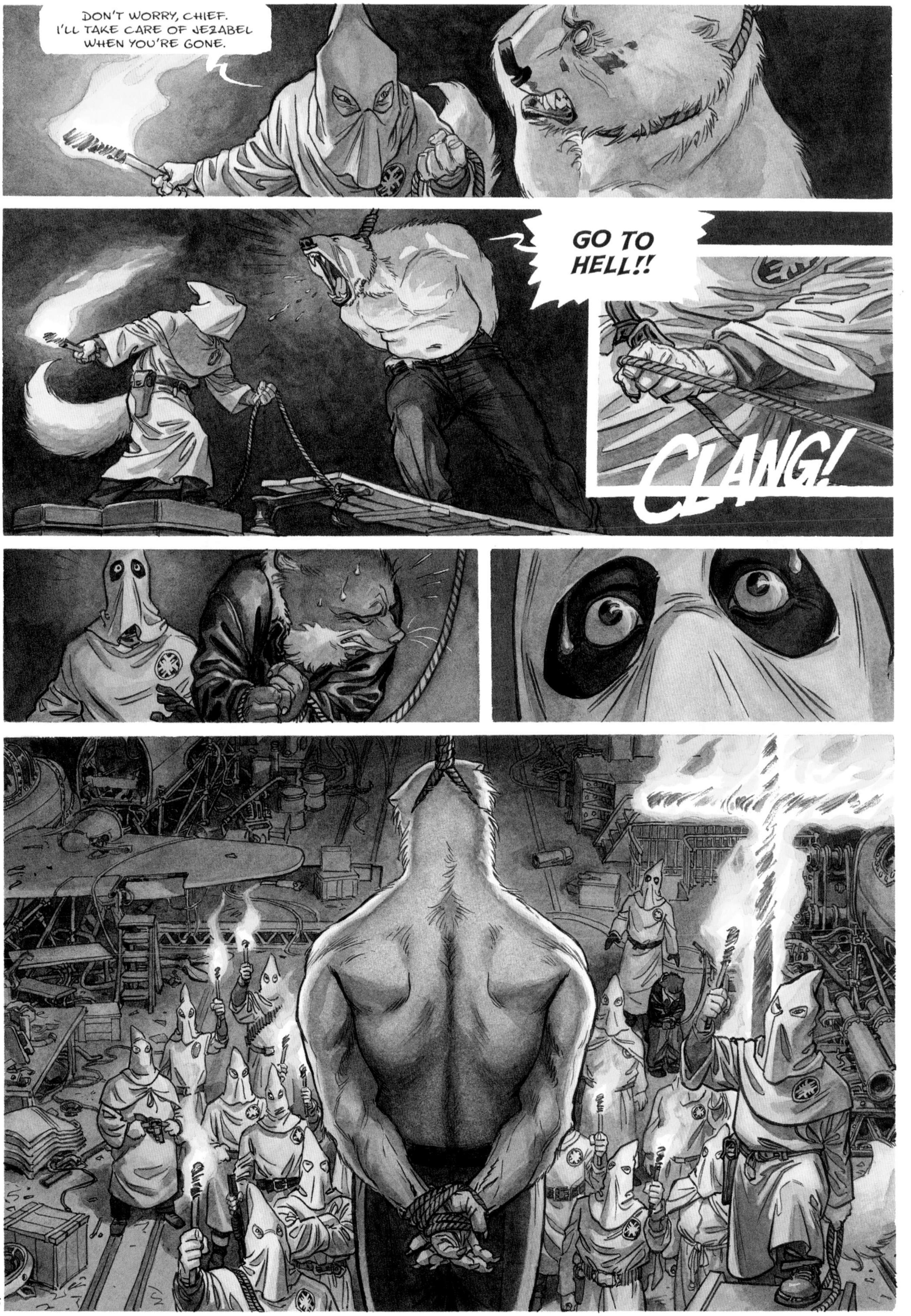
DON'T WORRY, CHIEF. I'LL TAKE CARE OF JEZABEL WHEN YOU'RE GONE.
GO TO HELL!!
CLANG!

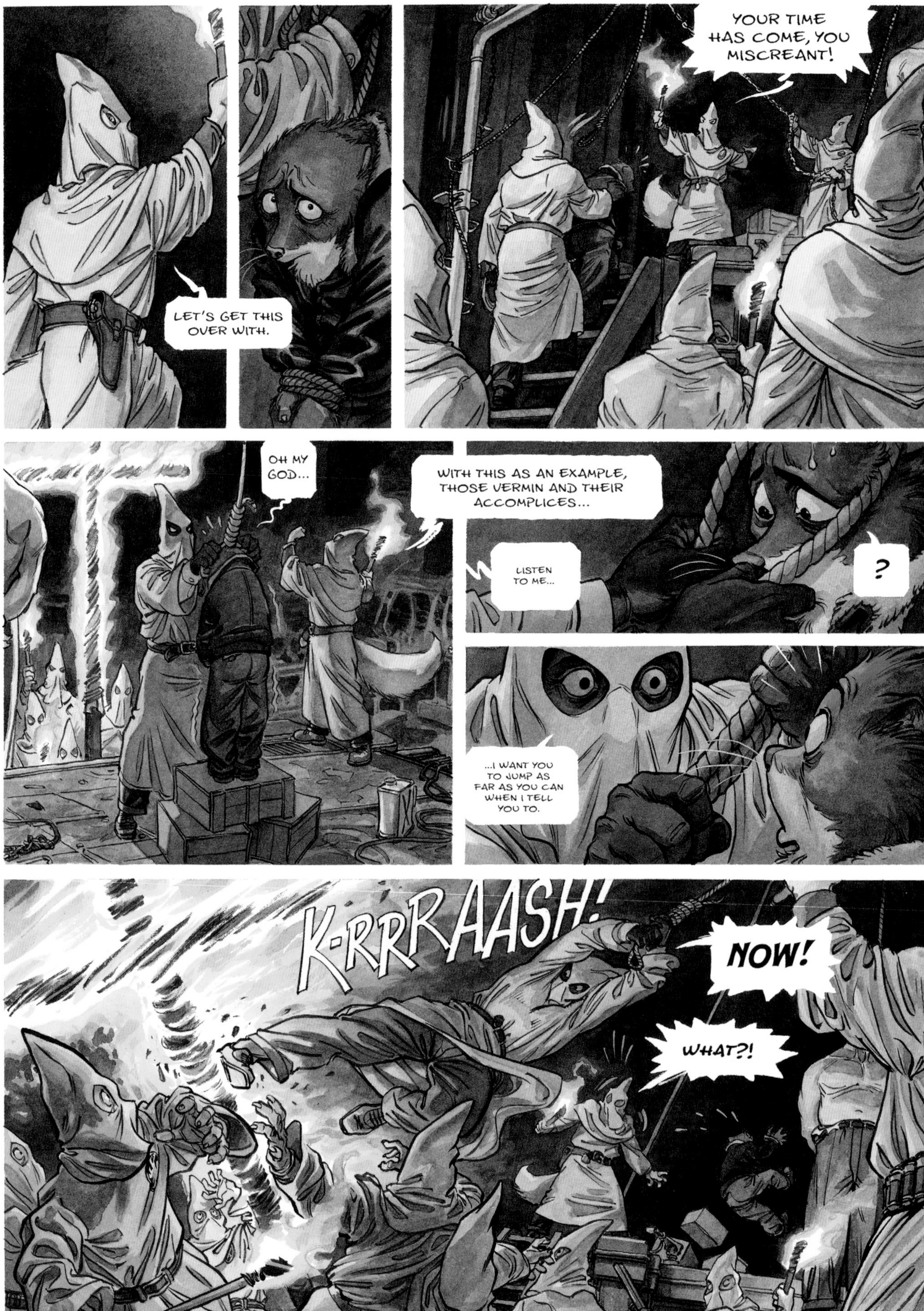

LET'S GET THIS OVER WITH.
YOUR TIME HAS COME, YOU MISCREANT!
OH MY GOD...
WITH THIS AS AN EXAMPLE, THOSE VERMIN AND THEIR ACCOMPLICES...
LISTEN TO ME...
?
...I WANT YOU TO JUMP AS FAR AS YOU CAN WHEN I TELL YOU TO.
K-RRRAASH!
NOW!
WHAT?!
36

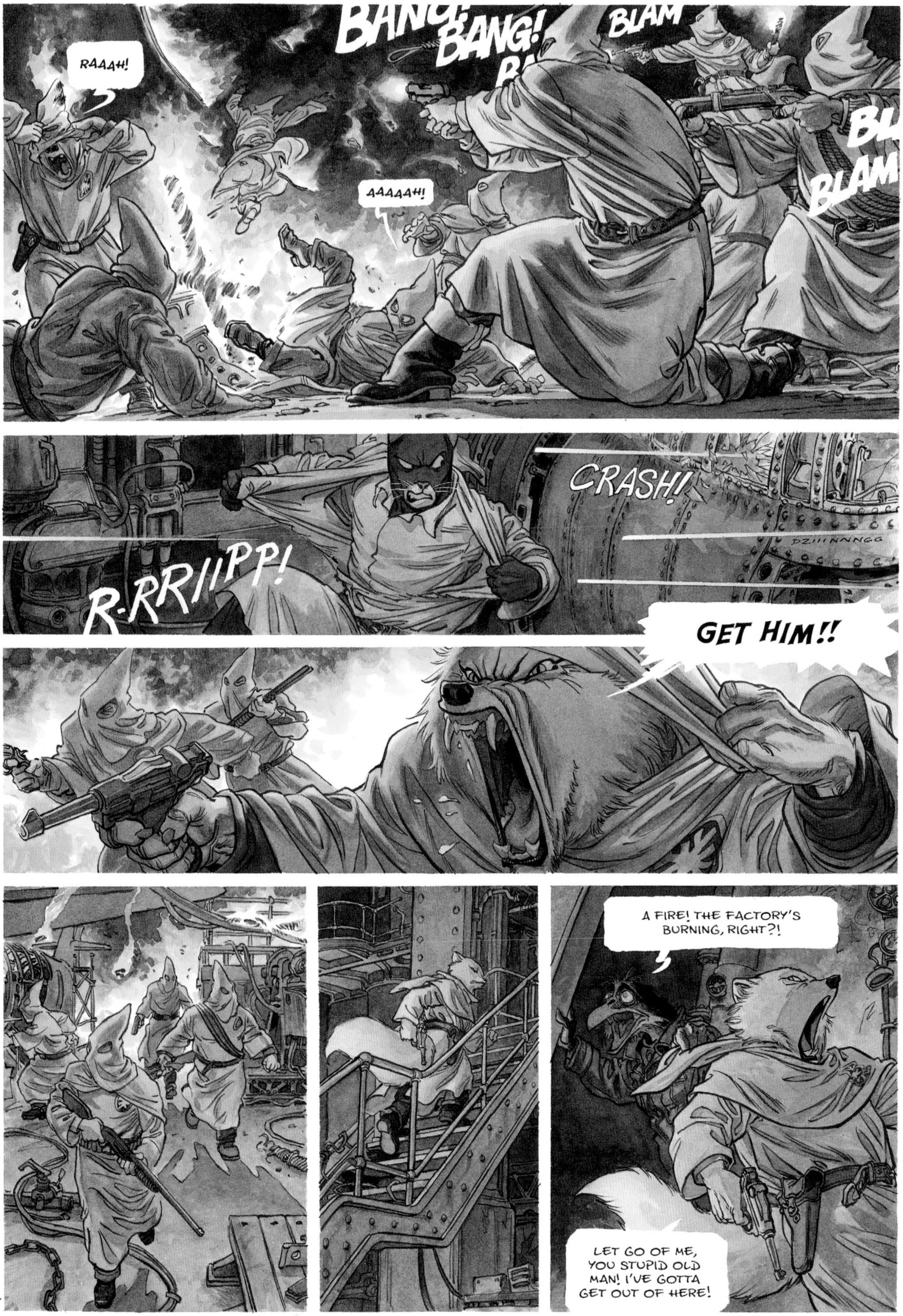

RAAAH!
AAAAAH!
BANG! BANG!
BLAM
BLAM
CRASH!
DZIIINNNGG
R-RRIIPP!
GET HIM!!
A FIRE! THE FACTORY'S BURNING, RIGHT?!
LET GO OF ME, YOU STUPID OLD MAN! I'VE GOTTA GET OUT OF HERE!

37

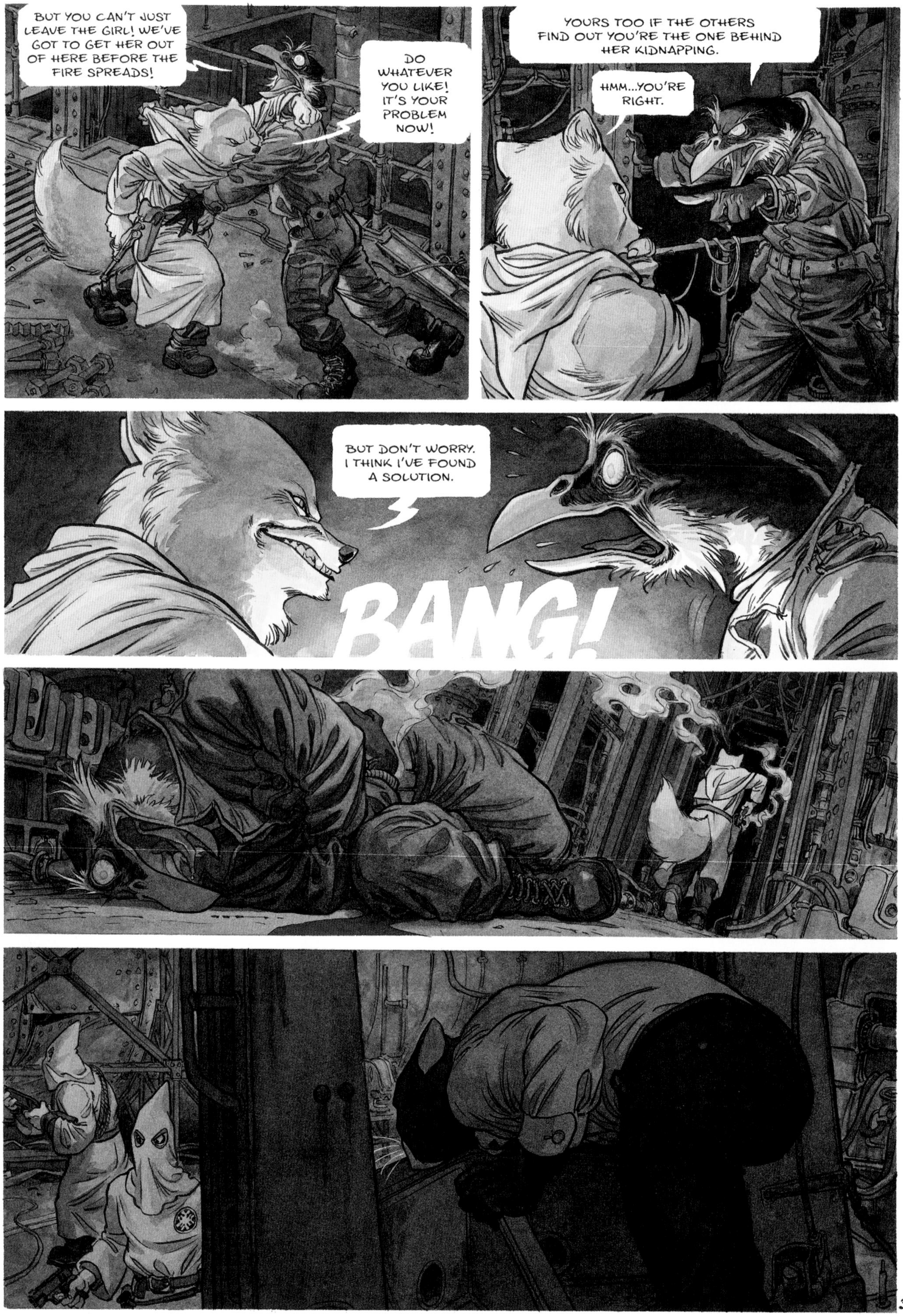
BUT YOU CAN'T JUST LEAVE THE GIRL! WE'VE GOT TO GET HER OUT OF HERE BEFORE THE FIRE SPREADS!
DO WHATEVER YOU LIKE! IT'S YOUR PROBLEM NOW!
YOURS TOO IF THE OTHERS FIND OUT YOU'RE THE ONE BEHIND HER KIDNAPPING.
HMM...YOU'RE RIGHT.
BUT DON'T WORRY. I THINK I'VE FOUND A SOLUTION.
BANG!
38

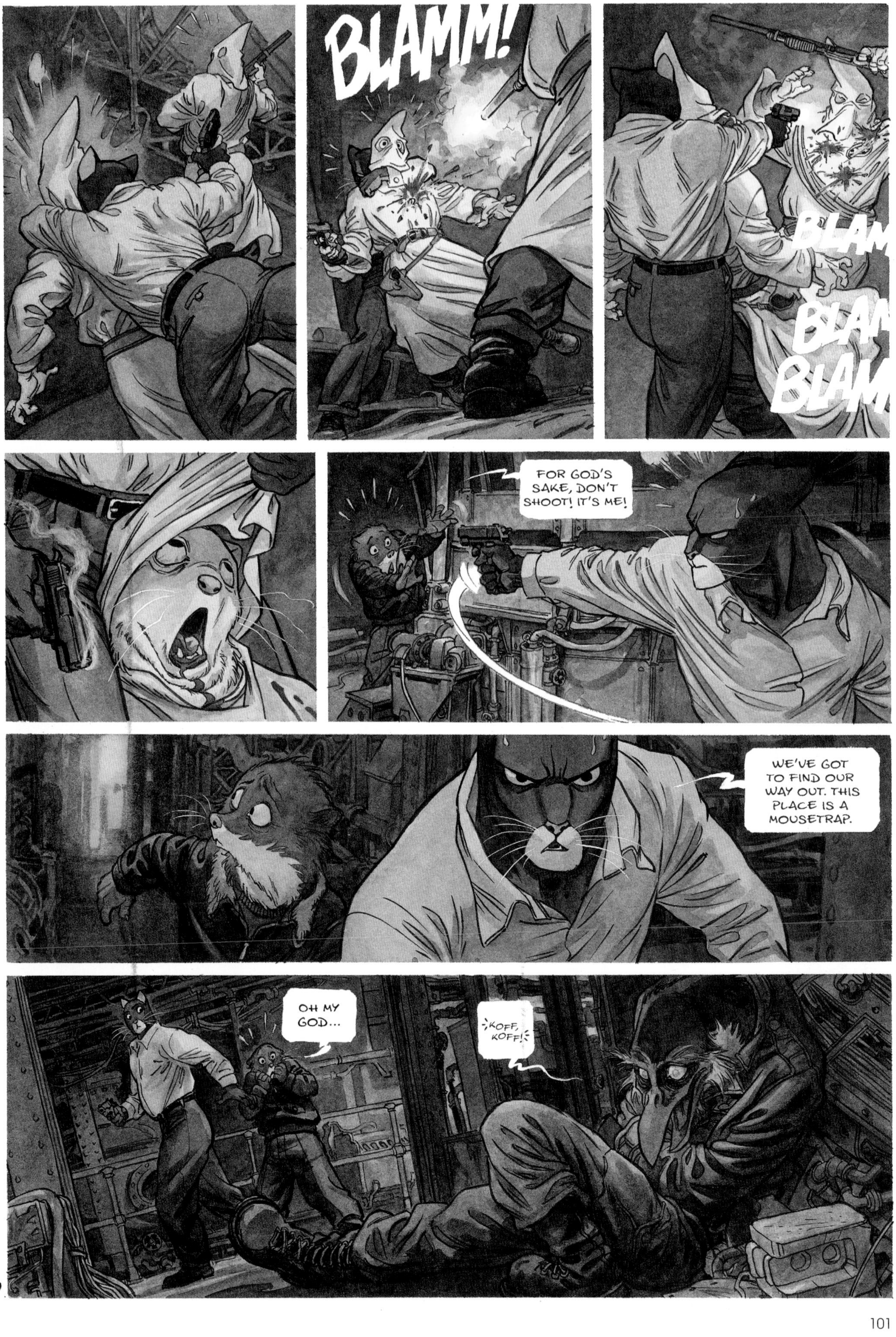
BLAMM!
BLAM
BLAM
BLAM
FOR GOD'S SAKE, DON'T SHOOT! IT'S ME!
WE'VE GOT TO FIND OUR WAY OUT. THIS PLACE IS A MOUSETRAP.
OH MY GOD...
¡KOFF, KOFF!

39

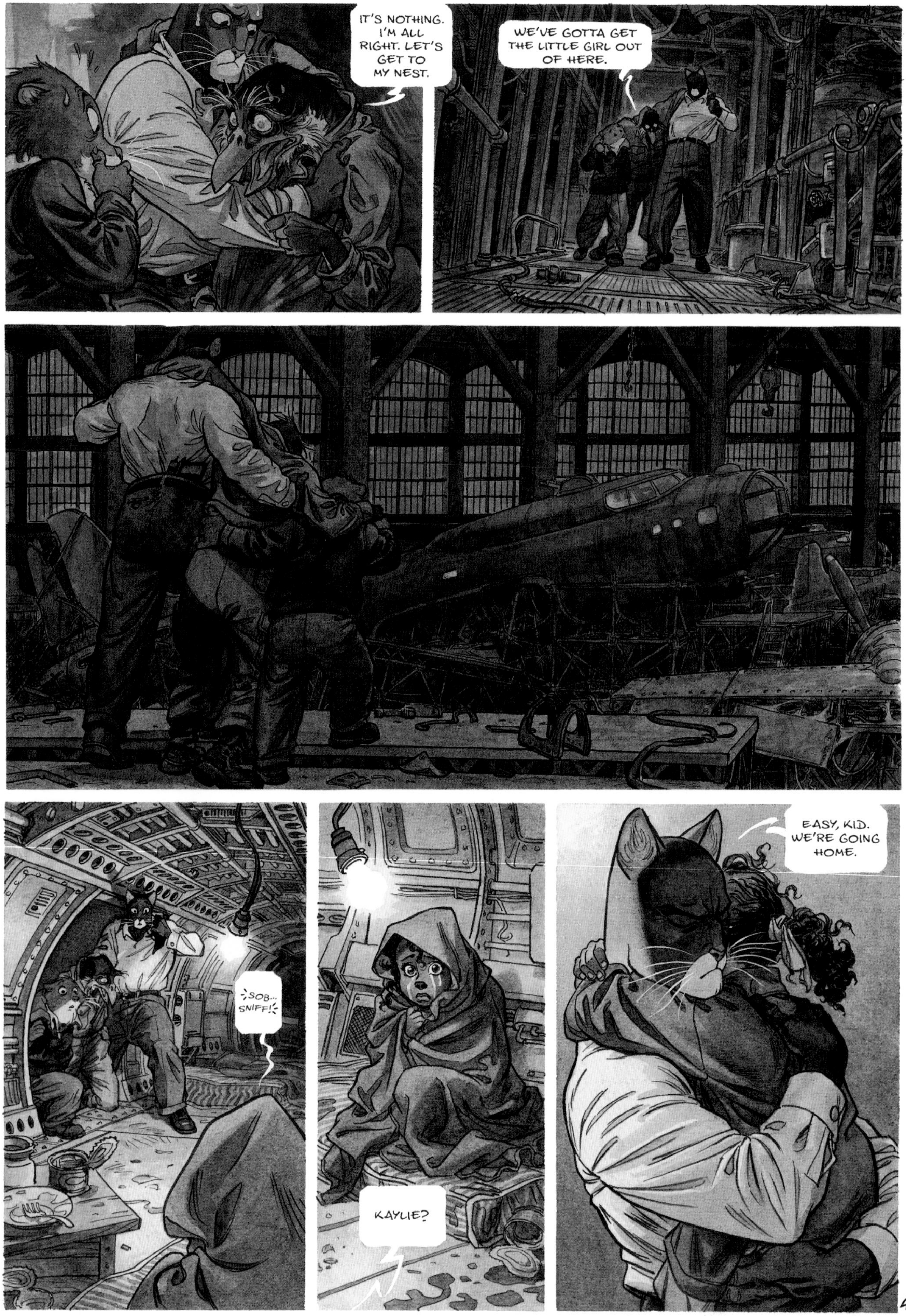
IT'S NOTHING. I'M ALL RIGHT. LET'S GET TO MY NEST.
WE'VE GOTTA GET THE LITTLE GIRL OUT OF HERE.
SOB... SNIFF!
KAYLIE?
EASY, KID. WE'RE GOING HOME.
40

BLACKSAD! YOU STILL HERE?

YES, COTTEN.

TELL ME--HAVE YOU EVER BEEN TO A CASINO? IT MUST BE BEAUTIFUL...ALL THOSE LIGHTS...THE SOUND OF MONEY FLOWING LIKE A WATERFALL... ⸰KOFF, KOFF!⸰ THE FOX PROMISED HE'D TAKE ME IF I HELPED OUT. BUT I'M AFRAID HE ISN'T A MAN OF HIS WORD, IS HE?

COTTEN, I'D HEARD THAT BIRDS OF YOUR KIND GO CRAZY OVER THINGS THAT SHINE, BUT YOUR CASE IS DOWNRIGHT PATHOLOGICAL...

I'VE BROUGHT YOU TO THE GIRL, SO NOW YOU'VE GOT TO PROMISE ME SOMETHING. PROMISE ME YOU'LL TAKE ME TO LAS VEGAS...

ALL RIGHT, FAIR ENOUGH. WE'LL GO TO THAT DAMN DESERT.

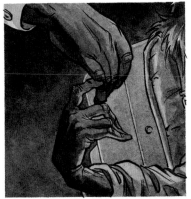

HURRY! WE'VE GOT TO TAKE OFF IF WE DON'T WANNA FRY!!

41

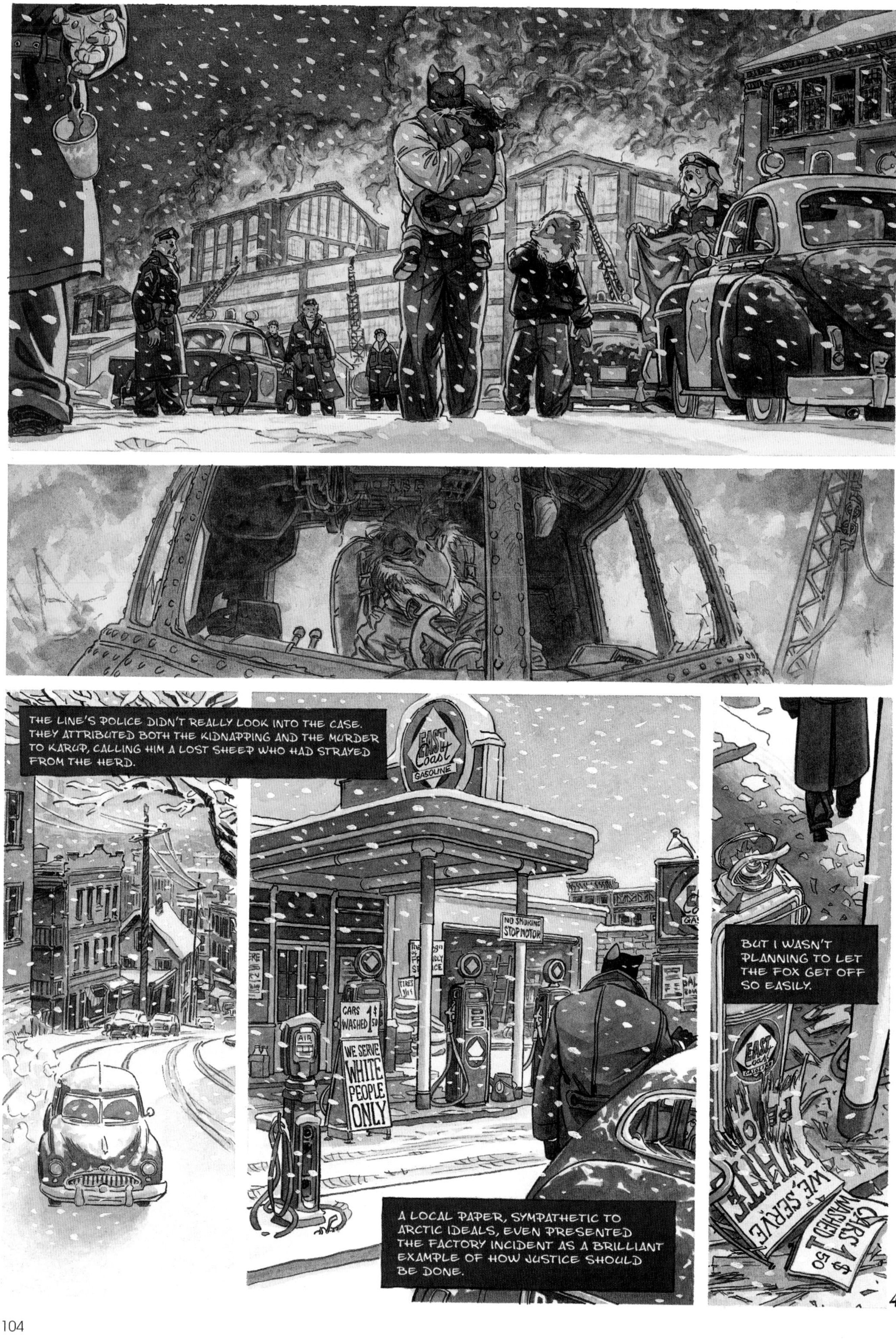
THE LINE'S POLICE DIDN'T REALLY LOOK INTO THE CASE. THEY ATTRIBUTED BOTH THE KIDNAPPING AND THE MURDER TO KARUP, CALLING HIM A LOST SHEEP WHO HAD STRAYED FROM THE HERD.
EAST Coast GASOLINE
NO SMOKING STOP MOTOR
CARS WASHED 1$ 50
AIR
WE SERVE WHITE PEOPLE ONLY
A LOCAL PAPER, SYMPATHETIC TO ARCTIC IDEALS, EVEN PRESENTED THE FACTORY INCIDENT AS A BRILLIANT EXAMPLE OF HOW JUSTICE SHOULD BE DONE.
BUT I WASN'T PLANNING TO LET THE FOX GET OFF SO EASILY.
42

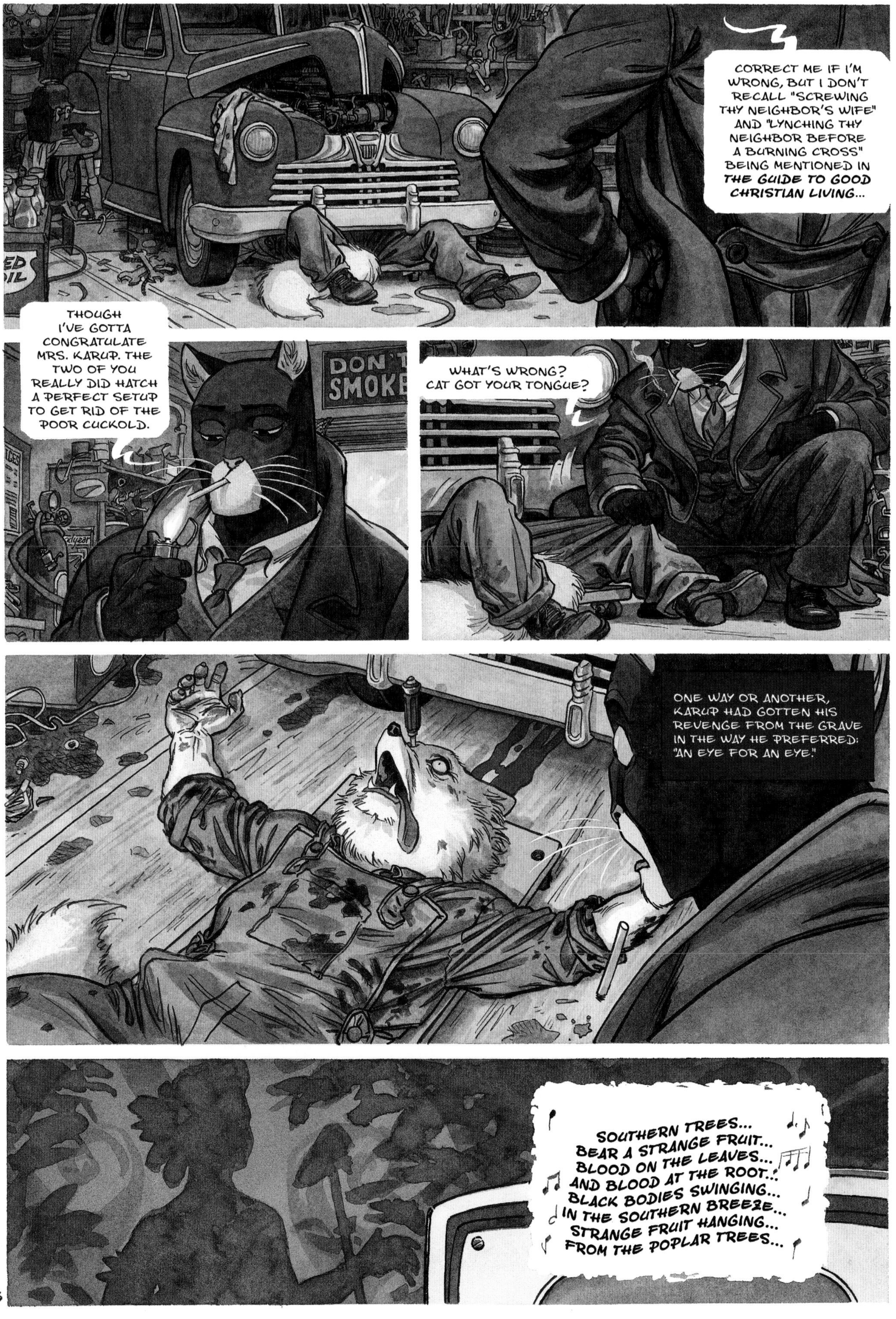
CORRECT ME IF I'M WRONG, BUT I DON'T RECALL "SCREWING THY NEIGHBOR'S WIFE" AND "LYNCHING THY NEIGHBOR BEFORE A BURNING CROSS" BEING MENTIONED IN THE GUIDE TO GOOD CHRISTIAN LIVING...
THOUGH I'VE GOTTA CONGRATULATE MRS. KARUP. THE TWO OF YOU REALLY DID HATCH A PERFECT SETUP TO GET RID OF THE POOR CUCKOLD.
DON'T SMOKE
WHAT'S WRONG? CAT GOT YOUR TONGUE?
ONE WAY OR ANOTHER, KARUP HAD GOTTEN HIS REVENGE FROM THE GRAVE IN THE WAY HE PREFERRED: "AN EYE FOR AN EYE."
SOUTHERN TREES... BEAR A STRANGE FRUIT... BLOOD ON THE LEAVES... AND BLOOD AT THE ROOT... BLACK BODIES SWINGING... IN THE SOUTHERN BREEZE... STRANGE FRUIT HANGING... FROM THE POPLAR TREES...
43

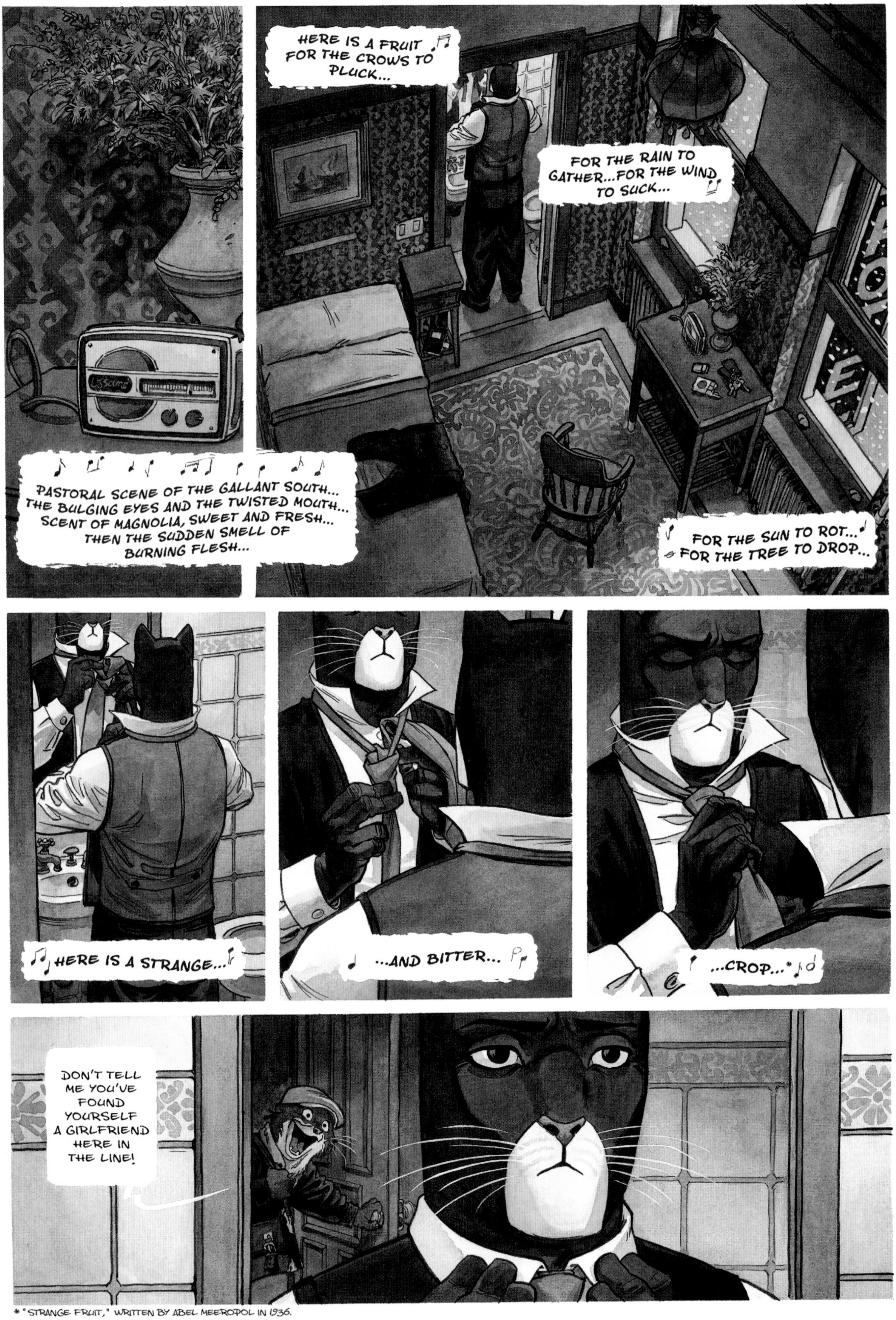
PASTORAL SCENE OF THE GALLANT SOUTH... THE BULGING EYES AND THE TWISTED MOUTH... SCENT OF MAGNOLIA, SWEET AND FRESH... THEN THE SUDDEN SMELL OF BURNING FLESH...
HERE IS A FRUIT FOR THE CROWS TO PLUCK...
FOR THE RAIN TO GATHER...FOR THE WIND TO SUCK...
FOR THE SUN TO ROT... FOR THE TREE TO DROP...
HERE IS A STRANGE...
...AND BITTER...
...CROP...*
DON'T TELL ME YOU'VE FOUND YOURSELF A GIRLFRIEND HERE IN THE LINE!

44

* "STRANGE FRUIT," WRITTEN BY ABEL MEEROPOL IN 1936.

WHERE YA GOIN', ALL DRESSED UP LIKE THAT?

TO A FUNERAL.

WELL, THAT SHOULD BE FUN...LUCKY FOR YOU YOUR GOOD FRIEND WEEK IS HERE FULL OF GOOD VIBES.

I'VE FINALLY BEEN ABLE TO DEVELOP THE PICTURES. MAN, I'M TELLING YOU, THEY ARE WORKS OF PURE ART!

WANNA SEE THE MERRY WIDOW IN ACTION?

I'M AFRAID I WON'T BE SHOCKED--

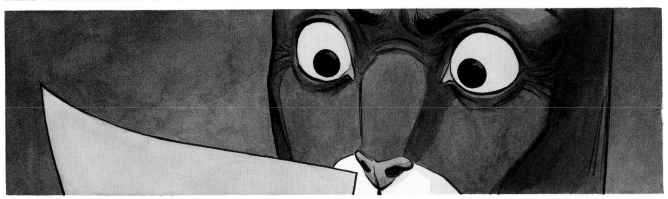

WEEKLY, CALL YOUR PAPER AND TELL THEM TO DIG UP ALL THEY CAN ON KARUP'S FIRST WIFE.

107

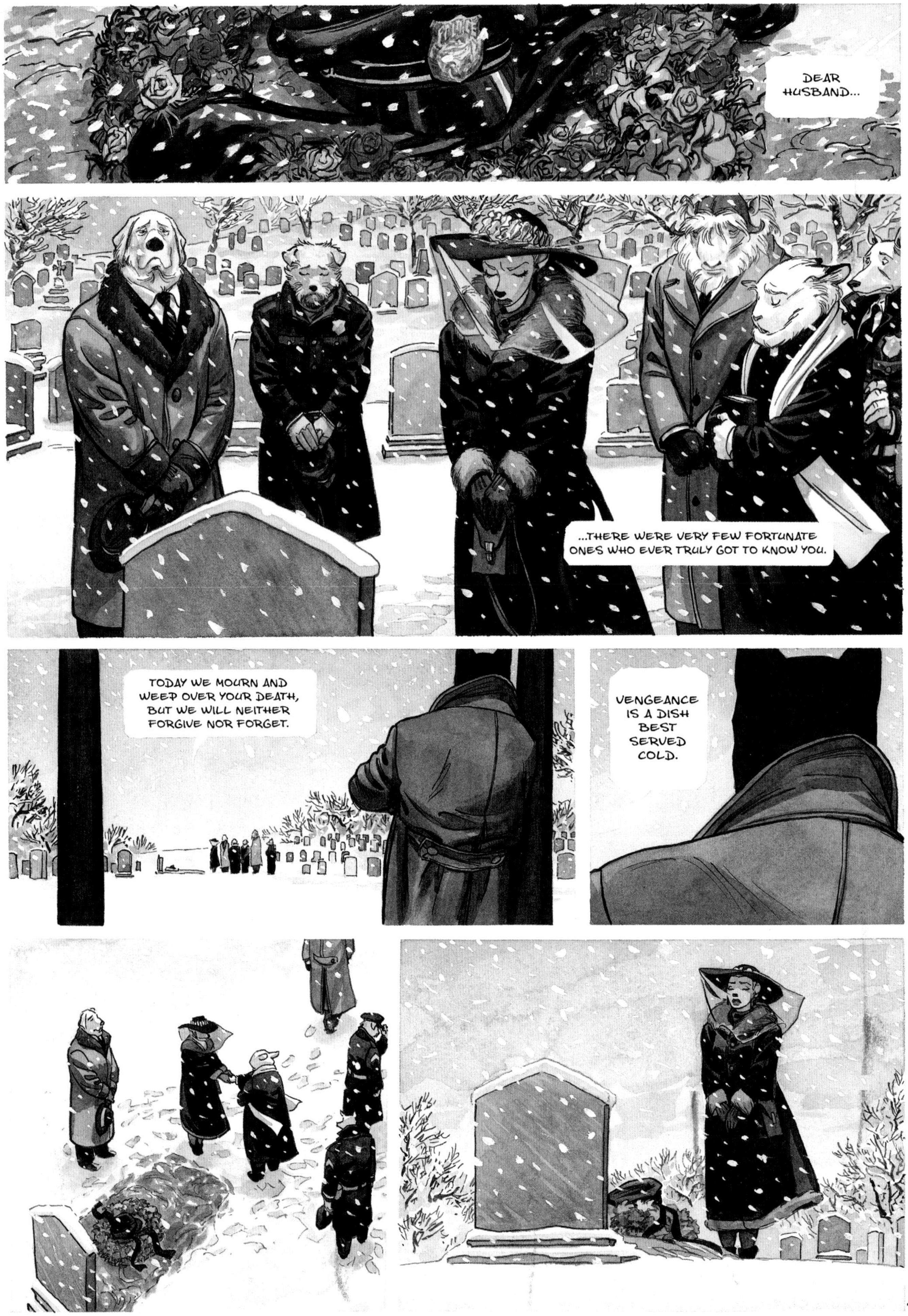
DEAR HUSBAND...
...THERE WERE VERY FEW FORTUNATE ONES WHO EVER TRULY GOT TO KNOW YOU.
TODAY WE MOURN AND WEEP OVER YOUR DEATH, BUT WE WILL NEITHER FORGIVE NOR FORGET.
VENGEANCE IS A DISH BEST SERVED COLD.
46

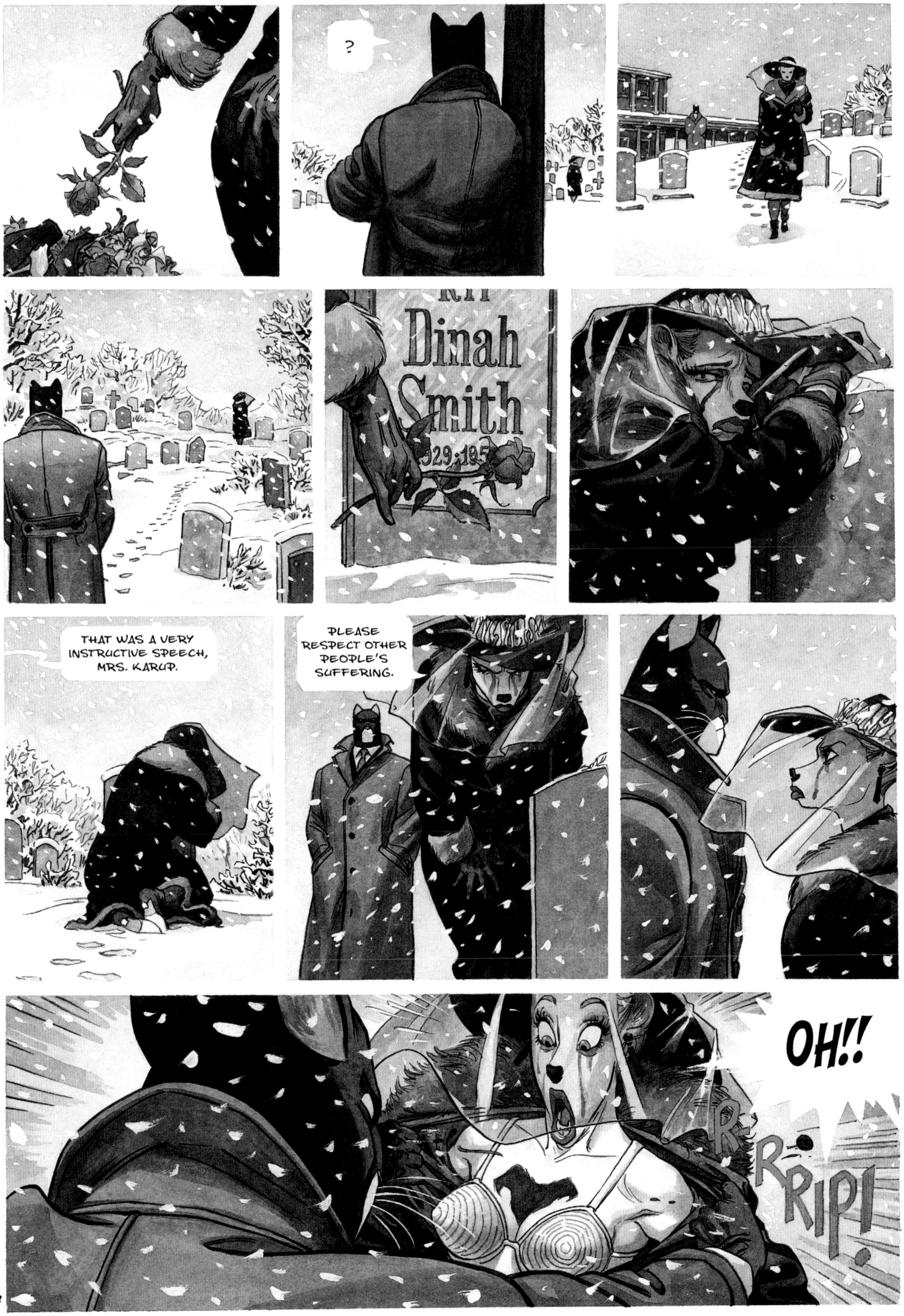
?
Dinah
Smith
THAT WAS A VERY INSTRUCTIVE SPEECH, MRS. KARUP.
PLEASE RESPECT OTHER PEOPLE'S SUFFERING.
OH!!
RRRIP!

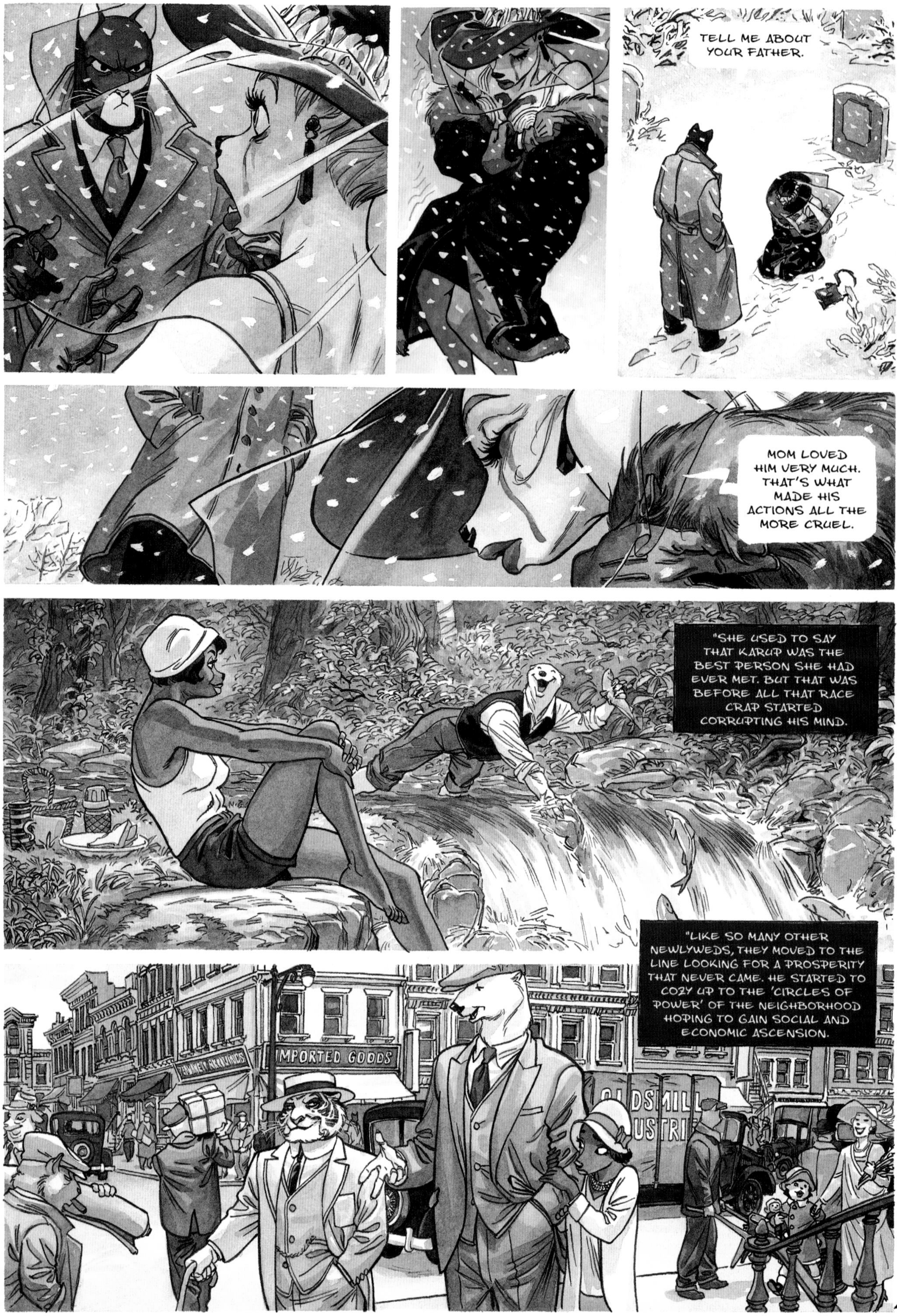
TELL ME ABOUT YOUR FATHER.
MOM LOVED HIM VERY MUCH. THAT'S WHAT MADE HIS ACTIONS ALL THE MORE CRUEL.
"SHE USED TO SAY THAT KARUP WAS THE BEST PERSON SHE HAD EVER MET. BUT THAT WAS BEFORE ALL THAT RACE CRAP STARTED CORRUPTING HIS MIND.
"LIKE SO MANY OTHER NEWLYWEDS, THEY MOVED TO THE LINE LOOKING FOR A PROSPERITY THAT NEVER CAME. HE STARTED TO COZY UP TO THE 'CIRCLES OF POWER' OF THE NEIGHBORHOOD HOPING TO GAIN SOCIAL AND ECONOMIC ASCENSION.
IMPORTED GOODS
48

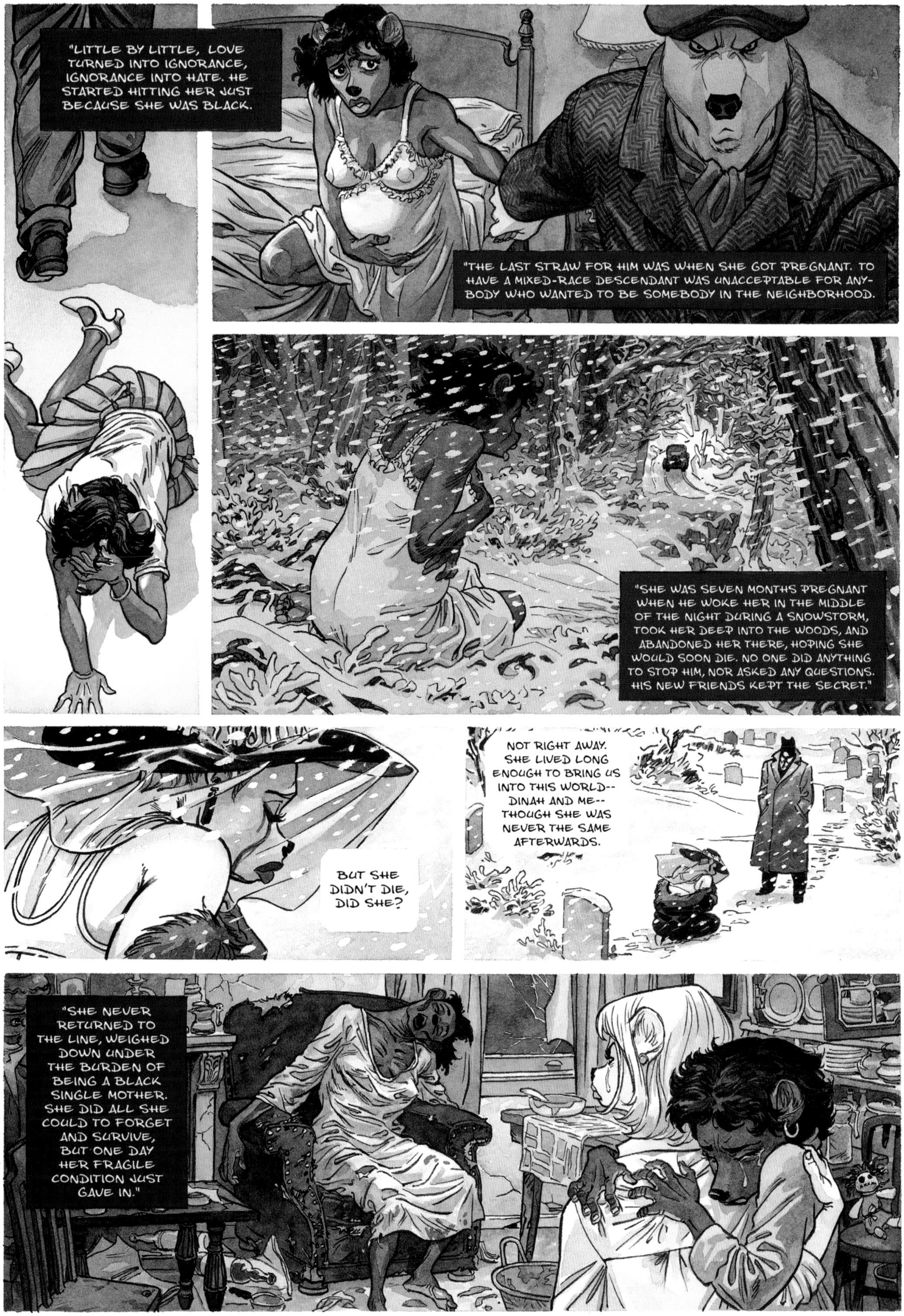
"LITTLE BY LITTLE, LOVE TURNED INTO IGNORANCE, IGNORANCE INTO HATE. HE STARTED HITTING HER JUST BECAUSE SHE WAS BLACK.
"THE LAST STRAW FOR HIM WAS WHEN SHE GOT PREGNANT. TO HAVE A MIXED-RACE DESCENDANT WAS UNACCEPTABLE FOR ANYBODY WHO WANTED TO BE SOMEBODY IN THE NEIGHBORHOOD.
"SHE WAS SEVEN MONTHS PREGNANT WHEN HE WOKE HER IN THE MIDDLE OF THE NIGHT DURING A SNOWSTORM, TOOK HER DEEP INTO THE WOODS, AND ABANDONED HER THERE, HOPING SHE WOULD SOON DIE. NO ONE DID ANYTHING TO STOP HIM, NOR ASKED ANY QUESTIONS. HIS NEW FRIENDS KEPT THE SECRET."
BUT SHE DIDN'T DIE, DID SHE?
NOT RIGHT AWAY. SHE LIVED LONG ENOUGH TO BRING US INTO THIS WORLD-- DINAH AND ME-- THOUGH SHE WAS NEVER THE SAME AFTERWARDS.
"SHE NEVER RETURNED TO THE LINE, WEIGHED DOWN UNDER THE BURDEN OF BEING A BLACK SINGLE MOTHER. SHE DID ALL SHE COULD TO FORGET AND SURVIVE, BUT ONE DAY HER FRAGILE CONDITION JUST GAVE IN."
49

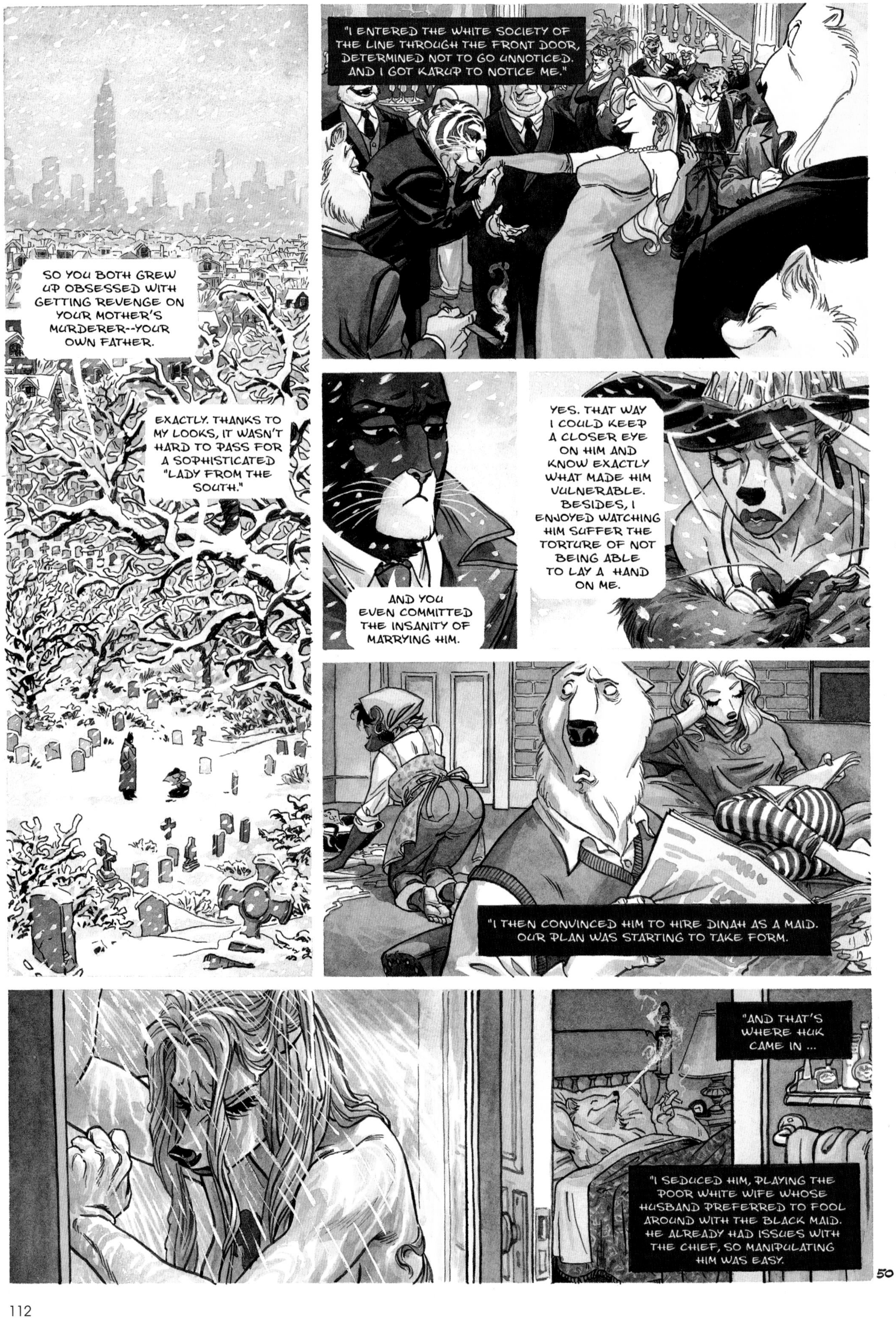
"I ENTERED THE WHITE SOCIETY OF THE LINE THROUGH THE FRONT DOOR, DETERMINED NOT TO GO UNNOTICED. AND I GOT KARUP TO NOTICE ME."
SO YOU BOTH GREW UP OBSESSED WITH GETTING REVENGE ON YOUR MOTHER'S MURDERER--YOUR OWN FATHER.
EXACTLY. THANKS TO MY LOOKS, IT WASN'T HARD TO PASS FOR A SOPHISTICATED "LADY FROM THE SOUTH."
AND YOU EVEN COMMITTED THE INSANITY OF MARRYING HIM.
YES. THAT WAY I COULD KEEP A CLOSER EYE ON HIM AND KNOW EXACTLY WHAT MADE HIM VULNERABLE. BESIDES, I ENJOYED WATCHING HIM SUFFER THE TORTURE OF NOT BEING ABLE TO LAY A HAND ON ME.
"I THEN CONVINCED HIM TO HIRE DINAH AS A MAID. OUR PLAN WAS STARTING TO TAKE FORM.
"AND THAT'S WHERE HUK CAME IN ...
"I SEDUCED HIM, PLAYING THE POOR WHITE WIFE WHOSE HUSBAND PREFERRED TO FOOL AROUND WITH THE BLACK MAID. HE ALREADY HAD ISSUES WITH THE CHIEF, SO MANIPULATING HIM WAS EASY.
50

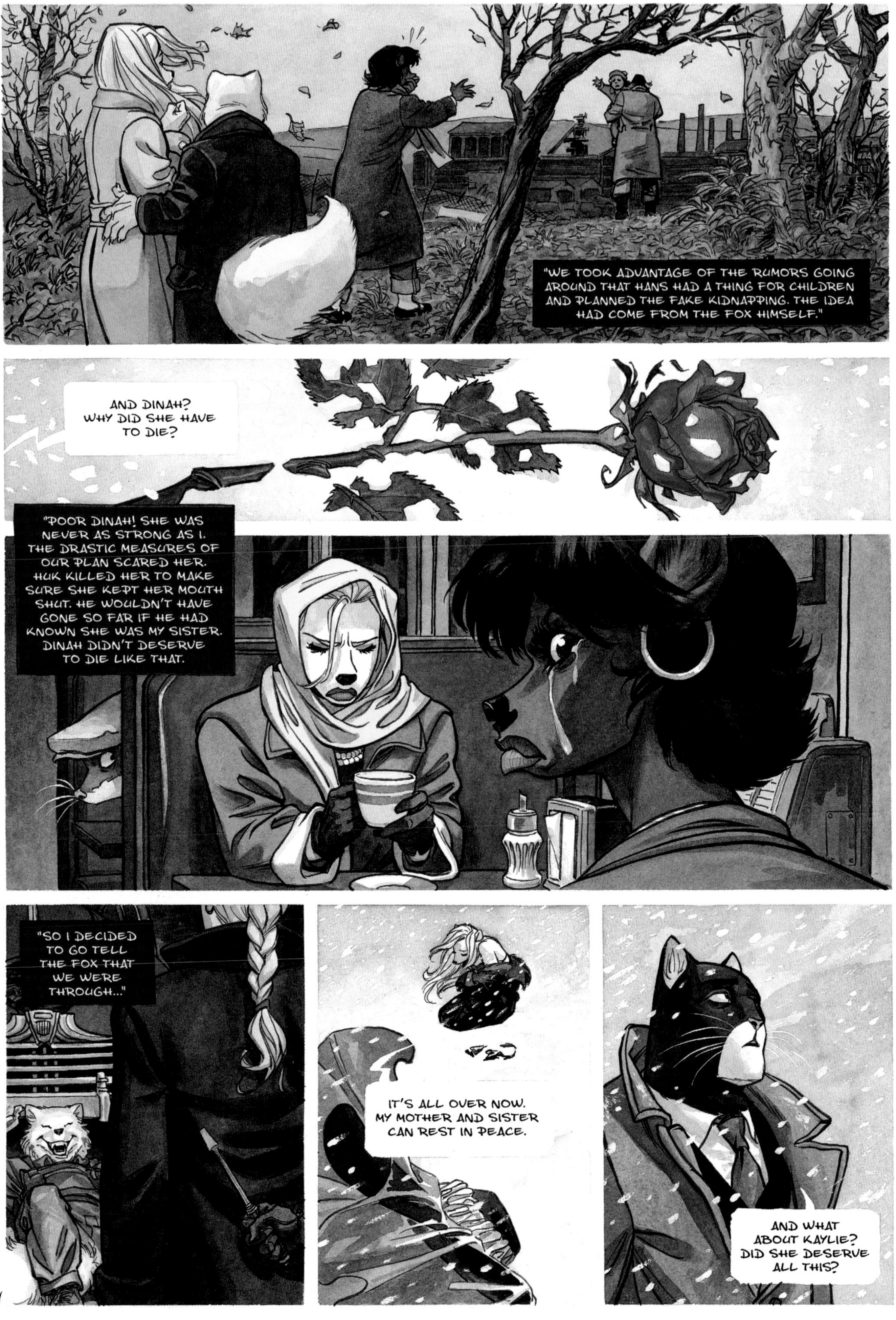
"WE TOOK ADVANTAGE OF THE RUMORS GOING AROUND THAT HANS HAD A THING FOR CHILDREN AND PLANNED THE FAKE KIDNAPPING. THE IDEA HAD COME FROM THE FOX HIMSELF."
AND DINAH? WHY DID SHE HAVE TO DIE?
"POOR DINAH! SHE WAS NEVER AS STRONG AS I. THE DRASTIC MEASURES OF OUR PLAN SCARED HER. HUK KILLED HER TO MAKE SURE SHE KEPT HER MOUTH SHUT. HE WOULDN'T HAVE GONE SO FAR IF HE HAD KNOWN SHE WAS MY SISTER. DINAH DIDN'T DESERVE TO DIE LIKE THAT.
"SO I DECIDED TO GO TELL THE FOX THAT WE WERE THROUGH..."
IT'S ALL OVER NOW. MY MOTHER AND SISTER CAN REST IN PEACE.
AND WHAT ABOUT KAYLIE? DID SHE DESERVE ALL THIS?
51

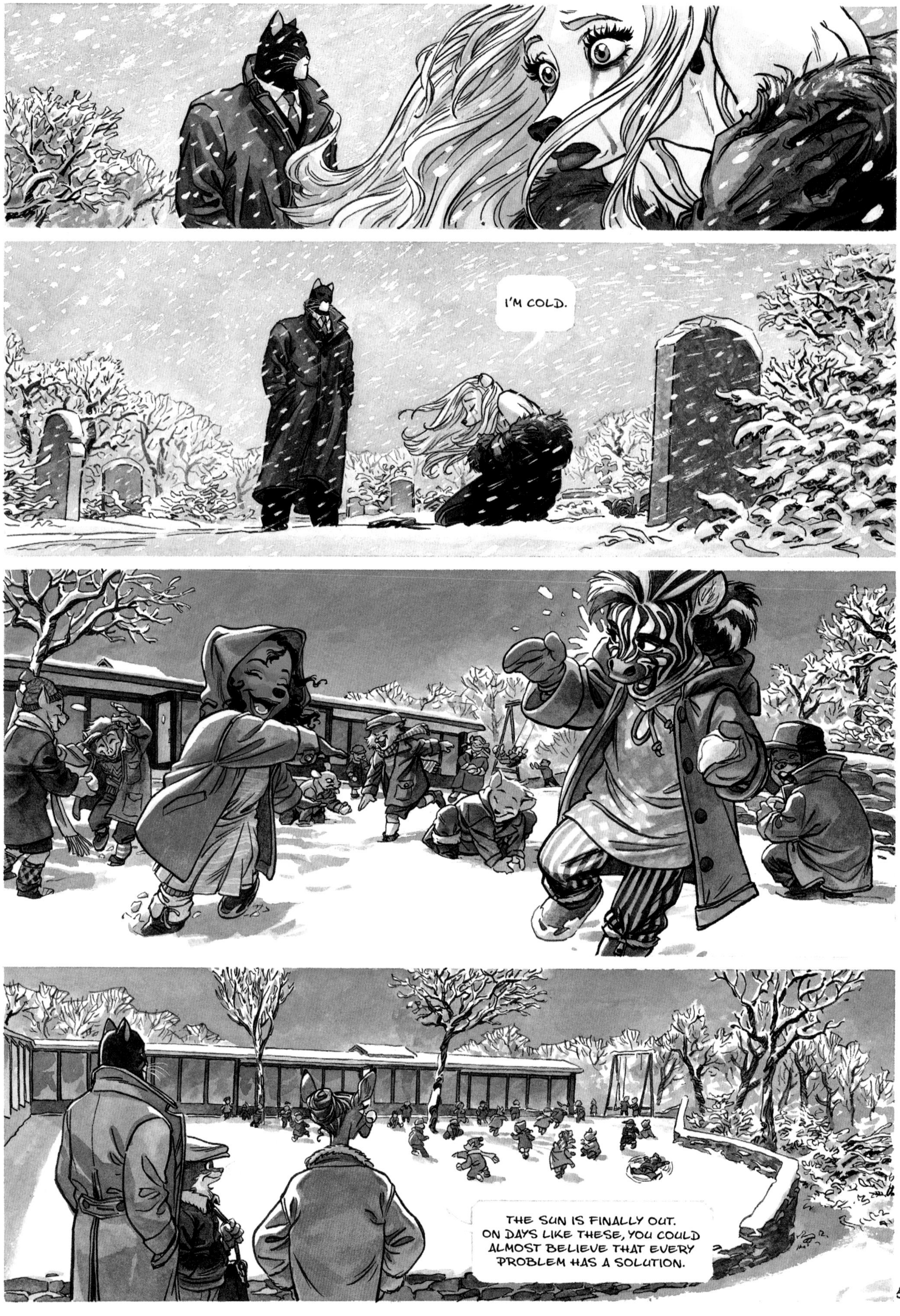
I'M COLD.
THE SUN IS FINALLY OUT.
ON DAYS LIKE THESE, YOU COULD
ALMOST BELIEVE THAT EVERY
PROBLEM HAS A SOLUTION.
52

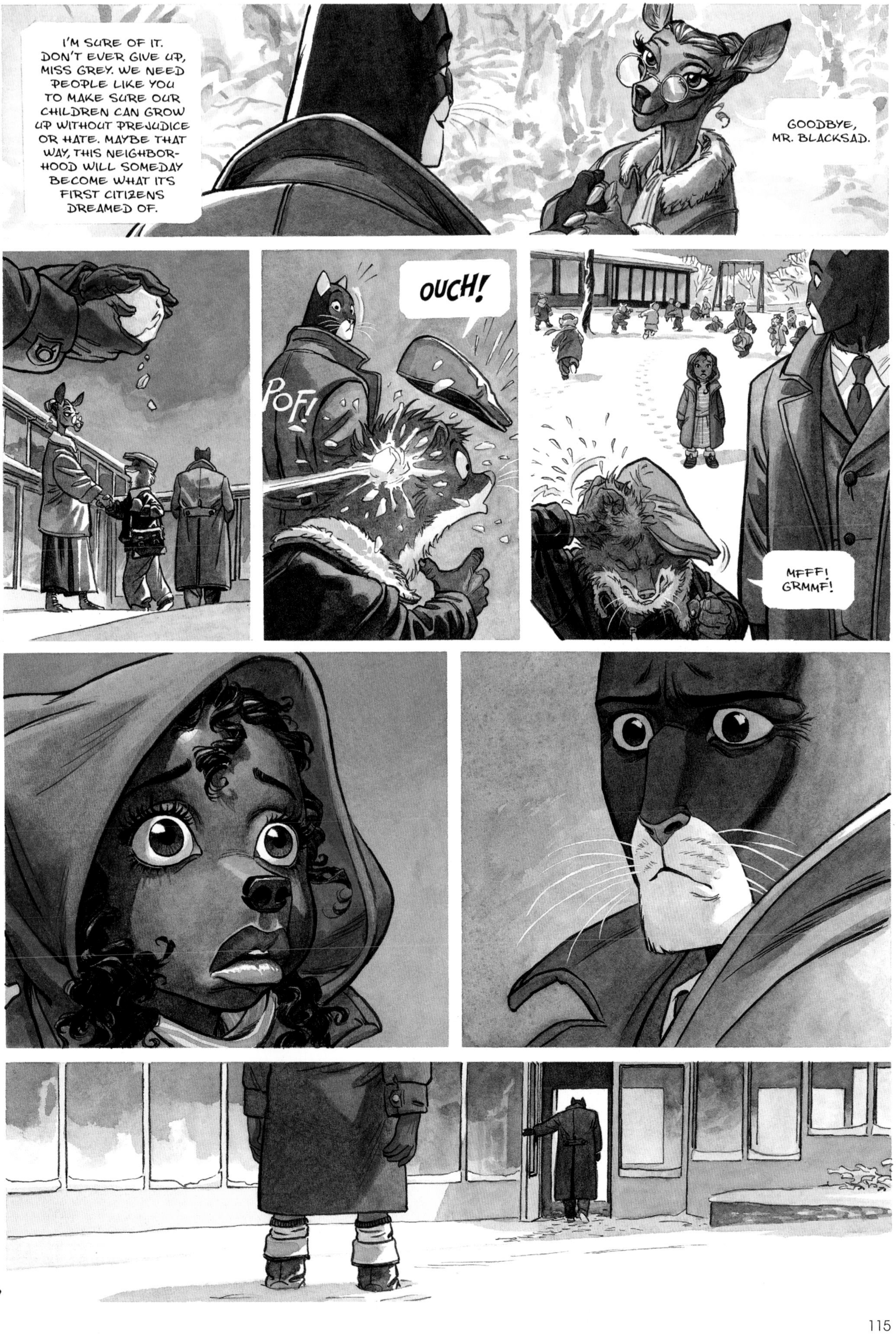
I'M SURE OF IT. DON'T EVER GIVE UP, MISS GREY. WE NEED PEOPLE LIKE YOU TO MAKE SURE OUR CHILDREN CAN GROW UP WITHOUT PREJUDICE OR HATE. MAYBE THAT WAY, THIS NEIGHBOR-HOOD WILL SOMEDAY BECOME WHAT ITS FIRST CITIZENS DREAMED OF.
GOODBYE, MR. BLACKSAD.
OUCH!
POF!
MFFF! GRMMF!
53

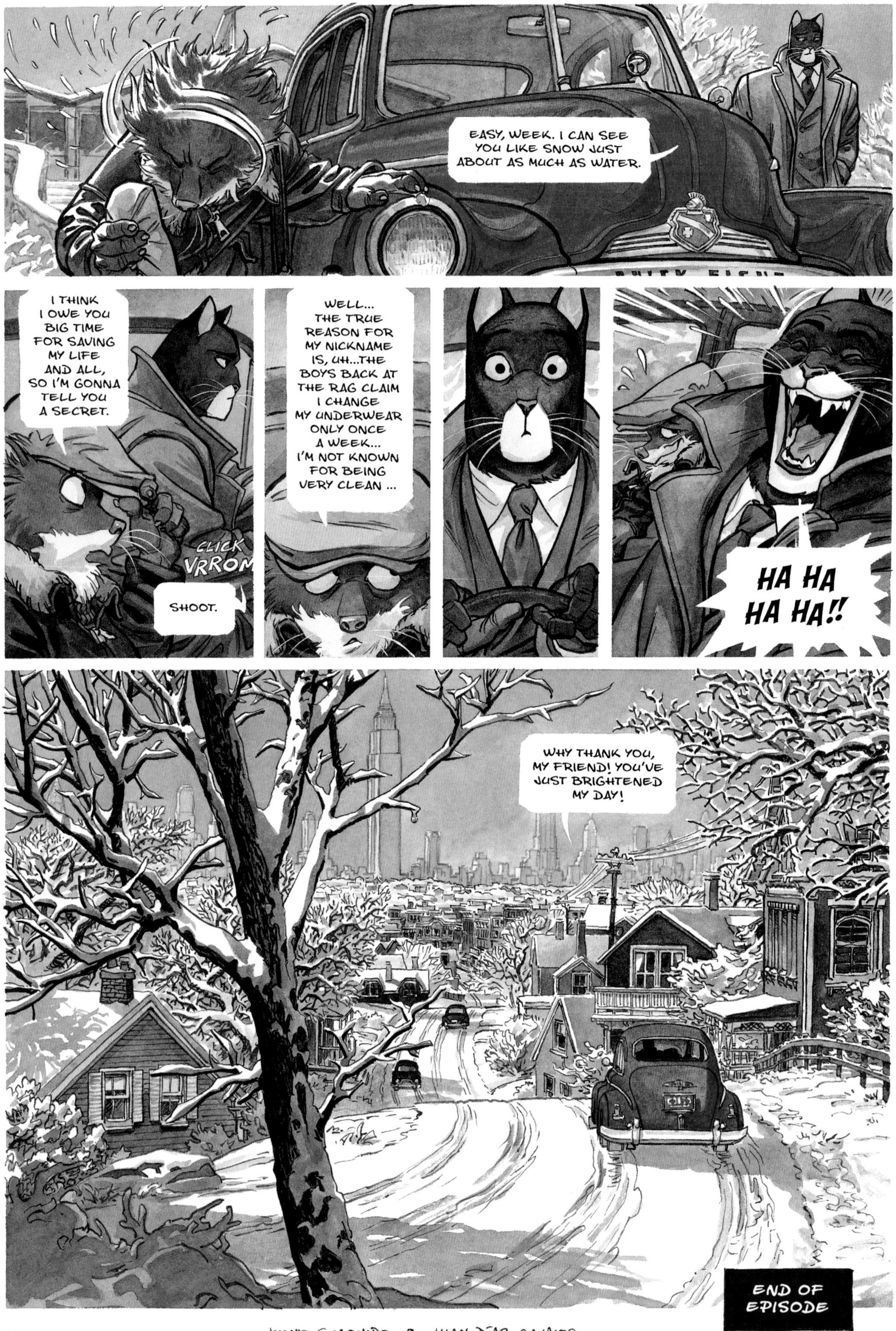
EASY, WEEK. I CAN SEE YOU LIKE SNOW JUST ABOUT AS MUCH AS WATER.
I THINK I OWE YOU BIG TIME FOR SAVING MY LIFE AND ALL, SO I'M GONNA TELL YOU A SECRET.
CLICK
VRROM
SHOOT.
WELL... THE TRUE REASON FOR MY NICKNAME IS, UH...THE BOYS BACK AT THE RAG CLAIM I CHANGE MY UNDERWEAR ONLY ONCE A WEEK... I'M NOT KNOWN FOR BEING VERY CLEAN ...
HA HA HA HA!!
WHY THANK YOU, MY FRIEND! YOU'VE JUST BRIGHTENED MY DAY!
END OF EPISODE

JUANJO GUARNIDO & JUAN DÍAZ CANALES
2003

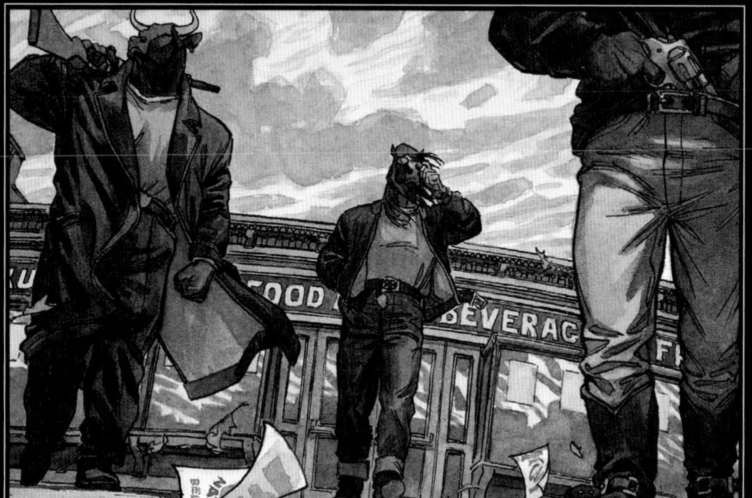
FOOD

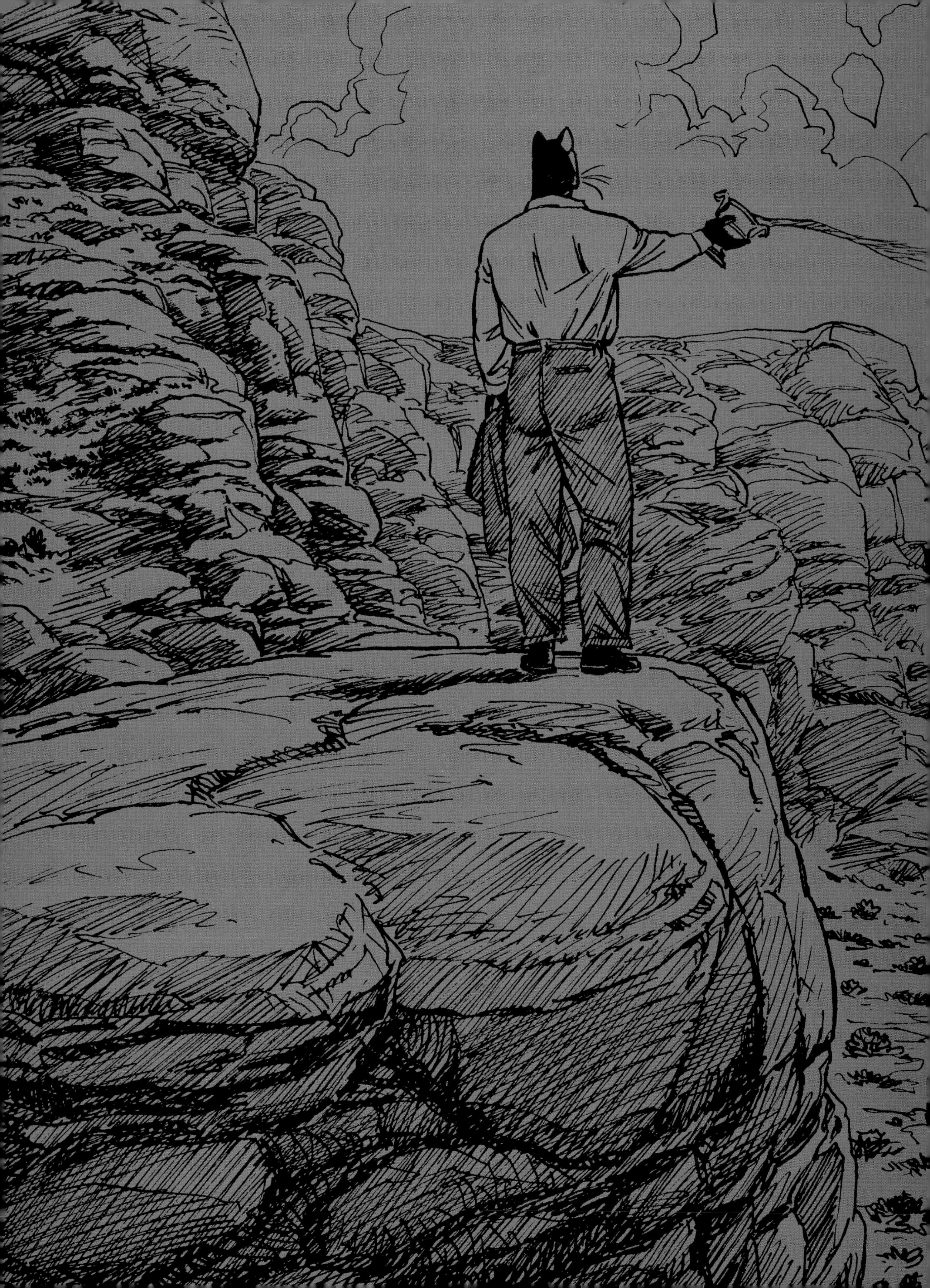

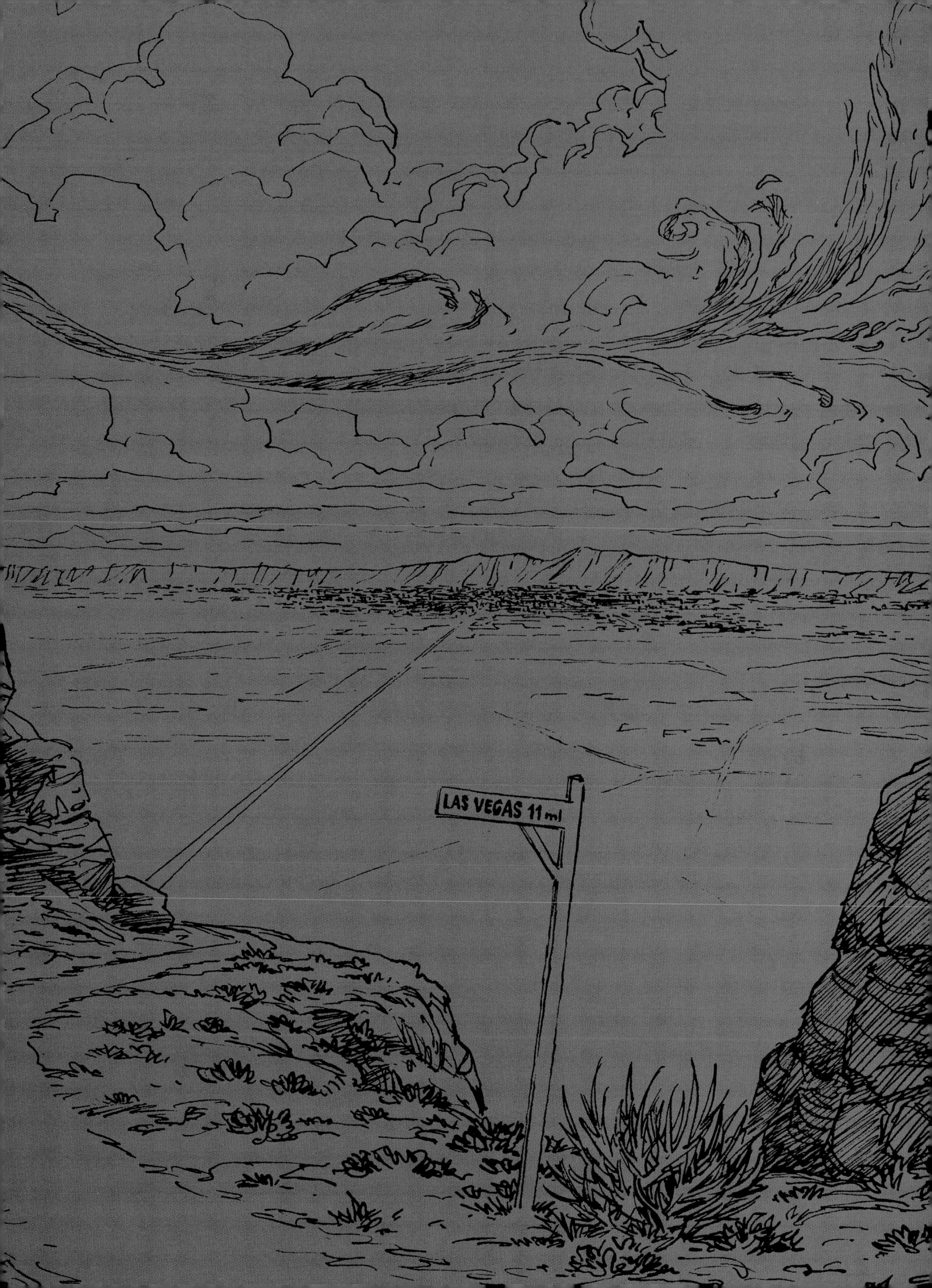
LAS VEGAS 11 mi

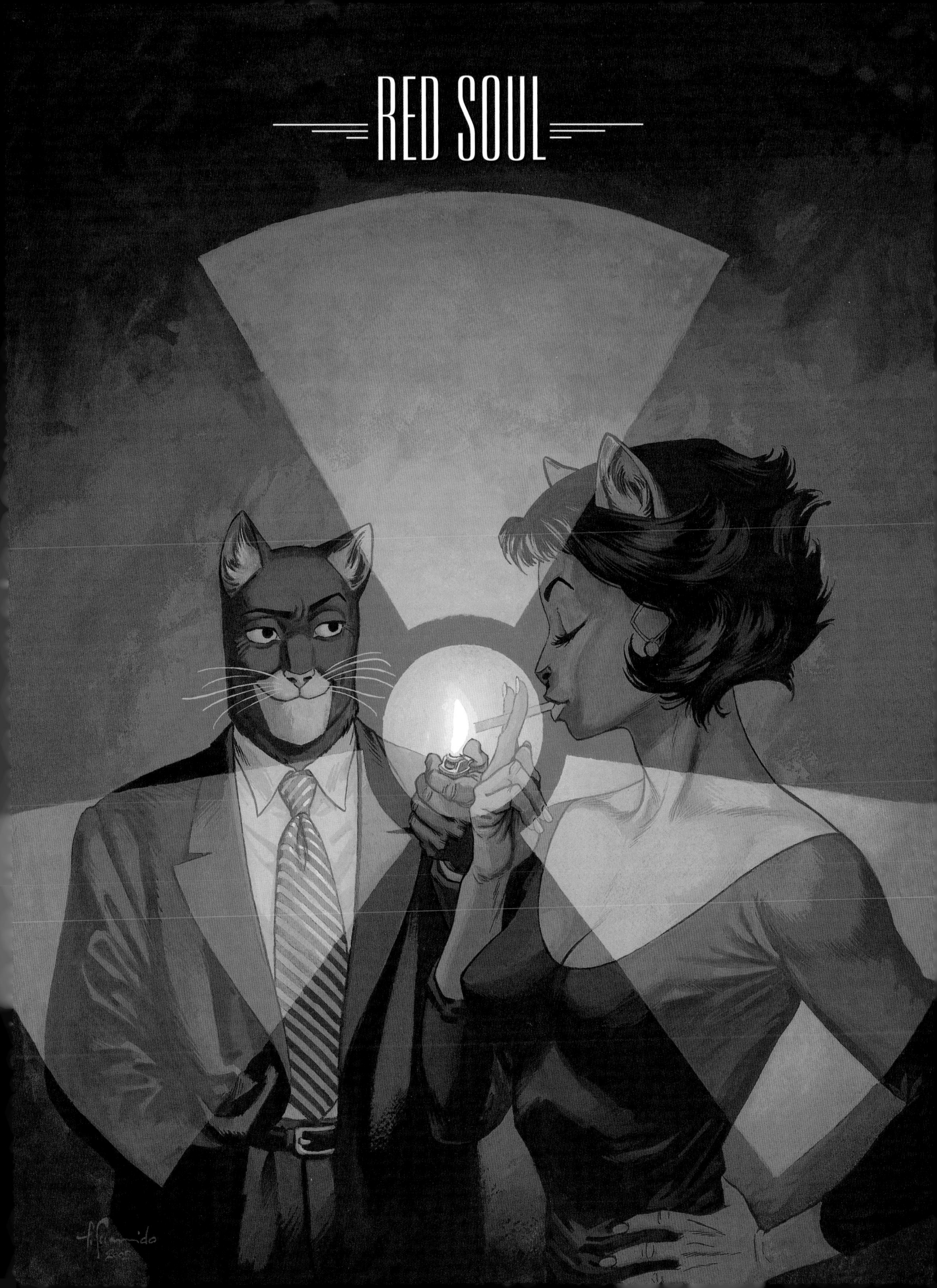
RED SOUL

Preceding:
The original cover to this album as
published by Dargaud, November 2005

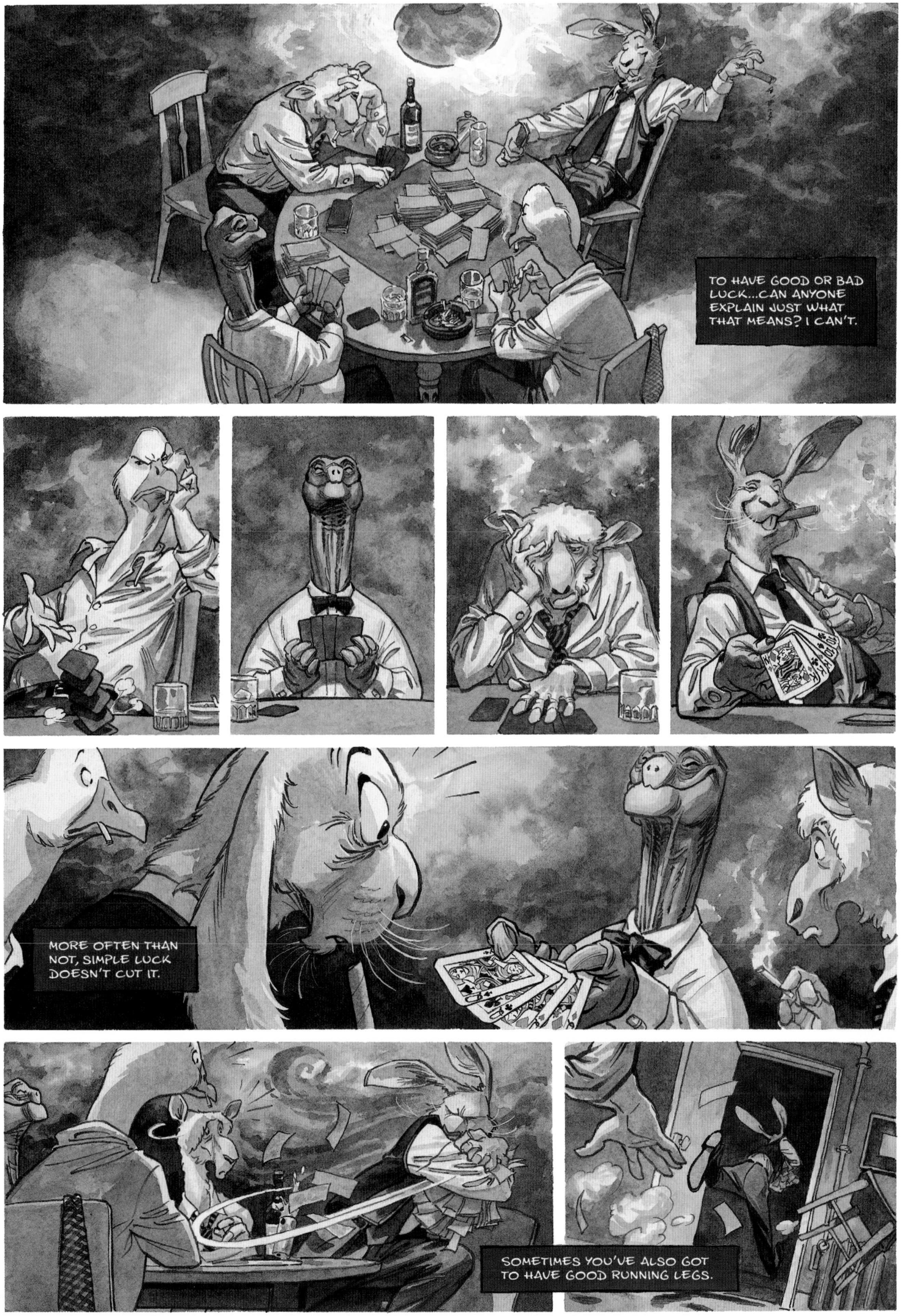
TO HAVE GOOD OR BAD LUCK...CAN ANYONE EXPLAIN JUST WHAT THAT MEANS? I CAN'T.
MORE OFTEN THAN NOT, SIMPLE LUCK DOESN'T CUT IT.
SOMETIMES YOU'VE ALSO GOT TO HAVE GOOD RUNNING LEGS.

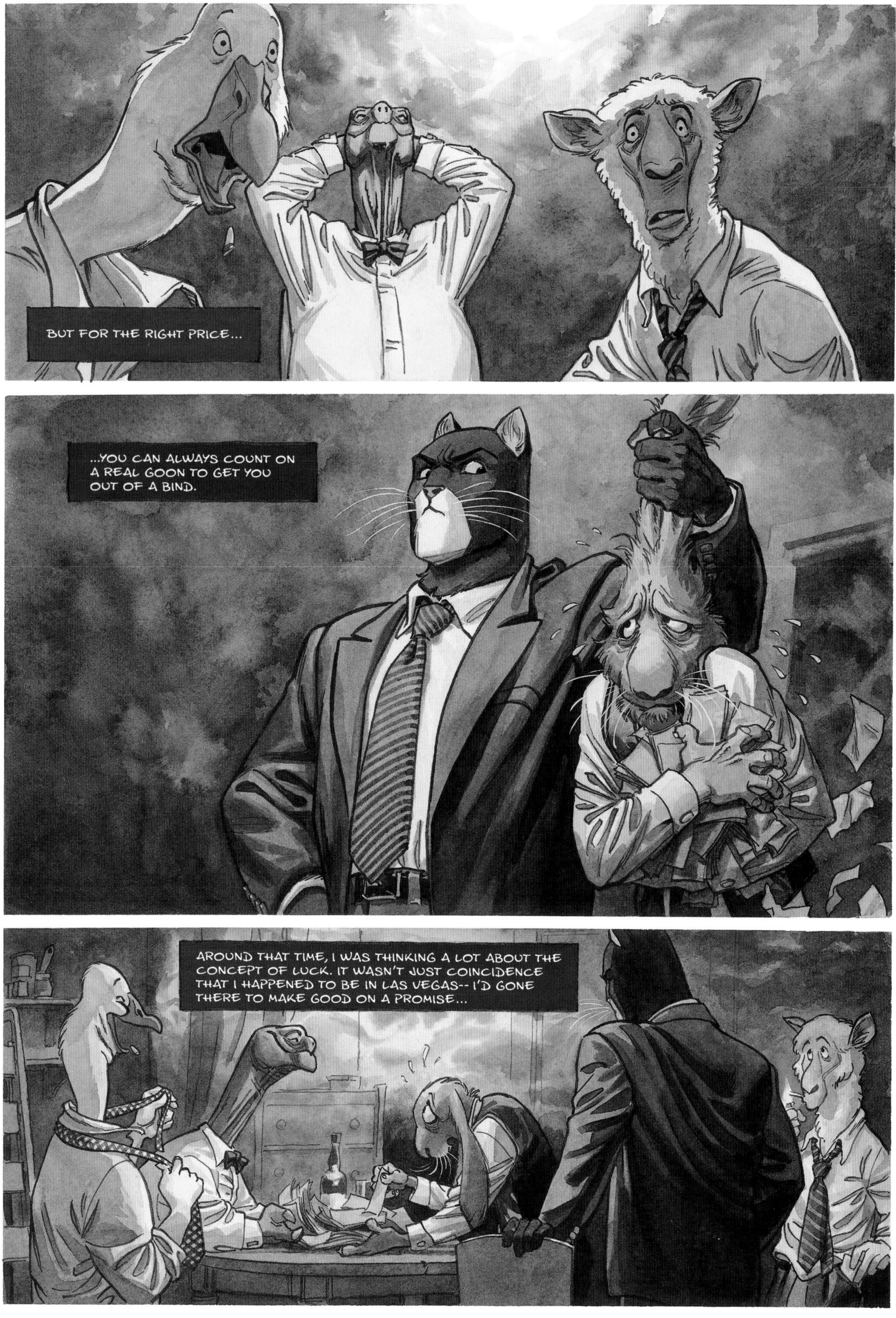
BUT FOR THE RIGHT PRICE...
...YOU CAN ALWAYS COUNT ON A REAL GOON TO GET YOU OUT OF A BIND.
AROUND THAT TIME, I WAS THINKING A LOT ABOUT THE CONCEPT OF LUCK. IT WASN'T JUST COINCIDENCE THAT I HAPPENED TO BE IN LAS VEGAS-- I'D GONE THERE TO MAKE GOOD ON A PROMISE...
2

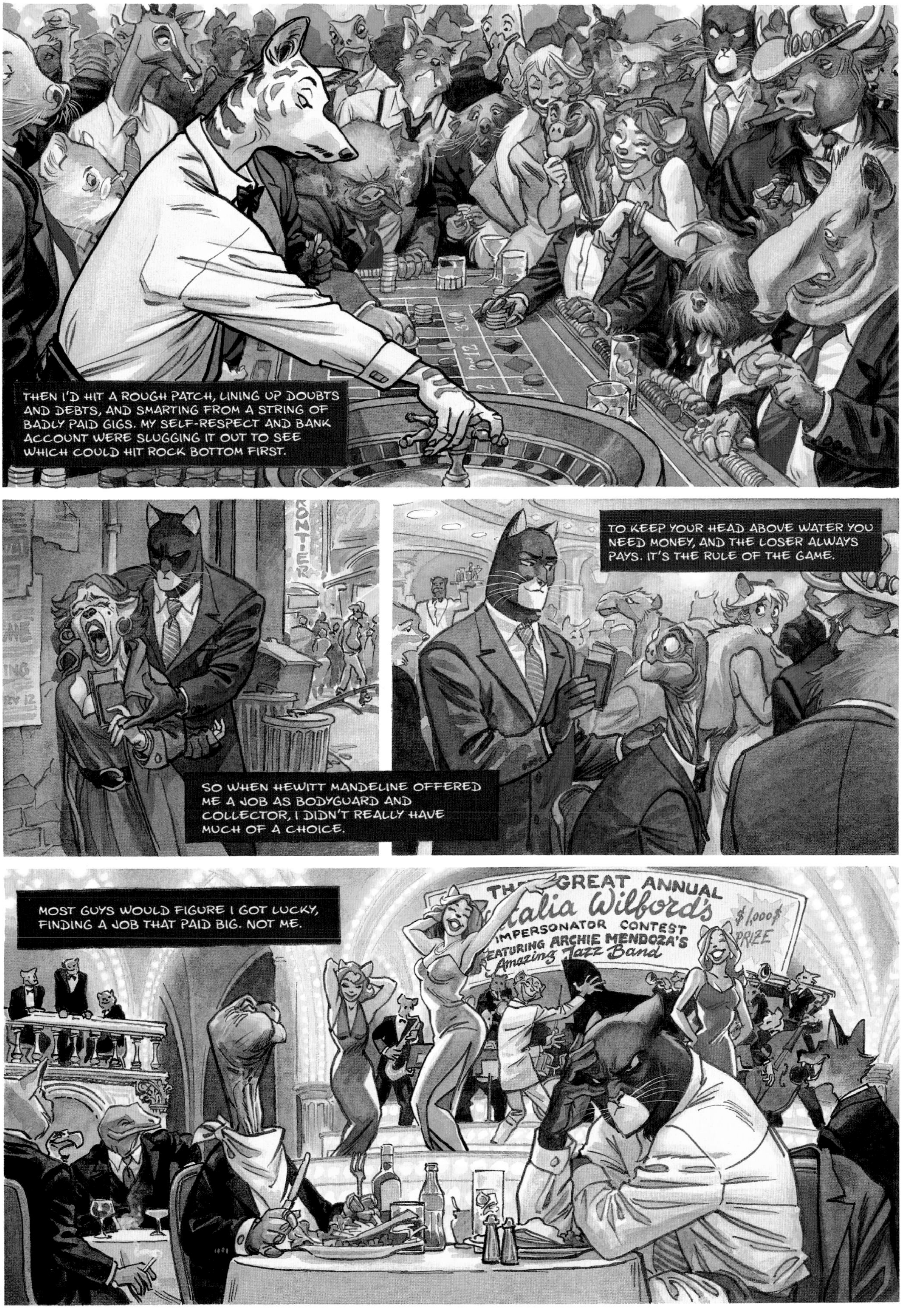
THEN I'D HIT A ROUGH PATCH, LINING UP DOUBTS AND DEBTS, AND SMARTING FROM A STRING OF BADLY PAID GIGS. MY SELF-RESPECT AND BANK ACCOUNT WERE SLUGGING IT OUT TO SEE WHICH COULD HIT ROCK BOTTOM FIRST.
SO WHEN HEWITT MANDELINE OFFERED ME A JOB AS BODYGUARD AND COLLECTOR, I DIDN'T REALLY HAVE MUCH OF A CHOICE.
TO KEEP YOUR HEAD ABOVE WATER YOU NEED MONEY, AND THE LOSER ALWAYS PAYS. IT'S THE RULE OF THE GAME.
MOST GUYS WOULD FIGURE I GOT LUCKY, FINDING A JOB THAT PAID BIG. NOT ME.
GREAT ANNUAL
IMPERSONATOR CONTEST
ARCHIE MENDOZA'S
Amazing Jazz Band
$1,000$ PRIZE

3

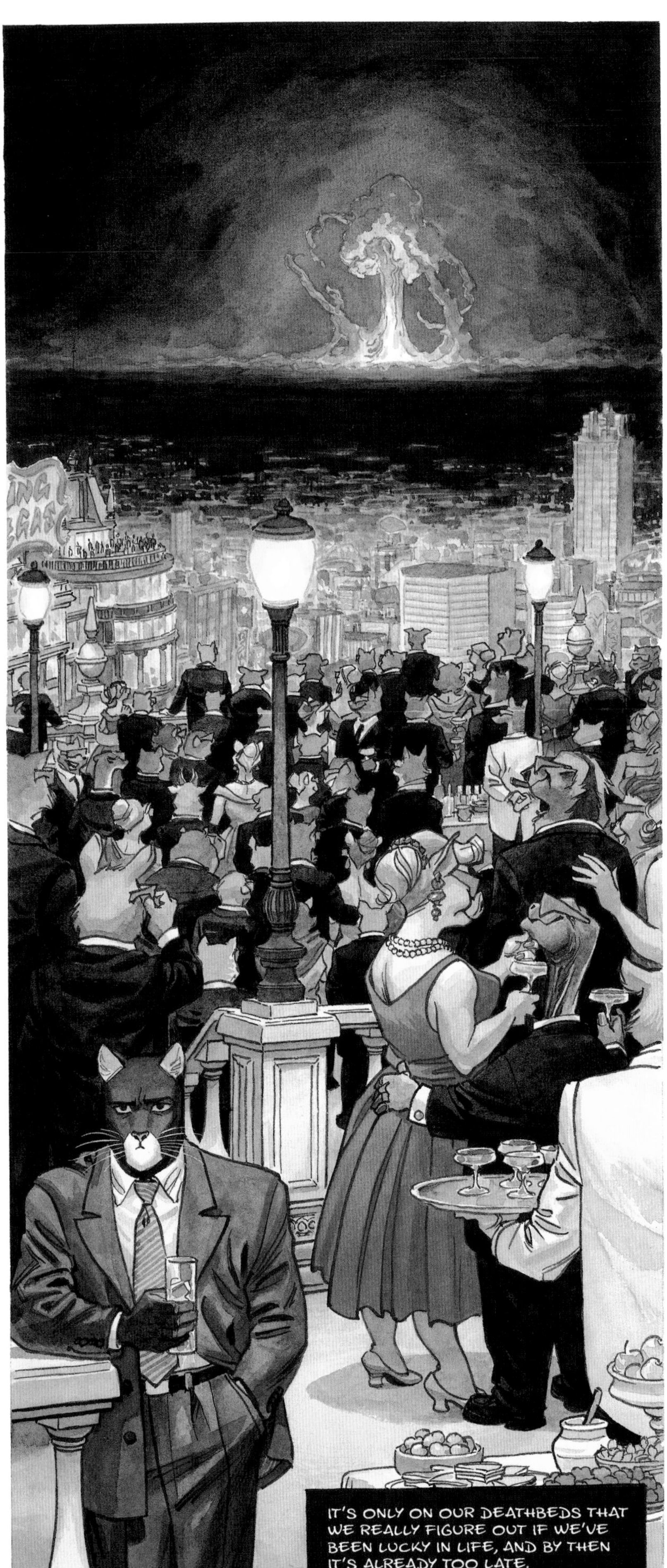
IT'S ONLY ON OUR DEATHBEDS THAT WE REALLY FIGURE OUT IF WE'VE BEEN LUCKY IN LIFE, AND BY THEN IT'S ALREADY TOO LATE.

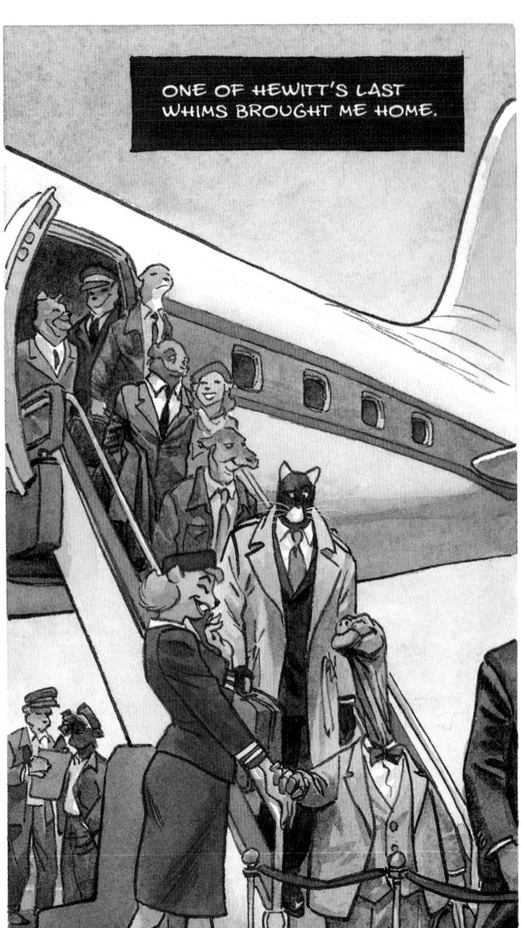
ONE OF HEWITT'S LAST WHIMS BROUGHT ME HOME.

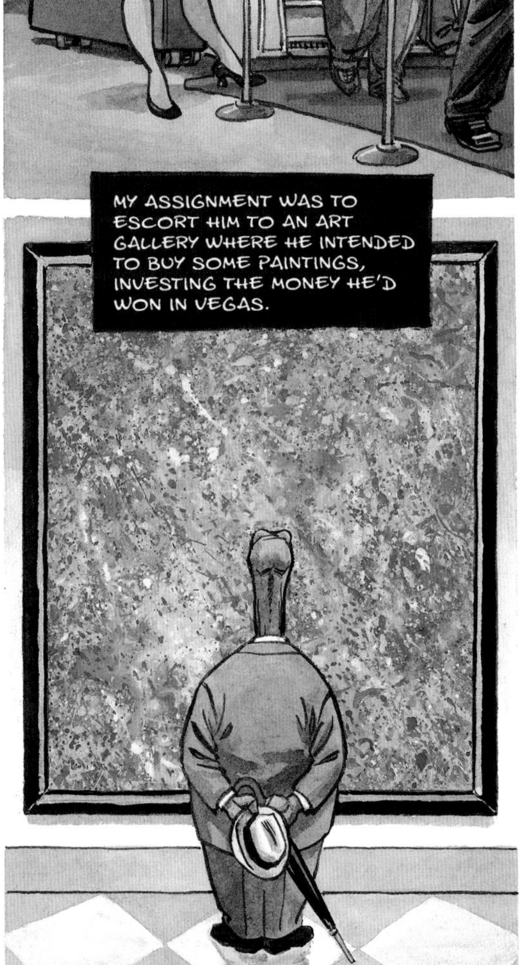
MY ASSIGNMENT WAS TO ESCORT HIM TO AN ART GALLERY WHERE HE INTENDED TO BUY SOME PAINTINGS, INVESTING THE MONEY HE'D WON IN VEGAS.
4

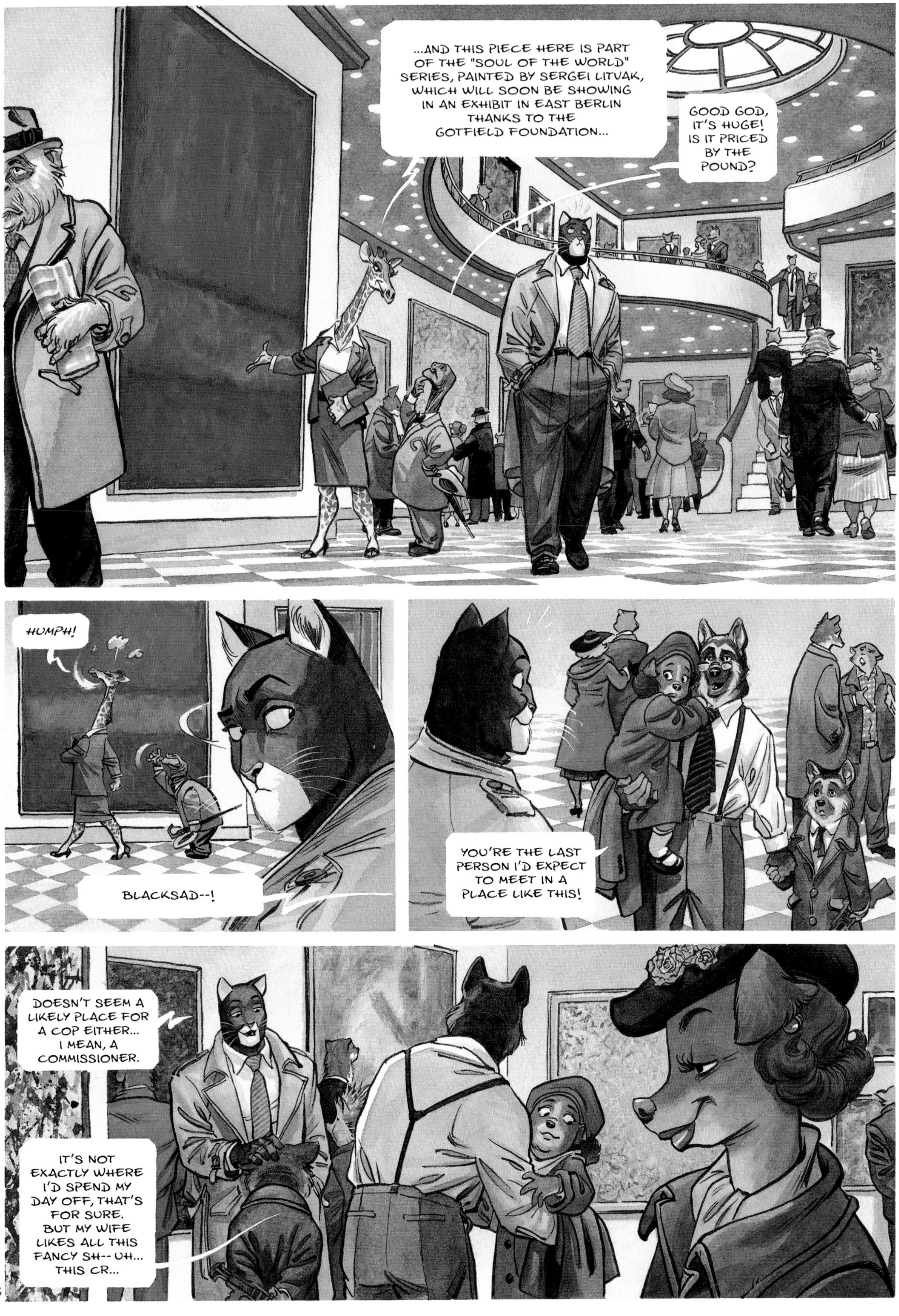
...AND THIS PIECE HERE IS PART OF THE "SOUL OF THE WORLD" SERIES, PAINTED BY SERGEI LITVAK, WHICH WILL SOON BE SHOWING IN AN EXHIBIT IN EAST BERLIN THANKS TO THE GOTFIELD FOUNDATION...
GOOD GOD, IT'S HUGE! IS IT PRICED BY THE POUND?
HUMPH!
BLACKSAD--!
YOU'RE THE LAST PERSON I'D EXPECT TO MEET IN A PLACE LIKE THIS!
DOESN'T SEEM A LIKELY PLACE FOR A COP EITHER... I MEAN, A COMMISSIONER.
IT'S NOT EXACTLY WHERE I'D SPEND MY DAY OFF, THAT'S FOR SURE. BUT MY WIFE LIKES ALL THIS FANCY SH-- UH... THIS CR...
5

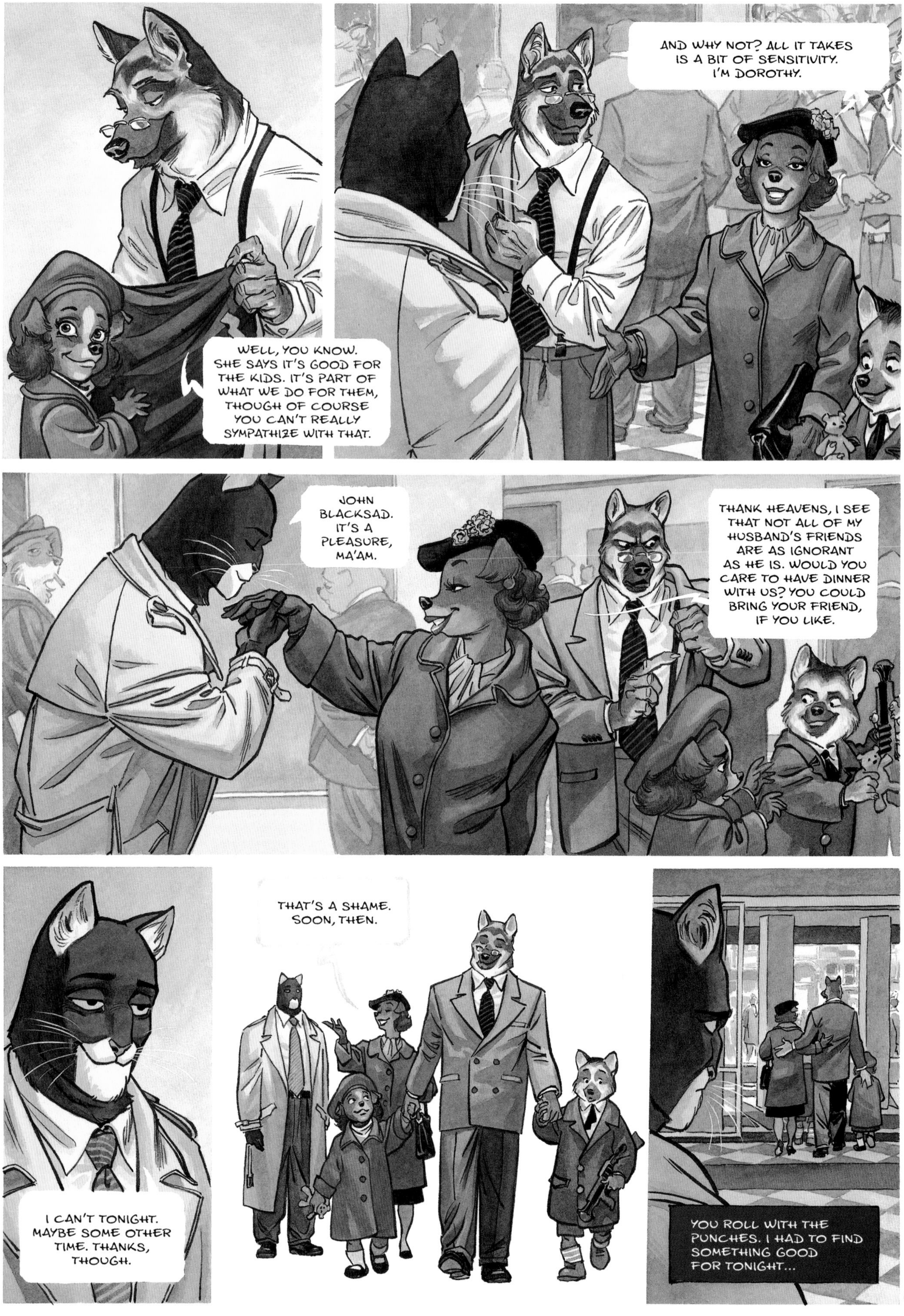
WELL, YOU KNOW. SHE SAYS IT'S GOOD FOR THE KIDS. IT'S PART OF WHAT WE DO FOR THEM, THOUGH OF COURSE YOU CAN'T REALLY SYMPATHIZE WITH THAT.
AND WHY NOT? ALL IT TAKES IS A BIT OF SENSITIVITY. I'M DOROTHY.
JOHN BLACKSAD. IT'S A PLEASURE, MA'AM.
THANK HEAVENS, I SEE THAT NOT ALL OF MY HUSBAND'S FRIENDS ARE AS IGNORANT AS HE IS. WOULD YOU CARE TO HAVE DINNER WITH US? YOU COULD BRING YOUR FRIEND, IF YOU LIKE.
I CAN'T TONIGHT. MAYBE SOME OTHER TIME. THANKS, THOUGH.
THAT'S A SHAME. SOON, THEN.
YOU ROLL WITH THE PUNCHES. I HAD TO FIND SOMETHING GOOD FOR TONIGHT...
6

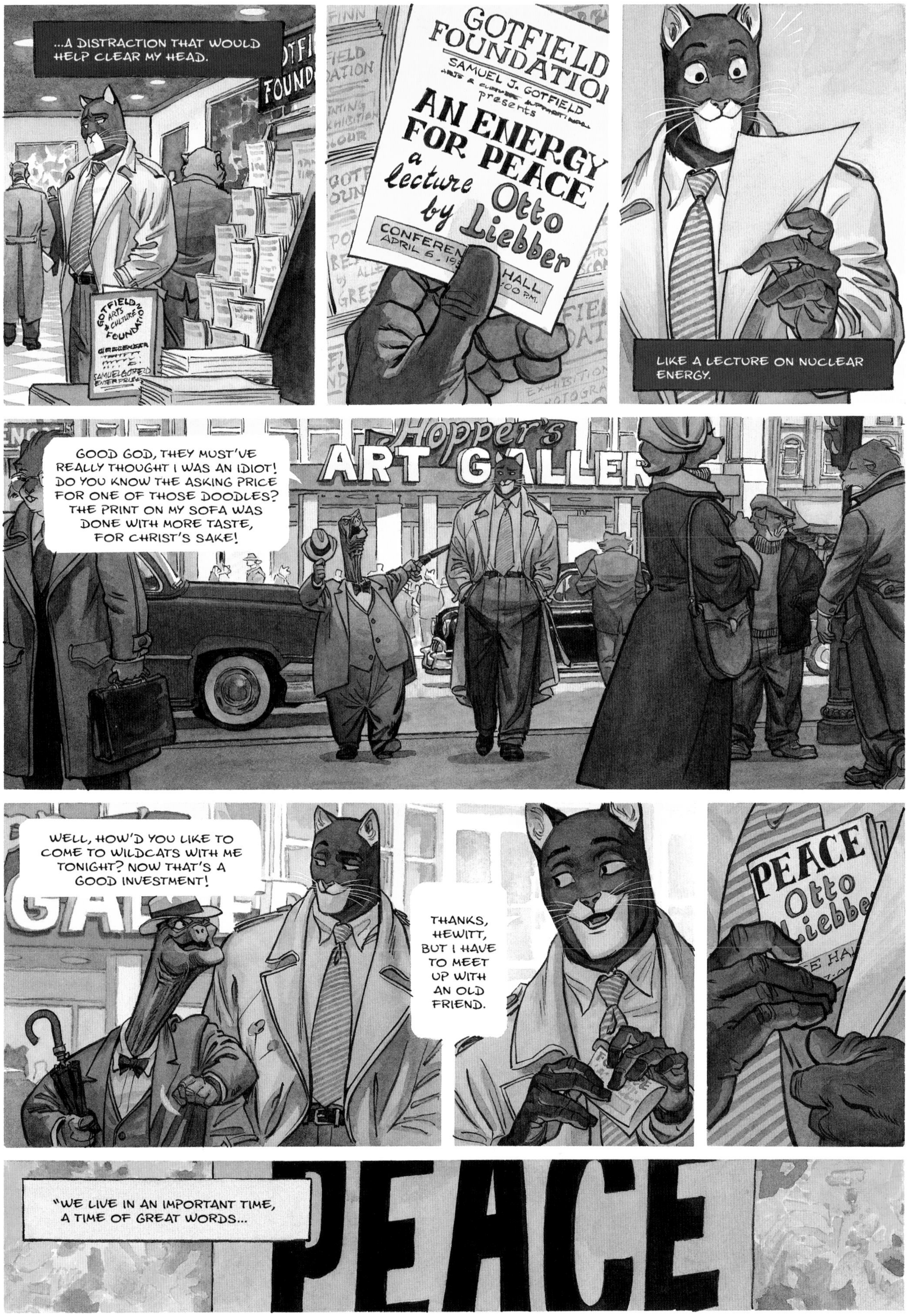
...A DISTRACTION THAT WOULD HELP CLEAR MY HEAD.
GOTFIELD FOUNDATION
SAMUEL J. GOTFIELD presents
AN ENERGY FOR PEACE
a lecture by Otto Liebber
LIKE A LECTURE ON NUCLEAR ENERGY.
Hopper's
ART GALLER
GOOD GOD, THEY MUST'VE REALLY THOUGHT I WAS AN IDIOT! DO YOU KNOW THE ASKING PRICE FOR ONE OF THOSE DOODLES? THE PRINT ON MY SOFA WAS DONE WITH MORE TASTE, FOR CHRIST'S SAKE!
WELL, HOW'D YOU LIKE TO COME TO WILDCATS WITH ME TONIGHT? NOW THAT'S A GOOD INVESTMENT!
THANKS, HEWITT, BUT I HAVE TO MEET UP WITH AN OLD FRIEND.
PEACE
Otto
"WE LIVE IN AN IMPORTANT TIME, A TIME OF GREAT WORDS...
PEACE
7

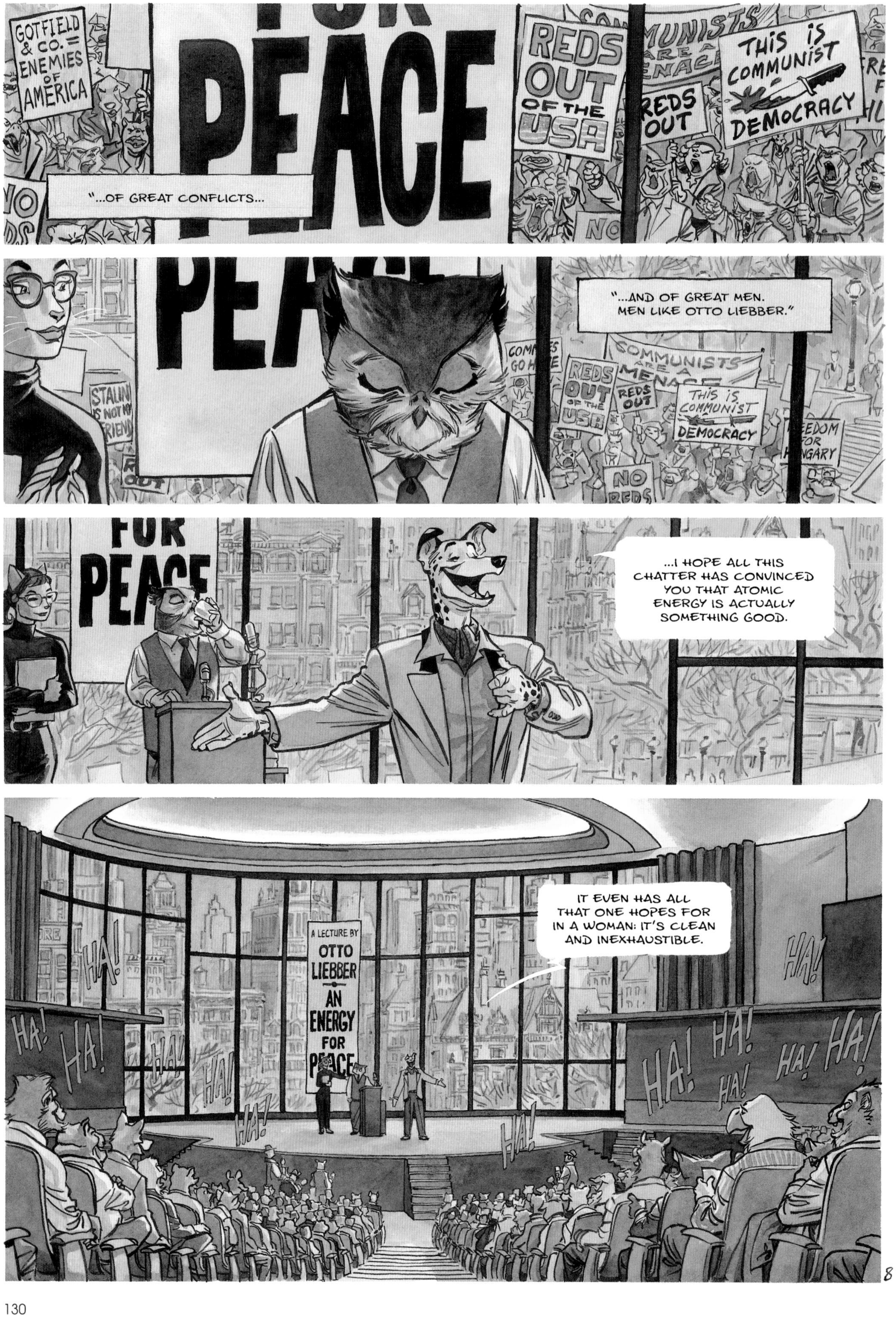
GOTFIELD & CO. = ENEMIES OF AMERICA
PEACE
REDS OUT OF THE USA
COMMUNISTS ARE A MENACE
REDS OUT
THIS IS COMMUNIST DEMOCRACY
"...OF GREAT CONFLICTS...
"...AND OF GREAT MEN.
MEN LIKE OTTO LIEBBER."
STALIN IS NOT MY FRIEND
NO REDS
FREEDOM FOR HUNGARY
FOR PEACE
...I HOPE ALL THIS CHATTER HAS CONVINCED YOU THAT ATOMIC ENERGY IS ACTUALLY SOMETHING GOOD.
A LECTURE BY OTTO LIEBBER
AN ENERGY FOR PEACE
IT EVEN HAS ALL THAT ONE HOPES FOR IN A WOMAN: IT'S CLEAN AND INEXHAUSTIBLE.
HA! HA! HA! HA! HA! HA! HA! HA! HA! HA! HA! HA!
8

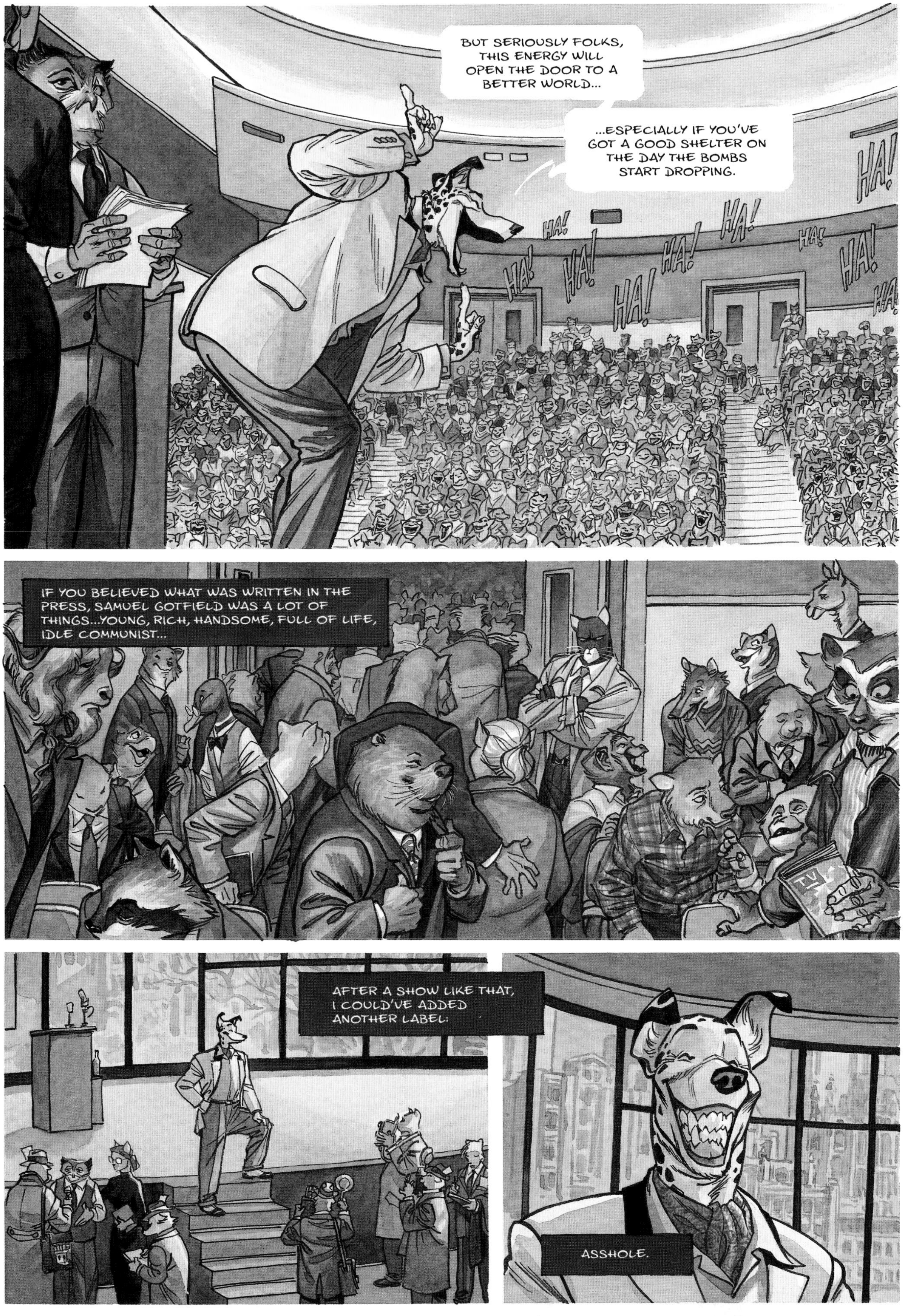
BUT SERIOUSLY FOLKS, THIS ENERGY WILL OPEN THE DOOR TO A BETTER WORLD...
...ESPECIALLY IF YOU'VE GOT A GOOD SHELTER ON THE DAY THE BOMBS START DROPPING.
HA! HA! HA! HA! HA! HA! HA! HA! HA! HA!
IF YOU BELIEVED WHAT WAS WRITTEN IN THE PRESS, SAMUEL GOTFIELD WAS A LOT OF THINGS...YOUNG, RICH, HANDSOME, FULL OF LIFE, IDLE COMMUNIST...
TV
AFTER A SHOW LIKE THAT, I COULD'VE ADDED ANOTHER LABEL:
ASSHOLE.

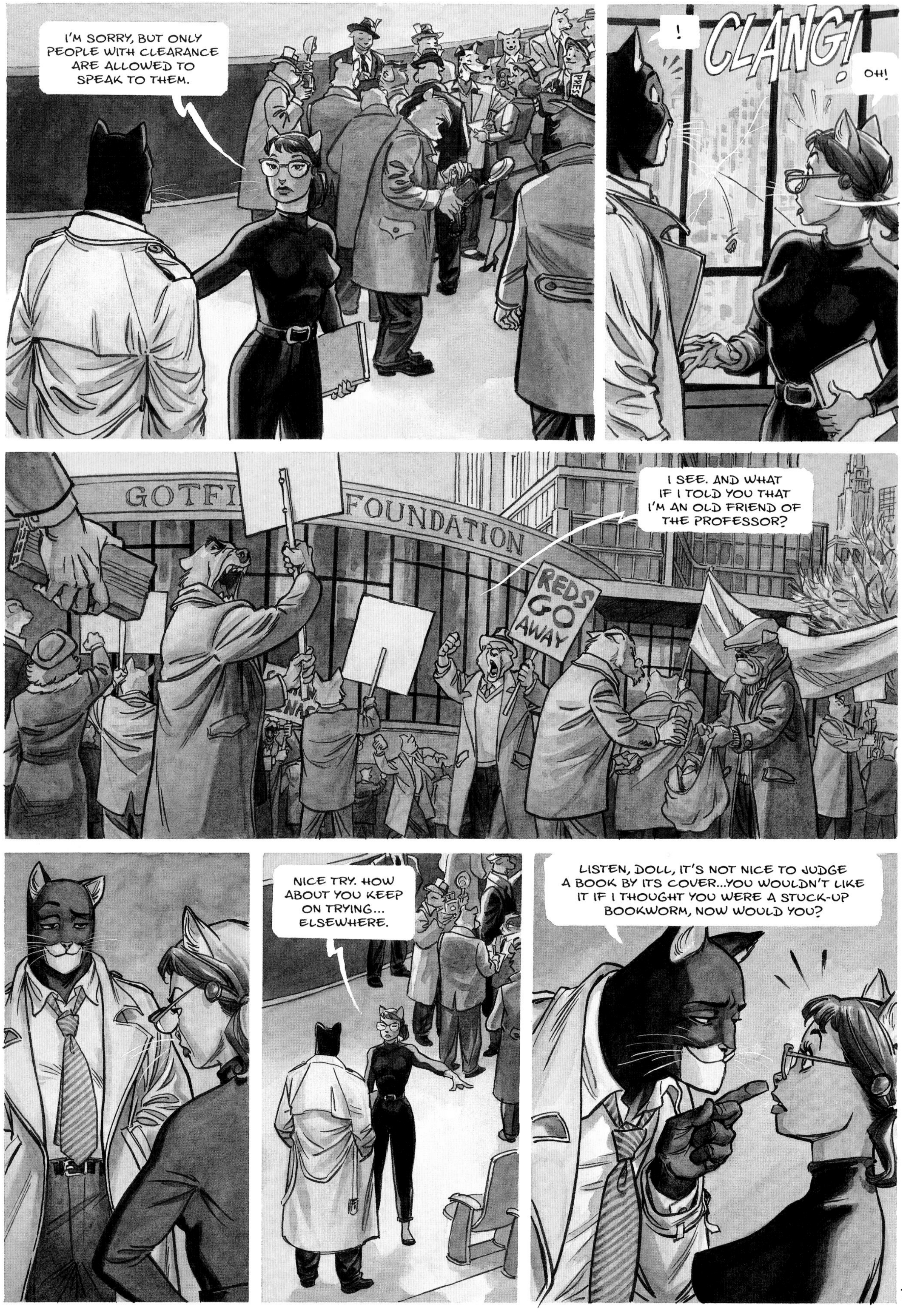
I'M SORRY, BUT ONLY PEOPLE WITH CLEARANCE ARE ALLOWED TO SPEAK TO THEM.
PRESS
!
CLANG!
OH!
GOTFI
FOUNDATION
I SEE. AND WHAT IF I TOLD YOU THAT I'M AN OLD FRIEND OF THE PROFESSOR?
REDS GO AWAY
NICE TRY. HOW ABOUT YOU KEEP ON TRYING... ELSEWHERE.
LISTEN, DOLL, IT'S NOT NICE TO JUDGE A BOOK BY ITS COVER...YOU WOULDN'T LIKE IT IF I THOUGHT YOU WERE A STUCK-UP BOOKWORM, NOW WOULD YOU?
10

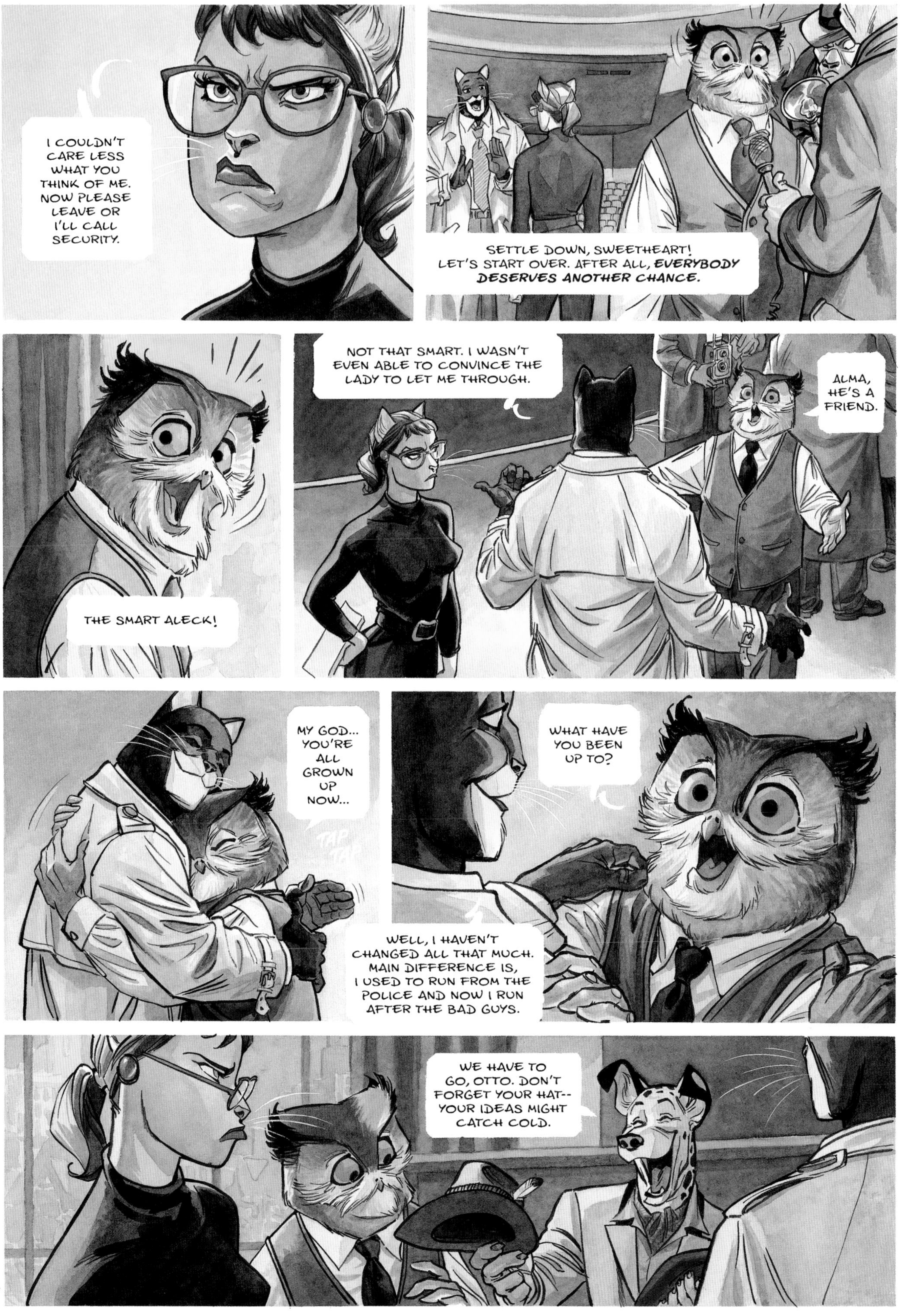
I COULDN'T CARE LESS WHAT YOU THINK OF ME. NOW PLEASE LEAVE OR I'LL CALL SECURITY.
SETTLE DOWN, SWEETHEART! LET'S START OVER. AFTER ALL, **EVERYBODY DESERVES ANOTHER CHANCE.**
THE SMART ALECK!
NOT THAT SMART. I WASN'T EVEN ABLE TO CONVINCE THE LADY TO LET ME THROUGH.
ALMA, HE'S A FRIEND.
MY GOD... YOU'RE ALL GROWN UP NOW...
TAP TAP
WHAT HAVE YOU BEEN UP TO?
WELL, I HAVEN'T CHANGED ALL THAT MUCH. MAIN DIFFERENCE IS, I USED TO RUN FROM THE POLICE AND NOW I RUN AFTER THE BAD GUYS.
WE HAVE TO GO, OTTO. DON'T FORGET YOUR HAT-- YOUR IDEAS MIGHT CATCH COLD.
11

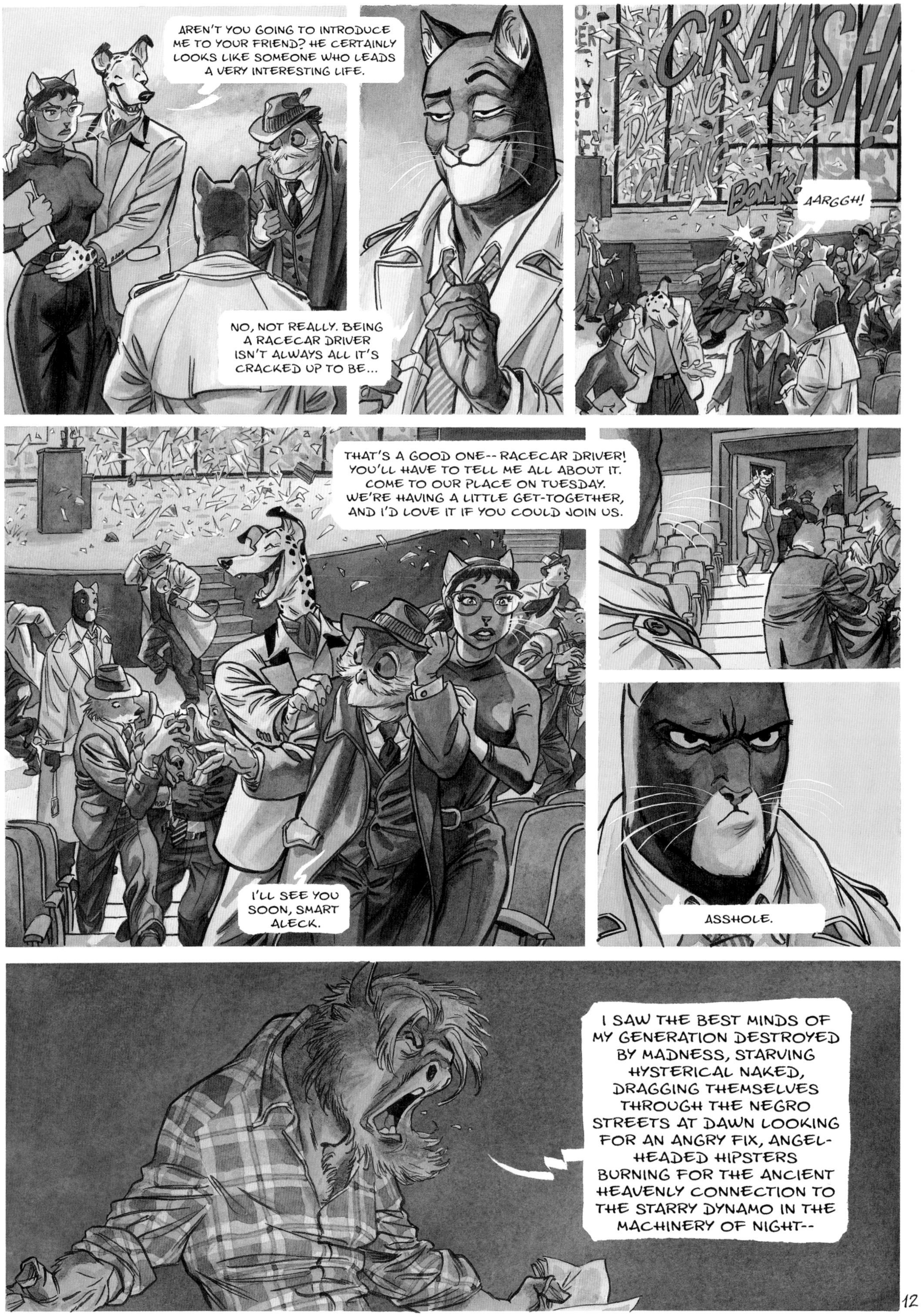

AREN'T YOU GOING TO INTRODUCE ME TO YOUR FRIEND? HE CERTAINLY LOOKS LIKE SOMEONE WHO LEADS A VERY INTERESTING LIFE.
NO, NOT REALLY. BEING A RACECAR DRIVER ISN'T ALWAYS ALL IT'S CRACKED UP TO BE...
CRAASH!
DZING
CLING
BONK!
AARGGH!
THAT'S A GOOD ONE-- RACECAR DRIVER! YOU'LL HAVE TO TELL ME ALL ABOUT IT. COME TO OUR PLACE ON TUESDAY. WE'RE HAVING A LITTLE GET-TOGETHER, AND I'D LOVE IT IF YOU COULD JOIN US.
I'LL SEE YOU SOON, SMART ALECK.
ASSHOLE.
I SAW THE BEST MINDS OF MY GENERATION DESTROYED BY MADNESS, STARVING HYSTERICAL NAKED, DRAGGING THEMSELVES THROUGH THE NEGRO STREETS AT DAWN LOOKING FOR AN ANGRY FIX, ANGEL-HEADED HIPSTERS BURNING FOR THE ANCIENT HEAVENLY CONNECTION TO THE STARRY DYNAMO IN THE MACHINERY OF NIGHT--
12

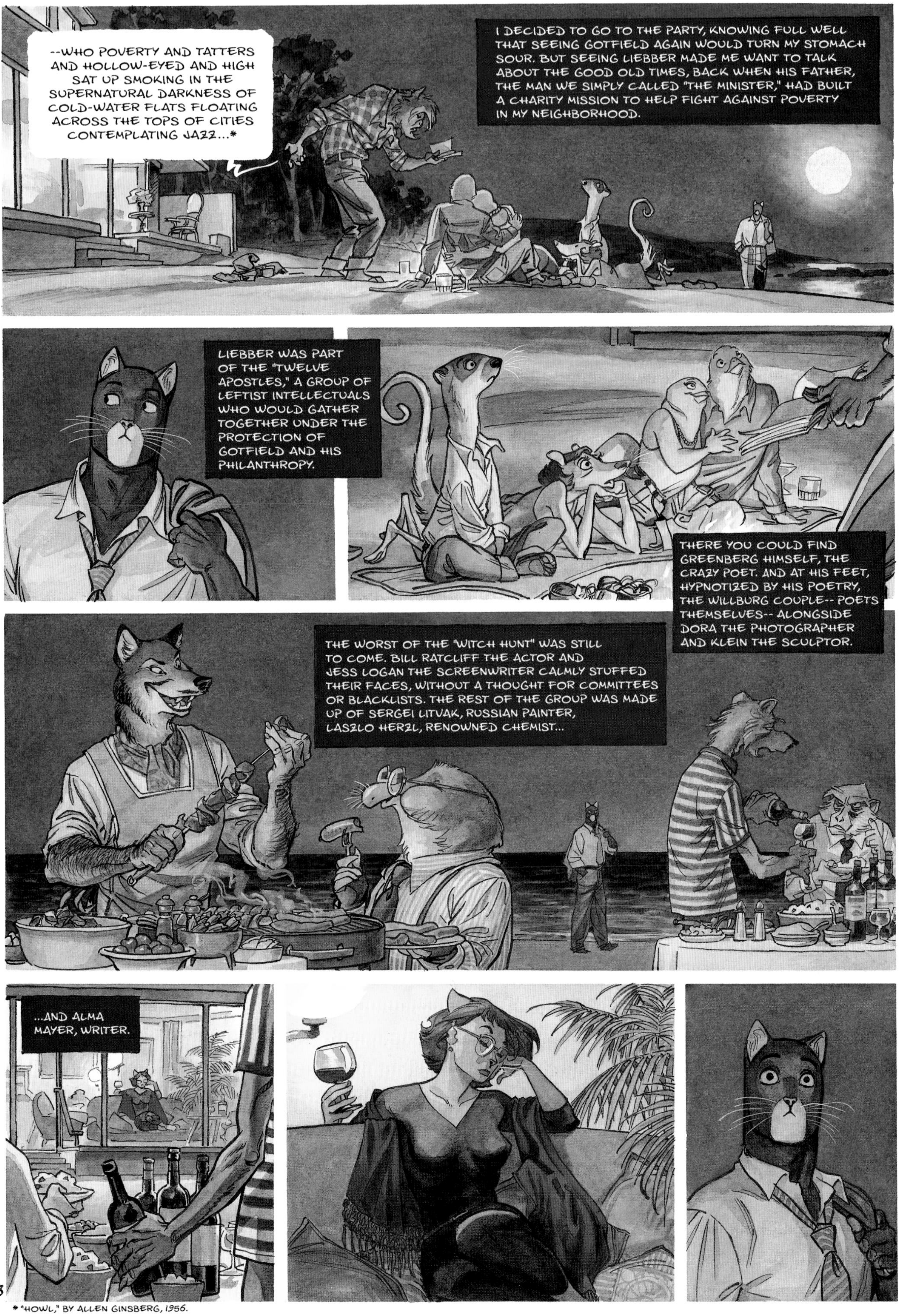
--WHO POVERTY AND TATTERS AND HOLLOW-EYED AND HIGH SAT UP SMOKING IN THE SUPERNATURAL DARKNESS OF COLD-WATER FLATS FLOATING ACROSS THE TOPS OF CITIES CONTEMPLATING JAZZ...*
I DECIDED TO GO TO THE PARTY, KNOWING FULL WELL THAT SEEING GOTFIELD AGAIN WOULD TURN MY STOMACH SOUR. BUT SEEING LIEBBER MADE ME WANT TO TALK ABOUT THE GOOD OLD TIMES, BACK WHEN HIS FATHER, THE MAN WE SIMPLY CALLED "THE MINISTER," HAD BUILT A CHARITY MISSION TO HELP FIGHT AGAINST POVERTY IN MY NEIGHBORHOOD.
LIEBBER WAS PART OF THE "TWELVE APOSTLES," A GROUP OF LEFTIST INTELLECTUALS WHO WOULD GATHER TOGETHER UNDER THE PROTECTION OF GOTFIELD AND HIS PHILANTHROPY.
THERE YOU COULD FIND GREENBERG HIMSELF, THE CRAZY POET. AND AT HIS FEET, HYPNOTIZED BY HIS POETRY, THE WILLBURG COUPLE-- POETS THEMSELVES-- ALONGSIDE DORA THE PHOTOGRAPHER AND KLEIN THE SCULPTOR.
THE WORST OF THE "WITCH HUNT" WAS STILL TO COME. BILL RATCLIFF THE ACTOR AND JESS LOGAN THE SCREENWRITER CALMLY STUFFED THEIR FACES, WITHOUT A THOUGHT FOR COMMITTEES OR BLACKLISTS. THE REST OF THE GROUP WAS MADE UP OF SERGEI LITVAK, RUSSIAN PAINTER, LASZLO HERZL, RENOWNED CHEMIST...
...AND ALMA MAYER, WRITER.
13

* "HOWL," BY ALLEN GINSBERG, 1956.

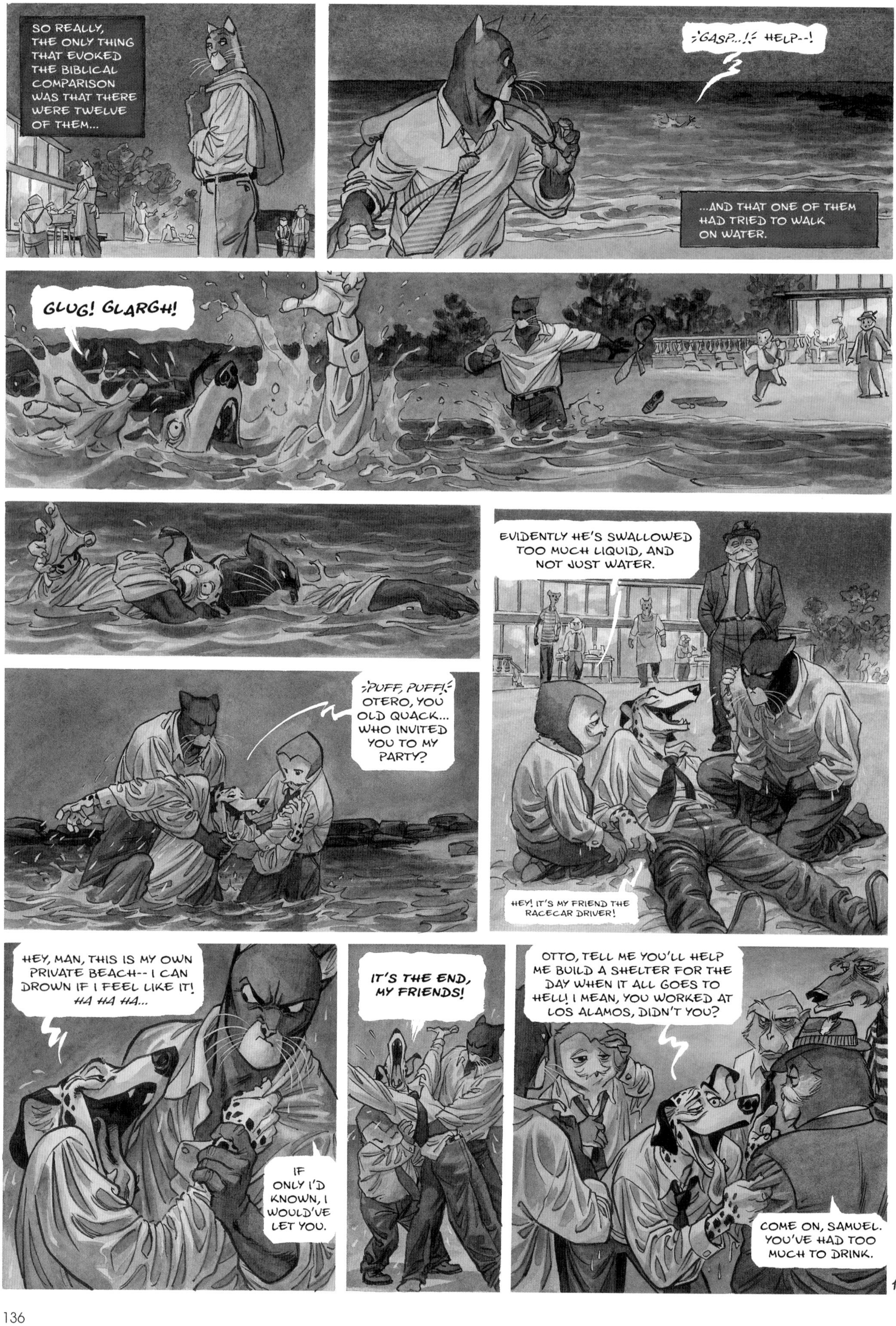

SO REALLY, THE ONLY THING THAT EVOKED THE BIBLICAL COMPARISON WAS THAT THERE WERE TWELVE OF THEM...
GASP...! HELP--!
...AND THAT ONE OF THEM HAD TRIED TO WALK ON WATER.
GLUG! GLARGH!
EVIDENTLY HE'S SWALLOWED TOO MUCH LIQUID, AND NOT JUST WATER.
PUFF, PUFF! OTERO, YOU OLD QUACK... WHO INVITED YOU TO MY PARTY?
HEY! IT'S MY FRIEND THE RACECAR DRIVER!
HEY, MAN, THIS IS MY OWN PRIVATE BEACH-- I CAN DROWN IF I FEEL LIKE IT! HA HA HA...
IF ONLY I'D KNOWN, I WOULD'VE LET YOU.
IT'S THE END, MY FRIENDS!
OTTO, TELL ME YOU'LL HELP ME BUILD A SHELTER FOR THE DAY WHEN IT ALL GOES TO HELL! I MEAN, YOU WORKED AT LOS ALAMOS, DIDN'T YOU?
COME ON, SAMUEL. YOU'VE HAD TOO MUCH TO DRINK.
14

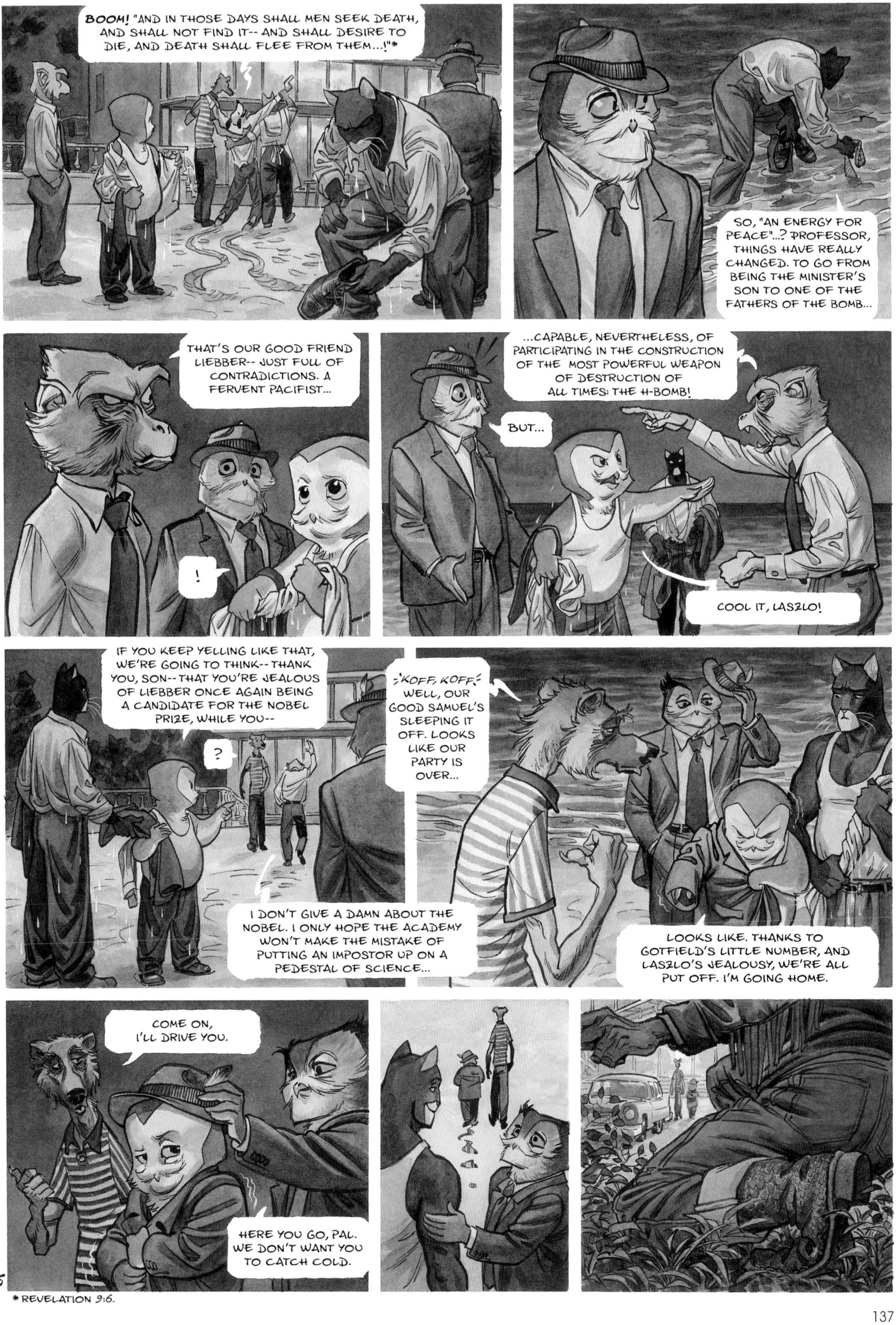
BOOM! "AND IN THOSE DAYS SHALL MEN SEEK DEATH, AND SHALL NOT FIND IT-- AND SHALL DESIRE TO DIE, AND DEATH SHALL FLEE FROM THEM...!"*
SO, "AN ENERGY FOR PEACE"...? PROFESSOR, THINGS HAVE REALLY CHANGED. TO GO FROM BEING THE MINISTER'S SON TO ONE OF THE FATHERS OF THE BOMB...
THAT'S OUR GOOD FRIEND LIEBBER-- JUST FULL OF CONTRADICTIONS. A FERVENT PACIFIST...
!
...CAPABLE, NEVERTHELESS, OF PARTICIPATING IN THE CONSTRUCTION OF THE MOST POWERFUL WEAPON OF DESTRUCTION OF ALL TIMES: THE H-BOMB!
BUT...
COOL IT, LASZLO!
IF YOU KEEP YELLING LIKE THAT, WE'RE GOING TO THINK-- THANK YOU, SON-- THAT YOU'RE JEALOUS OF LIEBBER ONCE AGAIN BEING A CANDIDATE FOR THE NOBEL PRIZE, WHILE YOU--
?
I DON'T GIVE A DAMN ABOUT THE NOBEL. I ONLY HOPE THE ACADEMY WON'T MAKE THE MISTAKE OF PUTTING AN IMPOSTOR UP ON A PEDESTAL OF SCIENCE...
KOFF, KOFF WELL, OUR GOOD SAMUEL'S SLEEPING IT OFF. LOOKS LIKE OUR PARTY IS OVER...
LOOKS LIKE. THANKS TO GOTFIELD'S LITTLE NUMBER, AND LASZLO'S JEALOUSY, WE'RE ALL PUT OFF. I'M GOING HOME.
COME ON, I'LL DRIVE YOU.
HERE YOU GO, PAL. WE DON'T WANT YOU TO CATCH COLD.
15

* REVELATION 9:6.

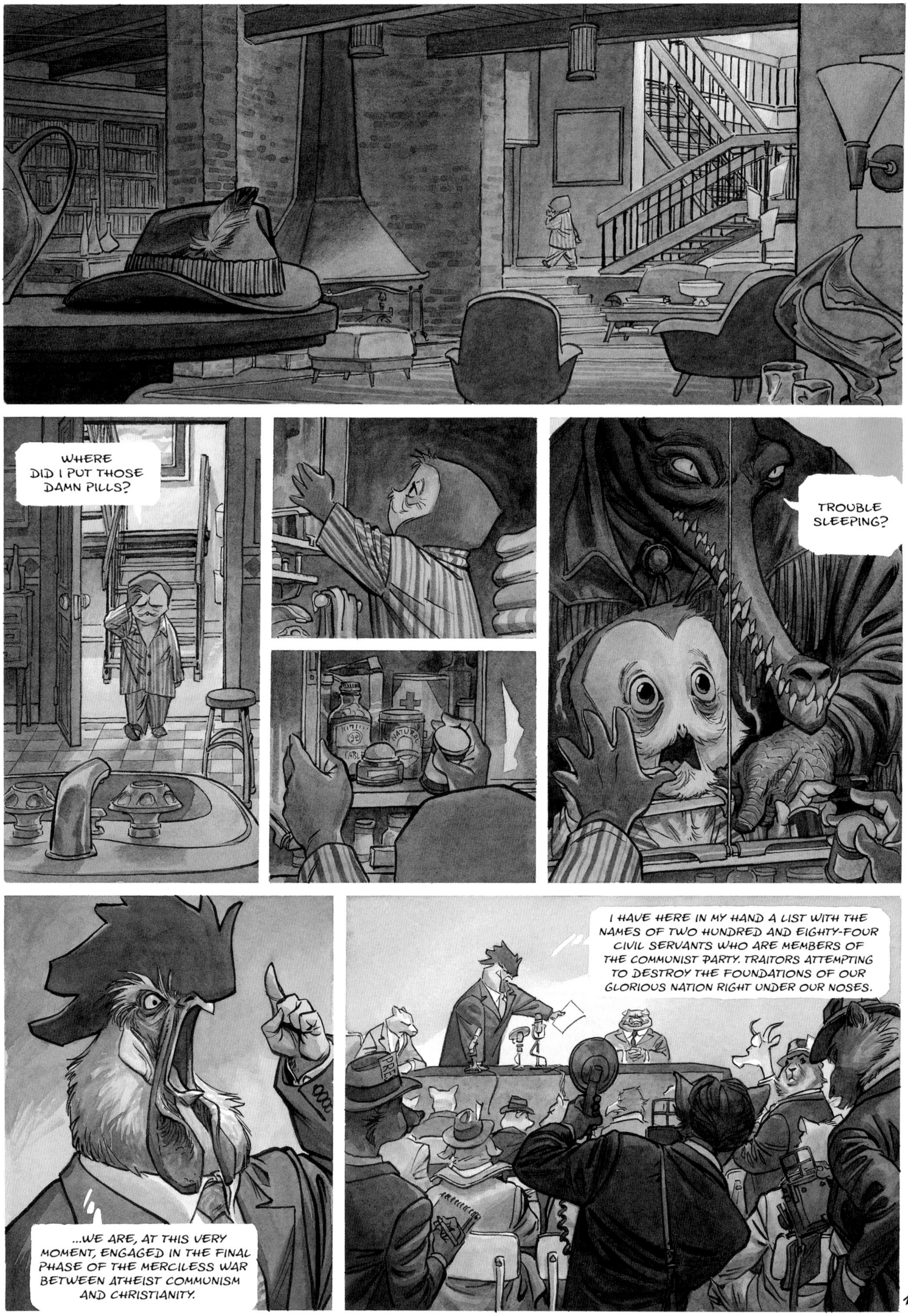
WHERE DID I PUT THOSE DAMN PILLS?
TROUBLE SLEEPING?
...WE ARE, AT THIS VERY MOMENT, ENGAGED IN THE FINAL PHASE OF THE MERCILESS WAR BETWEEN ATHEIST COMMUNISM AND CHRISTIANITY.
I HAVE HERE IN MY HAND A LIST WITH THE NAMES OF TWO HUNDRED AND EIGHTY-FOUR CIVIL SERVANTS WHO ARE MEMBERS OF THE COMMUNIST PARTY. TRAITORS ATTEMPTING TO DESTROY THE FOUNDATIONS OF OUR GLORIOUS NATION RIGHT UNDER OUR NOSES.
16

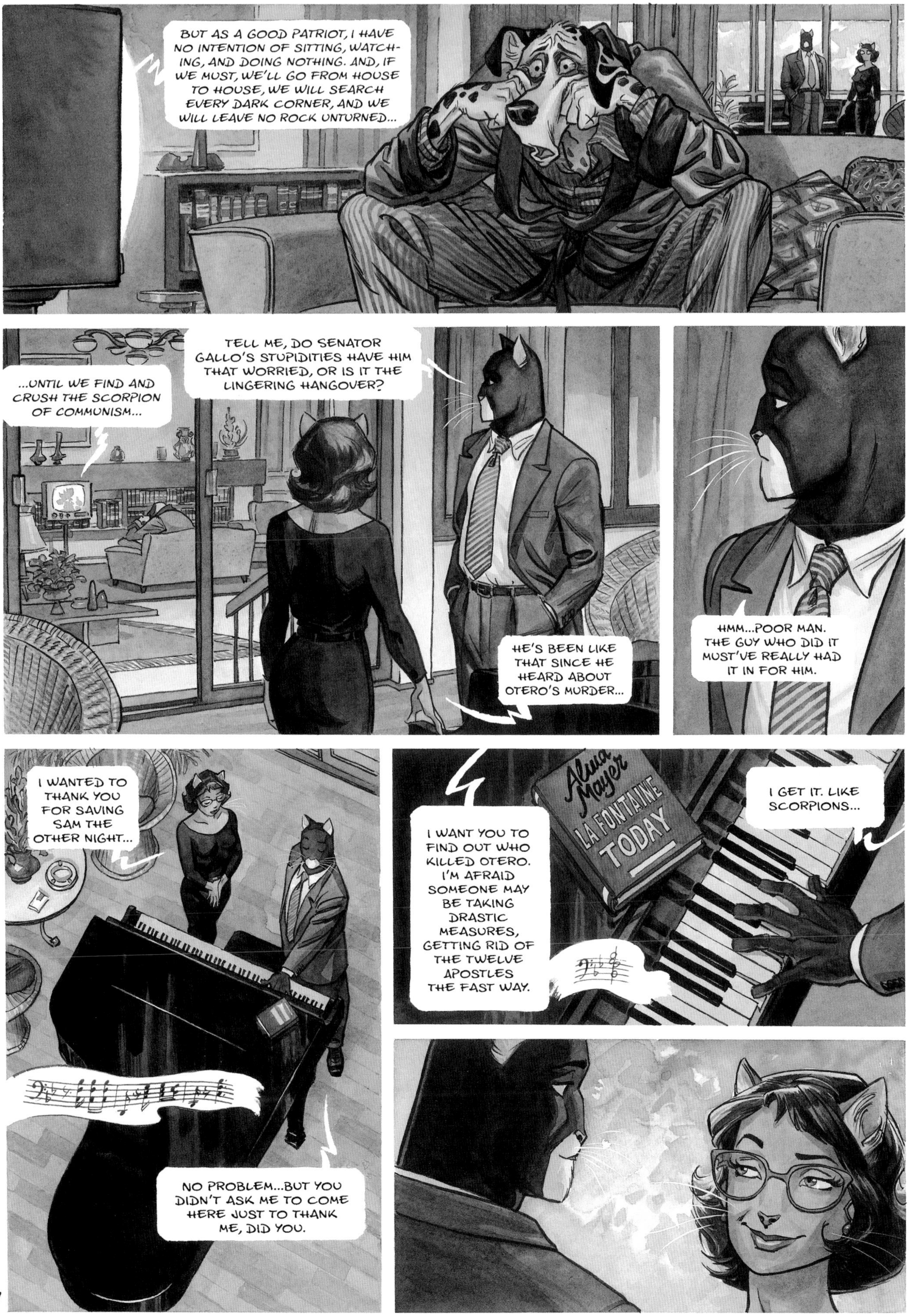
BUT AS A GOOD PATRIOT, I HAVE NO INTENTION OF SITTING, WATCHING, AND DOING NOTHING. AND, IF WE MUST, WE'LL GO FROM HOUSE TO HOUSE, WE WILL SEARCH EVERY DARK CORNER, AND WE WILL LEAVE NO ROCK UNTURNED...
...UNTIL WE FIND AND CRUSH THE SCORPION OF COMMUNISM...
TELL ME, DO SENATOR GALLO'S STUPIDITIES HAVE HIM THAT WORRIED, OR IS IT THE LINGERING HANGOVER?
HE'S BEEN LIKE THAT SINCE HE HEARD ABOUT OTERO'S MURDER...
HMM...POOR MAN. THE GUY WHO DID IT MUST'VE REALLY HAD IT IN FOR HIM.
I WANTED TO THANK YOU FOR SAVING SAM THE OTHER NIGHT...
NO PROBLEM...BUT YOU DIDN'T ASK ME TO COME HERE JUST TO THANK ME, DID YOU.
Alma Mayer
LA FONTAINE TODAY
I WANT YOU TO FIND OUT WHO KILLED OTERO. I'M AFRAID SOMEONE MAY BE TAKING DRASTIC MEASURES, GETTING RID OF THE TWELVE APOSTLES THE FAST WAY.
I GET IT. LIKE SCORPIONS...
17

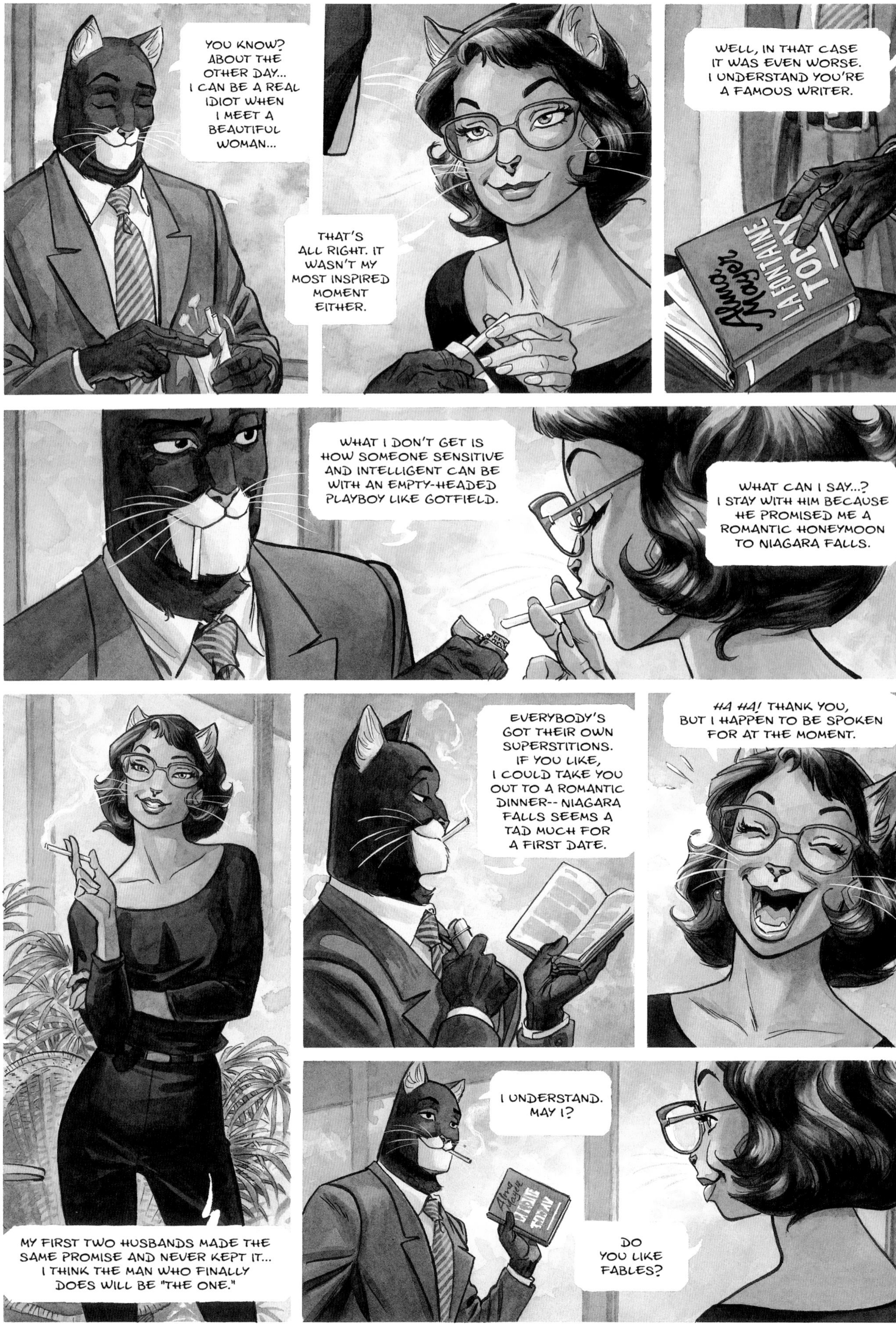
YOU KNOW? ABOUT THE OTHER DAY... I CAN BE A REAL IDIOT WHEN I MEET A BEAUTIFUL WOMAN...
THAT'S ALL RIGHT. IT WASN'T MY MOST INSPIRED MOMENT EITHER.
WELL, IN THAT CASE IT WAS EVEN WORSE. I UNDERSTAND YOU'RE A FAMOUS WRITER.
Alma Mayer LA FONTAINE TODAY
WHAT I DON'T GET IS HOW SOMEONE SENSITIVE AND INTELLIGENT CAN BE WITH AN EMPTY-HEADED PLAYBOY LIKE GOTFIELD.
WHAT CAN I SAY...? I STAY WITH HIM BECAUSE HE PROMISED ME A ROMANTIC HONEYMOON TO NIAGARA FALLS.
MY FIRST TWO HUSBANDS MADE THE SAME PROMISE AND NEVER KEPT IT... I THINK THE MAN WHO FINALLY DOES WILL BE "THE ONE."
EVERYBODY'S GOT THEIR OWN SUPERSTITIONS. IF YOU LIKE, I COULD TAKE YOU OUT TO A ROMANTIC DINNER-- NIAGARA FALLS SEEMS A TAD MUCH FOR A FIRST DATE.
HA HA! THANK YOU, BUT I HAPPEN TO BE SPOKEN FOR AT THE MOMENT.
I UNDERSTAND. MAY I?
DO YOU LIKE FABLES?
18

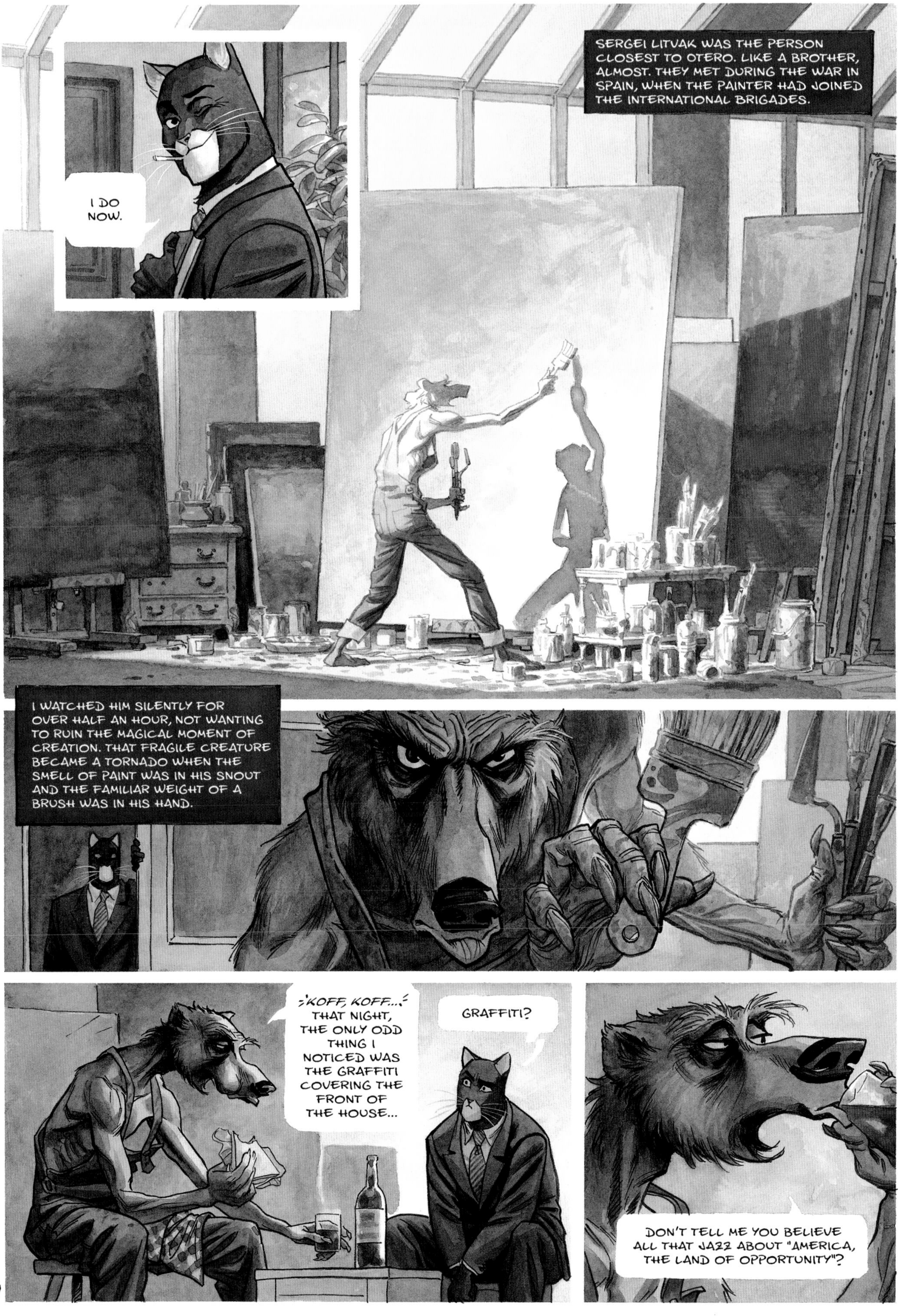
SERGEI LITVAK WAS THE PERSON CLOSEST TO OTERO. LIKE A BROTHER, ALMOST. THEY MET DURING THE WAR IN SPAIN, WHEN THE PAINTER HAD JOINED THE INTERNATIONAL BRIGADES.
I DO NOW.
I WATCHED HIM SILENTLY FOR OVER HALF AN HOUR, NOT WANTING TO RUIN THE MAGICAL MOMENT OF CREATION. THAT FRAGILE CREATURE BECAME A TORNADO WHEN THE SMELL OF PAINT WAS IN HIS SNOUT AND THE FAMILIAR WEIGHT OF A BRUSH WAS IN HIS HAND.
KOFF, KOFF... THAT NIGHT, THE ONLY ODD THING I NOTICED WAS THE GRAFFITI COVERING THE FRONT OF THE HOUSE...
GRAFFITI?
DON'T TELL ME YOU BELIEVE ALL THAT JAZZ ABOUT "AMERICA, THE LAND OF OPPORTUNITY"?
19

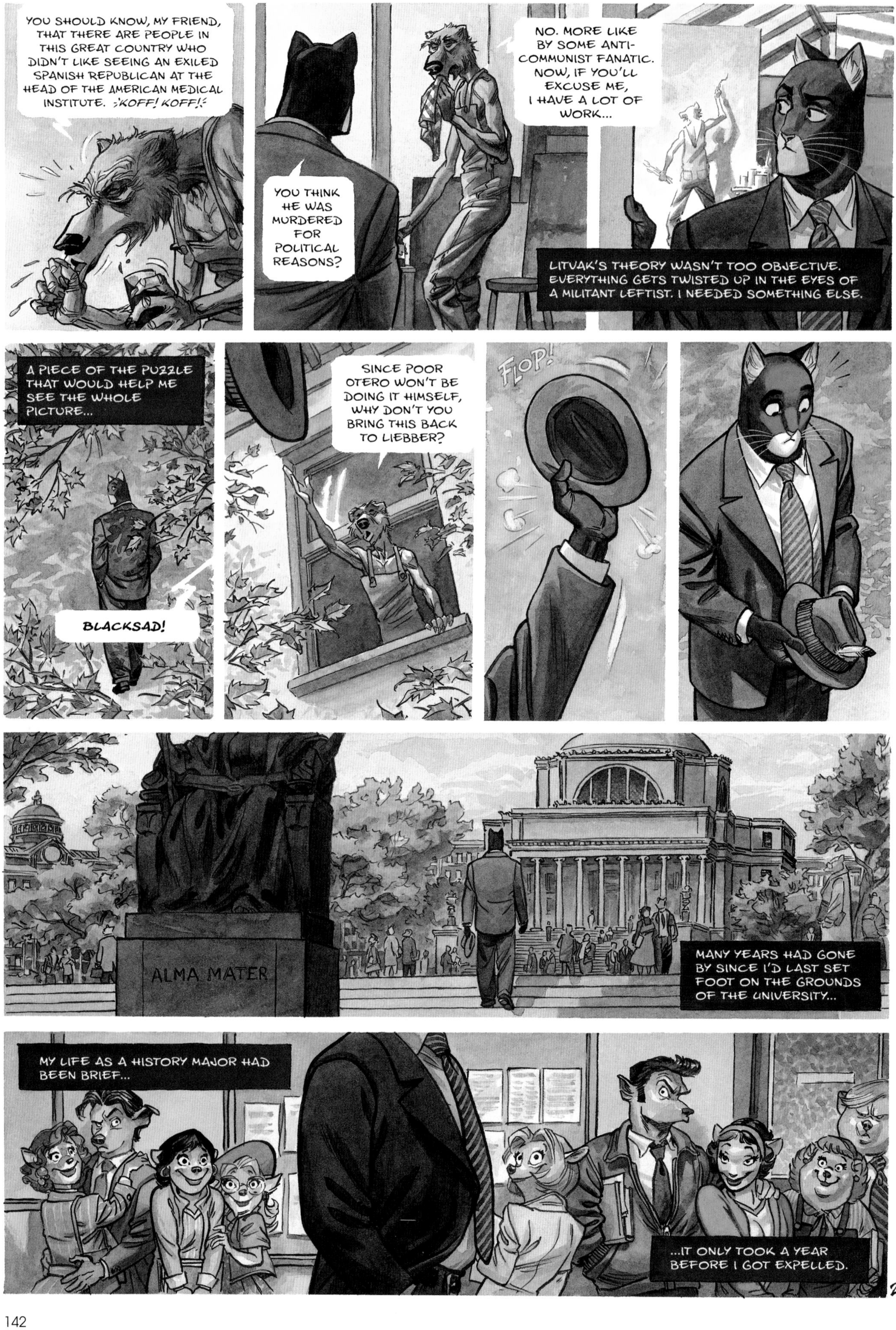

YOU SHOULD KNOW, MY FRIEND, THAT THERE ARE PEOPLE IN THIS GREAT COUNTRY WHO DIDN'T LIKE SEEING AN EXILED SPANISH REPUBLICAN AT THE HEAD OF THE AMERICAN MEDICAL INSTITUTE. ¡KOFF! KOFF!
YOU THINK HE WAS MURDERED FOR POLITICAL REASONS?
NO. MORE LIKE BY SOME ANTI-COMMUNIST FANATIC. NOW, IF YOU'LL EXCUSE ME, I HAVE A LOT OF WORK...
LITVAK'S THEORY WASN'T TOO OBJECTIVE. EVERYTHING GETS TWISTED UP IN THE EYES OF A MILITANT LEFTIST. I NEEDED SOMETHING ELSE.
A PIECE OF THE PUZZLE THAT WOULD HELP ME SEE THE WHOLE PICTURE...
BLACKSAD!
SINCE POOR OTERO WON'T BE DOING IT HIMSELF, WHY DON'T YOU BRING THIS BACK TO LIEBBER?
FLOP!
ALMA MATER
MANY YEARS HAD GONE BY SINCE I'D LAST SET FOOT ON THE GROUNDS OF THE UNIVERSITY...
MY LIFE AS A HISTORY MAJOR HAD BEEN BRIEF...
...IT ONLY TOOK A YEAR BEFORE I GOT EXPELLED.
20

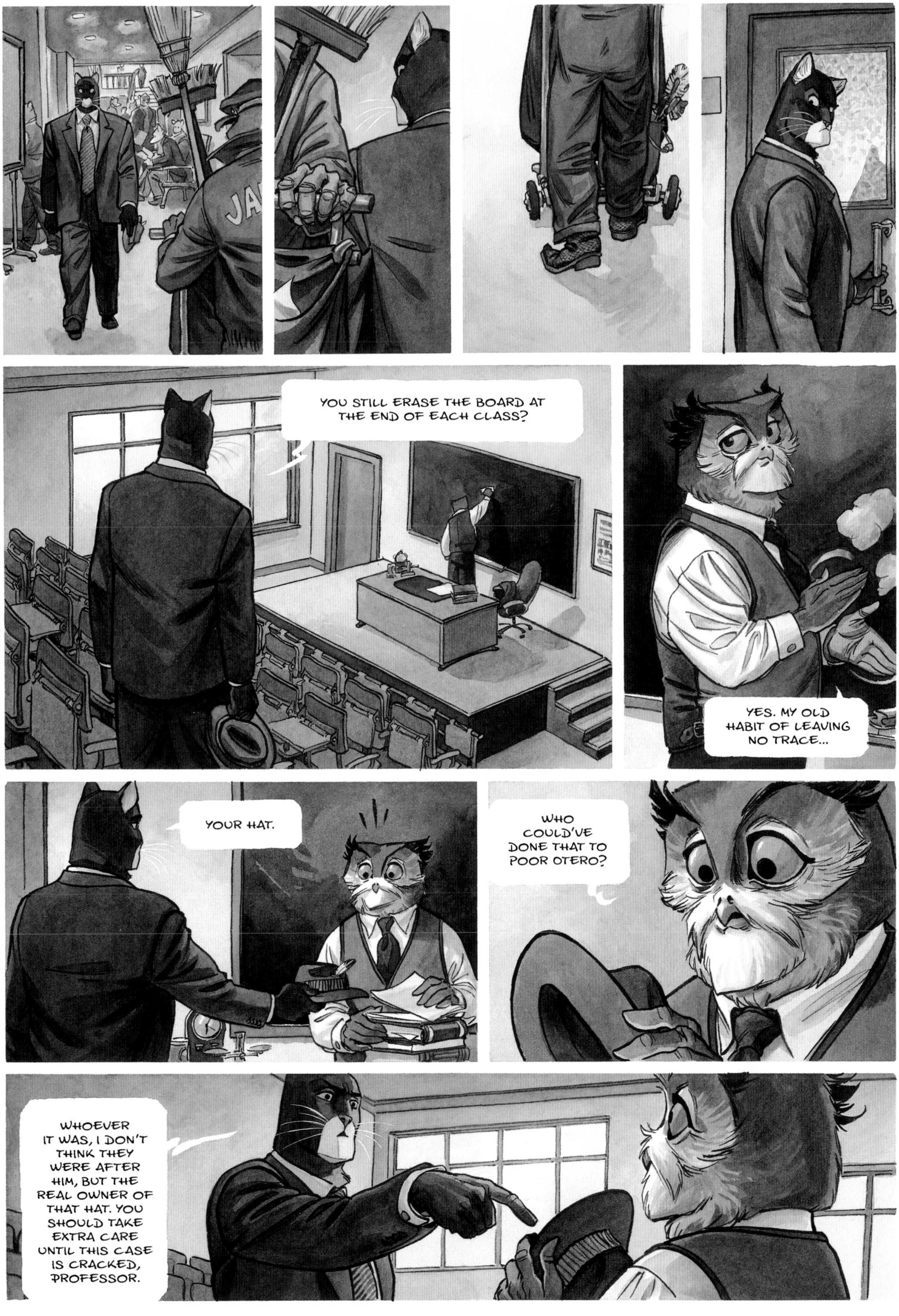
YOU STILL ERASE THE BOARD AT THE END OF EACH CLASS?
YES. MY OLD HABIT OF LEAVING NO TRACE...
YOUR HAT.
WHO COULD'VE DONE THAT TO POOR OTERO?
WHOEVER IT WAS, I DON'T THINK THEY WERE AFTER HIM, BUT THE REAL OWNER OF THAT HAT. YOU SHOULD TAKE EXTRA CARE UNTIL THIS CASE IS CRACKED, PROFESSOR.

21

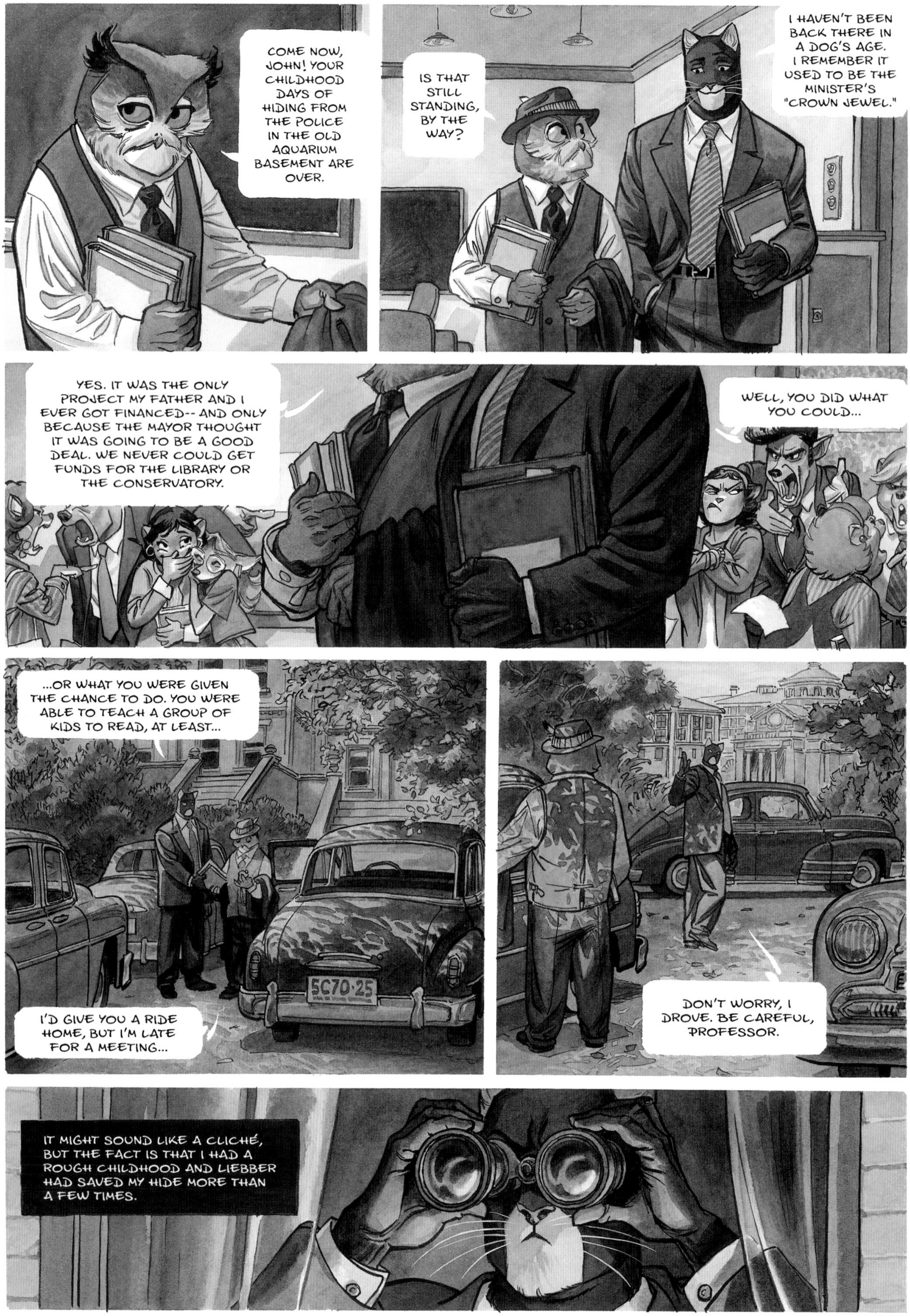

COME NOW, JOHN! YOUR CHILDHOOD DAYS OF HIDING FROM THE POLICE IN THE OLD AQUARIUM BASEMENT ARE OVER.
IS THAT STILL STANDING, BY THE WAY?
I HAVEN'T BEEN BACK THERE IN A DOG'S AGE. I REMEMBER IT USED TO BE THE MINISTER'S "CROWN JEWEL."
YES. IT WAS THE ONLY PROJECT MY FATHER AND I EVER GOT FINANCED-- AND ONLY BECAUSE THE MAYOR THOUGHT IT WAS GOING TO BE A GOOD DEAL. WE NEVER COULD GET FUNDS FOR THE LIBRARY OR THE CONSERVATORY.
WELL, YOU DID WHAT YOU COULD...
...OR WHAT YOU WERE GIVEN THE CHANCE TO DO. YOU WERE ABLE TO TEACH A GROUP OF KIDS TO READ, AT LEAST...
5C70·25
I'D GIVE YOU A RIDE HOME, BUT I'M LATE FOR A MEETING...
DON'T WORRY, I DROVE. BE CAREFUL, PROFESSOR.
IT MIGHT SOUND LIKE A CLICHÉ, BUT THE FACT IS THAT I HAD A ROUGH CHILDHOOD AND LIEBBER HAD SAVED MY HIDE MORE THAN A FEW TIMES.
22

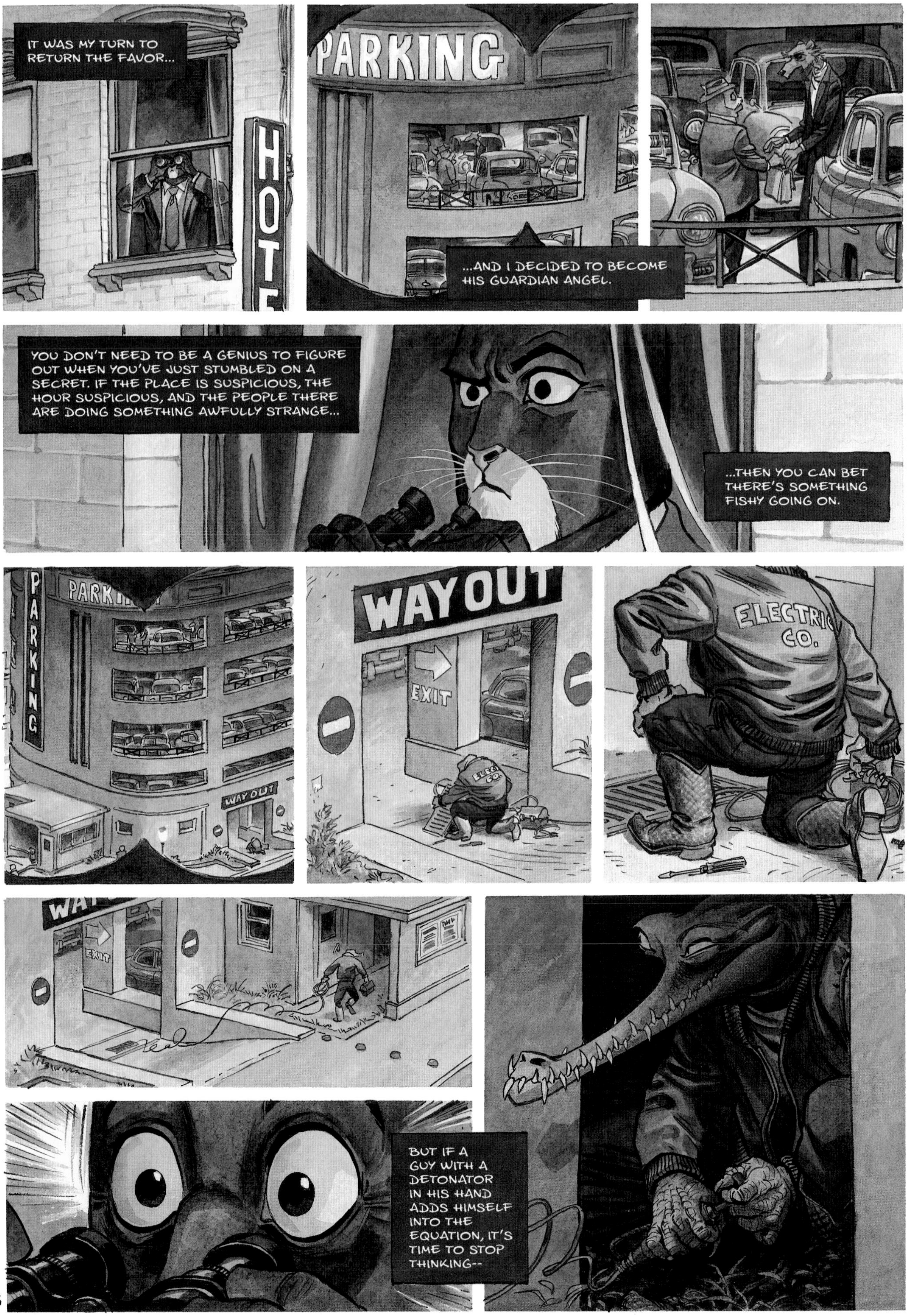
IT WAS MY TURN TO RETURN THE FAVOR...
PARKING
HOTE
...AND I DECIDED TO BECOME HIS GUARDIAN ANGEL.
YOU DON'T NEED TO BE A GENIUS TO FIGURE OUT WHEN YOU'VE JUST STUMBLED ON A SECRET. IF THE PLACE IS SUSPICIOUS, THE HOUR SUSPICIOUS, AND THE PEOPLE THERE ARE DOING SOMETHING AWFULLY STRANGE...
...THEN YOU CAN BET THERE'S SOMETHING FISHY GOING ON.
PARKING
WAY OUT
WAY OUT
EXIT
ELECTRIC CO.
EXIT
BUT IF A GUY WITH A DETONATOR IN HIS HAND ADDS HIMSELF INTO THE EQUATION, IT'S TIME TO STOP THINKING--
23

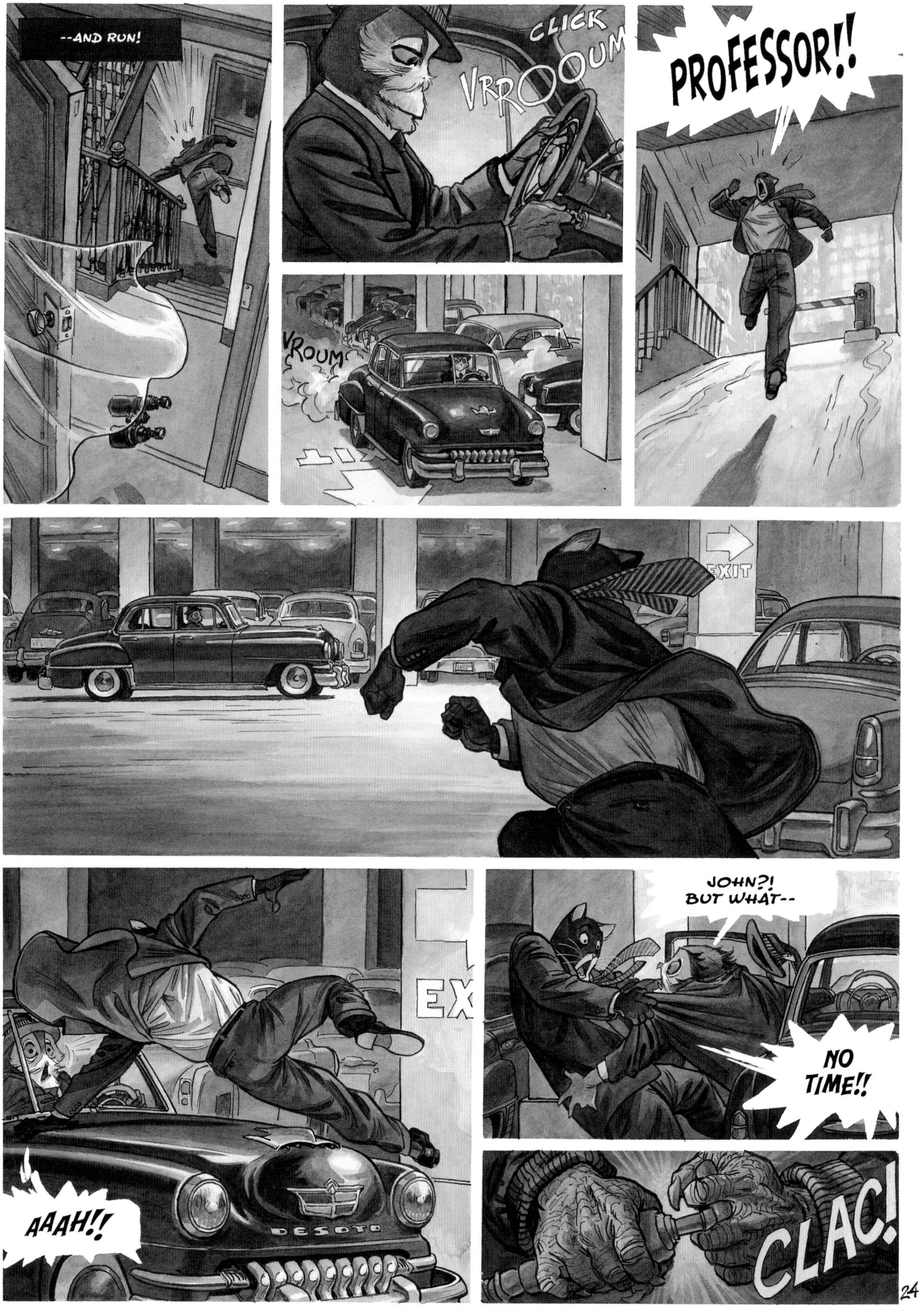
--AND RUN!
CLICK
VRROOUM
VROUM
PROFESSOR!!
EXIT
EX
AAAH!!
DESOTO
JOHN?! BUT WHAT--
NO TIME!!
CLAC!
24

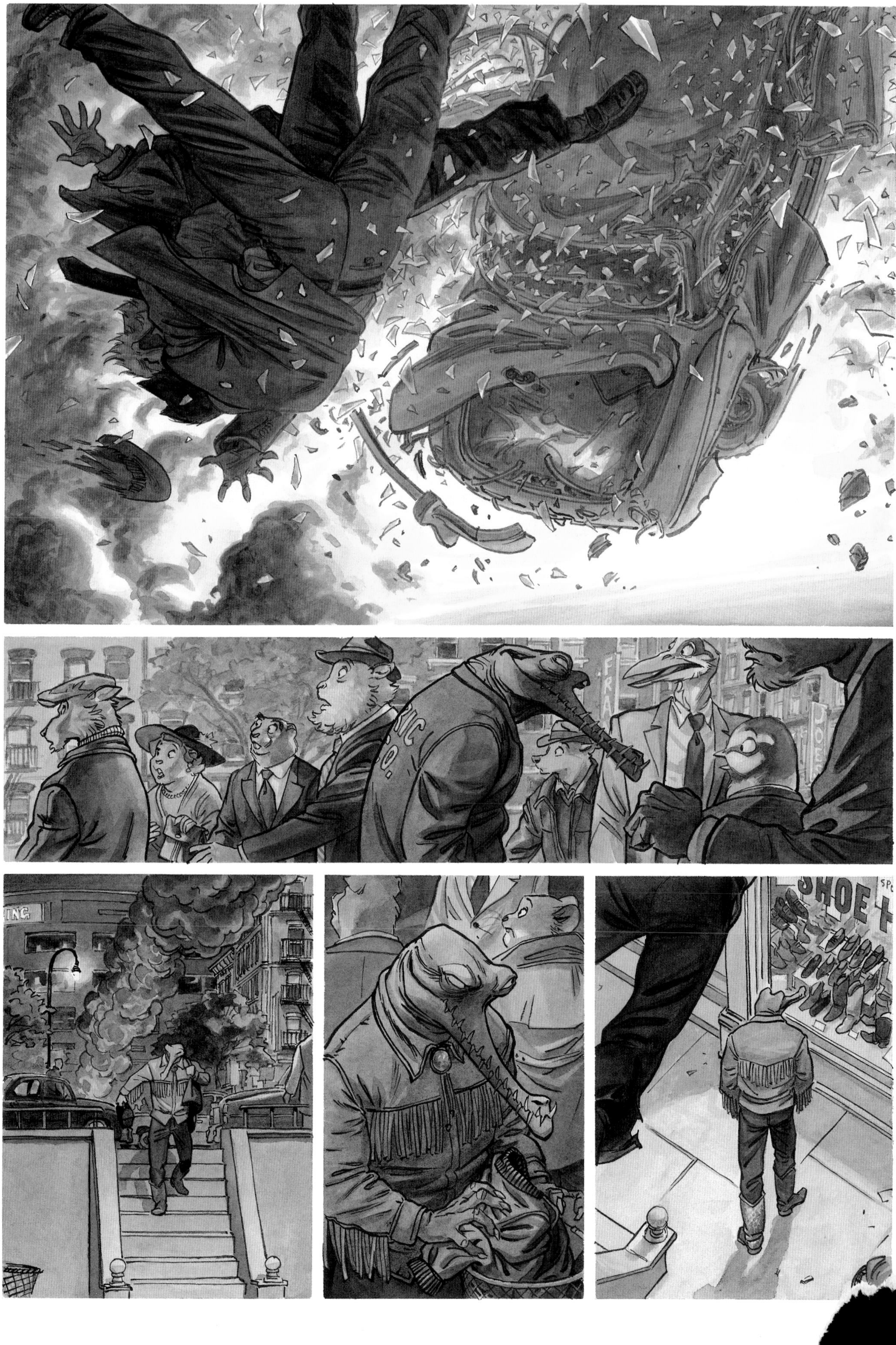
SHOE

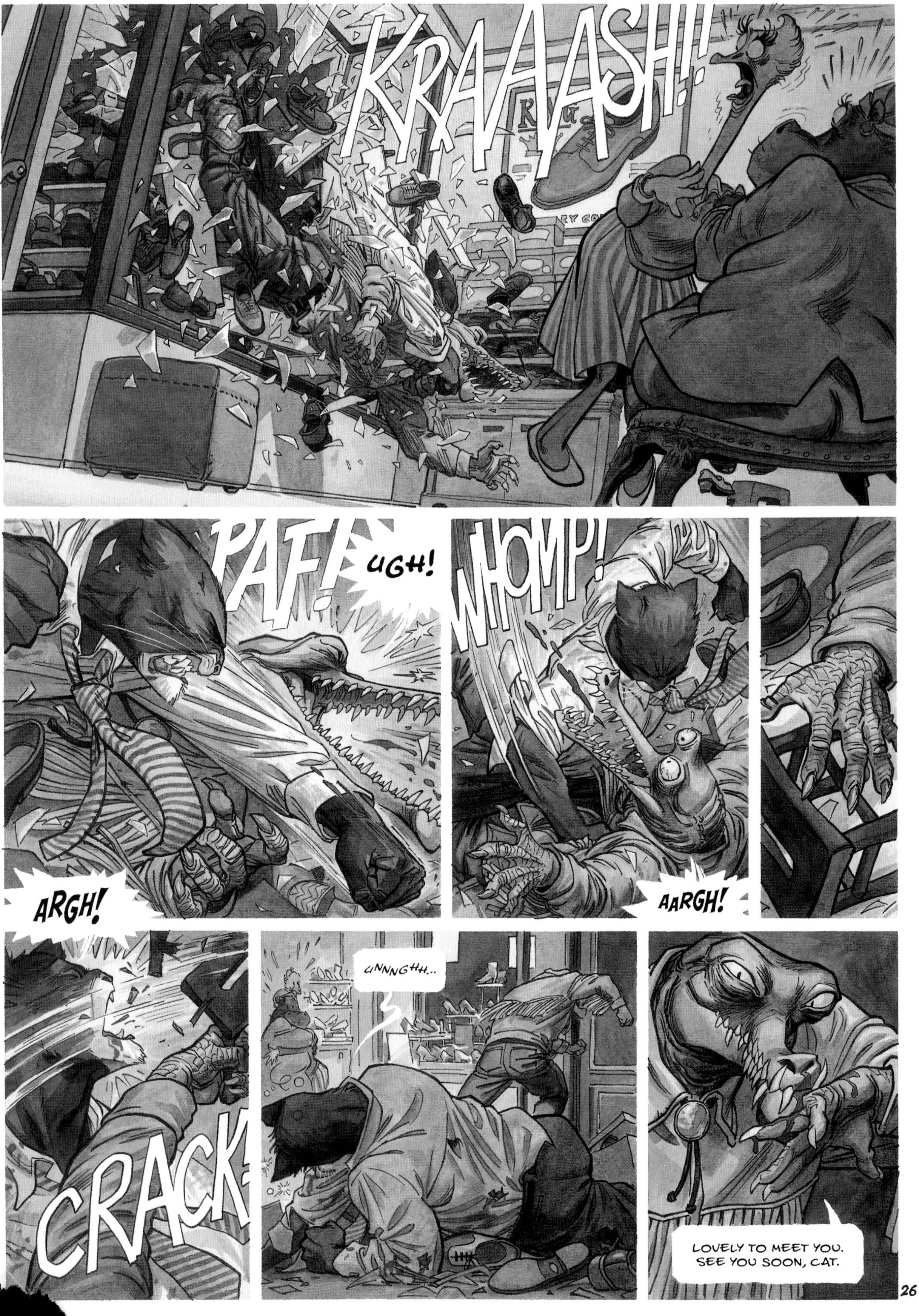
KRAAASH!!
PAF!
UGH!
ARGH!
WHOMP!
AARGH!
CRACK!
UNNNGHH...
LOVELY TO MEET YOU. SEE YOU SOON, CAT.

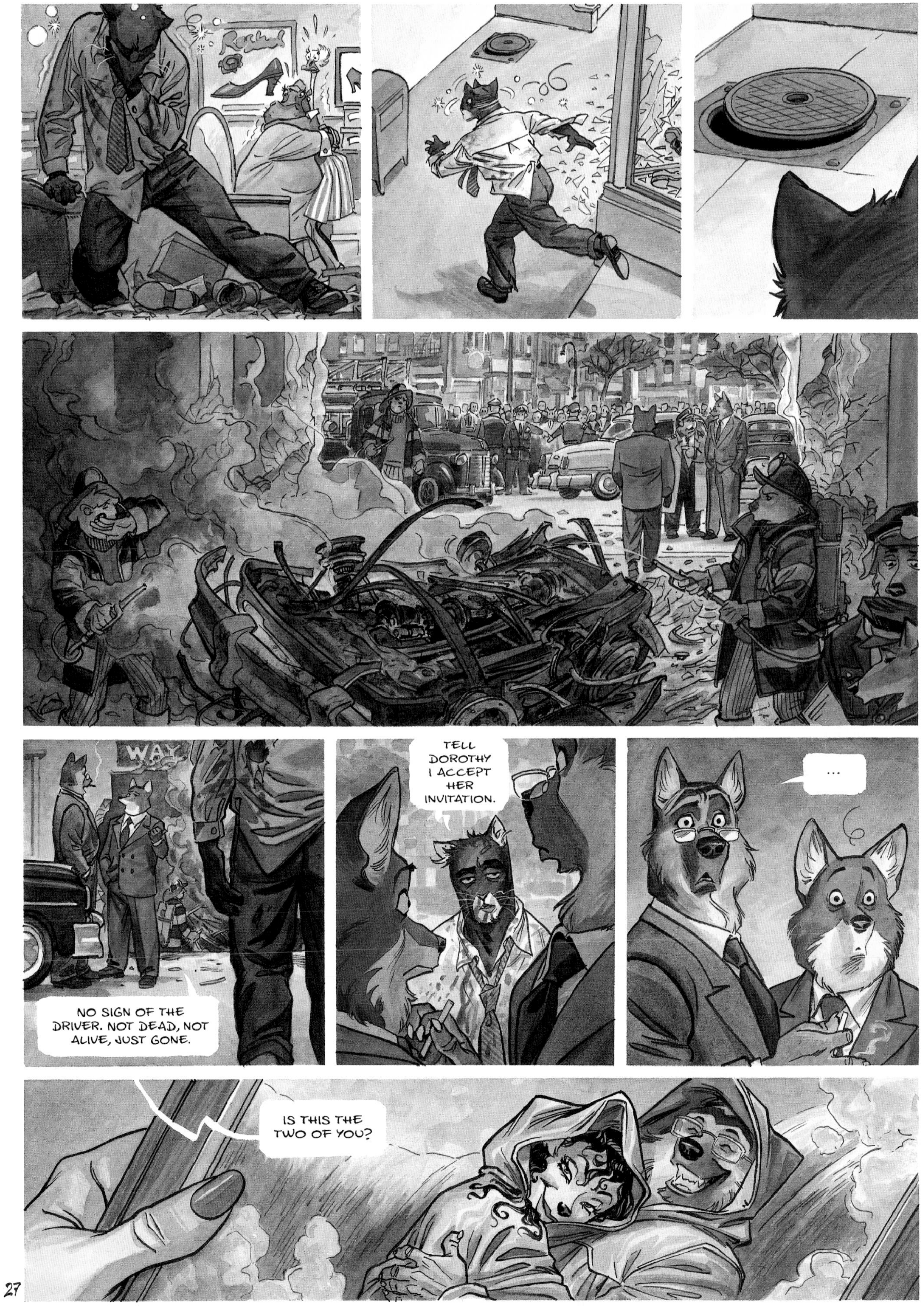
WAY
NO SIGN OF THE DRIVER. NOT DEAD, NOT ALIVE, JUST GONE.
TELL DOROTHY I ACCEPT HER INVITATION.
...
IS THIS THE TWO OF YOU?
27

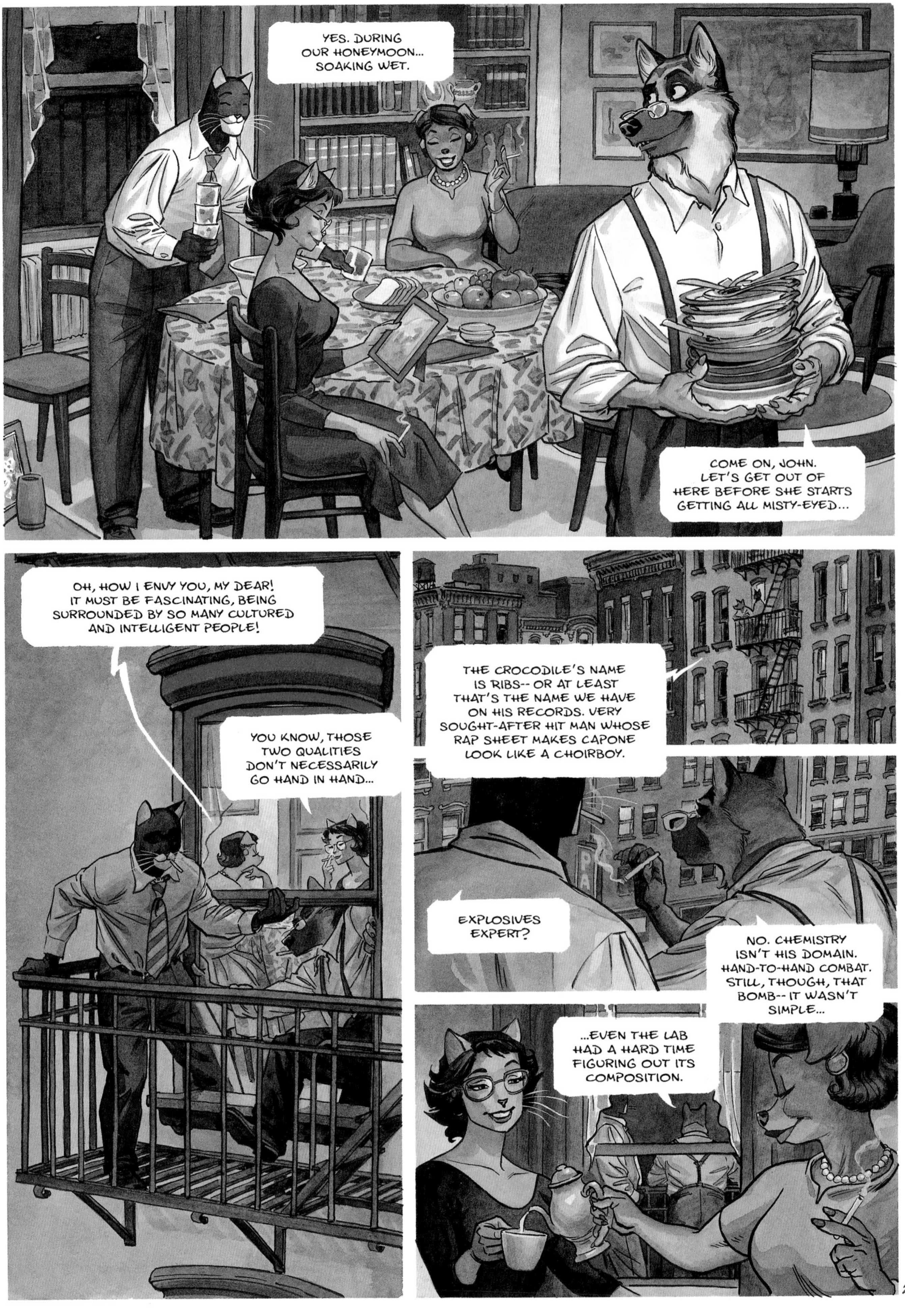
YES. DURING OUR HONEYMOON... SOAKING WET.
COME ON, JOHN. LET'S GET OUT OF HERE BEFORE SHE STARTS GETTING ALL MISTY-EYED...
OH, HOW I ENVY YOU, MY DEAR! IT MUST BE FASCINATING, BEING SURROUNDED BY SO MANY CULTURED AND INTELLIGENT PEOPLE!
YOU KNOW, THOSE TWO QUALITIES DON'T NECESSARILY GO HAND IN HAND...
THE CROCODILE'S NAME IS RIBS-- OR AT LEAST THAT'S THE NAME WE HAVE ON HIS RECORDS. VERY SOUGHT-AFTER HIT MAN WHOSE RAP SHEET MAKES CAPONE LOOK LIKE A CHOIRBOY.
EXPLOSIVES EXPERT?
NO. CHEMISTRY ISN'T HIS DOMAIN. HAND-TO-HAND COMBAT. STILL, THOUGH, THAT BOMB-- IT WASN'T SIMPLE...
...EVEN THE LAB HAD A HARD TIME FIGURING OUT ITS COMPOSITION.
28

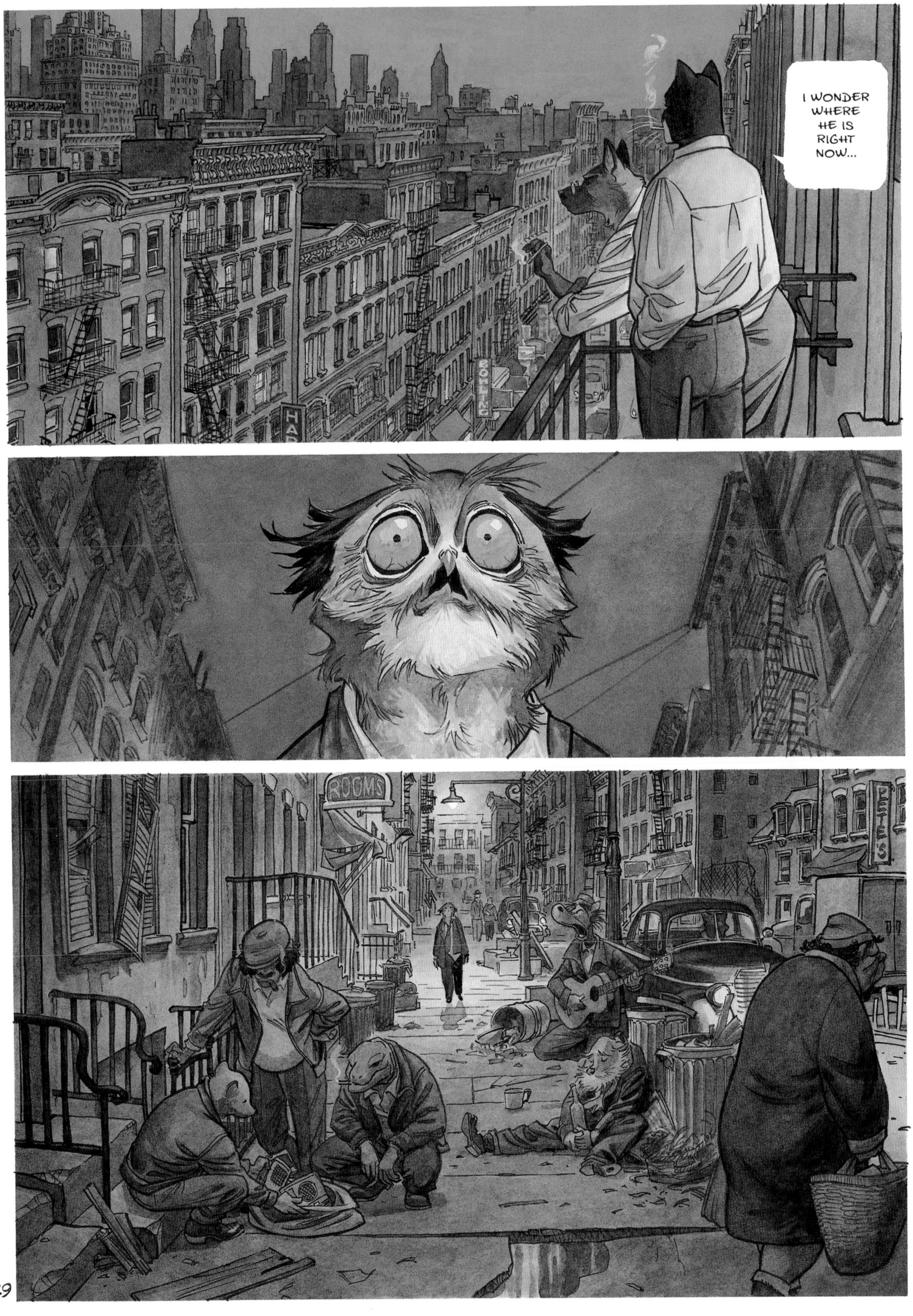
I WONDER WHERE HE IS RIGHT NOW...
ROOMS
PETE'S

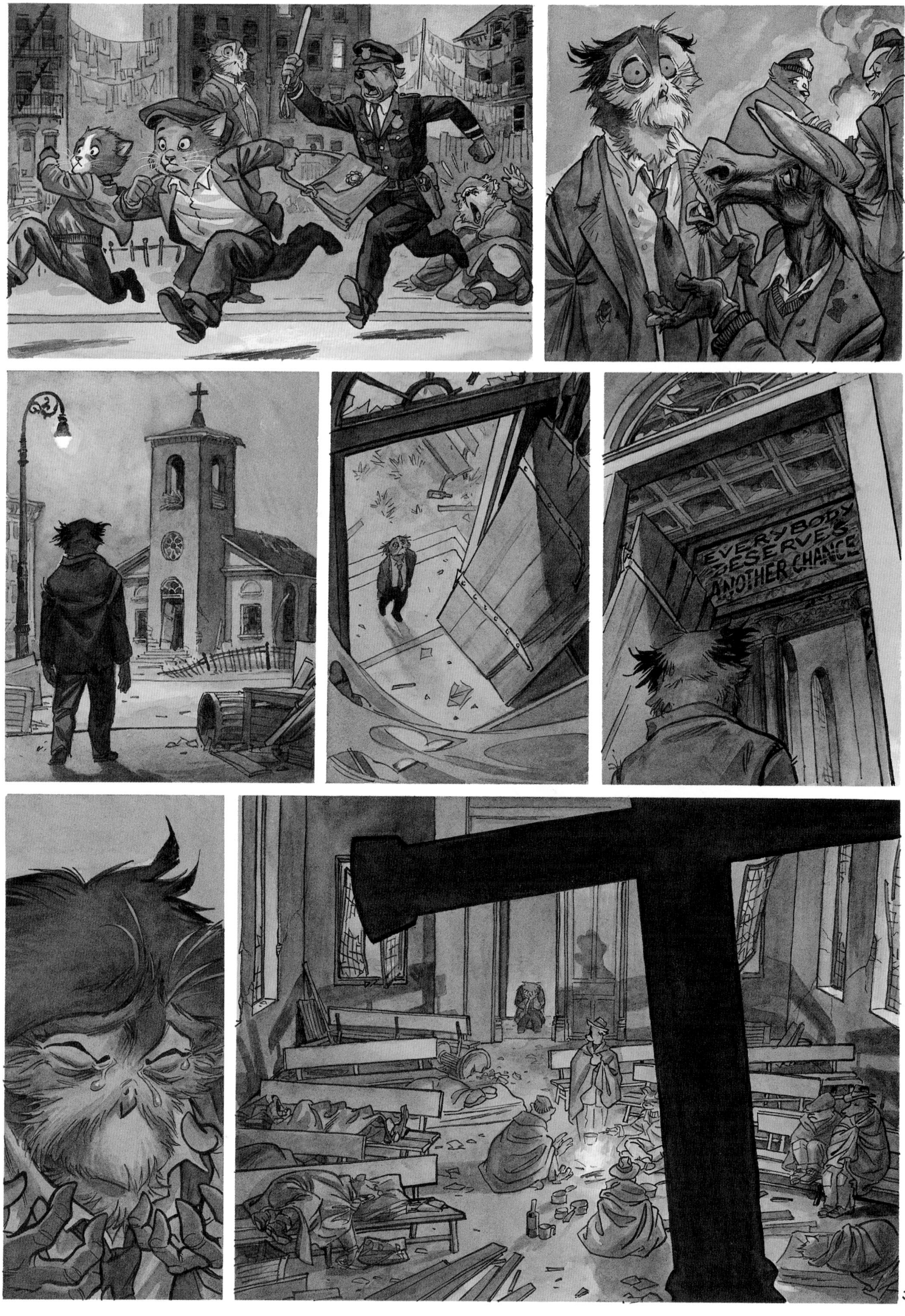
EVERYBODY DESERVES ANOTHER CHANCE
30

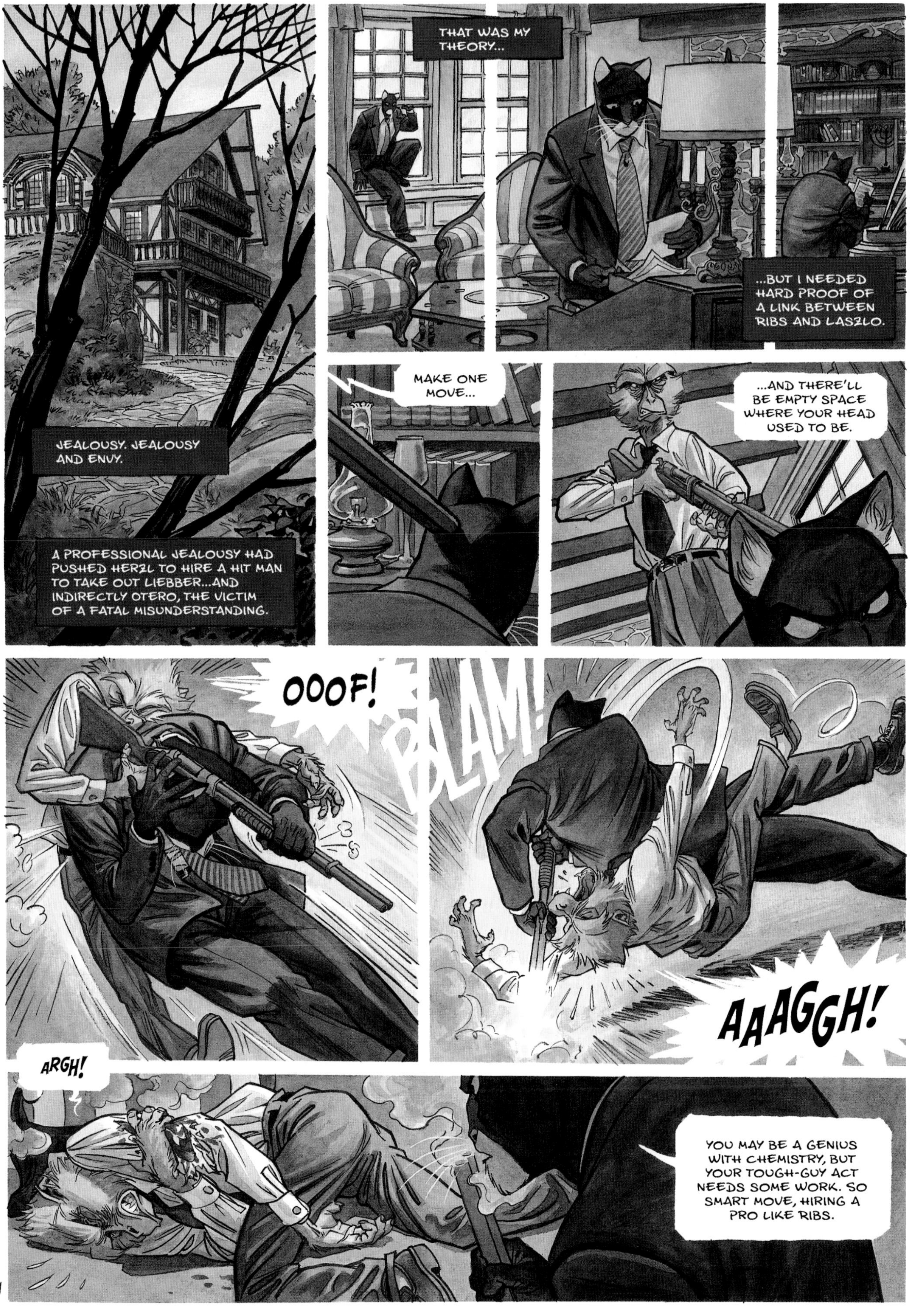
JEALOUSY. JEALOUSY AND ENVY.
A PROFESSIONAL JEALOUSY HAD PUSHED HERZL TO HIRE A HIT MAN TO TAKE OUT LIEBBER...AND INDIRECTLY OTERO, THE VICTIM OF A FATAL MISUNDERSTANDING.
THAT WAS MY THEORY...
...BUT I NEEDED HARD PROOF OF A LINK BETWEEN RIBS AND LASZLO.
MAKE ONE MOVE...
...AND THERE'LL BE EMPTY SPACE WHERE YOUR HEAD USED TO BE.
OOOF!
BLAM!
AAAGGH!
ARGH!
YOU MAY BE A GENIUS WITH CHEMISTRY, BUT YOUR TOUGH-GUY ACT NEEDS SOME WORK. SO SMART MOVE, HIRING A PRO LIKE RIBS.
31

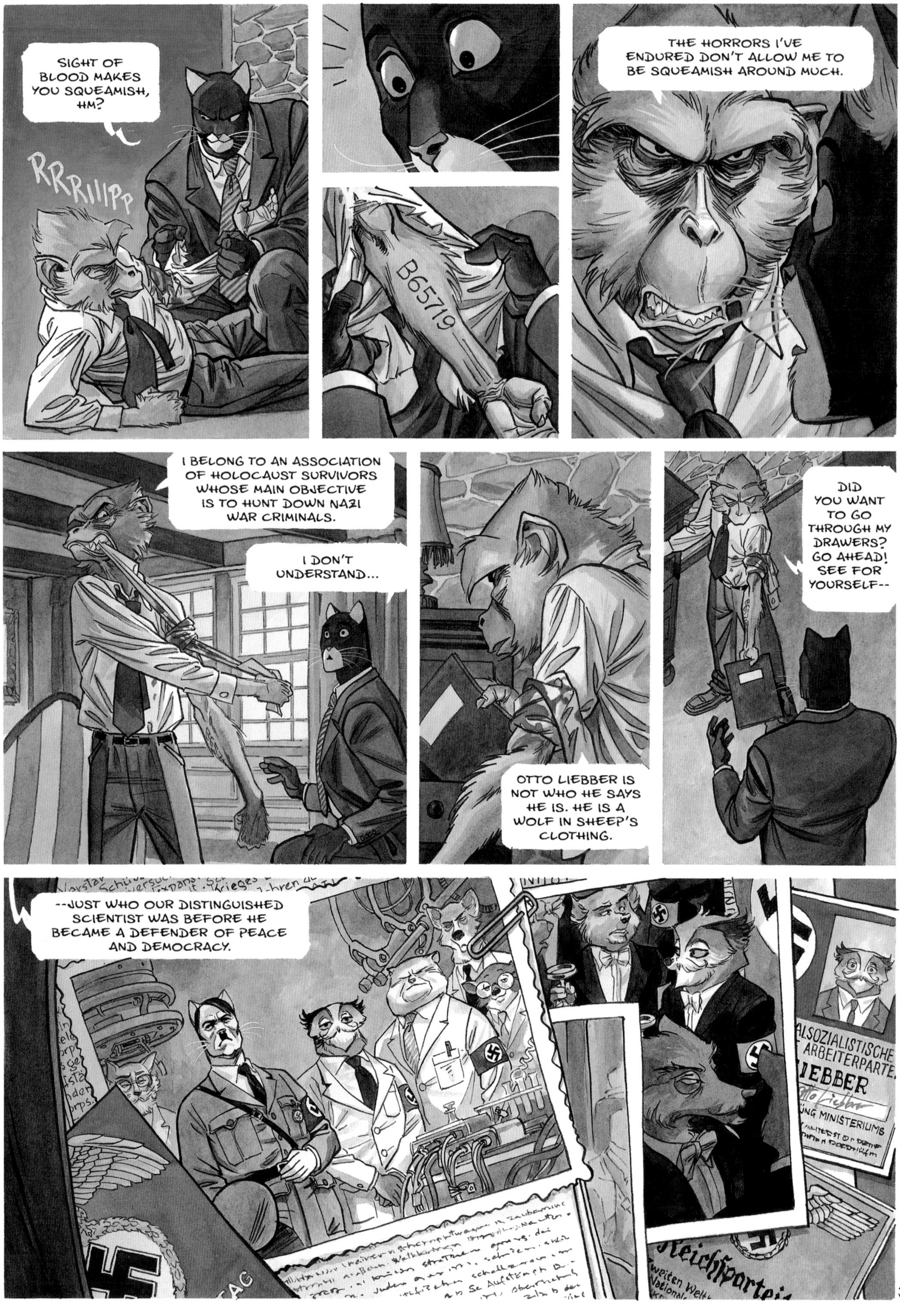
SIGHT OF BLOOD MAKES YOU SQUEAMISH, HM?
RRRIIIPP
B65719
THE HORRORS I'VE ENDURED DON'T ALLOW ME TO BE SQUEAMISH AROUND MUCH.
I BELONG TO AN ASSOCIATION OF HOLOCAUST SURVIVORS WHOSE MAIN OBJECTIVE IS TO HUNT DOWN NAZI WAR CRIMINALS.
I DON'T UNDERSTAND...
OTTO LIEBBER IS NOT WHO HE SAYS HE IS. HE IS A WOLF IN SHEEP'S CLOTHING.
DID YOU WANT TO GO THROUGH MY DRAWERS? GO AHEAD! SEE FOR YOURSELF--
--JUST WHO OUR DISTINGUISHED SCIENTIST WAS BEFORE HE BECAME A DEFENDER OF PEACE AND DEMOCRACY.
ALSOZIALISTISCHE ARBEITERPARTE
LIEBBER
UNG MINISTERIUMS
Reichspartei
32

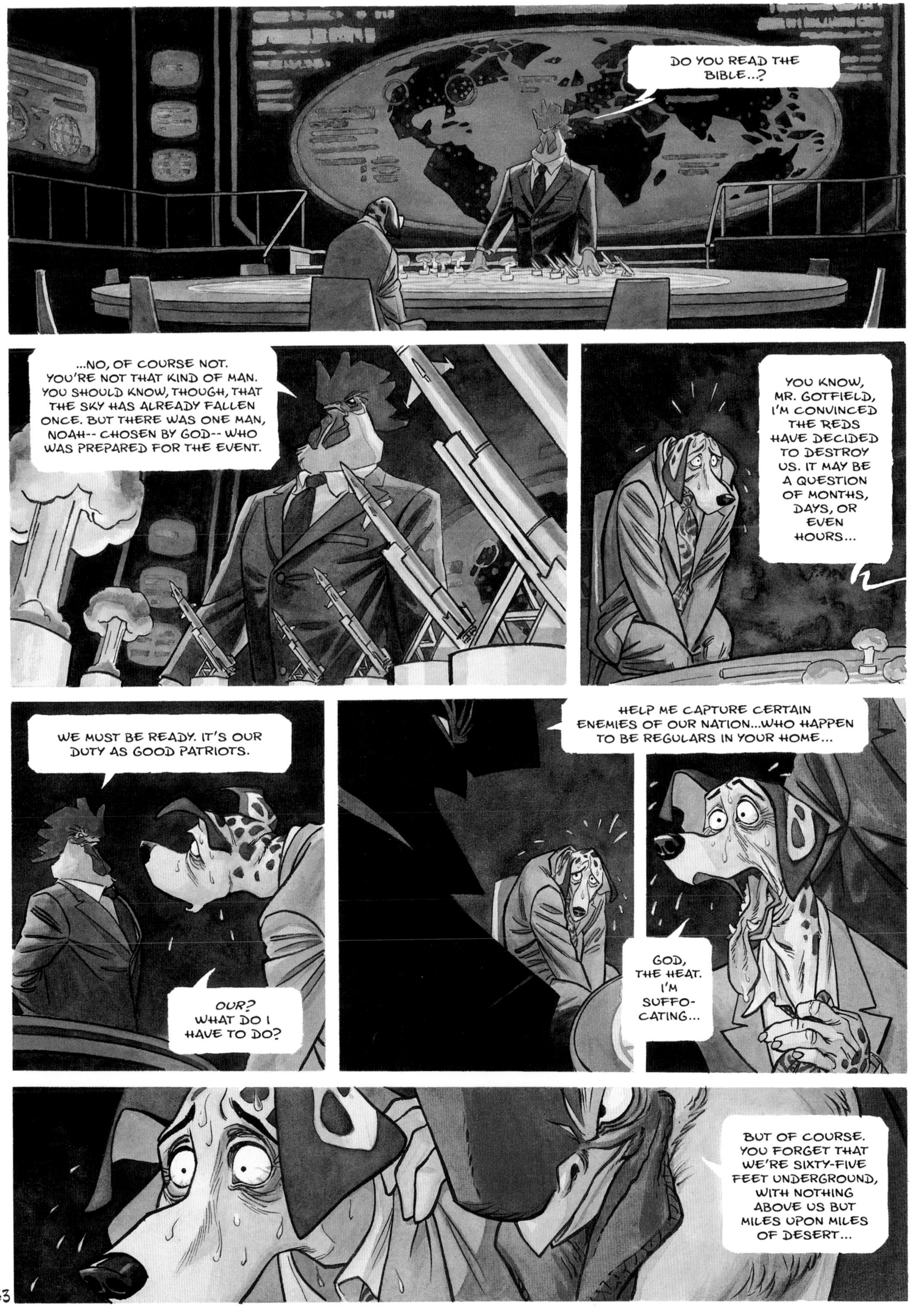
DO YOU READ THE BIBLE...?
...NO, OF COURSE NOT. YOU'RE NOT THAT KIND OF MAN. YOU SHOULD KNOW, THOUGH, THAT THE SKY HAS ALREADY FALLEN ONCE. BUT THERE WAS ONE MAN, NOAH-- CHOSEN BY GOD-- WHO WAS PREPARED FOR THE EVENT.
YOU KNOW, MR. GOTFIELD, I'M CONVINCED THE REDS HAVE DECIDED TO DESTROY US. IT MAY BE A QUESTION OF MONTHS, DAYS, OR EVEN HOURS...
WE MUST BE READY. IT'S OUR DUTY AS GOOD PATRIOTS.
OUR? WHAT DO I HAVE TO DO?
HELP ME CAPTURE CERTAIN ENEMIES OF OUR NATION...WHO HAPPEN TO BE REGULARS IN YOUR HOME...
GOD, THE HEAT. I'M SUFFOCATING...
BUT OF COURSE. YOU FORGET THAT WE'RE SIXTY-FIVE FEET UNDERGROUND, WITH NOTHING ABOVE US BUT MILES UPON MILES OF DESERT...
33

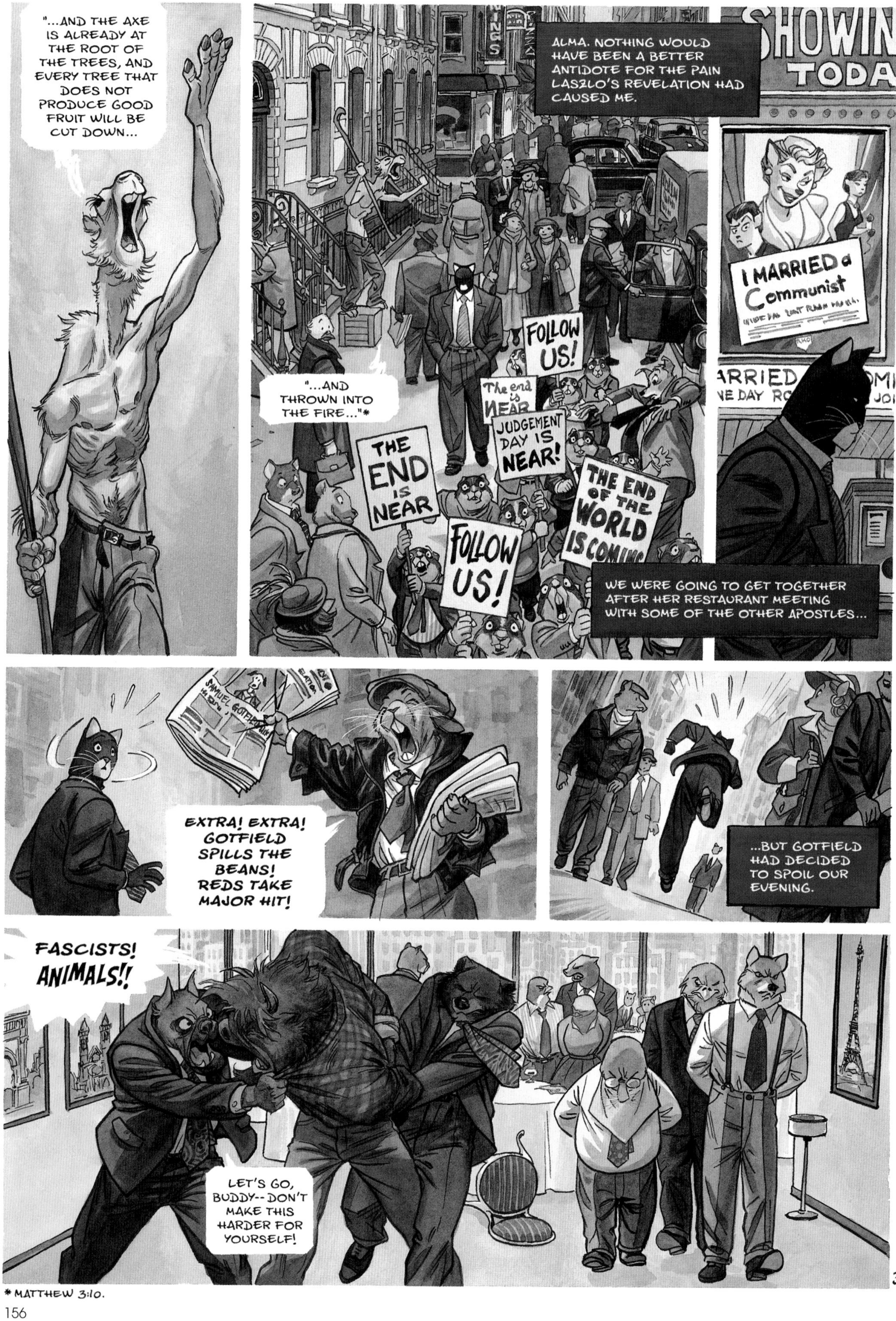
"...AND THE AXE IS ALREADY AT THE ROOT OF THE TREES, AND EVERY TREE THAT DOES NOT PRODUCE GOOD FRUIT WILL BE CUT DOWN...
ALMA. NOTHING WOULD HAVE BEEN A BETTER ANTIDOTE FOR THE PAIN LASZLO'S REVELATION HAD CAUSED ME.
SHOWIN
TODA
I MARRIED a Communist
ARRIED
"...AND THROWN INTO THE FIRE..."*
FOLLOW US!
The end is NEAR
JUDGEMENT DAY IS NEAR!
THE END IS NEAR
THE END OF THE WORLD IS COMING
FOLLOW US!
WE WERE GOING TO GET TOGETHER AFTER HER RESTAURANT MEETING WITH SOME OF THE OTHER APOSTLES...
EXTRA! EXTRA! GOTFIELD SPILLS THE BEANS! REDS TAKE MAJOR HIT!
...BUT GOTFIELD HAD DECIDED TO SPOIL OUR EVENING.
FASCISTS! ANIMALS!!
LET'S GO, BUDDY-- DON'T MAKE THIS HARDER FOR YOURSELF!
34

* MATTHEW 3:10.

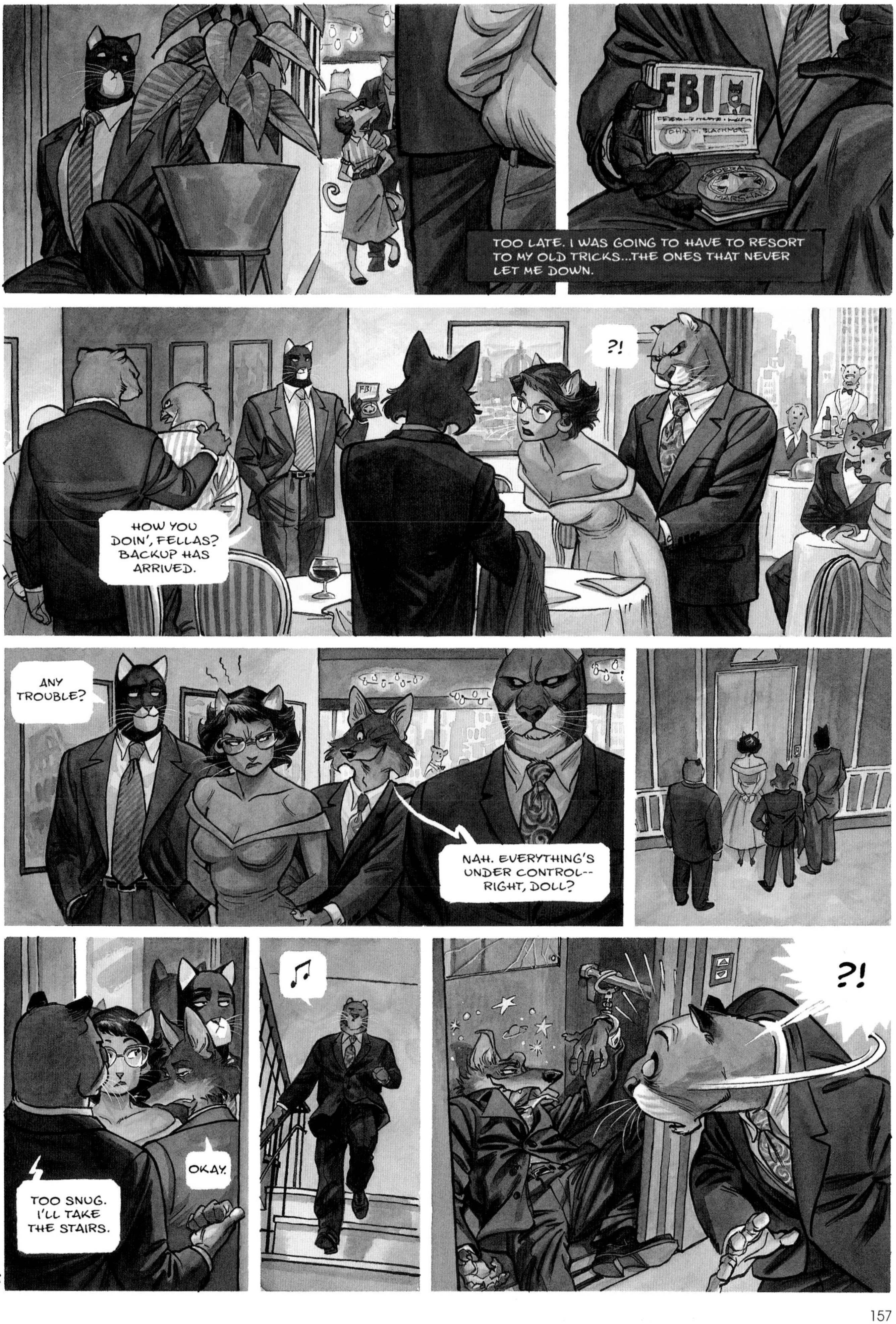
FBI
JOHN H. BLACKMORE
FEDERAL MARSHAL
TOO LATE. I WAS GOING TO HAVE TO RESORT TO MY OLD TRICKS...THE ONES THAT NEVER LET ME DOWN.
?!
HOW YOU DOIN', FELLAS? BACKUP HAS ARRIVED.
ANY TROUBLE?
NAH. EVERYTHING'S UNDER CONTROL--RIGHT, DOLL?
TOO SNUG. I'LL TAKE THE STAIRS.
OKAY.
♪
?!
35

GAAH! THE DEVIL--?!

SHHH! NOT A PEEP, WEEKLY!

WHOA! WHAT'S THIS? TROUBLE WITH A SCORNED HUSBAND, HUH?! I SEE YOU'RE MAKIN' YOUR JOB A LITTLE MORE "PERSONAL"...

SHUT YOUR DIRTY MOUTH. I NEED TO HIDE HER HERE FOR A FEW DAYS. WE'VE GOT THE FBI ON OUR TRAIL...

MMFF!

THE FBI?! BLACKSAD...WHY ARE YOU DOING THIS TO ME?

TAKE IT EASY-- IT'LL BE FINE. WEREN'T YOU ON YOUR WAY OUT?

YEAH, BUT... UH...

UHM...

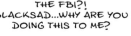

OFF YOU GO. HAVE A GOOD DAY-- I OWE YOU ONE!

36

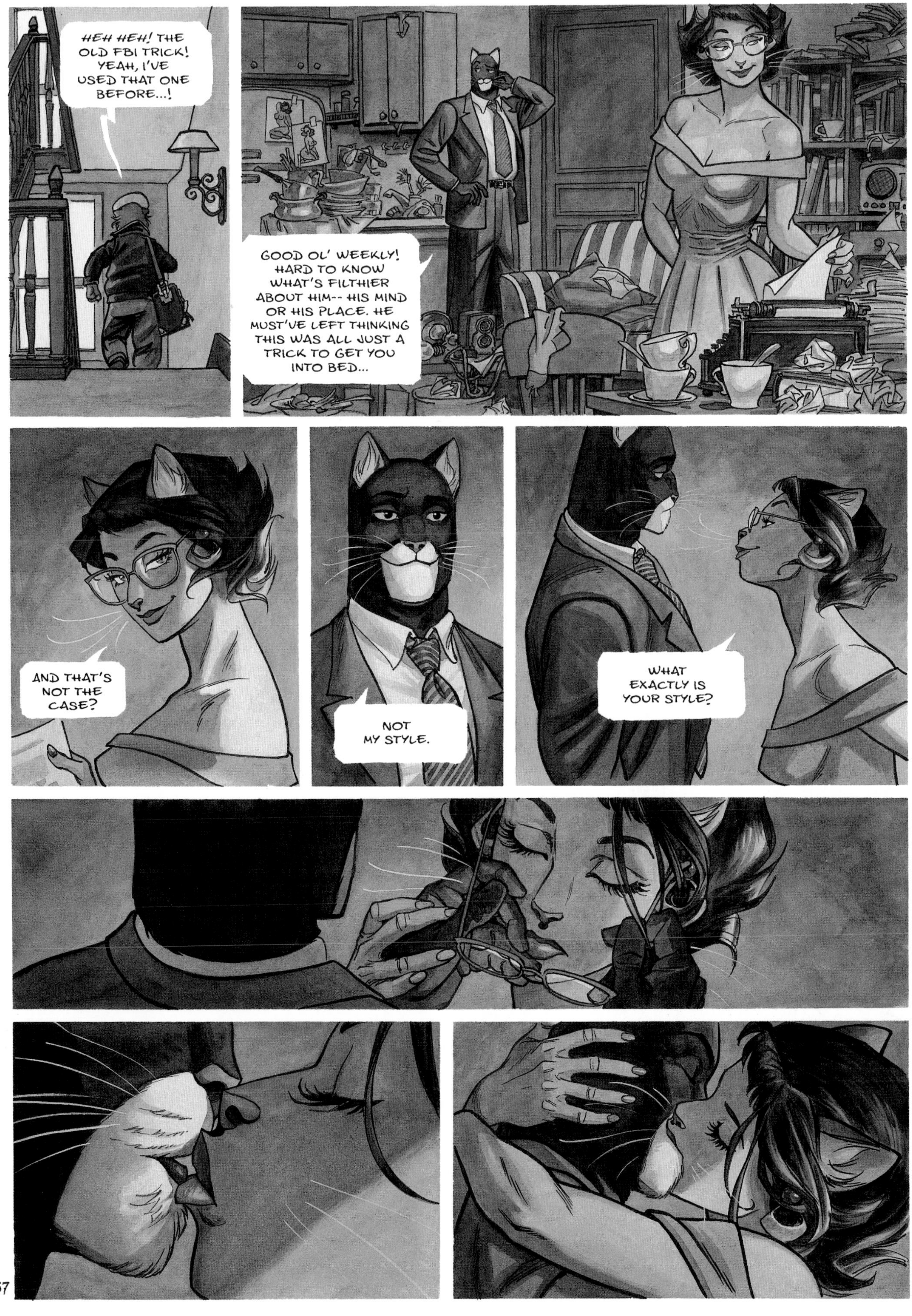
HEH HEH! THE OLD FBI TRICK! YEAH, I'VE USED THAT ONE BEFORE...!
GOOD OL' WEEKLY! HARD TO KNOW WHAT'S FILTHIER ABOUT HIM-- HIS MIND OR HIS PLACE. HE MUST'VE LEFT THINKING THIS WAS ALL JUST A TRICK TO GET YOU INTO BED...
AND THAT'S NOT THE CASE?
NOT MY STYLE.
WHAT EXACTLY IS YOUR STYLE?

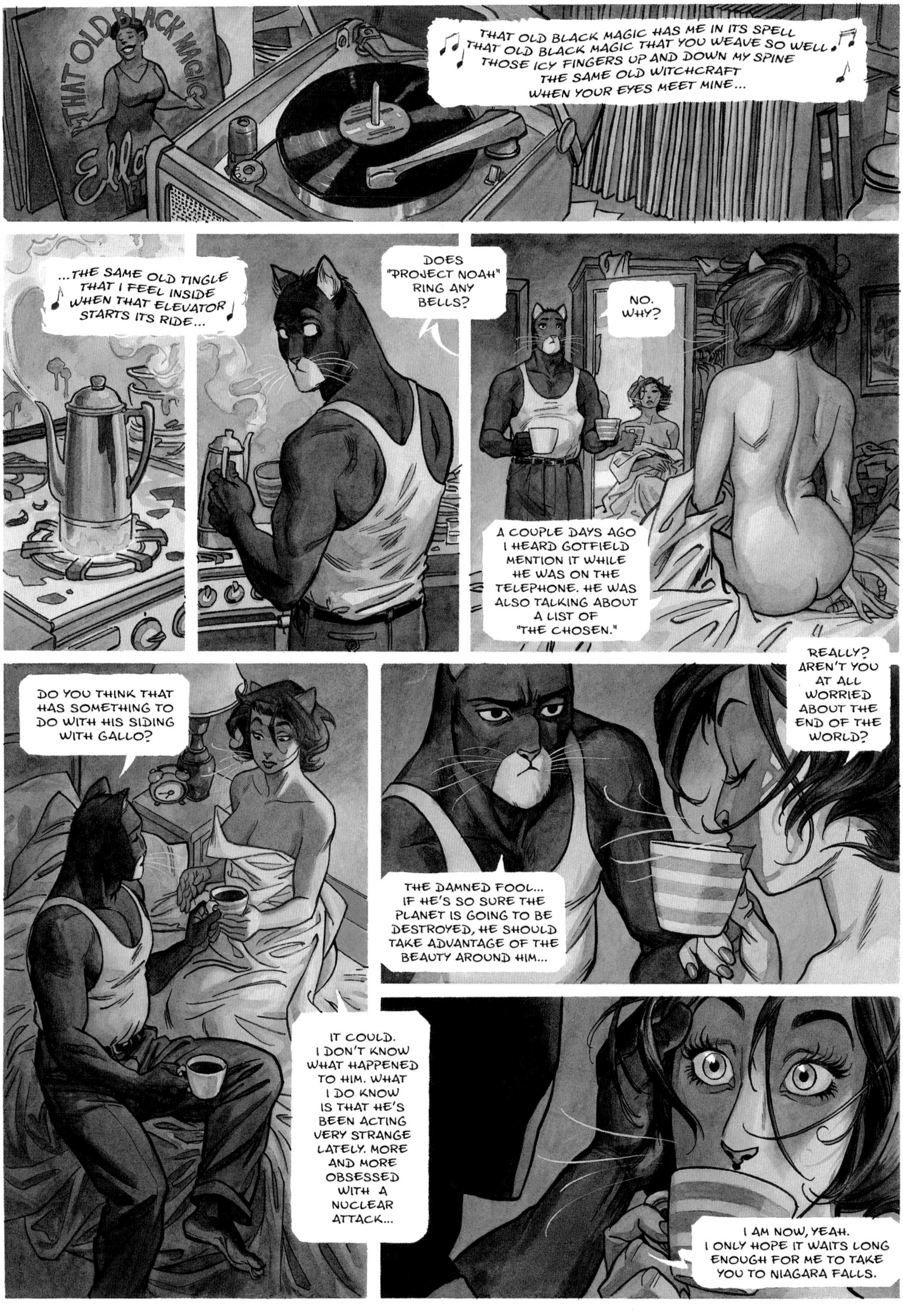
THAT OLD BLACK MAGIC
Ella
THAT OLD BLACK MAGIC HAS ME IN ITS SPELL THAT OLD BLACK MAGIC THAT YOU WEAVE SO WELL THOSE ICY FINGERS UP AND DOWN MY SPINE THE SAME OLD WITCHCRAFT WHEN YOUR EYES MEET MINE...
...THE SAME OLD TINGLE THAT I FEEL INSIDE WHEN THAT ELEVATOR STARTS ITS RIDE...
DOES "PROJECT NOAH" RING ANY BELLS?
NO. WHY?
A COUPLE DAYS AGO I HEARD GOTFIELD MENTION IT WHILE HE WAS ON THE TELEPHONE. HE WAS ALSO TALKING ABOUT A LIST OF "THE CHOSEN."
DO YOU THINK THAT HAS SOMETHING TO DO WITH HIS SIDING WITH GALLO?
IT COULD. I DON'T KNOW WHAT HAPPENED TO HIM. WHAT I DO KNOW IS THAT HE'S BEEN ACTING VERY STRANGE LATELY. MORE AND MORE OBSESSED WITH A NUCLEAR ATTACK...
THE DAMNED FOOL... IF HE'S SO SURE THE PLANET IS GOING TO BE DESTROYED, HE SHOULD TAKE ADVANTAGE OF THE BEAUTY AROUND HIM...
REALLY? AREN'T YOU AT ALL WORRIED ABOUT THE END OF THE WORLD?
I AM NOW, YEAH. I ONLY HOPE IT WAITS LONG ENOUGH FOR ME TO TAKE YOU TO NIAGARA FALLS.
38

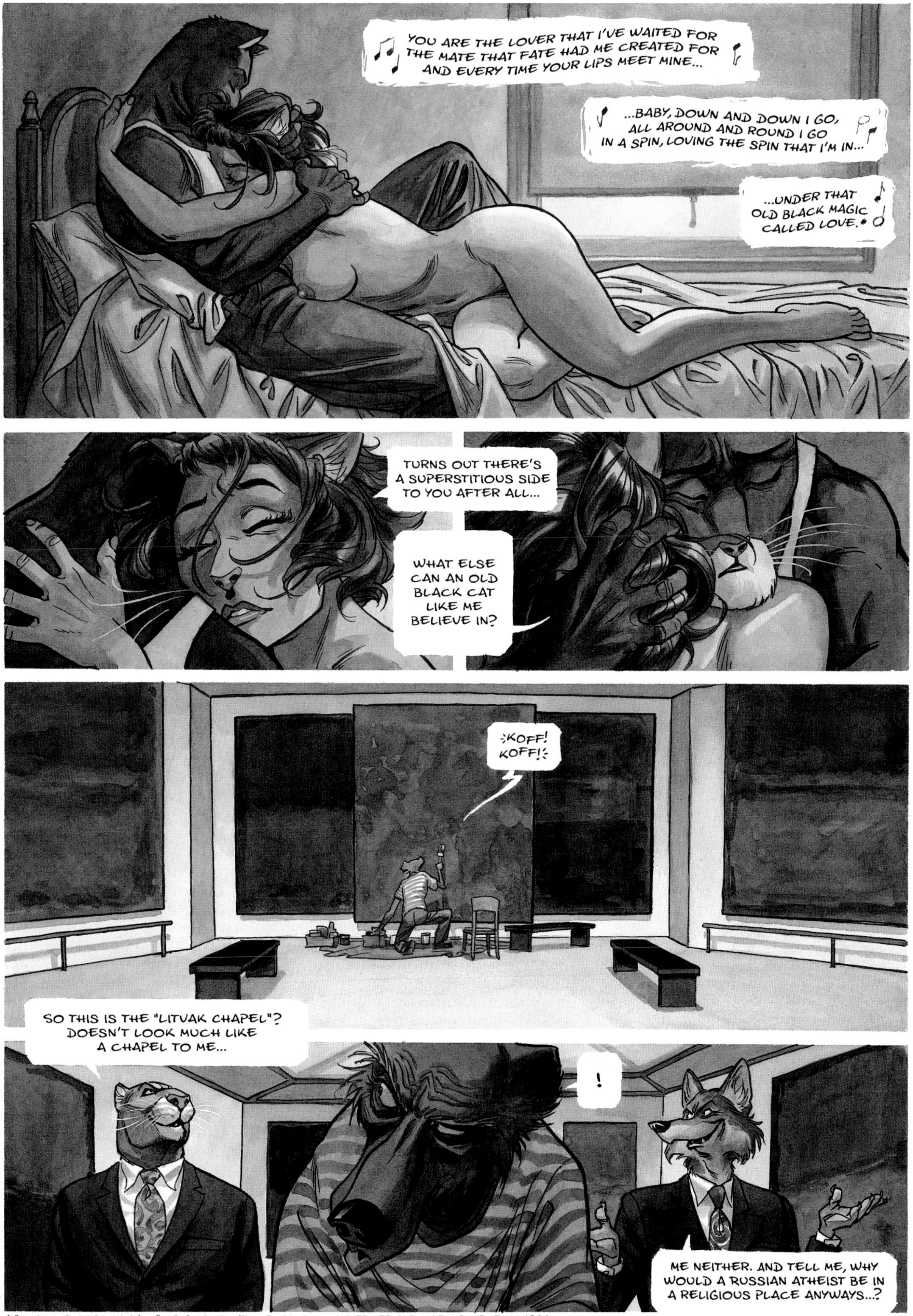

YOU ARE THE LOVER THAT I'VE WAITED FOR THE MATE THAT FATE HAD ME CREATED FOR AND EVERY TIME YOUR LIPS MEET MINE...
...BABY, DOWN AND DOWN I GO, ALL AROUND AND ROUND I GO IN A SPIN, LOVING THE SPIN THAT I'M IN...
...UNDER THAT OLD BLACK MAGIC CALLED LOVE.*
TURNS OUT THERE'S A SUPERSTITIOUS SIDE TO YOU AFTER ALL...
WHAT ELSE CAN AN OLD BLACK CAT LIKE ME BELIEVE IN?
KOFF! KOFF!
SO THIS IS THE "LITVAK CHAPEL"? DOESN'T LOOK MUCH LIKE A CHAPEL TO ME...
!
ME NEITHER. AND TELL ME, WHY WOULD A RUSSIAN ATHEIST BE IN A RELIGIOUS PLACE ANYWAYS...?
39

* "THAT OLD BLACK MAGIC," ORIGINALLY WRITTEN BY JOHNNY MERCER AND HAROLD ARLEN IN 1942.

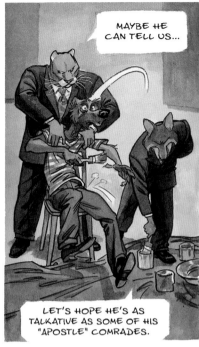

MAYBE HE CAN TELL US...

LET'S HOPE HE'S AS TALKATIVE AS SOME OF HIS "APOSTLE" COMRADES.

YEAH, BUDDY...'CAUSE THANKS TO THEM, WE KNOW WHAT YOU'RE UP TO-- YOU AND YOUR FRIEND LIEBBER...

YOU KNOW HOW THIS WORKS. YOU TELL US WHERE THE OLD GUY IS, AND WE'LL LET YOU KEEP DRAWING ON THE WALLS.

GO TO HELL!

I DON'T THINK SO, RED! HELL IS WHERE YOU'RE HEADED IF YOU DON'T COOPERATE!

GO AHEAD! IF YOU THINK THREATENING ME IS GOING TO ACHIEVE ANYTHING, YOU'RE WRONG... I'M TOO OLD AND TOO SICK TO BE AFRAID OF DYING...

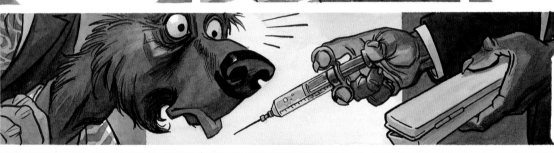

WHO SAID ANYTHING ABOUT DYING? WHY USE FORCE WHEN TRUTH SERUMS EXIST?

YOU GODDAMN BASTARDS!

SAY, HE DOESN'T LOOK TOO GOOD...

...NOT TOO GOOD AT ALL...

SHIT! DAMN GEEZER GOT HIS WAY AFTER ALL.

HUH...HEADS OR TAILS FOR WHO TYPES UP THE REPORT?

40

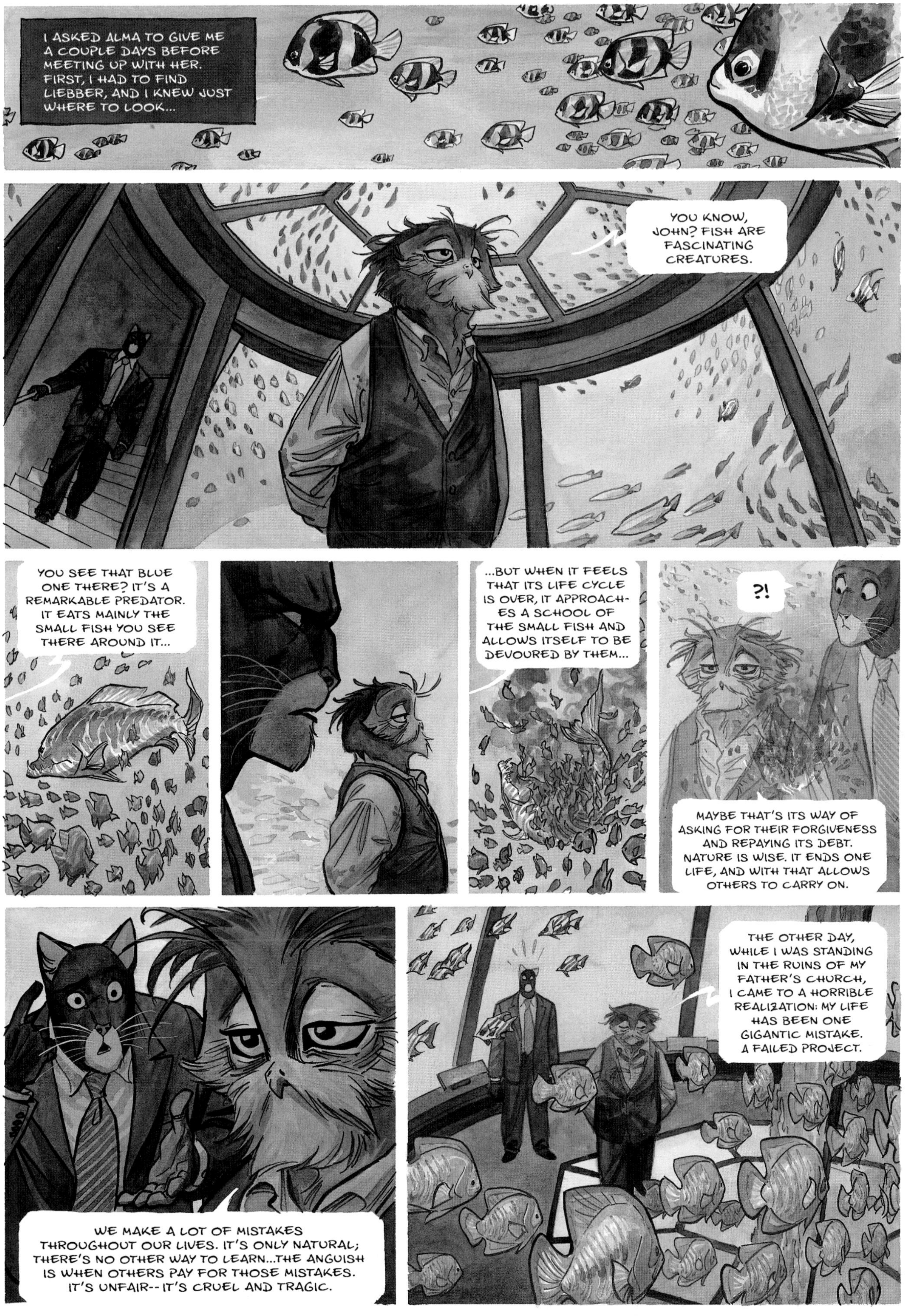
I ASKED ALMA TO GIVE ME A COUPLE DAYS BEFORE MEETING UP WITH HER. FIRST, I HAD TO FIND LIEBBER, AND I KNEW JUST WHERE TO LOOK...
YOU KNOW, JOHN? FISH ARE FASCINATING CREATURES.
YOU SEE THAT BLUE ONE THERE? IT'S A REMARKABLE PREDATOR. IT EATS MAINLY THE SMALL FISH YOU SEE THERE AROUND IT...
...BUT WHEN IT FEELS THAT ITS LIFE CYCLE IS OVER, IT APPROACH-ES A SCHOOL OF THE SMALL FISH AND ALLOWS ITSELF TO BE DEVOURED BY THEM...
?!
MAYBE THAT'S ITS WAY OF ASKING FOR THEIR FORGIVENESS AND REPAYING ITS DEBT. NATURE IS WISE. IT ENDS ONE LIFE, AND WITH THAT ALLOWS OTHERS TO CARRY ON.
WE MAKE A LOT OF MISTAKES THROUGHOUT OUR LIVES. IT'S ONLY NATURAL; THERE'S NO OTHER WAY TO LEARN...THE ANGUISH IS WHEN OTHERS PAY FOR THOSE MISTAKES. IT'S UNFAIR-- IT'S CRUEL AND TRAGIC.
41
THE OTHER DAY, WHILE I WAS STANDING IN THE RUINS OF MY FATHER'S CHURCH, I CAME TO A HORRIBLE REALIZATION: MY LIFE HAS BEEN ONE GIGANTIC MISTAKE. A FAILED PROJECT.

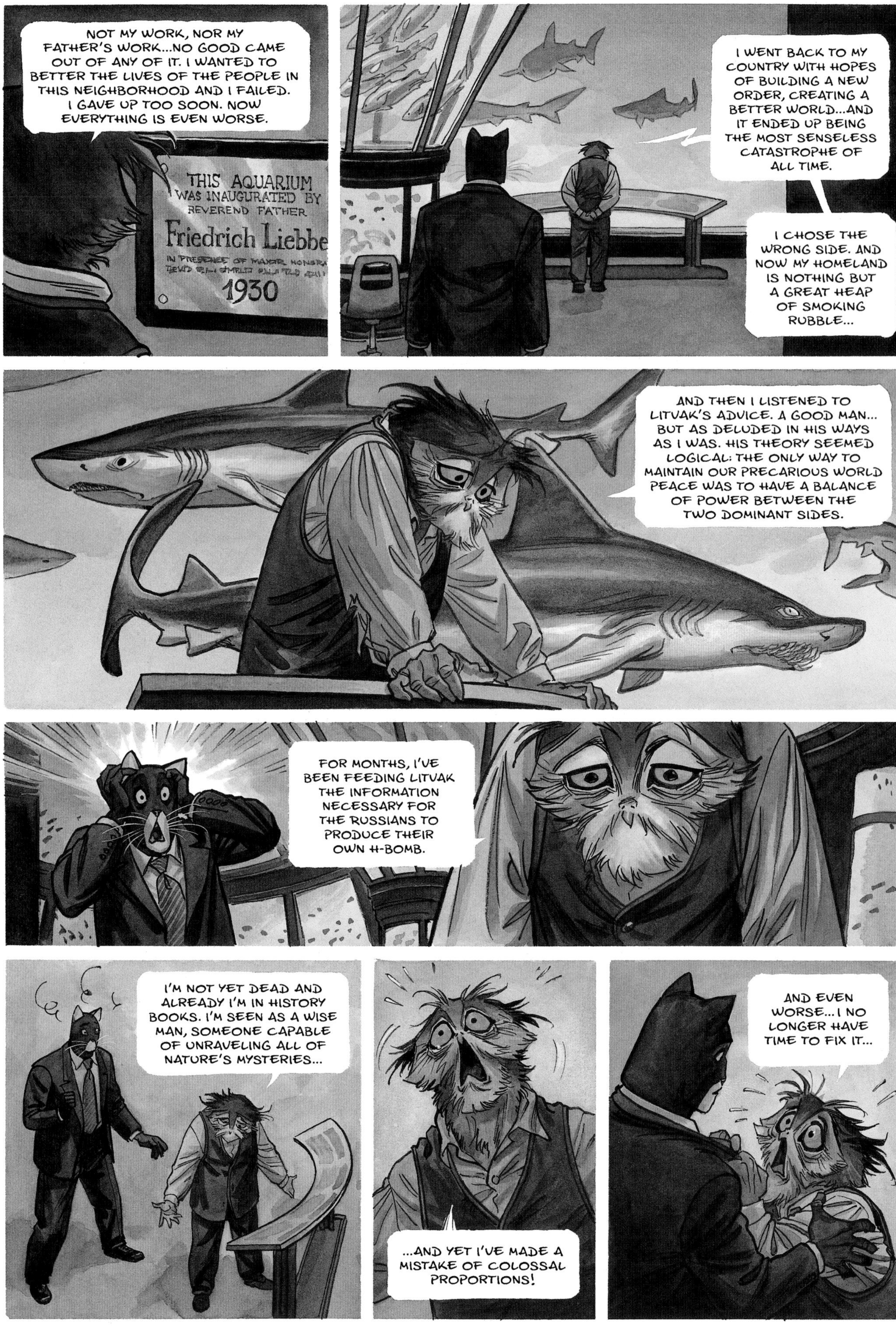
NOT MY WORK, NOR MY FATHER'S WORK...NO GOOD CAME OUT OF ANY OF IT. I WANTED TO BETTER THE LIVES OF THE PEOPLE IN THIS NEIGHBORHOOD AND I FAILED. I GAVE UP TOO SOON. NOW EVERYTHING IS EVEN WORSE.
THIS AQUARIUM
WAS INAUGURATED BY
REVEREND FATHER
Friedrich Liebbe
1930
I WENT BACK TO MY COUNTRY WITH HOPES OF BUILDING A NEW ORDER, CREATING A BETTER WORLD...AND IT ENDED UP BEING THE MOST SENSELESS CATASTROPHE OF ALL TIME.
I CHOSE THE WRONG SIDE. AND NOW MY HOMELAND IS NOTHING BUT A GREAT HEAP OF SMOKING RUBBLE...
AND THEN I LISTENED TO LITVAK'S ADVICE. A GOOD MAN... BUT AS DELUDED IN HIS WAYS AS I WAS. HIS THEORY SEEMED LOGICAL: THE ONLY WAY TO MAINTAIN OUR PRECARIOUS WORLD PEACE WAS TO HAVE A BALANCE OF POWER BETWEEN THE TWO DOMINANT SIDES.
FOR MONTHS, I'VE BEEN FEEDING LITVAK THE INFORMATION NECESSARY FOR THE RUSSIANS TO PRODUCE THEIR OWN H-BOMB.
I'M NOT YET DEAD AND ALREADY I'M IN HISTORY BOOKS. I'M SEEN AS A WISE MAN, SOMEONE CAPABLE OF UNRAVELING ALL OF NATURE'S MYSTERIES...
...AND YET I'VE MADE A MISTAKE OF COLOSSAL PROPORTIONS!
AND EVEN WORSE... I NO LONGER HAVE TIME TO FIX IT...
42

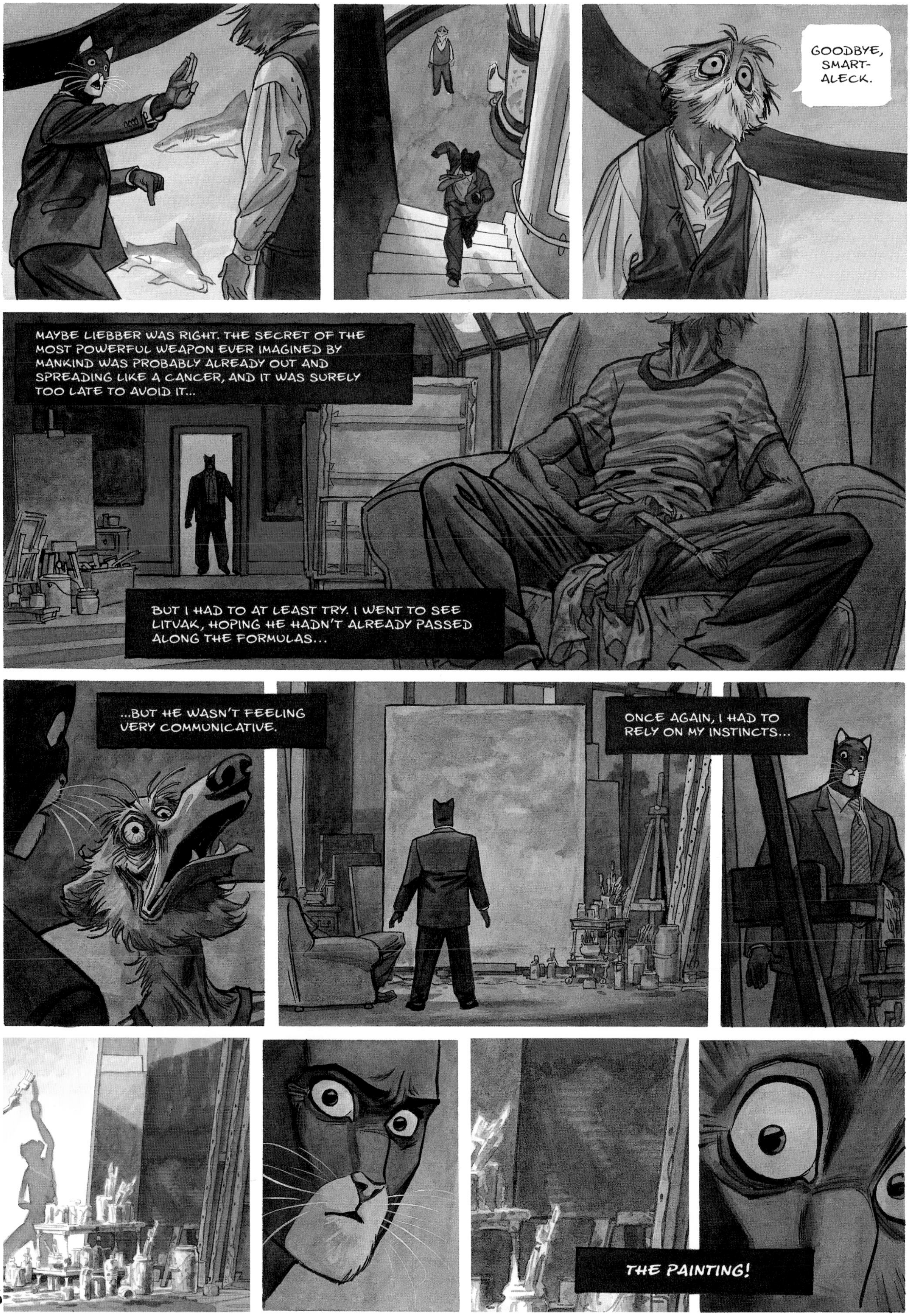
GOODBYE, SMART-ALECK.
MAYBE LIEBBER WAS RIGHT. THE SECRET OF THE MOST POWERFUL WEAPON EVER IMAGINED BY MANKIND WAS PROBABLY ALREADY OUT AND SPREADING LIKE A CANCER, AND IT WAS SURELY TOO LATE TO AVOID IT...
BUT I HAD TO AT LEAST TRY. I WENT TO SEE LITVAK, HOPING HE HADN'T ALREADY PASSED ALONG THE FORMULAS...
...BUT HE WASN'T FEELING VERY COMMUNICATIVE.
ONCE AGAIN, I HAD TO RELY ON MY INSTINCTS...
THE PAINTING!

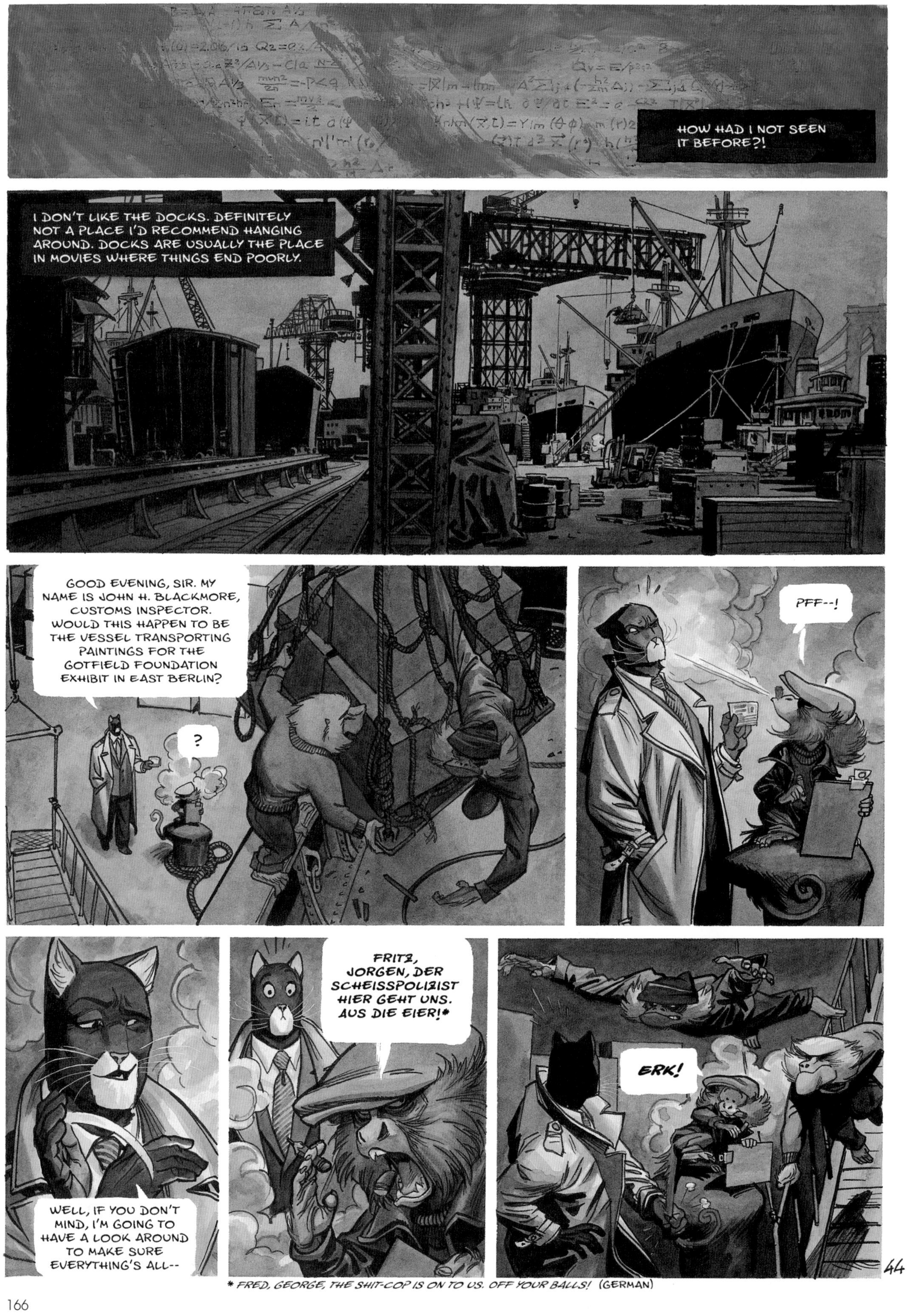
HOW HAD I NOT SEEN IT BEFORE?!
I DON'T LIKE THE DOCKS. DEFINITELY NOT A PLACE I'D RECOMMEND HANGING AROUND. DOCKS ARE USUALLY THE PLACE IN MOVIES WHERE THINGS END POORLY.
GOOD EVENING, SIR. MY NAME IS JOHN H. BLACKMORE, CUSTOMS INSPECTOR. WOULD THIS HAPPEN TO BE THE VESSEL TRANSPORTING PAINTINGS FOR THE GOTFIELD FOUNDATION EXHIBIT IN EAST BERLIN?
?
PFF--!
WELL, IF YOU DON'T MIND, I'M GOING TO HAVE A LOOK AROUND TO MAKE SURE EVERYTHING'S ALL--
FRITZ, JORGEN, DER SCHEISSPOLIZIST HIER GEHT UNS. AUS DIE EIER!*
ERK!
44

* FRED, GEORGE, THE SHIT-COP IS ON TO US. OFF YOUR BALLS! (GERMAN)

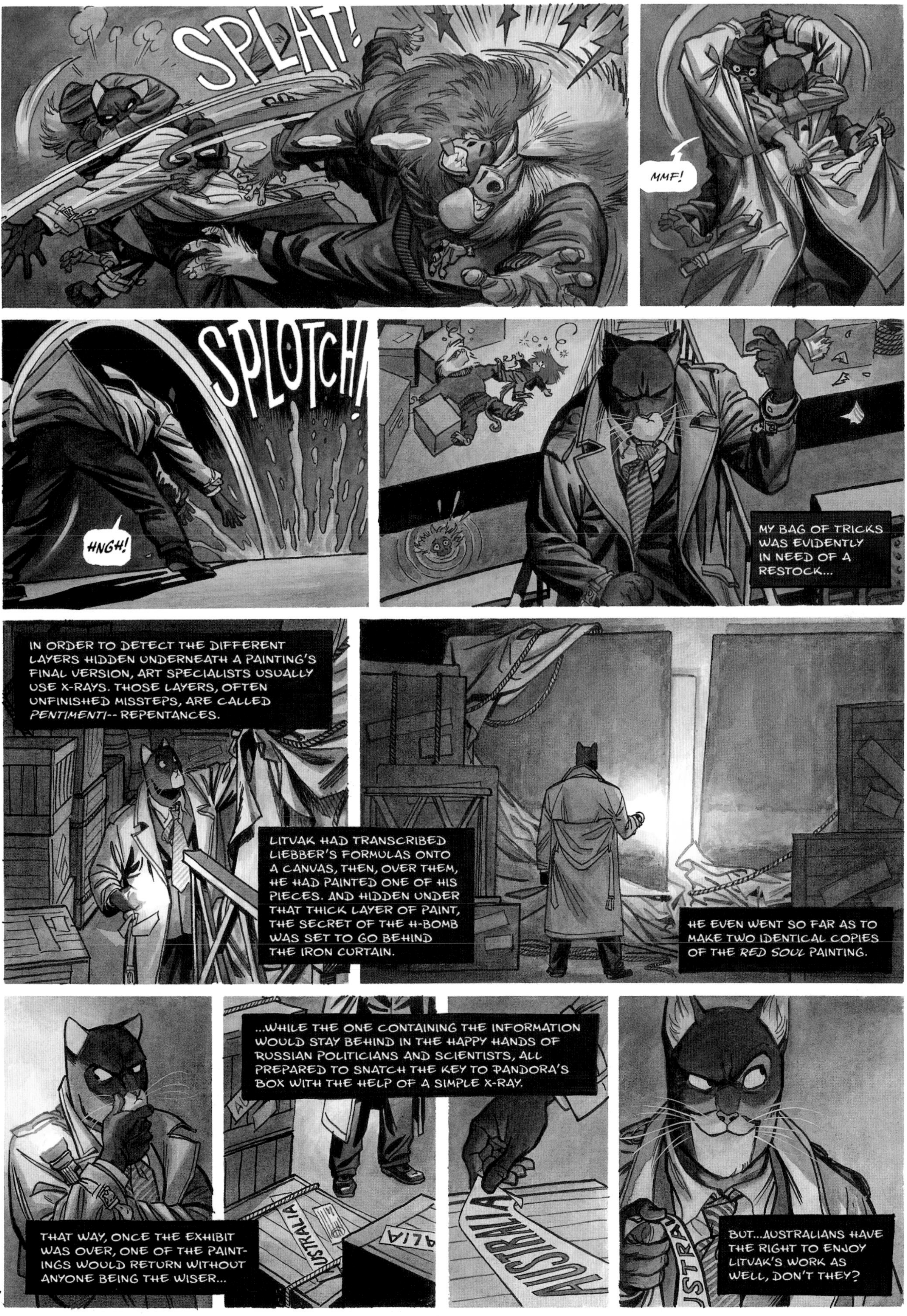
SPLAT!
MMF!
SPLOTCH!
HNGH!
MY BAG OF TRICKS WAS EVIDENTLY IN NEED OF A RESTOCK...
IN ORDER TO DETECT THE DIFFERENT LAYERS HIDDEN UNDERNEATH A PAINTING'S FINAL VERSION, ART SPECIALISTS USUALLY USE X-RAYS. THOSE LAYERS, OFTEN UNFINISHED MISSTEPS, ARE CALLED *PENTIMENTI*-- REPENTANCES.
LITVAK HAD TRANSCRIBED LIEBBER'S FORMULAS ONTO A CANVAS, THEN, OVER THEM, HE HAD PAINTED ONE OF HIS PIECES. AND HIDDEN UNDER THAT THICK LAYER OF PAINT, THE SECRET OF THE H-BOMB WAS SET TO GO BEHIND THE IRON CURTAIN.
HE EVEN WENT SO FAR AS TO MAKE TWO IDENTICAL COPIES OF THE *RED SOUL* PAINTING.
THAT WAY, ONCE THE EXHIBIT WAS OVER, ONE OF THE PAINTINGS WOULD RETURN WITHOUT ANYONE BEING THE WISER...
...WHILE THE ONE CONTAINING THE INFORMATION WOULD STAY BEHIND IN THE HAPPY HANDS OF RUSSIAN POLITICIANS AND SCIENTISTS, ALL PREPARED TO SNATCH THE KEY TO PANDORA'S BOX WITH THE HELP OF A SIMPLE X-RAY.
AUSTRALIA
BUT...AUSTRALIANS HAVE THE RIGHT TO ENJOY LITVAK'S WORK AS WELL, DON'T THEY?
45

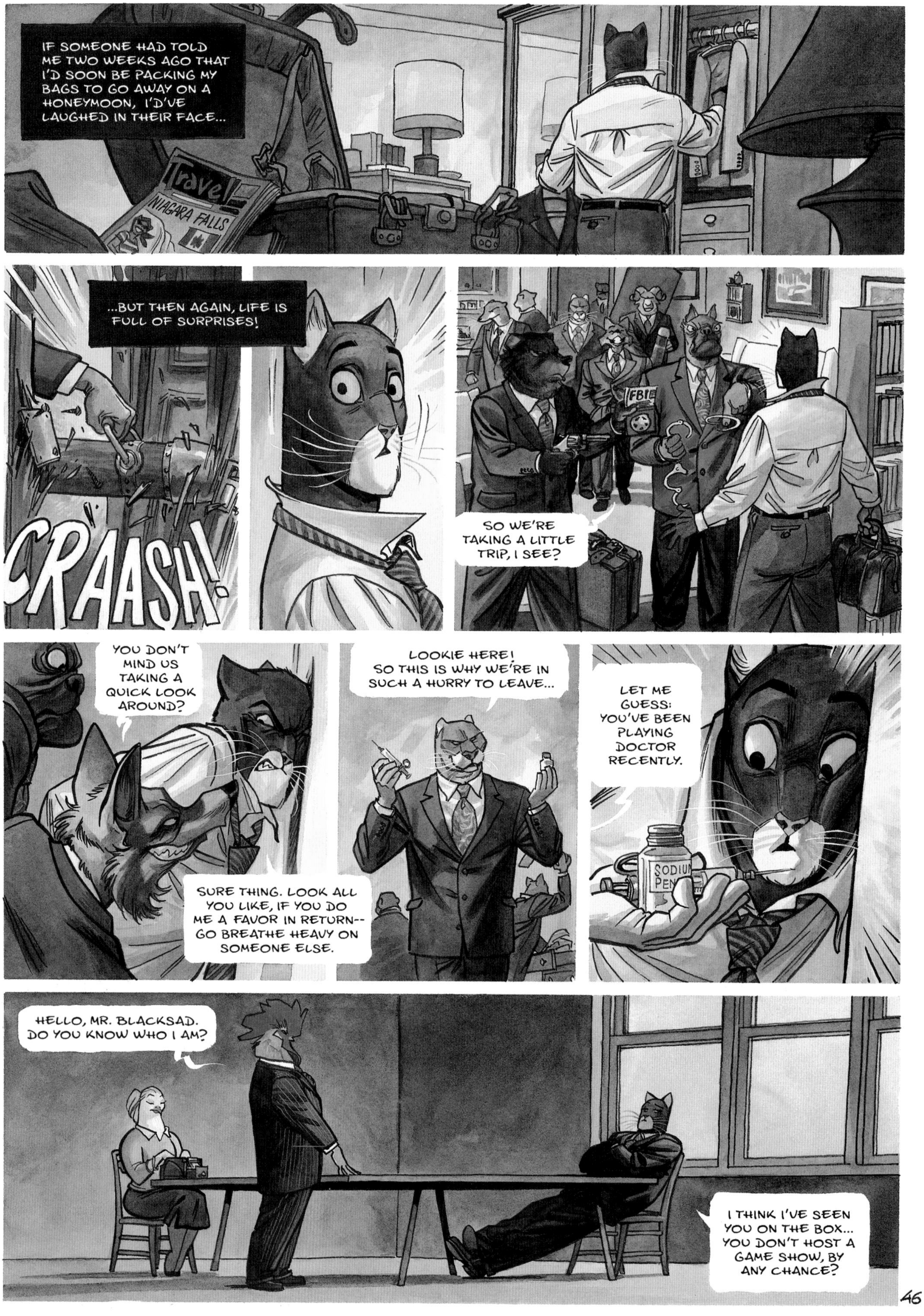
IF SOMEONE HAD TOLD ME TWO WEEKS AGO THAT I'D SOON BE PACKING MY BAGS TO GO AWAY ON A HONEYMOON, I'D'VE LAUGHED IN THEIR FACE...
Travel
NIAGARA FALLS
...BUT THEN AGAIN, LIFE IS FULL OF SURPRISES!
CRAASH!
FBI
SO WE'RE TAKING A LITTLE TRIP, I SEE?
YOU DON'T MIND US TAKING A QUICK LOOK AROUND?
SURE THING. LOOK ALL YOU LIKE, IF YOU DO ME A FAVOR IN RETURN-- GO BREATHE HEAVY ON SOMEONE ELSE.
LOOKIE HERE! SO THIS IS WHY WE'RE IN SUCH A HURRY TO LEAVE...
LET ME GUESS: YOU'VE BEEN PLAYING DOCTOR RECENTLY.
HELLO, MR. BLACKSAD. DO YOU KNOW WHO I AM?
I THINK I'VE SEEN YOU ON THE BOX... YOU DON'T HOST A GAME SHOW, BY ANY CHANCE?
46

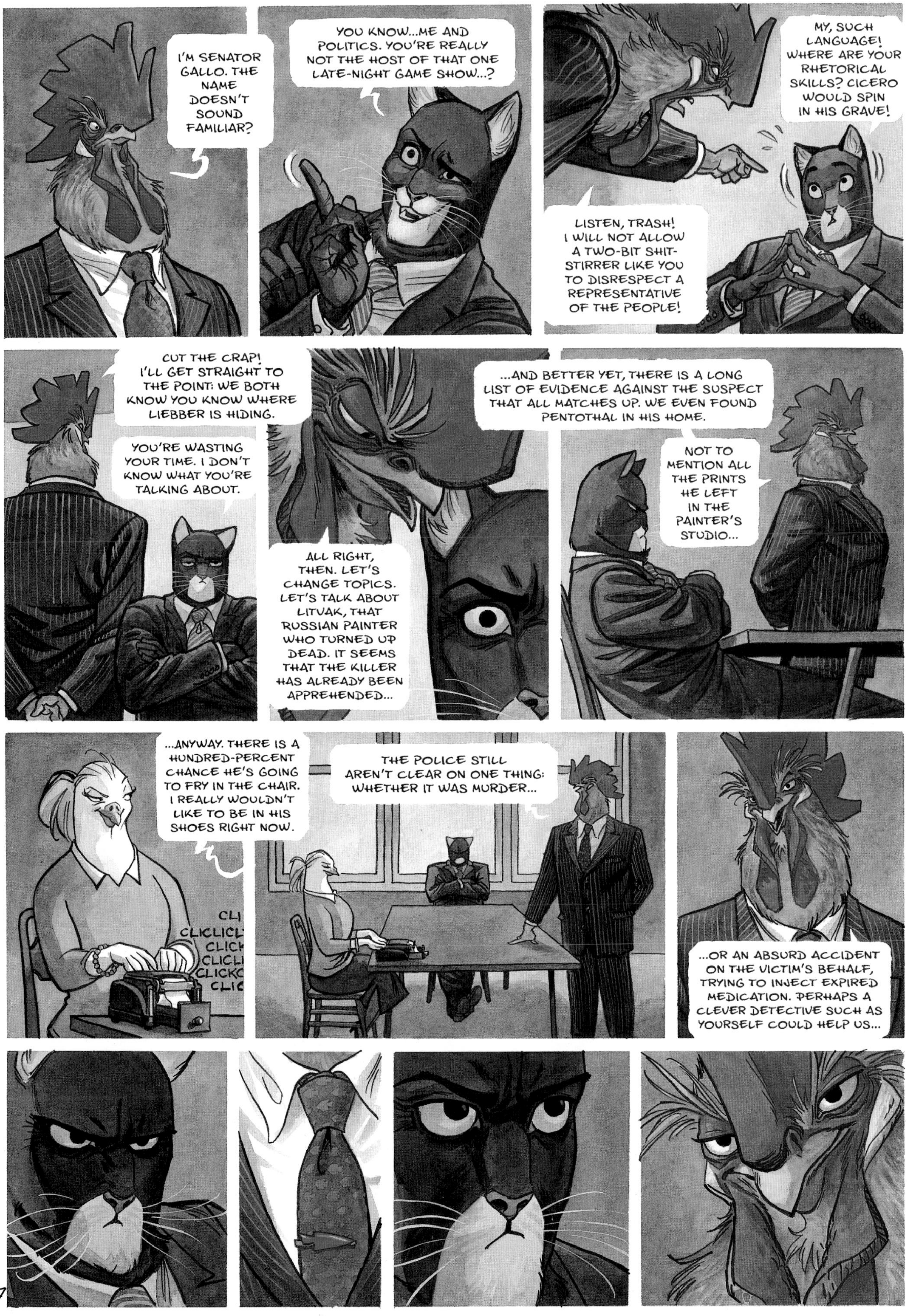
I'M SENATOR GALLO. THE NAME DOESN'T SOUND FAMILIAR?
YOU KNOW...ME AND POLITICS. YOU'RE REALLY NOT THE HOST OF THAT ONE LATE-NIGHT GAME SHOW...?
LISTEN, TRASH! I WILL NOT ALLOW A TWO-BIT SHIT-STIRRER LIKE YOU TO DISRESPECT A REPRESENTATIVE OF THE PEOPLE!
MY, SUCH LANGUAGE! WHERE ARE YOUR RHETORICAL SKILLS? CICERO WOULD SPIN IN HIS GRAVE!
CUT THE CRAP! I'LL GET STRAIGHT TO THE POINT: WE BOTH KNOW YOU KNOW WHERE LIEBBER IS HIDING.
YOU'RE WASTING YOUR TIME. I DON'T KNOW WHAT YOU'RE TALKING ABOUT.
ALL RIGHT, THEN. LET'S CHANGE TOPICS. LET'S TALK ABOUT LITVAK, THAT RUSSIAN PAINTER WHO TURNED UP DEAD. IT SEEMS THAT THE KILLER HAS ALREADY BEEN APPREHENDED...
...AND BETTER YET, THERE IS A LONG LIST OF EVIDENCE AGAINST THE SUSPECT THAT ALL MATCHES UP. WE EVEN FOUND PENTOTHAL IN HIS HOME.
NOT TO MENTION ALL THE PRINTS HE LEFT IN THE PAINTER'S STUDIO...
...ANYWAY. THERE IS A HUNDRED-PERCENT CHANCE HE'S GOING TO FRY IN THE CHAIR. I REALLY WOULDN'T LIKE TO BE IN HIS SHOES RIGHT NOW.
CLI CLICLICL CLICK CLICLI CLICKC CLI
THE POLICE STILL AREN'T CLEAR ON ONE THING: WHETHER IT WAS MURDER...
...OR AN ABSURD ACCIDENT ON THE VICTIM'S BEHALF, TRYING TO INJECT EXPIRED MEDICATION. PERHAPS A CLEVER DETECTIVE SUCH AS YOURSELF COULD HELP US...
47

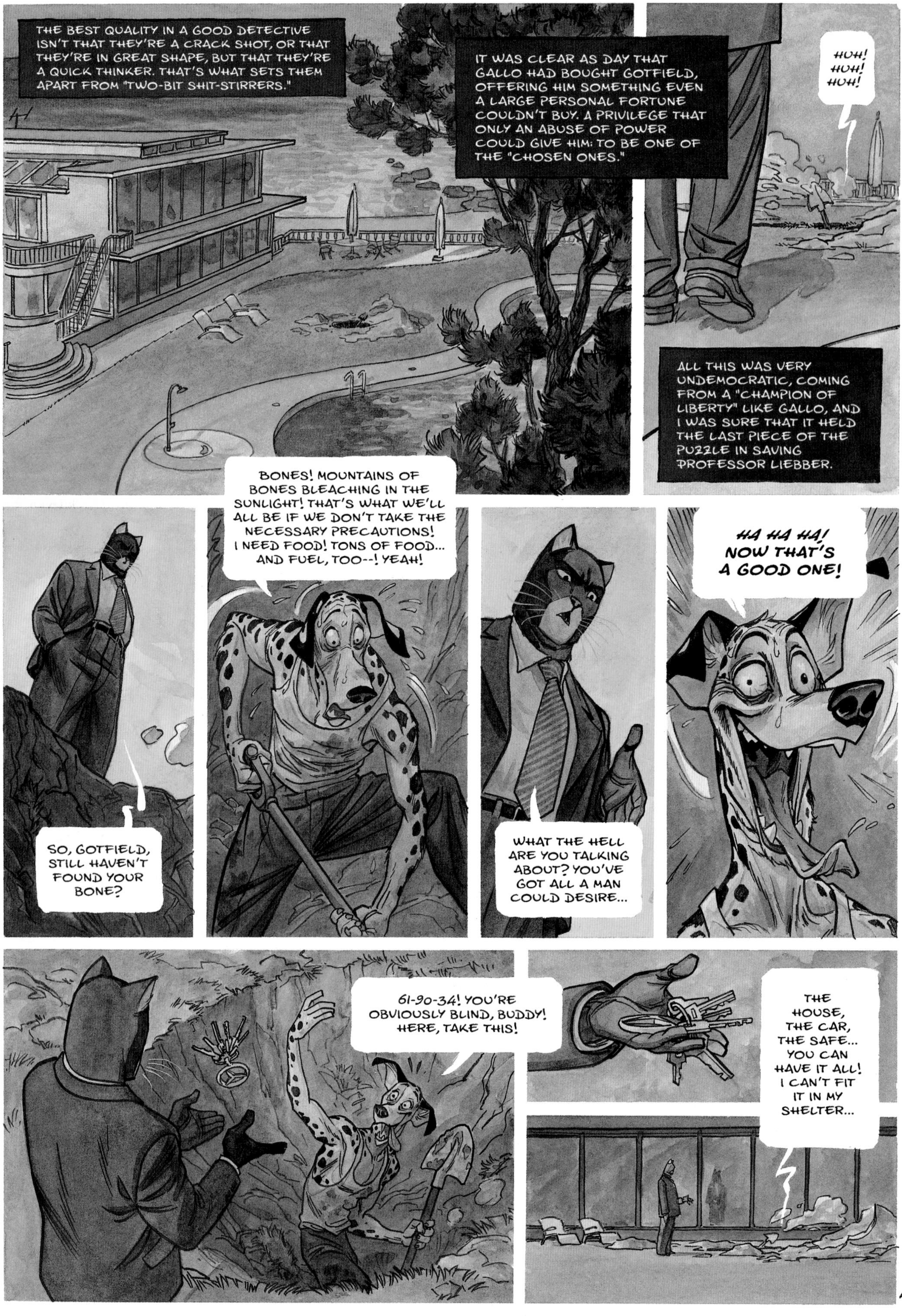

THE BEST QUALITY IN A GOOD DETECTIVE ISN'T THAT THEY'RE A CRACK SHOT, OR THAT THEY'RE IN GREAT SHAPE, BUT THAT THEY'RE A QUICK THINKER. THAT'S WHAT SETS THEM APART FROM "TWO-BIT SHIT-STIRRERS."
IT WAS CLEAR AS DAY THAT GALLO HAD BOUGHT GOTFIELD, OFFERING HIM SOMETHING EVEN A LARGE PERSONAL FORTUNE COULDN'T BUY. A PRIVILEGE THAT ONLY AN ABUSE OF POWER COULD GIVE HIM: TO BE ONE OF THE "CHOSEN ONES."
HUH! HUH! HUH!
ALL THIS WAS VERY UNDEMOCRATIC, COMING FROM A "CHAMPION OF LIBERTY" LIKE GALLO, AND I WAS SURE THAT IT HELD THE LAST PIECE OF THE PUZZLE IN SAVING PROFESSOR LIEBBER.
SO, GOTFIELD, STILL HAVEN'T FOUND YOUR BONE?
BONES! MOUNTAINS OF BONES BLEACHING IN THE SUNLIGHT! THAT'S WHAT WE'LL ALL BE IF WE DON'T TAKE THE NECESSARY PRECAUTIONS! I NEED FOOD! TONS OF FOOD... AND FUEL, TOO--! YEAH!
WHAT THE HELL ARE YOU TALKING ABOUT? YOU'VE GOT ALL A MAN COULD DESIRE...
HA HA HA! NOW THAT'S A GOOD ONE!
61-90-34! YOU'RE OBVIOUSLY BLIND, BUDDY! HERE, TAKE THIS!
THE HOUSE, THE CAR, THE SAFE... YOU CAN HAVE IT ALL! I CAN'T FIT IT IN MY SHELTER...
48

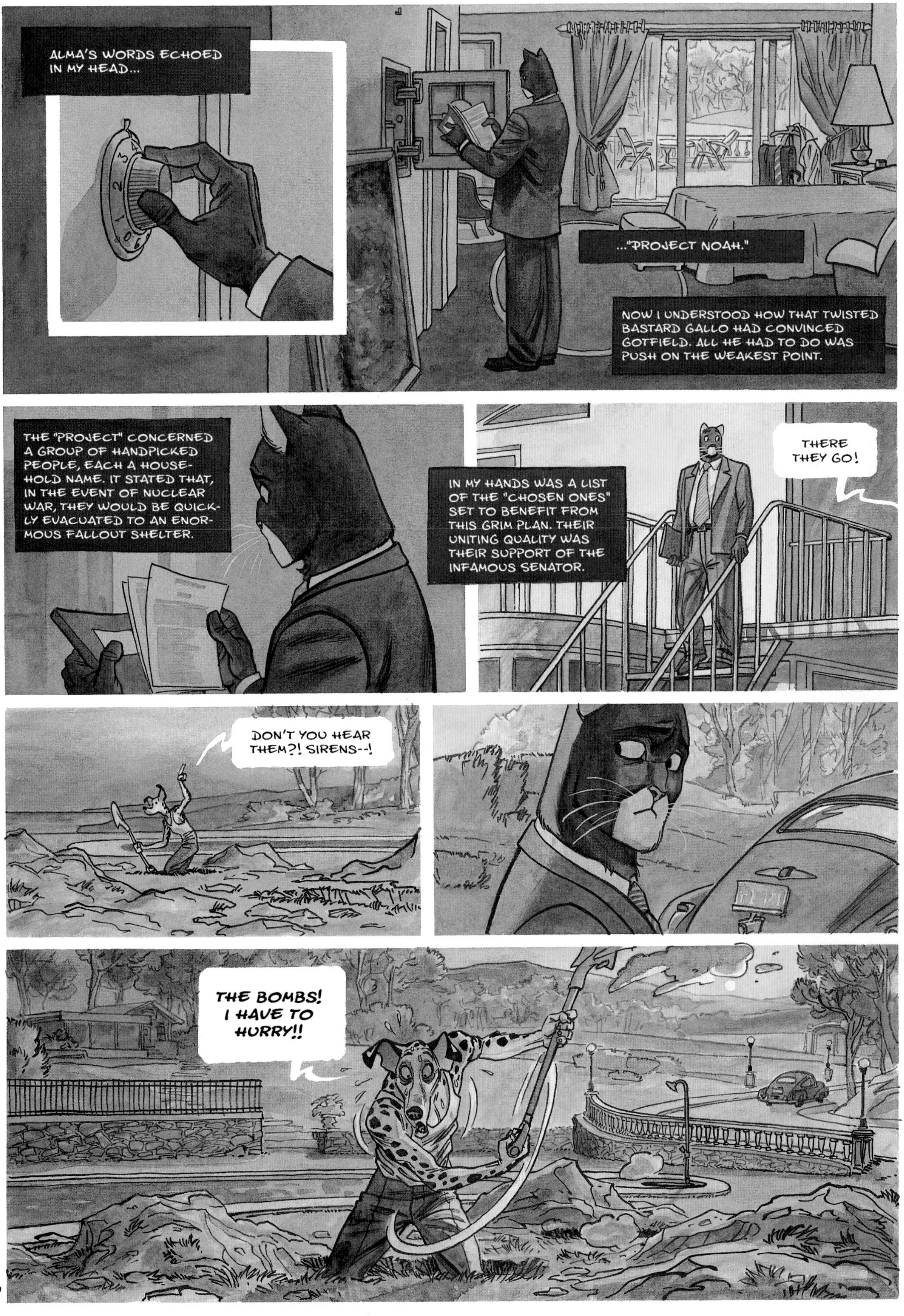
ALMA'S WORDS ECHOED IN MY HEAD...
..."PROJECT NOAH."
NOW I UNDERSTOOD HOW THAT TWISTED BASTARD GALLO HAD CONVINCED GOTFIELD. ALL HE HAD TO DO WAS PUSH ON THE WEAKEST POINT.
THE "PROJECT" CONCERNED A GROUP OF HANDPICKED PEOPLE, EACH A HOUSE-HOLD NAME. IT STATED THAT, IN THE EVENT OF NUCLEAR WAR, THEY WOULD BE QUICK-LY EVACUATED TO AN ENOR-MOUS FALLOUT SHELTER.
IN MY HANDS WAS A LIST OF THE "CHOSEN ONES" SET TO BENEFIT FROM THIS GRIM PLAN. THEIR UNITING QUALITY WAS THEIR SUPPORT OF THE INFAMOUS SENATOR.
THERE THEY GO!
DON'T YOU HEAR THEM?! SIRENS--!
THE BOMBS! I HAVE TO HURRY!!

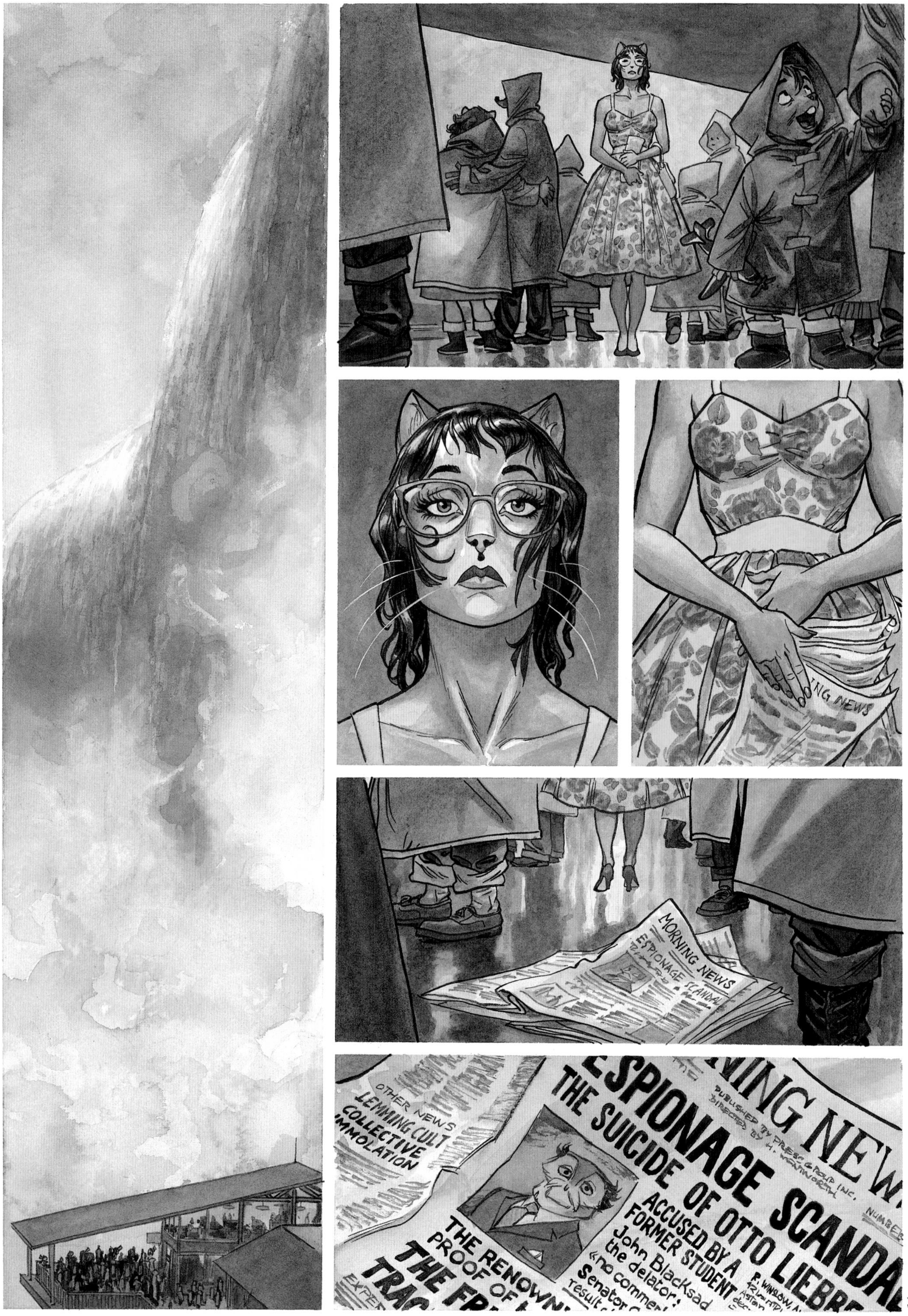
MORNING NEWS
ESPIONAGE SCANDAL
OTHER NEWS
LEMMING CULT
COLLECTIVE
IMMOLATION
ESPIONAGE SCANDAL
THE SUICIDE OF OTTO LIEBER
ACCUSED BY A FORMER STUDENT
John Blacksad
the delator:
«no comment
PUBLISHED BY PRESS GROUP INC.

50

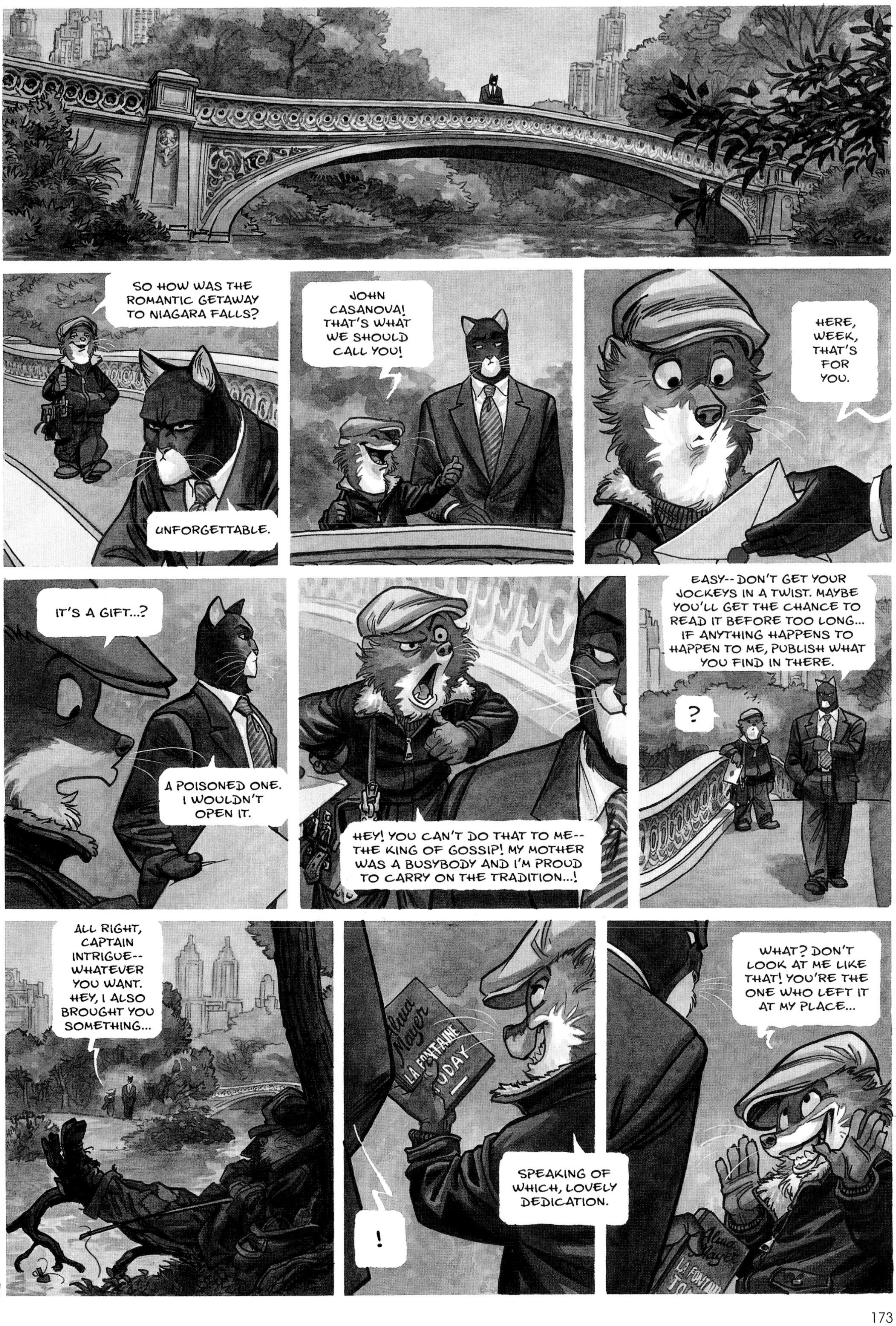
SO HOW WAS THE ROMANTIC GETAWAY TO NIAGARA FALLS?
UNFORGETTABLE.
JOHN CASANOVA! THAT'S WHAT WE SHOULD CALL YOU!
HERE, WEEK, THAT'S FOR YOU.
IT'S A GIFT...?
A POISONED ONE. I WOULDN'T OPEN IT.
HEY! YOU CAN'T DO THAT TO ME-- THE KING OF GOSSIP! MY MOTHER WAS A BUSYBODY AND I'M PROUD TO CARRY ON THE TRADITION...!
EASY-- DON'T GET YOUR JOCKEYS IN A TWIST. MAYBE YOU'LL GET THE CHANCE TO READ IT BEFORE TOO LONG... IF ANYTHING HAPPENS TO HAPPEN TO ME, PUBLISH WHAT YOU FIND IN THERE.
?
ALL RIGHT, CAPTAIN INTRIGUE-- WHATEVER YOU WANT. HEY, I ALSO BROUGHT YOU SOMETHING...
Alma Mayer
LA FONTAINE TODAY
SPEAKING OF WHICH, LOVELY DEDICATION.
!
WHAT? DON'T LOOK AT ME LIKE THAT! YOU'RE THE ONE WHO LEFT IT AT MY PLACE...
51

WEEKLY WAS HEADED HOME WITH A REAL TICKING TIME BOMB. THAT ENVELOPE CONTAINED THE LIST OF THOSE IN "PROJECT NOAH"-- AND WHO JUST HAPPENED TO BE INFLUENTIAL SUPPORTERS OF GALLO AND THE MAJORITY PARTY.

IN ORDER TO WIPE MY RECORD AND AVOID BEING FRAMED FOR LITVAK'S MURDER, I HAD THREATENED THE "INCORRUPTIBLE" SENATOR GALLO WITH MAKING THIS LIST PUBLIC, WHICH WOULD HAVE OUTED A HELL OF A LOT OF PEOPLE AND DELIGHTED REPORTERS AND THE MINORITY PARTY.

THE SENATOR ULTIMATELY AGREED TO STAGE A STORY ABOUT LIEBBER'S SUICIDE RATHER THAN TEST PUBLIC OPINION. IT WAS PUBLIC OPINION THAT HE SO LOVED TO MANIPULATE, AFTER ALL.

I ALSO HAD TO PAY A HEAVY PRICE-- DURING THE NEGOTIATIONS, GALLO KEPT ME LOCKED UP FOR TWO WEEKS. ENOUGH TIME TO MISS MY DATE WITH ALMA.

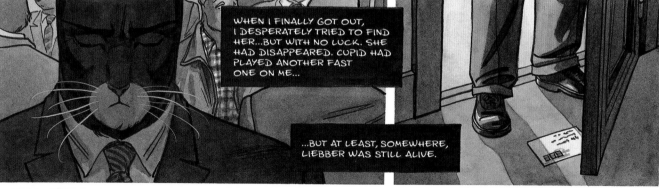

WHEN I FINALLY GOT OUT, I DESPERATELY TRIED TO FIND HER...BUT WITH NO LUCK. SHE HAD DISAPPEARED. CUPID HAD PLAYED ANOTHER FAST ONE ON ME...

...BUT AT LEAST, SOMEWHERE, LIEBBER WAS STILL ALIVE.

My dear friend,

All my life I've searched for a way to give meaning to my existence by trying to serve society as best as I could.

52

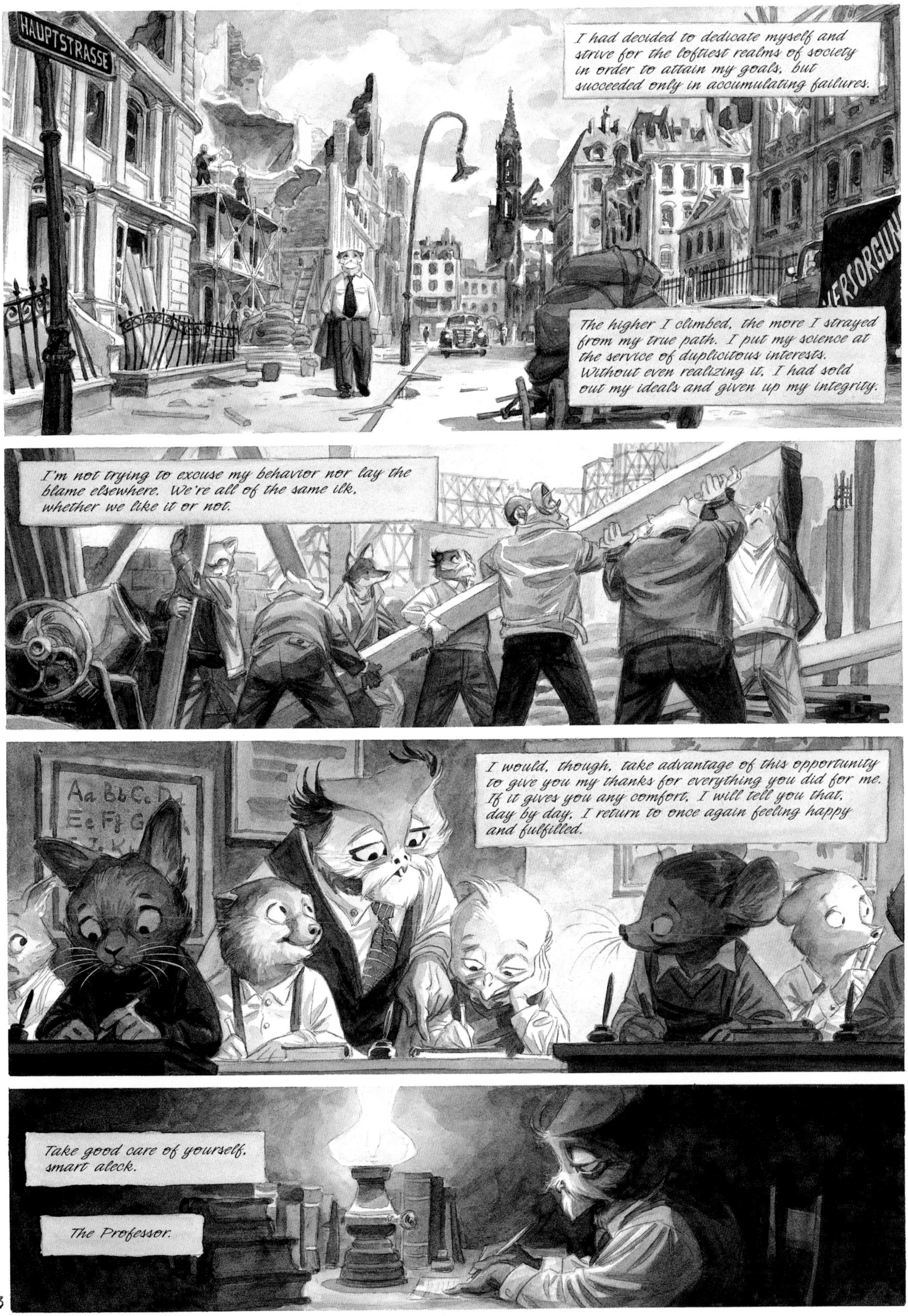
HAUPTSTRASSE
I had decided to dedicate myself and strive for the loftiest realms of society in order to attain my goals, but succeeded only in accumulating failures.
The higher I climbed, the more I strayed from my true path. I put my science at the service of duplicitous interests. Without even realizing it, I had sold out my ideals and given up my integrity.
I'm not trying to excuse my behavior nor lay the blame elsewhere. We're all of the same ilk, whether we like it or not.
I would, though, take advantage of this opportunity to give you my thanks for everything you did for me. If it gives you any comfort, I will tell you that, day by day, I return to once again feeling happy and fulfilled.
Take good care of yourself, smart aleck.
The Professor.

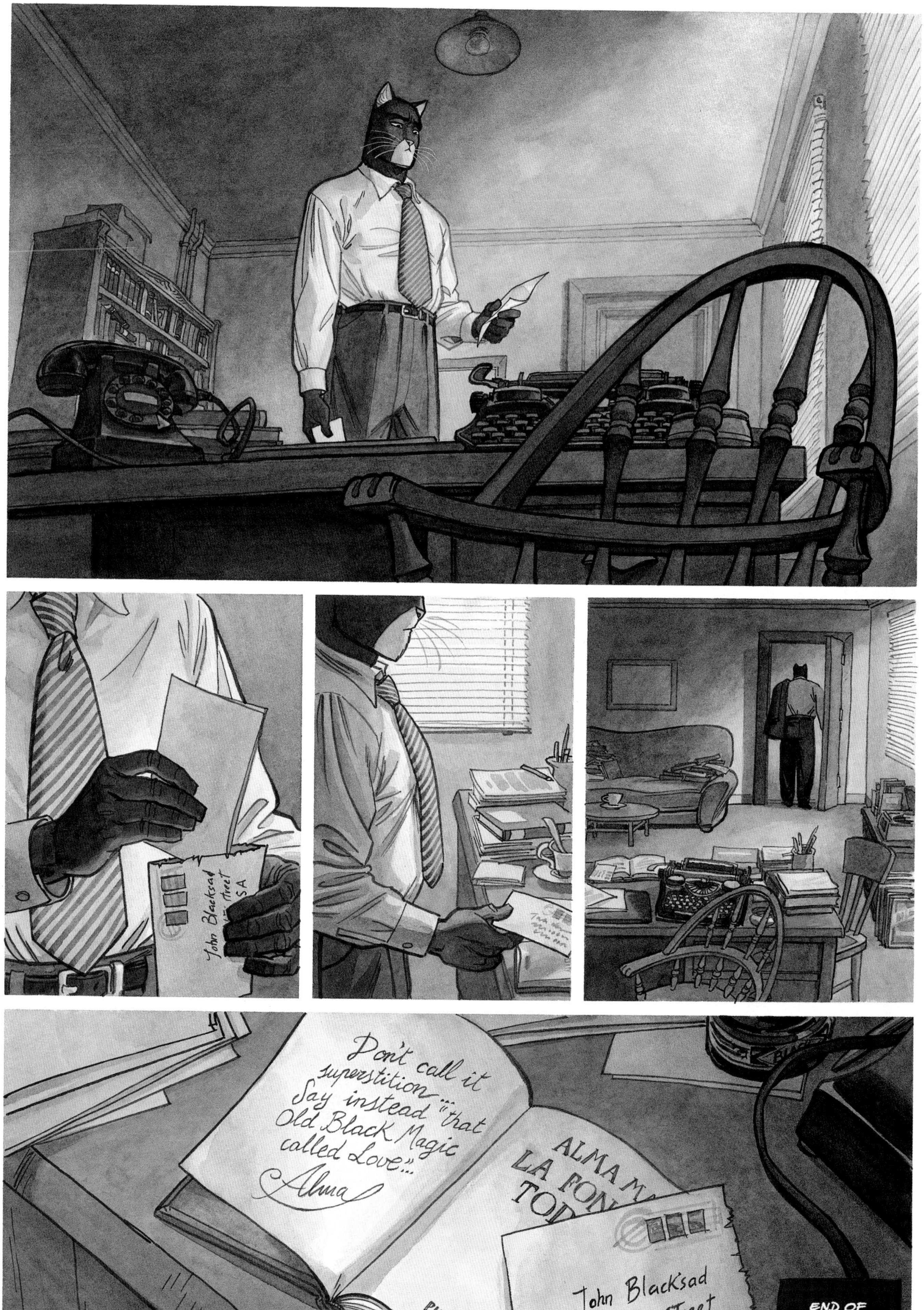
Don't call it superstition... Say instead "that Old Black Magic called Love"...
Alma
ALMA M
LA FON
TOD
John Blacksad
ton Street
END OF EPISODE

Juanjo Guarnido & Juan Díaz Canales
-2005-

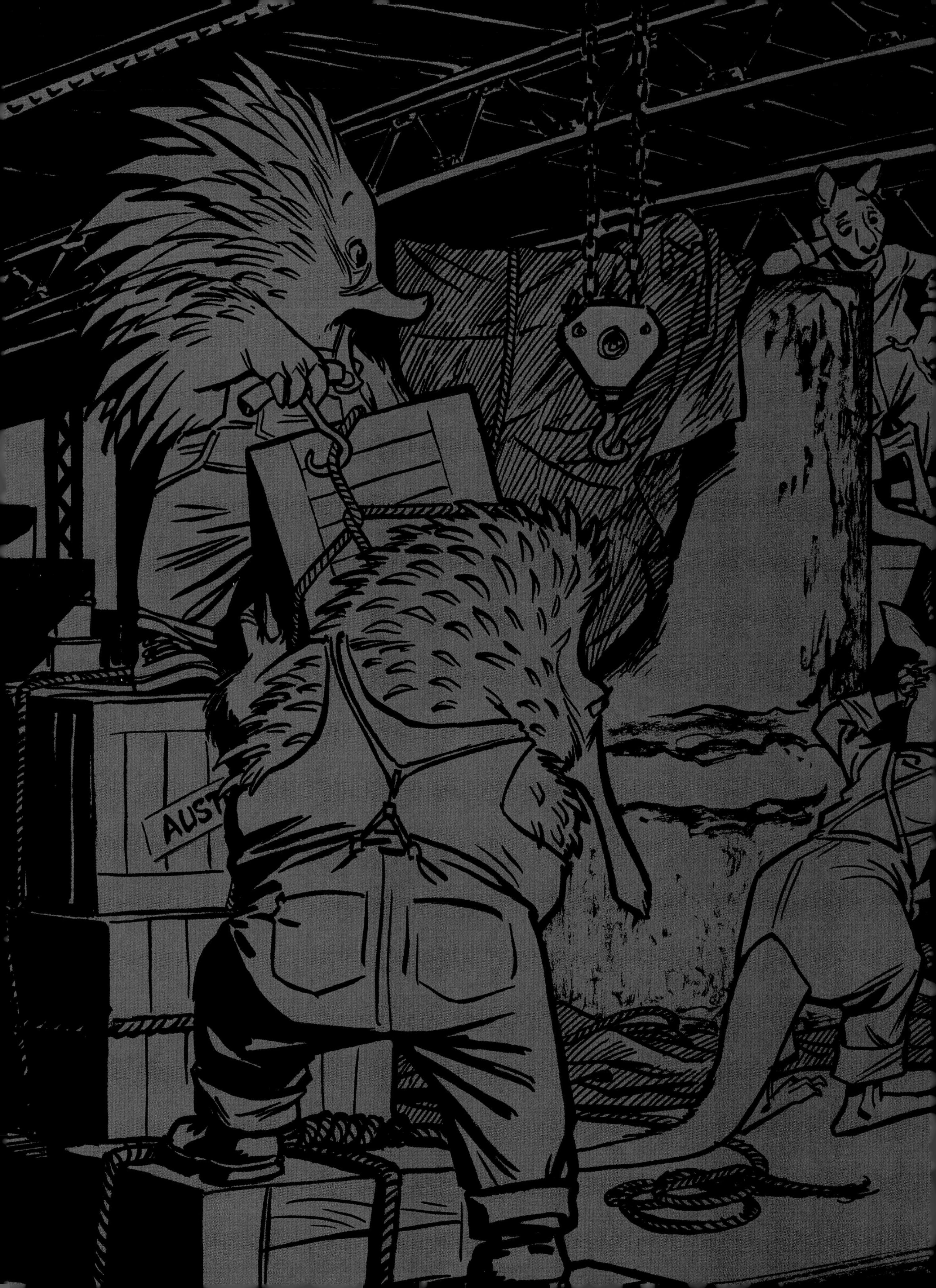
AUST

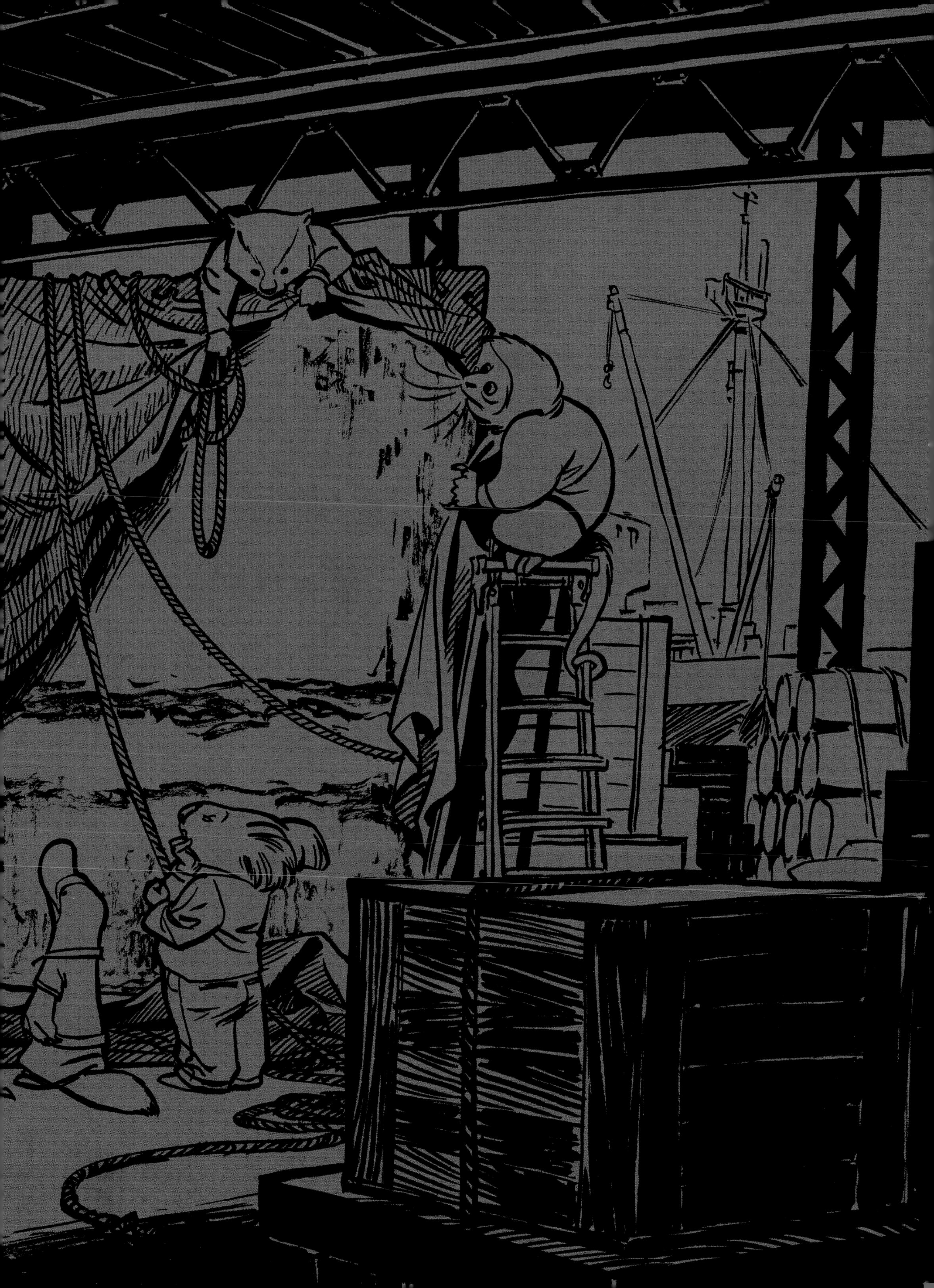

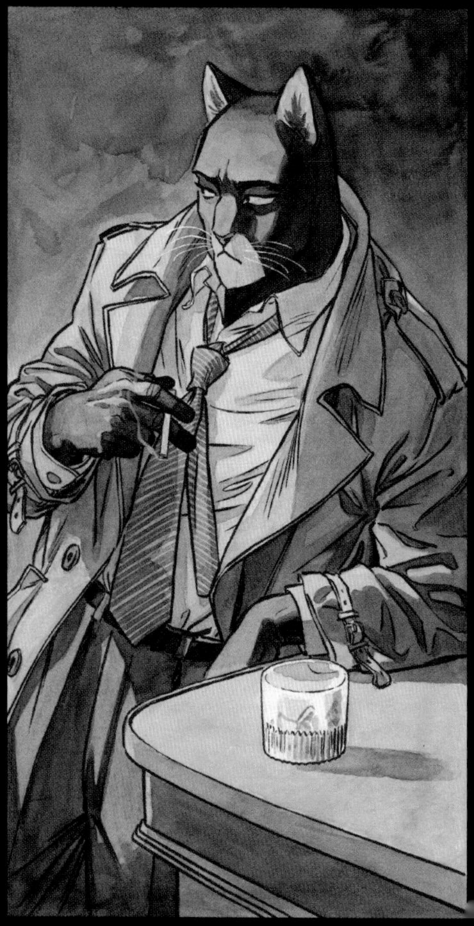

JUAN DÍAZ CANALES

Born in Madrid in 1972, Díaz Canales was a comics enthusiast from the very beginning. In 1990, at the age of eighteen, he found his first job doing layouts for the Spanish animation studio Lapiz Azul (Blue Pencil), where he met Juanjo Guarnido. The two quickly formed a close friendship, and continued to stay in contact—trading ideas with the aim of creating a comic-book series together—after Guarnido moved to Paris in 1993.

Díaz Canales studied the fine arts at Universidad Complutense de Madrid until 1996, when he finished his education and founded the studio Tridente Animación with three of his colleagues. Through this studio, and his position there as art director, he has done storyboard, layout, and directing work for various animated European and American television shows and films. Around this same time, he continued to develop the comics project with Guarnido, both of them inspired by the hard-boiled style of detective novels and films of the 1930s.

This project eventually took form as *Blacksad: Somewhere within the Shadows*, and was first published in French by Dargaud in November of 2000. Though it was their first comics album, the collaboration proved an immense critical and commercial success; it won a variety of prestigious comics awards and was soon translated into sixteen different languages. Two subsequent *Blacksad* albums have been published to date, in 2003 and 2005, and the fourth will be published in Europe in 2010.

In addition to *Blacksad*, Díaz Canales writes the humor series *Les patriciens* (The Patricians) for comics illustrator Gabor and their French publisher Glénat. He is happily married to fellow comics author Teresa Valero, and they have three lovely children. He currently lives and works in Madrid.

JUANJO GUARNIDO

Guarnido was born in Salobreña, a town on the Spanish Mediterranean coast, in 1967. After spending much of his childhood sketching the area and reading comics, he moved north to Granada with his family. There he studied painting and obtained his diploma from La Universidad de Granada's School of Fine Arts.

During his years at school he collaborated on comics fanzines and had illustrations published by Comics Forum, the division of Planeta DeAgostini that produced and printed Spanish translations of Marvel Comics stories. While Guarnido hoped to transition from there to work for Marvel UK, and then to its parent company in the states—like his contemporaries Carlos Pacheco and Salvador Larroca would—it was not to be. So, believing the Spanish comics market was too small to allow him to make a living, he turned to animation.

In 1990, at the age of twenty-three, Guarnido moved to Madrid and found work at the Lapiz Azul and Milímetros animation studios, doing layouts and storyboards for such television shows as *Tintin*, *Adventures of Sonic the Hedgehog*, and *The Pink Panther*. His first day at Lapiz Azul, he met Juan Díaz Canales, who shared his passion for the comics medium, and the two became fast friends. Three years later, Guarnido was hired by the Walt Disney satellite studio in Montreuil, France, and moved to Paris.

There he quickly rose in the ranks, going from layout work (*A Goofy Movie*, *The Hunchback of Notre Dame*) to lead character animation (Hades in *Hercules*; Tarzan's father and Sabor in *Tarzan*; and Helga in *Atlantis: The Lost Empire*). Simultaneously, he and Díaz Canales refined their plans for a collaboration aimed at the respected Franco-Belgian *bande dessinée* market, and worked towards the publication of *Blacksad: Somewhere within the Shadows* in 2000.

Though the French Disney studio closed in 2003, Guarnido is now able to work in comics full time, illustrating the series *Sorcelleries* (Witchcrafts), written by Teresa Valero, alongside covers for the series *Voyageur* and his work on *Blacksad*. He currently lives and works in Paris, and is a proud father of three.

Brought to you by

MIKE RICHARDSON president and publisher NEIL HANKERSON executive vice president
TOM WEDDLE chief financial officer RANDY STRADLEY vice president of publishing
MICHAEL MARTENS vice president of business development ANITA NELSON vice president of marketing, sales, and licensing DAVID SCROGGY vice president of product development DALE LAFOUNTAIN vice president of information technology DARLENE VOGEL director of purchasing KEN LIZZI general counsel DAVEY ESTRADA editorial director SCOTT ALLIE senior managing editor   CHRIS WARNER senior books editor
DIANA SCHUTZ executive editor CARY GRAZZINI director of design and production
LIA RIBACCHI art director CARA NIECE director of scheduling

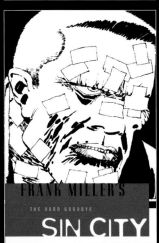

HELLBOY LIBRARY EDITION VOLUME ONE

Mike Mignola

Hellboy is one of the most celebrated comics series in recent years, created by the ultimate artists' artist and a great storyteller whose work is in turns haunting, hilarious, and spellbinding. *Hellboy* Volume 1 collects the first two story arcs—*Seed of Destruction* and *Wake the Devil*—with the original introductions by Robert Bloch and Alan Moore.
ISBN 978-1-59307-910-9 $49.99

THE GOON: CHINATOWN

Eric Powell

Dark Horse is very proud to present the first original graphic novel from Eisner Award–laden swami Eric Powell. Witness the Goon's formative backstory of love, loss, and extortion—a lengthy tale that demanded to be told in this uninterrupted format.
ISBN 978-1-59307-833-1 $19.99

SIN CITY VOLUME ONE: THE HARD GOODBYE

Frank Miller

This critically acclaimed triumph—honored by both an Eisner Award and the prestigious National Cartoonists' Award—combines pulp intensity with the gritty graphic storytelling that only Miller can deliver. Sin City is the place: tough as leather and dry as tinder. Love is the fuel, and the now-infamous character Marv has the match, not to mention a "condition." He's gunning after Goldie's killer, so it's time to watch this town burn!
ISBN 978-1-59307-293-3 $17.00

NOIR

The biggest names in comics crime fiction assemble for an anthology of original tales of murder and deceit, presented in glorious black and white! Featuring original work from creators including Rick Geary, Brian Azzarello, Ed Brubaker, Chris Offutt, and Dean Motter, this latest in Dark Horse's Eisner Award–nominated series of anthologies by top creators explores the dark, lonely side of the street.
ISBN 978-1-59582-358-8 $12.99

AVAILABLE AT YOUR LOCAL COMICS SHOP OR BOOKSTORE
TO FIND A COMICS SHOP IN YOUR AREA, CALL 1-888-266-4226

For more information or to order direct: •On the web: darkhorse.com •E-mail: mailorder@darkhorse.com •Phone: 1-800-862-0052 Mon.–Fri. 9 AM to 5 PM Pacific Time.

THE ART OF USAGI YOJIMBO

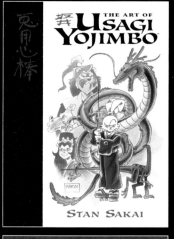

This showcase of the work of multi-award-winning creator Stan Sakai features scores of never-before-seen pieces, a long-out-of-print twelve-page primer illustrating how Stan creates each *Usagi* story, forty-eight full-color pages of Stan's beautiful painted artwork, a gallery section in which some of the biggest names in comics pay tribute to their favorite rabbit *ronin*, and more!
ISBN 978-1-59307-493-7 $29.99

DRAWING DOWN THE MOON: THE ART OF CHARLES VESS

For over thirty years, the fantasy art of Charles Vess has been acclaimed worldwide, his rich palette, striking compositions, and lavish detail second to none in the field. Vess has been the illustrator of choice for countless publishers and writers, including Neil Gaiman, Susanna Clarke, and George R. R. Martin. Embodying the timeless approach of the golden age of illustration, Vess's work is breathtakingly singular and gorgeously evocative.
ISBN 978-1-59307-813-3 $39.99

LONELY HEART: THE ART OF TARA MCPHERSON

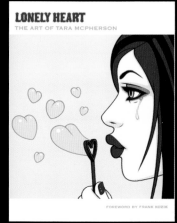

The compelling paintings and posters of Tara McPherson are a tour de force of creative tension, at once heartfelt and heartbreaking. Tara's array of work includes numerous gig posters for rock bands, including Green Day, Modest Mouse, and Death Cab for Cutie, and advertising and editorial illustrations for a diverse group of clients. Her prints and paintings have been exhibited in galleries all over the world. *Lonely Heart* is the first printed collection of McPherson's seductive, thought-provoking work.
ISBN 978-1-59582-102-7 $19.99

CREEPY ARCHIVES VOLUME TWO

This vein-chilling volume showcases work by some of the best artists to ever work in the comics medium, including Alex Toth, Gray Morrow, Reed Crandall, John Severin, and others. Each archive volume of *Creepy* is packed with stories that run the gamut of gruesome subject matter, from reimagined horror classics such as "The Cask of Amontillado," to spectacularly mind-twisting shorts such as "The Thing in the Pit," or the macabre maritime yarn "Drink Deep."
ISBN 978-1-59582-168-3 $49.99